D0457567

AUG 1 8 2020

NO LONGER PROPERTY OF
SEATTLE PUBLIC LIBRARY

ALSO BY DAVID STOUT

Carolina Skeletons
Night of the Ice Storm
The Dog Hermit
Night of the Devil
The Boy in the Box

THE KIDNAP YEARS

The Astonishing True History of
the Forgotten Kidnapping Epidemic
That Shook Depression-Era America

DAVID STOUT

sourcebooks

Copyright © 2020 by David Stout
Cover and internal design © 2020 by Sourcebooks
Cover design by Sarah Brody
Cover images © New York Times Co./Getty Images,
 Bettmann/Getty Images, STILLFX/Getty Images
Internal design by Ashley Holstrom

Sourcebooks and the colophon are registered trademarks of Sourcebooks.

All rights reserved. No part of this book may be reproduced in any form or by
any electronic or mechanical means including information storage and retrieval
systems—except in the case of brief quotations embodied in critical articles or
reviews—without permission in writing from its publisher, Sourcebooks.

This publication is designed to provide accurate and authoritative information in regard
to the subject matter covered. It is sold with the understanding that the publisher is
not engaged in rendering legal, accounting, or other professional service. If legal advice
or other expert assistance is required, the services of a competent professional person
should be sought.—*From a Declaration of Principles Jointly Adopted by a Committee
of the American Bar Association and a Committee of Publishers and Associations*

All brand names and product names used in this book are trademarks,
registered trademarks, or trade names of their respective holders. Sourcebooks
is not associated with any product or vendor in this book.

Published by Sourcebooks
P.O. Box 4410, Naperville, Illinois 60567-4410
(630) 961-3900
sourcebooks.com

Library of Congress Cataloging-in-Publication Data
Names: Stout, David, author.
Title: The kidnap years : the astonishing true history of the forgotten
kidnapping epidemic that shook Depression-era America / David Stout.
Description: Naperville, Illinois : Sourcebooks, [2020] |
Includes bibliographical references and index.
Identifiers: LCCN 2019032997 | (hardcover)
Subjects: LCSH: Kidnapping—United States—History—20th
century. | Crime—United States—History—20th century.
Classification: LCC HV6598 .S76 2020 | DDC 364.15/4097309043—
dc23 LC record available at https://lccn.loc.gov/2019032997

Printed and bound in the United States of America.
SB 10 9 8 7 6 5 4 3 2 1

For Rita, my rock and my light

TABLE OF CONTENTS

INTRODUCTION

One winter day a long time ago, a handsome woman in her early forties was found dead in a snowbank off a highway in northwestern Pennsylvania. She had been strangled. The homicide was big news around Erie, Pennsylvania, where I grew up. The killer, it was soon revealed, was a man the victim had begun dating after her marriage turned to ashes. For weeks, the crime was grist for newspaper headlines and chatter in barbershops and saloons. It was even featured in the true-crime pulp magazines of the era.

The victim was my mother's sister.

I recall the coffin being wheeled out of a candle-scented church as a choir sang farewell and my aunt's relatives stood grim-faced, some with tears on their cheeks. I was in college at the time, old enough to understand that I had been granted wisdom not bestowed on everyone. I understood that a murder spreads an indelible stain, dividing the lives of people close to it into Before and After.

So began my interest in crime. It is an interest that has only deepened with the passage of years. It has compelled me to read scholarly tomes as well as lurid accounts of sensational cases. It has drawn me to courtrooms and prisons and to the death house in Texas, where I witnessed the execution of a pathetic, dirt-poor man who had raped and killed his ex-wife and her niece in a drunken rage.

————

My preoccupation with crime was known to my editors during my newspaper career. Thus, on January 12, 1974, an arctic cold Saturday in Buffalo, my bosses at the *Buffalo Evening News* sent me to the Federal Building for a somber announcement by the resident FBI agent. The fourteen-year-old son of a wealthy doctor in Jamestown, New York, sixty miles southwest of Buffalo, had been kidnapped the previous Tuesday. Three teenagers had been arrested Friday, and most of the ransom money had been recovered in the home of one of them.

But the boy was still missing.

The FBI agent told reporters that the bureau had entered the case because the victim had been missing for more than twenty-four hours. Ergo, there was a presumption under the Lindbergh Law that he might have been taken across state lines, so the feds were authorized to assist the local cops.

I knew about the 1932 kidnapping and murder of the infant son of legendary aviator Charles A. Lindbergh. So I assumed that horrible crime inspired the law.

Not exactly.

I was surprised to learn that, despite acquiring its informal name from the Lindbergh crime, the Federal Kidnapping Act of 1932 was a reaction to a string of abductions that began before the Lindbergh baby was even born and continued while he was still squirming happily in his crib.[*]

———————

[*]   Originally, the law gave the FBI jurisdiction when a victim was missing for seven
      days on the presumption that the victim might have been taken across state lines. In
      1956, the law was amended to shorten the FBI's waiting period to twenty-four hours.

There were so many kidnappings in Depression-era America that newspapers listed the less sensational cases in small type, the way real estate transactions or baseball trades were rendered. There were so many kidnappings that some public officials wondered aloud if they were witnessing an epidemic.

In fact, they were.

From New Jersey to California, in big cities and hamlets, men and women sat by a telephone (if the household had one) or waited for a postman's knock, praying that whoever had stolen a loved one would give instructions for the victim's deliverance. There was usually a demand for money, sometimes for a fantastic sum, other times for a small amount that might even be negotiated down. It *was* possible to put a dollar sign on the value of a life.

A family's ordeal might last for hours and end happily. Or it might go on for days, with the relatives knowing that as time passed, hope ebbed. For some people, the ring of the phone or the knock on the door brought heartbreak and bottomless sorrow—the very emotions visited upon the family in Jamestown, New York, in 1974.

———

There was never much mystery behind the Jamestown case. The instructions for delivering the ransom were simple and unimaginative, giving investigators plenty of time to stake out the drop site and photograph whoever picked up the money. The ransom demand was a mere $15,000, a fraction of what the doctor's family could have paid.

The amateurish nature of the scheme had caused investigators to

---

If it is learned that the victim was never taken out of state, the FBI will defer to local authorities, although nothing prevents the FBI from offering its help. The law does not apply when a child is taken by a parent, as in a custody dispute, unless a child is taken abroad. The law has evolved in other ways that I shall touch upon.

suspect early on that the crime was the work of local teenage dim bulbs. Sure enough, teachers at the area high school easily identified the youth who had been photographed picking up the money. He was a supervisor at a teen center where the doctor's son had said he was going just before he vanished. The voice on a tape-recorded call to the doctor's home was recognized as that of a nineteen-year-old high school dropout who hung out at the teen center.

When two eighteen-year-olds were arrested, they admitted they'd done something wrong under the guidance of the nineteen-year-old, but they swore they hadn't signed on for anything that might bring harm to the boy.

Ominously, the nineteen-year-old, in whose home the ransom money was found, kept quiet about the boy's whereabouts. Searchers combed the snowy woods around Jamestown on Saturday and Sunday until the boy's body was found lashed to a tree. He had been beaten to death, probably with a metal pipe or a hammer judging by the wounds to his head.

Since the kidnapping and slaying had obviously occurred within New York State, the FBI bowed out, leaving the state prosecutors and courts to mete out justice. The two eighteen-year-olds got off with light punishment. But it was the nineteen-year-old who got the biggest break of all. When he went to trial on kidnapping and murder charges, his lawyer argued that there was insufficient evidence to convict him of murder. After all, no one had seen the suspect with the victim from the time he vanished until his body was found in the woods.

The jurors pronounced themselves hopelessly deadlocked, so a deal was worked out under which the nineteen-year-old pleaded guilty just to kidnapping, which meant a sentence of eight to twenty-five years instead of the twenty-five-to-life term he could have gotten for the murder count alone.

Had I been on the jury, I would have tried to cut through the fog. "Let's use our common sense," I would have said. "Of course he killed the kid. If he didn't, who the hell *did*?"

But the truth doesn't always count for much in a courtroom, as some lawyers try to inject reasonable doubt into cases in which there is none.[*]

———————

Viewing a time in history from the vantage point of the present is a bit like being in an airplane and gazing at the ground from two miles up. It is too easy to miss the trees while looking at the forest. Most of the kidnappings from long ago are little remembered today, but they defined the times as much as bank robberies and speakeasies and panhandling.

They spurred new laws and new law-enforcement techniques, like criminal profiling. They brought out the best qualities in some lawmen, like endless persistence and ingenuity, and the worst in others: carelessness, cruelty, even brutality.

Indirectly, the kidnappings also helped to expose the corruption, the moral rot, that infected city hall and police headquarters in some communities in the 1930s, as shown by the fact that some victims were rescued by gangsters while complacent or corrupt police officers watched from the sidelines. Eventually, public disgust helped to spur reforms as people belatedly realized that the mobsters among them were not just colorful rogues but robbers, parasites, pimps, even killers—the kind of people who made kidnapping profitable.

Some people who survived kidnappings were able to treat their

———————

[*]   I can hear some lawyers clucking in disapproval, as though I don't know what I'm
       talking about. I think I do.

times in captivity as excellent adventures (once they had bathed and changed clothes). But most were emotionally scarred, even if they did not realize it at first. Others were damaged for life.

———————

As the false glitz of the 1920s yielded to the crushing poverty of the 1930s, kidnappings became so frequent in the United States that newspapers could scarcely keep up with them, as evidenced by a front-page article in the *New York Times* on Tuesday, July 25, 1933. The article reported[1] the arrest of several Chicago gangsters for the kidnapping of a St. Paul, Minnesota, beer mogul who had been freed after a ransom payment. The article noted that lawmen expected to link the gang to another Midwest kidnapping. And it alluded to an attempted kidnapping on Long Island.

The article was continued on page 4, a "jump page" in newspaper parlance. There was also an article on page 4 about the kidnappings of an Oklahoma oil tycoon and the son of a politician in Albany, New York. There was a report about a Philadelphia real estate broker who was shot dead in a bungled kidnapping attempt. Finally, there was a list, rather like a scoreboard, of *some* recent cases in which victims were rescued and suspects were apprehended:

> Mrs. E. L. (Zeke) Caress, Los Angeles; Dec. 20, 1930, three in prison for life, twenty-two, and ten years.
>
> Sidney Mann, New York; Oct. 13, 1931; three in prison for life, fifty, and twenty years.
>
> Mrs. Nell Quinlan Donnelly, Kansas City; Dec. 16, 1931; two in prison for life; one for thirty-five years.
>
> Fred de Filippi and Adhemar Huughe, Illinois; winter, 1931; two in prison for forty-two years; one for twenty; two others for two years.

Benjamin P. Bower, Denver; Jan. 8, 1932; three in prison for six and one-half years.

James DeJute, Niles, Ohio; March 2, 1932; two in prison for life.

Haskell Bohn, St. Paul; June 30, 1932; suspect awaiting trial.

Jackie Russell, Brooklyn; Sept. 30, 1932; two in prison for four to twenty-five years.

Mr. and Mrs. Max Gecht, Chicago; Dec. 10, 1932, two in prison for life.

Ernest Schoening, Pleasantville, N.J.; Dec. 27, 1932; five in prison for five to twenty years.

Charles Boettcher Jr., Denver; Feb. 12, 1933; two in prison for twenty-six and sixteen years.

John Factor, Chicago; April 12, 1933; two suspects held.

Peggy McMath, Harwichport, Mass.; May 2, 1933; kidnapper in prison for twenty-four years.

Mary McElroy, Kansas City; May 27, 1933; two held; two more sought.

John King Ottley, Atlanta, Ga.; July 5, 1933; guard arrested.

August Luer, Alton, Ill.; July 10, 1933; four men and two women under arrest, after confession by one of the men.[2]

What spawned the kidnapping epidemic? Prohibition, which was ostensibly intended to eradicate domestic violence, workplace injuries, and other social ills associated with drunkenness, has been blamed not just for creating a vast new liquor-supply business for organized crime but for fostering, even glamorizing, a general spirit of lawlessness. But it can also be argued that the approaching *end* of Prohibition contributed to the spate of kidnappings. After all, what was an honest bootlegger or rumrunner to do when his trade became obsolete?*

Or perhaps something much deeper was going on. For all the talk about economic inequality in twenty-first century America, the chasm between rich and poor was far wider in the 1930s. A man was lucky to have a job, any job, while less fortunate men were standing in bread lines and housewives were serving ketchup sandwiches for dinner and boiling bones to make thin soup.

And if a person was born to wealth, he or she might be hated by those on the bottom rung of society. Almost surely, some kidnapping victims suffered because they had what their abductors could never have: money and self-esteem. And freedom from worry, perhaps that above all. Nowadays, people know that recessions come and go, that prosperity will return as surely as the seasons will change. But in the Great Depression, that kind of optimism, that certainty, was inconceivable to many people.

Travel back in time via newspaper microfilm to the 1930s, and you sense the fear and sorrow and violence of those years. In the depths of the Depression, bank robbers roamed the country. They were new Robin Hoods to some Americans, especially those who lost their savings when banks failed or were terrified of losing their homes or farms to foreclosure.

---

*   Prohibition, the law of the land from 1920 to 1933 after ratification of the Eighteenth
     Amendment to the Constitution, was also driven by political and social factors, like
     prejudice against immigrants from countries where drinking was the norm. After World
     War One, this bias was especially pronounced against people of German descent.
     Prohibition's enabling law forbade the manufacture, sale, or transportation of alcoholic
     beverages in the United States or importing and exporting them. But possession or
     consumption was not forbidden. Thus, some pharmacists were happy to dispense
     "prescriptions" for medicinal whiskey, and grape growers profited from selling wine
     for "religious" rites. And while home stills were officially illegal, they were not hard
     to buy or build. By the early 1930s, there was a growing recognition that the "noble
     experiment" had failed, even though alcohol-related deaths had declined. The Eighteenth
     Amendment was repealed by the Twenty-First Amendment, ratified on December 5,
     1933.

To read the news from that time is to sense that the very fabric of American society was being torn apart. President Franklin D. Roosevelt's famous line, "The only thing we have to fear is fear itself," delivered at his first inauguration in 1933, offered a flicker of hope to a people in need of hope. It just wasn't true.

"Every day, the children seemed to grow more pale and thin," an impoverished Chicago city street sweeper said a few weeks after FDR took office. "I was working only four days a week and had received no pay for months."[**]

The street sweeper was explaining to the police why he fed his starving family meat from a dead pig he had found in an alley behind a restaurant. He sampled the meat, and it didn't seem to harm him. So his wife and their ten children also ate. Soon, two of his children died of food poisoning. Within days, two more of the children were dead. When the street sweeper told his story, he was said to be gravely ill, as were his wife and some of their remaining children. I wanted to know if the mother and father and their children survived, but I could not find out. Not long after the initial reports, the newspapers in Chicago and elsewhere seemed to tire of the family's ordeal. Or perhaps the journalists simply lost track; the family was Italian, and the name was spelled at least two ways in the coverage.

Besides, the Great Depression offered countless stories of suffering and death. No need to dwell on the troubles of a lowly street sweeper and his family, not when some broken men were committing suicide and others were abandoning their families and hopping freight trains to nowhere.

———————————

[**] Reported by the Associated Press on March 29, 1933, and published in numerous newspapers.

Not all kidnappings stirred public revulsion. On the contrary, a juicy gangland kidnapping could be as entertaining as a newspaper photo of a slain mobster with his head resting in a bowl of pasta and his blood mingling with spilled wine.

Newspaper reporters and editors indulged in considerable levity as they chronicled the snatches and ransom negotiations involving people on the wrong side of the law. Even the *New York Times*, that stuffy bastion of good taste and prudery, got into the spirit now and then. Reporting on one case in the thirties, the *Times* noted lightheartedly that Basil Banghart, a Chicago gangster and machine-gun artist known to friend and foe as "the Owl," had been sentenced to ninety-nine years in prison for his role in a kidnapping. (A fellow mobster explained Banghart's nickname: "He had big, slow-blinking eyes—and he was wise.")[3]

Around the same time, the newspaper noted breezily, another Windy City miscreant, Charles "Ice Wagon" Connors, was kidnapped and "taken for a ride" to a patch of woods where he was shot to death by former associates after a falling out—over money, of all things. (In mob legend, Connors acquired his nickname as a good-natured joke: a getaway car he was driving collided with an ice-delivery truck after a robbery. The historical record is unclear as to whether he got away anyhow.)

The laughter stopped on the night of March 1, 1932, with the most famous kidnapping in U.S. history, that of twenty-month-old Charles Augustus Lindbergh Jr., stolen from his parents' home in Hopewell in rural west-central New Jersey. It was called "the crime of the century."[*] It is hard to imagine, in our age of debunking and social media sniping,

---

[*]   The Lindbergh crime inherited that title from the 1924 abduction and murder of a
      Chicago boy by Nathan Leopold and Richard Loeb, two spoiled young men from rich
      families who wanted to experience the thrill of killing. They were saved from the electric
      chair by famed lawyer Clarence Darrow and sentenced to life plus ninety-nine years in
      prison. Loeb was stabbed to death by another inmate in 1936. Leopold was paroled in
      1958 and died in 1971.

the adoration that was heaped upon Charles Lindbergh after his epic 1927 flight to Paris. He was idolized for his great courage in flying alone over the Atlantic Ocean, for his matinee idol good looks, for a half smile that suggested an underlying modesty and not the aloofness that really lay behind the façade.

"Had not Charles A. Lindbergh flown the Atlantic...a federal kidnapping statute might not yet have been enacted," a commentator observed[4] after the anti-kidnapping law was passed by lawmakers and signed by President Herbert Hoover in June 1932.

Yes, the ordeal of the Lindberghs roused Congress from its torpor. But well before March 1, 1932, it seemed that people who were not necessarily famous nationally but were well-to-do—brewers, bankers, builders, and merchants—were in danger, as were their children.

While there is no empirical way to gauge a nation's collective emotion, it may be that the kidnapping and slaying of the golden curled Lindbergh baby caused more grief, revulsion, and yearning for retribution than any other crime against a private citizen, adult or child, ever.

Charles Lindbergh Jr. was an adorable baby. His heroic father was the son of a former congressman. Charles Lindbergh's shy, pretty wife, Anne, was the daughter of Dwight Morrow, a wealthy banker, former ambassador to Mexico, and briefly a Republican senator from New Jersey before his unexpected death in 1931 at age fifty-eight.

Before the Lindbergh horror, enactment of a federal kidnapping law was hardly a sure thing. The U.S. attorney general, William D. Mitchell, argued against it on grounds that it would increase federal spending and make the states too dependent on Washington.

But with the discovery of the Lindbergh baby's body on May 12, 1932, things changed literally overnight. On May 13, President Hoover, ignoring the reality that the U.S. government had no jurisdiction over kidnappings, ordered federal law enforcement agencies to aid state and local investigators "until the criminals are implacably brought to justice."[5]

Representative Charles Eaton, a New Jersey Republican, was similarly outraged, declaring after the baby was found dead that the Lindbergh family was "the symbol of all that is holy and best in our nation and civilization."[6]

The chaplain of the House of Representatives, the Reverend J. S. Montgomery, offered a prayer for the child, then urged lawmakers to "arouse the public conscience, that a slight atonement may be made, by smiting murderers and outlaws into the dust."

At the dawn of the 1930s, taking a kidnapping victim across a state line was a smart tactic. In that predigital era, there wasn't much coordination and cooperation among the police and courts of the states. Most states did not have statewide police forces. Potential witnesses in a state to which a victim was taken were beyond the subpoena reach of courts in a state where the kidnapping had taken place. Laws against kidnapping varied from state to state. Extradition was cumbersome. Fewer than half of American households had telephones.

And sadly, some local cops augmented their modest incomes by taking money in return for not chasing criminals too aggressively.

What became known as the Lindbergh Law was sponsored by Missouri lawmakers Senator Roscoe Conkling Patterson, a Republican, and Representative John Joseph Cochran, a Democrat from St. Louis. A number of kidnappings had taken place around Kansas City and St. Louis. Both cities were influenced by, some would say *run* by, organized crime. A lot of kidnappings were carried out by professional criminals who had branched out from gambling, bootlegging, and other illicit enterprises.

But some kidnappings were the work of amateurs, driven to desperation because they had no jobs and no prospects. And some people plumbed the depths of human cruelty by posing as kidnappers, sending ransom demands to relatives of the victims while knowing nothing of the victims' whereabouts.

What made Kansas City, Missouri, and St. Louis such hotbeds of kidnapping? The first city, of course, is next door to the identically named city in the state of Kansas. St. Louis, which sits on the Mississippi River, was even more ideally situated. Kidnappers could take a bridge across the river and be in Illinois in minutes. And for kidnappers with boats, the mighty river offered access to the entire Midwest. Thus, St. Louis, which was known in frontier days as the "Gateway to the West," could have been dubbed "the Kidnap Turnstile" in the 1930s.

"Kidnapping is the feature crime of the present time," Walter B. Weisenberger, president of the St. Louis Chamber of Commerce, told the Senate Judiciary Committee as he urged federal anti-kidnapping legislation days after the Lindbergh infant was stolen. "It is a crime that men with some of the best brains in this country have gone into, because it offers big returns and reasonable safeguards."[7]

Some of the best brains in the country? Perhaps Weisenberger exaggerated the intellects of most kidnappers. But there was no denying that they were an industrious lot. The St. Louis police chief, Joseph Gerk, claimed to have collected statistics from cities nationwide in 1931. He told Congress he had counted 279 kidnappings that year, in the course of which thirteen victims were killed and sixty-nine kidnappers captured and convicted.[8]

But those numbers were unreliable, as Gerk acknowledged. He had sent questionnaires to the police in 948 cities but received replies from just 501. States and cities did not routinely share information with one another, as indicated by the limited cooperation for Gerk's survey.

The day after the Lindbergh kidnapping, a *New York Times* article offered a partial list of the most recent kidnappings in various states:

Illinois, 49; Michigan, 26; California, 25; Indiana, 20. And so on. The following day, attributing its figures somewhat vaguely to "authorities," the paper reported that more than two thousand persons had been abducted in the country in the previous two years.[9]

No doubt, many kidnappings went unreported, as some of the victims were criminals themselves, grabbed by rival gangsters, then sold back to their own gangs if they were lucky.

And if they weren't lucky? A Chicago detective testifying before the House Judiciary Committee in February 1932 let the lawmakers imagine what could happen if negotiations fell through. He told of a raid on a kidnapping ring's lair that included a "torture chamber," which apparently had been used frequently and which "hinted at almost unbelievable horrors," as the *Times* put it.[10]

Items found in the lair included vats of lime, cans of gasoline, and diving suits.

Why diving suits? Apparently, a captive would be stuffed into one, then lowered to the bottom of the Chicago River and "only infrequently allowed to have air," the *Times* reported. Upon being brought up from the cold and total darkness, the victim would presumably have been willing to do whatever his captors desired: agree to stay out of his captors' territory, beg his employers to pay a big ransom, or both.

And here, the inescapable question: were some kidnappers mean-spirited enough to leave victims at the river bottom until the bubbles stopped?

———

Justice was more streamlined in the 1930s. The courts were far less cluttered by appeals; defendants' rights that we take for granted today did not yet exist. And if numbers are any indication, there was far less ambivalence about capital punishment. In the 1930s, there were 167 executions a year on average, more than in any other decade before or since, according to the Death Penalty Information Center, a Washington nonprofit organization that collects and analyzes data on capital punishment.*

Here, some numbers are illuminating—and startling. In 1935, there were about 127 million Americans; in 2018, there were about 328 million. If executions were carried out nowadays at the same rate as they were in 1935, about 430 prisoners would have been put to death in 2018—roughly eight a week. But since the Supreme Court reinstated capital punishment in 1976, after a four-year hiatus, the highest total of executions in a single year was "only" 98 in 1999, as the Death Penalty Information Center notes.**

Why such a parade to the gallows, gas chamber, or electric chair at that point in history? Again, there were fewer grounds for appeals. Probably more important, some criminologists argued that the death penalty was necessary to prevent society from disintegrating.***

In the 1930s, the 1901 assassination of President William McKinley in Buffalo by an anarchist, Leon Czolgosz, was fresh in the memories of Americans of middle age and beyond. In Europe, dynasties had been toppled and social norms shattered by the Great War. The Russian Revolution had enflamed fears that "radicals" and "Bolsheviks" were working their mischief within the United States. In fact, there *were*

---

*   The organization is opposed to capital punishment, and its leadership has included people who are outspoken against the death penalty. But I have found the organization's data to be unfailingly reliable.

**   For more information, see www.deathpenaltyinfo.org.

*** Public support for capital punishment in the United States has fluctuated since the Supreme Court restored the death penalty in 1976 after a four-year hiatus. A Pew Research poll taken in June 2018 showed that 54 percent of Americans said they favored capital punishment, while 39 percent were opposed, according to the Death Penalty Information Center. The percentage in favor was up five points from the record-low 49 percent found by Pew Research in 2016. But the long-range trend shows a decline in support for the death penalty since 1996, when support peaked at 78 percent.

left-leaning Americans who wanted to bring about fundamental changes in government and society, although it is likely that few wanted to see blood running in the streets.

As a proud alumnus of the *New York Times*, I was struck by the tone of some of the newspaper's coverage of events during the 1930s.[*]

Riots in "Negro" neighborhoods stirred speculation that communists and other social agitators were responsible. The lynching of "a Negro" typically merited a few paragraphs, especially if it occurred in the South, where lynchings were too common to be newsworthy. If there was much reporting on whether racial unrest might be linked to the evils of segregation, bigotry, and poverty, I missed it. This was a time when the Ku Klux Klan was still thriving—and parading—and not just in the Old Confederacy.

Labor unrest was also blamed on communists rather than the desire of workers to have more job security and benefits, more food on the dinner table, and an extra sandwich in the lunch pail. Strikers and union organizers were beaten by company thugs who were euphemistically called "security guards."

———————

There was a man who both contributed to the harsh law-and-order atmosphere of the 1930s and fed off it. He was a dour Washington bachelor who had to overcome a childhood stutter and began his career as an obscure clerk. But he was anything but an unimaginative paper shuffler. He had a gift for organization. He also sensed that one could acquire power, sometimes *great* power, by filling a vacuum and by throwing himself into seemingly menial tasks that others avoided.

———————

[*]   As a subscriber to the *Times*, I have access to the newspaper's microfilm. In every
    instance in which I cite the *Times* as a source, I have read the article or articles cited.

When he took a low-level job in the Department of Justice, he saw a need for reliable, centralized information on crime. He also saw a national leadership vacuum in law enforcement. He would move deftly to fill it and to compile statistics that would eventually be helpful to criminologists and lawmen across the country—and to himself as he massaged numbers to attest to the importance of his own job.

He would use his considerable talents to become one of the most famous law enforcement officials and arguably one of the most important public figures in American history.

CHAPTER ONE

THE ORGANIZATION MAN

J. Edgar Hoover was born in Washington, DC, on New Year's Day, 1895, the youngest of three children of Dickerson Hoover, who worked for the U.S. Coast and Geodetic Survey, and his wife, Annie. Dickerson Hoover was hospitalized for a time because of mental illness, a taboo subject at the time, and Annie Hoover dominated the household, instilling in her children her own uncompromising ideas of Christian morality and right and wrong.

Young Edgar's first job was as a messenger boy in the Library of Congress. Soon, he was promoted to cataloger, then to clerk, a position in which he mastered the Dewey decimal system, which later became the basis for the filing system of the agency he would rule.

Attending classes at night, he earned his law degree from George Washington University in the capital and passed the bar exam. On July 26, 1917, when he was twenty-two, he became a clerk in the DOJ's

Bureau of Investigation.* One of his initial tasks was assembling a card file on suspected radicals and Bolsheviks.

Fears of these shadowy and threatening people were heightened on June 2, 1919, when a bomb exploded in front of the Washington home of the U.S. attorney general, A. Mitchell Palmer, demolishing the front of the house and rattling windows for many blocks around. The only casualty was the bomber himself, over whose remains Palmer's neighbor, Assistant Navy Secretary Franklin D. Roosevelt, had to step as he rushed to make sure Palmer was unhurt.

The incident helped to spur the attorney general's "Palmer raids," in which federal agents, acting with no regard for constitutional rights, arrested, harassed, and even deported people who were deemed radical, subversive, or...well...not sufficiently *American*.

In his new job in the Bureau of Investigation, Hoover impressed those around him by assembling a file of some *450,000* such people. He also impressed with his utterly serious demeanor and his impeccable wardrobe. He seemed marked for bigger things. His chance came with the 1923 death of President Warren G. Harding, under whose lax administration the Bureau of Investigation had been a haven for political hacks.

In fairness to Harding, the bureau's sorry state predated his lamentable tenure. Founded in 1908 during the presidency of Theodore Roosevelt, the bureau was supposed to be the DOJ's main weapon for combatting crimes that threatened national security so that the department would not have to "borrow" investigators from other agencies, like the Secret Service.** But the bureau quickly became a swamp of

---

*   The agency was known as the Bureau of Investigation until 1935, when "Federal" was added to the title. For the sake of simplicity, I shall refer to the agency later in this book as the Federal Bureau of Investigation or FBI.

**   The federal government was, of course, much smaller at that time, in terms of numbers of employees and agencies. There was not even a federal income tax until 1913.

incompetence as its "investigators" devoted themselves to crimes on Indian reservations and other obscure cases.

Roosevelt, who had been police commissioner of New York City for two years in the 1890s where he was frustrated by the corruption that permeated the force, wanted his attorney general, Charles Bonaparte, to improve the bureau.*** But cronyism persisted, either because Bonaparte wasn't strict enough or the culture was too deep-rooted or both.

Perhaps a hard-nosed outsider was needed.

———————

Harlan Fiske Stone, who became attorney general under President Calvin Coolidge in 1924, was determined to clean up the bureau. Commerce Secretary Herbert Hoover, a scandal-free holdover from the Harding administration, recommended J. Edgar Hoover (no relation) as "a lawyer of uncommon ability and character."[11]

Edgar was just twenty-nine. He was a bachelor (and would remain one for life) and was thus undistracted by problems at home. In short, he seemed perfect for the job, but he said he would take it only if it could be free of political influence and if he, as director, had power over hiring, firing, and promotions.

Stone agreed. So in 1924, the Federal Bureau of Investigation was reborn. At the time and for several years thereafter, its agents were not authorized to carry firearms, which may have been a good thing, considering how inept some of them were with weapons. Agents were not even authorized at first to make arrests, having to turn that chore over to local police. But Hoover envisioned larger roles for himself and his men (almost always *white* men), whose ranks he wanted to fill with lawyers and accountants.

———————

*** Bonaparte's grandfather, Jérôme Bonaparte, was the brother of Emperor Napoleon of France.

For someone who never ran for public office, Hoover had good political antennae. He sensed that crime would endure as a national issue and that declaring war against it could inflate reputations and boost careers. The crime of kidnapping offered great opportunities, especially after the Lindbergh baby was taken.

Hoover knew that people feared for their safety (the kidnapping of a prominent citizen typically spurred hirings of bodyguards and purchases of firearms), and he knew which victims and families had friends in the White House or a governor's mansion. Nor was he above sitting next to the FBI's kidnapping telephone hotline in truly big cases.

———

"Too many habitual criminals are at liberty," Hoover told a meeting of the International Association of Chiefs of Police in 1933, warning that lawbreakers were "roaming our streets and highways intent upon violence, kidnapping, murder or any crime that will enable them to inflict their bloody will upon society." He likened kidnappers to "sewer rats."[12]

Initially, the maximum punishment for interstate kidnapping under the Lindbergh Law was life in prison. But members of Congress sensed that more and more Americans did indeed believe in smiting murderers and outlaws into the dust, as the House chaplain had urged after the Lindbergh baby was found dead. So the Lindbergh Law was amended in 1934 to allow the death penalty to be imposed if the jury so recommended.

The lawmakers presumably wanted the ultimate punishment to be imposed on interstate kidnappers who killed their victims or did them great harm. And that is how the law has almost always been applied. The Death Penalty Information Center lists five defendants who have been put to death by the federal government for kidnapping. Four of those defendants killed their victims.

And then there was a luckless, dim-witted career criminal who broke out of an Oklahoma jail with another prisoner in November 1934. The pair drove into Texas, where they pulled off a robbery, then kidnapped two local policemen. The escapees drove a short distance before freeing the cops, unharmed.

One of the escapees was soon killed in a shootout. Within weeks, the surviving fugitive was caught in Oklahoma City and no doubt expected to go back behind bars for a long spell, a prospect that probably did not scare him. But the cops had been kidnapped in Texas, then driven into Oklahoma. Because they had been taken across a state line, the hapless fugitive was prosecuted under the Lindbergh Law and hanged in 1936, becoming the only kidnapper executed under the Lindbergh Law who hadn't killed a victim.*

The fugitive probably didn't deserve his fate. But not many people were voicing compassion for habitual criminals in those desperate times.

<hr>

Of course, you see similarities between then and now as you travel back to the 1930s via newspaper microfilm, following daily life. Presidents and governors and mayors wrestled with choices day after day, knowing they were living through history, *making* history, yet not knowing how it would turn out.

Then as now, there was no shortage of the sad and bizarre. A high school student hanged himself because he felt overwhelmed by pressure to succeed. A teenager killed his mother with an ax because he didn't want to weed the garden.

---

* In 1968, the Supreme Court struck down the section of the Lindbergh Law that allowed for the death penalty if a jury so recommended. The court reasoned that the provision denied a defendant his right to a fair trial, since he would be tempted to plead guilty rather than risk having jurors condemn him to death. In any event, only a relatively few crimes other than murder—treason or espionage, for instance—are punishable by death at present under federal or state law. And a defendant cannot be executed for kidnapping in and of itself.

This book is about kidnappings of long ago, but it can't be only about them. After all, some big-time criminals in that era were bank robbers *and* kidnappers.

And two major crimes of the era intersected in a way that seems unbelievable—except that it really happened. The central figure was a young woman named Mary McElroy whose father was a high official in Kansas City, Missouri. She was kidnapped by gunmen who invaded her home on Saturday, May 27, 1933, while she was enjoying a bubble bath. Her father paid a $30,000 ransom, and she was freed after a brief but deeply traumatizing captivity.

A few weeks later, Mary heard a rumor from one of her father's gangster friends that something big would happen at the Kansas City train station on the morning of Saturday, June 17, 1933. The prospect of excitement and danger had a moth-to-the-flame lure for her, so she persuaded a friendly gangster to accompany her to the station that morning.

As Mary and her companion sat in a car in the station parking lot, there was an explosion of gunfire about fifty yards from them. They were witnessing what would be called the Union Station Massacre: the death of an FBI agent, two Kansas City cops, an Oklahoma lawman, and the fugitive they were taking back to prison.

Immediately, J. Edgar Hoover proclaimed that the ambush had been carried out by the notorious bank robber Charles "Pretty Boy" Floyd and another thug, Adam Richetti. The pair had been trying to free the fugitive, who was their friend, according to Hoover.

Hoover was eager to link Floyd and Richetti, who were already wanted for robbery, to the Union Station Massacre. And he wanted the FBI to get them with as little help as possible from local police. That way, he could boast that his men had avenged the death of one of their own, the agent killed at the train station.

Yet Mary's gangster companion said he recognized two of the ambushers as brothers who worked for a Kansas City gangster, John Lazia, and that Floyd and Richetti were not there.

Floyd was gunned down in an Ohio cornfield in 1934. As Hoover had wanted, his agents were in on the kill. Richetti was captured in Ohio, convicted of murder in Missouri, and sentenced to death. He maintained his innocence in the Union Station shooting right up to the day in 1938 when he breathed in the cyanide in Missouri's new gas chamber.

The identity of the train station ambushers is a question that lingers to this day. Maybe the answer isn't important in the eternal scheme of things all these years later. Back then, the issue was vitally important to the FBI chieftain. For nothing—*nothing*—was more important to Hoover than image.

The mostly admiring press of the era helped Hoover paint himself as a lawman who was at once incorruptible and avuncular, as when he was happily pictured in the midst of children whom he christened junior crime fighters. That he was a wily and ruthless bureaucrat; that he could be tyrannical, petty, and vindictive; that he tried to avoid cases that looked like "losers" for his bureau—these were truths that were unknown to the general public for decades.

Journalists' treatment of Hoover in the 1930s seems remarkable, considering that he never subjected himself to the give-and-take of a news conference. (If he had, his volcanic temper might have erupted, since Hoover never learned to tolerate criticism. Years later, when he heard that the columnist Jack Anderson, whom he detested, might be preparing to write something unflattering, Hoover told associates that Anderson was "a flea-ridden dog" with a mind "lower than the regurgitated filth of vultures." On another occasion, Hoover told a confidant that Anderson was "lower than dog shit."[*]

In the 1930s, some reporters and lawmen had symbiotic relationships of a kind gone forever. If reporters got on the good side of police, they were alerted about raids and perp walks. In return, reporters sometimes wrote about lawmen in prose that smacked of gag-inducing hero worship, at least to my ear. They didn't write about police brutality, an idea whose time was yet to come.

Hoover has been rightly credited with injecting a degree of professionalism into an agency that had been a haven for incompetents. He oversaw the establishment of a national crime laboratory and instituted scientific methods still relied upon by police agencies. But early on, some of his agents were shockingly ignorant of basic investigative techniques.

And Hoover was not averse to more traditional, unsavory policing methods. In recent years, old memoranda in FBI files have surfaced in which the director demanded "physically vigorous" questioning of some suspects. Nor did Hoover and his acolytes shy away from occasional evidence tampering and perjury.

A half century after his death, Hoover remains a creature of baffling contradictions. He expressed Victorian views on sexual behavior (although suspicions about his personal proclivities persisted), yet he reveled in listening to tape recordings of public figures overheard in strange bedrooms. He railed against gangsters and racketeers while long denying *the very existence* of organized crime.[**]

---

[*]   For this vignette and numerous others about the FBI head, I am indebted to the late
        Curt Gentry, whose book *J. Edgar Hoover: The Man and the Secrets* is essential reading
        for anyone seeking a deeper understanding of Hoover's place in American history.
[**]   Various reasons have been offered for Hoover's willful myopia and semantic
        contradictions, including his preoccupation with choosing enemies whose defeat could

And while he warned his agents to take care in their personal relationships lest they create even a whiff of embarrassment for the bureau, he
was a familiar and very public figure at the Stork Club, the Midtown
Manhattan nightclub frequented by gossips, glitterati, and gangsters.
The club was owned by Sherman Billingsley, an ex-bootlegger, and one
of its most prominent regulars was Walter Winchell, the immensely
popular gossip columnist of the era who promoted Hoover's image and
got occasional scoops in return. And Hoover wasn't above turning to
shady figures for tips on which horse races might be fixed. (Betting on
the ponies was one of his pleasures.)

It is not too much to say that while he expressed hatred for criminals, Hoover *needed* them—killers, bank robbers, and kidnappers—as
targets for the national police force he was creating. And he *did* build a
national police force, something that probably would have horrified the
Founding Fathers, for better and worse.

———

In the early 1980s, when I was a journalist at the *Record* newspaper in
New Jersey, there was a resurgence of interest in the Lindbergh kidnapping. The widow of Bruno Hauptmann, the man who was convicted of
kidnapping and killing the Lindbergh baby and was executed in 1936,
sued in federal court in a vain attempt to show that her husband was
innocent.

Her suit went nowhere. But it brought a spirited response from
David Wilentz, who was a fiery little bantam rooster of a prosecutor
in 1935 when he convicted Hauptmann. Well into his senior years at
the time of the widow's suit but in possession of all his wits, Wilentz

---

be demonstrated by displaying scalps and statistics. Since organized crime could never
be entirely eradicated, no ultimate victory was possible.

rebutted the widow point by point. He said he had never doubted Hauptmann's guilt.

I lived in Englewood, New Jersey, from 1977 to 1987. My house was near a school that was once the mansion of Dwight Morrow, the banker, U.S. senator, and one-time ambassador to Mexico who was Charles Lindbergh's father-in-law.

My backyard abutted Brookside Cemetery. Every time I let my dogs out, they rushed to the cemetery fence and barked, as if to chase away ghosts. I found out later that Brookside is the resting place of Dwight Morrow and of a maid in the Morrow household who took her own life when she came under suspicion, unjustly it seems, soon after the Lindbergh baby was kidnapped.

Ghosts?

I don't believe in ghosts, or I don't think I do. Then again…

———

The more I have dug into the past, the more people I have found who deserve to be rescued from obscurity. They were not just pawns in Hoover's power games, not just stick figures in the purple prose of journalists of the time. Some of the people rest in manicured cemeteries, others in paupers' fields. For some, their ashes are sealed in urns or were scattered at sea.

When you gaze at photographs in newspaper microfilm from back then, the people are frozen in time, yet they almost seem alive again. Radiant brides on the society pages. Kindergarten children with crayons. A family huddled around the living room radio, ready to listen to—what? A detective story? One of Franklin Roosevelt's fireside chats? News of omens of war in Europe and the Orient?

Or perhaps there is news of yet another robbery or kidnapping or murder. One doesn't have to search hard to find images of grim-faced cops wearing rumpled suits and weary faces.

Even the children in the photographs are dead now or very old and frail. Their elders are all long gone, including the kidnapping victims and their abductors, cops and prosecutors. Gone, too, are the reporters and photographers who chronicled life back then, sometimes becoming actual players in kidnapping dramas in ways that seem inconceivable today.

As I said, I traveled back in time to meet the people in this book. I just had no idea how many would stay with me as I returned to the present. Ghosts?

CHAPTER TWO

FATHERS AND SONS

St. Louis
Wednesday, December 31, 1930

On New Year's Eve, 1930, Adolphus Busch Orthwein, a thirteen-year-old heir to the Anheuser-Busch beer empire, suddenly seemed too old for his nickname, "Buppie." For he was putting on a new blue serge suit for a dinner at his grandparents' estate just outside St. Louis, and the suit had long trousers instead of the knickers obligatory for preadolescent boys in that era.

Buppie's parents, Percy and Clara Orthwein, were going to a New Year's Eve party at the Bridlespur Hunt Club, made up of riding and fox-hunting devotees, so young Adolphus was to be driven by the Orthweins' chauffeur, Roy Yowell, to his grandparents' estate. The 281-acre tract was known as Grant's Farm because it was once owned by Ulysses S. Grant. It was anchored by a twenty-five-room mansion.

Percy Orthwein was an advertising executive, earning enough to make his family quite well off, and Clara was the second of three daughters of August Anheuser Busch Sr., the chief of the Anheuser-Busch beer empire, so the Orthweins were very rich indeed. The previous summer, they had moved into a two-story stone chateau built for them in the fashionable Huntleigh Village neighborhood. They were at ease in the world of country clubs and horse farms. (Clara's father had been a founder of the Bridlespur club in 1927.)

Buppie had already won several prizes at riding shows. He went to a private school. Yet he and his younger brother, Jimmie, were neither snobbish nor spoiled. They were beloved by the household help at Grant's Farm, where they were frequent guests. They seemed to be normal boys despite having been born to privilege—great privilege.

———

Adolphus Busch had come to the United States from Germany in the middle of the nineteenth century, settled in St. Louis, which had a large German population, and began selling beer-brewing supplies. One of Adolphus's best customers was a brewing company owned by another German-American, Eberhard Anheuser. Eberhard and his wife, Dorothea, had six children, including a daughter named Lilly, a lovely blonde.

Adolphus courted Lilly, and they married in 1861. They would have eight sons and five daughters. Adolphus and his father-in-law got along well, and they decided to go into business together. And so was born the Anheuser-Busch brewing empire. Adolphus Busch was an innovator; he had his beer pasteurized and shipped in refrigerated train cars from the St. Louis brewery to beer lovers far away. The beer, Budweiser, became an American institution.

Adolphus died in 1913 while visiting Germany. It fell to his son August—whose daughter Clara would marry Percy Orthwein—not just to run Anheuser-Busch as president and chief executive but to save it. When the Great War broke out in 1914, there was considerable anti-German sentiment in the United States, especially after America entered the conflict in 1917. August combatted this bigotry by flaunting his red, white, and blue American patriotism and promoting the city of St. Louis. His mother helped by opening a family estate in Pasadena, California, to disabled soldiers.

But there was a more existential threat to Anheuser-Busch: Prohibition. How to survive when your product is verboten? By diversifying: selling syrup for beer lovers to make beer in the sanctity of their homes, selling soft drinks, yeast, corn products. If Adolphus Busch and Eberhard Anheuser were creative entrepreneurs, August was the coolheaded yet imaginative businessman who kept it prospering.

The headlights pierced the darkness as the Lincoln limo carrying Buppie reached the outskirts of his parents' property and approached Lindbergh Boulevard, which had once been known as Denny Road. The name had been changed in honor of the famed aviator, who lived for a time in the city and named his famous monoplane the *Spirit of St. Louis.*

Buppie was in the front passenger seat. He was holding a gift for his grandfather: a new matchbox with a horse's head painted on the cover. The chauffeur was navigating the limo up a steep incline, getting ready to turn onto Lindbergh Boulevard, when a black man emerged from the trees. He ran to the rear of the limo and jumped onto the bumper.

Buppie was afraid. "Roy? Roy!"

The limo stopped. The man jumped off the bumper, opened the passenger side door, and pointed a revolver at the stunned chauffeur.

"Here, here's everything," Yowell said, fishing several dollars from a pocket and handing it over.

"You can take this too," Buppie said, offering the gunman the new matchbox.

The gunman ignored the boy's offer. "Get out!" he ordered the chauffeur.

Yowell did as commanded, and Buppie started to exit the limo also.

"You stay in!" the gunman said, getting behind the wheel and speeding off. He went only a short distance, then turned the limo around and, with the lights off, drove past the Orthwein property. A few hundred yards later, he stopped the limo, pulled the boy out, and led him to a car parked nearby.

"Get in and lie down on the back seat," the man said. As he drove away, he asked, "Are you Percy Orthwein's son?"

"Yes."

"Be quiet or I'll burn you."

Burn me?

Yowell ran back to the house and told Buppie's parents what had happened. Buppie's mother collapsed in hysteria. A doctor was summoned. Upon learning of the kidnapping, August Busch Sr. grabbed a pistol and drove to the home of his daughter Clara.

As one year was passing into history and another was dawning, there was chaos in the Orthwein home. Friends of the family who heard of the kidnapping abandoned their New Year's Eve plans and sped to the house in their party finery to offer consolation. Percy Orthwein and Yowell searched Lindbergh Boulevard, quickly finding the abandoned limousine.

The boy's uncle August Jr., who was thirty-one and known as "Gussie," brought two bloodhounds to the scene. They sniffed in vain as the chauffeur was driven by August Busch Sr. to St. Louis police headquarters.

Throughout the night, as friends of the Orthwein family came and went and reporters hovered like vultures, there was no word on the fate of Buppie. As the sun rose, radio stations broadcast the news of the kidnapping along with a plea from the boy's parents: return our son, and you will get a generous award, no questions asked.

The kidnapping stunned the people of St. Louis, where the Busches were social lions.

———

Percy Orthwein hadn't slept. He wondered if the dawn of a new day, the new year of 1931, would forever divide his life into Before and After.

It seemed an eternity ago that he and Clara were getting ready for a New Year's Eve party and Buppie was on his way to dinner with his grandfather.

Orthwein forced himself to think coldly. Surely, Buppie was worth more alive than dead.

Orthwein didn't know many Negroes. In St. Louis as in so many other communities, they had their own neighborhoods, their own schools, their own churches. No doubt, they loved their children, just as white folks loved theirs. Just because Buppie had been taken by a Negro didn't mean…

Around noon, the phone rang. Orthwein rushed to answer it. "Hello?"

"As father to father, I want to give you back your boy," a man said.

The caller was a Negro; Orthwein knew that from his voice, although like most white people in the segregated St. Louis of that era he had virtually no social contact with black people.

"You are worried about your son, and I am worried about mine," the caller went on, his voice almost breaking. "He is safe." The caller suggested he and Orthwein meet at once at the St. Louis County sheriff's office in Clayton.

Orthwein immediately called Harry Troll, a prominent St. Louis attorney who represented the Busch and Orthwein families. Within minutes, Orthwein, Troll, and Gussie Busch were headed to Clayton. When they got to the sheriff's office, they found only a deputy on duty. The party was bewildered.

Things fell into place minutes later when a black man and a young woman entered. The man was Pearl Abernathy, a real estate dealer well known among black people in St. Louis. He was accompanied by his niece, Elfrida Bobb.

Pearl Abernathy told a sad story. He had a son, Charles, who had followed him into the real estate business. Charles was just twenty-eight. He and his wife had seven children. He worried desperately over how to support his family since his real estate enterprise had gone broke.

A crazy dream began to form in Charles's mind. He knew that the Busch and Orthwein families would part with some money to get Buppie back. He hadn't thought out all the details—how much money to demand, how to collect it without getting caught, how to return the boy. But he knew that kidnappings were becoming common. The people pulling them off couldn't all be smarter than he was...

Pearl Abernathy had grown increasingly worried about his son's mental state, but he couldn't babysit him all the time. So on the morning of December 31, when Pearl saw Charles and sensed the deep depression he was in, he gave him $40. It was both a gift, from father to son, and a payoff. *Just leave me alone for a while, Charles. I have my own life.*

Charles's wife had been worried too, afraid that her husband was becoming unhinged. When she saw a white boy in her house on New Year's morning and her husband was gone, she was horrified. So she called Charles's father, Pearl, and he in turn called the Orthwein home to say he could get the boy back unharmed.

Orthwein and Troll listened to this sad tale, then demanded to know where Buppie was. They were told to wait a little while, then drive to Webster Groves, a suburb just to the west of St. Louis proper, and stop on Bacon Avenue near a nursing home that was a familiar landmark.

———————

Buppie had endured a terrifying night, not sure what was real and what was nightmare. Bound, he had been placed in an easy chair with a blanket over his head. The blanket smelled dirty, and it made his face too warm. Meanwhile, his feet were cold.

He knew that his captor had driven him to a place not far from the Orthwein home, and he knew that the man was black. From the movements of the man, and the way the footsteps never seemed far away, Buppie sensed that he was in a little house. He heard a baby cry, heard a dog barking, heard a cat meowing, heard a door open—to let the cat out, Buppie thought.

Slowly, the terror in Buppie's heart faded. The man wanted money; that must be the reason he'd taken him. Nothing else made sense.

The man hadn't hurt him, and he wasn't mean. The man fixed him scrambled eggs and took the blanket off long enough for Buppie to eat. The eggs weren't very good, nothing like what he would have had for dinner at his grandfather's!

With the blanket off him for a little while, Buppie saw that it was daylight. Then the blanket went over him again, and he was in the dark. Time passed; he couldn't tell how much. He didn't hear people noises anymore. He dozed off now and then. When he was awake, the man brought him an orange. It tasted better than the eggs. He slept again...

Footsteps! Not a dream!

The blanket was lifted from his head. "You're going home," a woman said as she untied him. "You know the nursing home on Bacon Avenue? Run there. Stop in front of it and wait. Go on now!"*

———

As the car approached the boy standing in front of the nursing home, Troll recognized him, though his face was almost black with dirt. "Percy, there's your son!"

Orthwein didn't wait for the car to come to a full stop. He leaped out and ran to Buppie.

"I've been waiting for you," Buppie said.

A joyous reunion followed at Grant's Farm. Household servants joined social elites in offering tearful prayers of thanks. Buppie was given a bath and good food and was sent to bed.

"Not a cent" had changed hands to secure Buppie Orthwein's freedom, Troll told a pack of reporters.[13]

Percy and Clara Orthwein were charitable as well as rich. They had not just promised a reward for the safe return of their son. They had even offered to help find a job for the abductor if he was impoverished. Charles Abernathy certainly was.

But the police were having none of it. Kidnapping was a *crime*, after all. For a short period, Pearl Abernathy was held as an accessory. And the police made it clear that they wanted Buppie's parents to cooperate in the prosecution of Charles Abernathy. But first the police had to find him. Having failed at kidnapping as well as real estate, the hapless Charles had vanished.

———

---

* The author has inserted dialogue for dramatic effect as it was reported in several newspapers at the time of the kidnapping, and as it was rendered in a December 28, 2013, reprise of the case by Tim O'Neil in the *St. Louis Post-Dispatch*.

Enter ace reporter Harry T. Brundidge of the *St. Louis Star*, one of
several newspapers that thrived in the city back then. By the time the
thirties began, he had exposed trafficking in fraudulent medical creden-
tials in the Midwest. He had worked as a deckhand on a ship sailing
between Havana and New Orleans to expose liquor smuggling. He had
interviewed Al Capone.

Brundidge had sources on both sides of the law, and he quickly
learned that Charles Abernathy was hiding in Kansas City, Missouri.
Brundidge tracked him down a few days after the kidnapping, interviewed him, and obtained his confession. His newspaper ran the scoop
on page 1. Soon afterward, Charles pleaded guilty to kidnapping and
robbery and was sentenced to fifteen years in state prison.

(There would also be heartbreak in the extended Busch family.
On New Year's Eve 1930, August Busch Sr. was sixty-five years old,
having celebrated his birthday just two days before. But he was not a
young sixty-five. The long days over the years had taken their toll, and
he was suffering from heart disease and gout. On February 13, 1934, he
would scribble a note saying, "Goodbye precious mommie and adorable
children" before killing himself with a revolver he kept by his bedside.)

―――――――――

Charles and Anne Lindbergh followed the Orthwein case from afar.
They had spent the Christmas and New Year holidays at the Englewood,
New Jersey, estate of Anne's parents, Dwight and Elizabeth Morrow.
A one-time partner at J. P. Morgan and one of the richest men in New
Jersey, Morrow was a former ambassador to Mexico (appointed by his
Amherst College classmate President Calvin Coolidge) and had just been
elected to the U.S. Senate. Soon, he would be talked about as a possible
Republican candidate for president.

Then as now a leafy community, Englewood would be much

busier later that year and forever after with the opening of the George Washington Bridge, spanning the nearby Hudson River and linking northern New Jersey with New York City.

Lindbergh and his wife were building a house of their own on a 390-acre tract near Hopewell, New Jersey, about sixty miles south of Englewood. The home was expected to be finished in the autumn of 1931. In Hopewell, Lindbergh hoped, he and his wife would find the privacy they so craved. Lindbergh had come to despise reporters and photographers, who seemed to follow his every move.

To be sure, the newspaper people could be annoying. But there was another factor at play, one the adoring public didn't understand. Lindbergh had a cool and distant personality. It was so appropriate, really, that he was an aviator, for he was comfortable being aloof. He was at ease around airplanes and engines, not around people.

Nor was Anne Lindbergh at home in the spotlight. Though from a prominent family and acquainted with some famous people, she was basically a shy person. No wonder the Lindberghs wanted privacy for themselves and their new son, Charles Augustus Lindbergh Jr., who by delightful coincidence had been born on his mother's twenty-fourth birthday, June 22, 1930.

Surely, the new homestead near Hopewell would offer seclusion... and safety.

CHAPTER THREE

THE DOCTOR

St. Louis
Monday, April 20, 1931

Lightning flared, and thunder rolled across the sky like barrels. Wind-driven rain mixed with hail lashed the windows of the three-story brick mansion on exclusive Portland Place, the home of Dr. Isaac Kelley. Forty-five years old, he was already recognized as the leading ear, nose, and throat specialist in St. Louis.

It was a perfect time to be snug and warm indoors, reading by the fireplace. Dr. Kelley and his wife, Kathleen, had a large book collection, and on a night like this, reading might be safer than listening to the radio. Over the weekend, a young woman in St. Louis had suffered a severe shock while adjusting her radio during a storm.

If he wanted to catch up with the news, Kelley had that evening's *St. Louis Post-Dispatch* to go through. The Monday paper had a darkly amusing item about the funeral of mobster Giuseppe "Joe the Boss" Masseria, who had been shot to death several days before at his favorite dining place in Brooklyn.

Masseria, forty-five, had traveled to Coney Island's Nuova Villa Tammaro restaurant in his heavily armored car. The armor plating and inch-thick glass protected him from snipers and street ambushers but not from the perfidy of his own bodyguards, who excused themselves from the table just before several assassins walked in to end Masseria's last meal. As Masseria lay in a puddle of chianti and his own blood, someone slipped an ace of spades between the fingers of his right hand. Was the so-called death card placed there by a rival gangster or by an insensitive tabloid photographer? No one could say.

But there was more somber news: yet another kidnapping in the Midwest. Fred J. Blumer, president of a beverage company in Monroe, Wisconsin, had endured more than a week in captivity during which he had been handcuffed and blindfolded.

On April 9, Blumer was grabbed in front of his home by three gunmen. Early on, the kidnappers contacted the secretary-treasurer of Blumer's company and demanded a ransom of $150,000. But in negotiations with the Blumer family, the demand was lowered to a mere $6,000. On their way to pick up the $6,000 from Blumer's brother, the kidnappers were intercepted near Winona, Illinois, by Chicago police, who had gleaned information on the kidnappers' moves through wiretaps.

After a gun battle, the kidnappers sped off without getting their money. Fred Blumer, who was fifty-one, was soon freed near Decatur, Illinois. Perhaps the kidnappers were amateurs who had panicked, or maybe they were members of an Iowa-based gang of bank robbers and beer runners, as a Chicago police lieutenant speculated, rather vaguely, in predicting quick arrests.* Regardless, the ordeal of Fred Blumer was

---

* The kidnapping of Fred J. Blumer was never solved. He died of a heart ailment on May 19, 1956, his seventy-seventh birthday.

enough to make people wonder how safe they were in their own homes
and neighborhoods.

———

The Kelleys' phone rang around nine o'clock that Monday night. The
man on the phone said his name was Holmes, that he and his nephew
were visiting from Chicago, and that the nephew had developed a sudden
and severe earache.

Kathleen heard snippets of her husband's end of the conversation,
enough to know that someone was ill and that he was giving instructions. "Oh, yes, I know him," her husband said. She presumed he was
referring to another doctor.

Kathleen was relieved when the conversation ended and her
husband settled back into his easy chair. It was no night to venture
outdoors! Besides, a recent sensational kidnapping had hit too close to
home, quite literally. One of Kathleen's sisters was married to William
Orthwein, a lawyer who was a cousin of Buppie Orthwein.

Isaac Kelley was Kathleen's second husband, her first husband
having died after only three years of marriage. The Kelleys had had two
daughters together, and Kathleen had a son from her first marriage.

Kathleen was the daughter of William Cullen McBride, a well-
to-do oil executive. Her inherited wealth and her husband's considerable income enabled the Kelleys to travel widely and belong to several
exclusive clubs. Knowing that they were blessed, the Kelleys gave generously to charities.

Around ten o'clock, Kelley told his wife the patient must not be as
bad off as first thought, as an hour had passed since the initial call. "I'm
glad I don't have to go out on a night like this," he said. Reflecting for a
moment, he added, "There was something very queer about that phone
call. They must be new to the area."[14]

Just then, the phone rang again. It was Holmes, calling back to say his nephew was worse. "I can bring him to your house," the caller said.

"No," the doctor said. "Keep him comfortable. I'll come to see you."

Kathleen heard her husband repeating the directions he was being given: "A filling station at the North and South road...two blocks east...a trestle...second house..."

Watching her husband don his raincoat and derby and fetch his medical kit, Kathleen was uneasy. "Are you sure you have to do this?" she asked. But she already knew the answer; her husband was a doctor, after all, and always willing to respond to an emergency.

———————

The windshield wipers on the Lincoln coupe could barely keep up with the rain as Dr. Kelley drove to the address Holmes had given him and pulled into the driveway. At first, he wondered if there had been a mistake: the house near the intersection of Oleta and Crescent Drives was dark save for a single window where the form of a man was silhouetted by a light.

For a moment, Kelley didn't know what to do. Holmes had said he would watch for the doctor and greet him. Kelley sounded the car horn to alert people inside. And just then, he heard another car pull into the driveway behind his own.

Trouble, he thought. Then the passenger side door was pulled open, and a man got inside.

"Back up and don't look at me," the man said as he pressed a gun barrel against Kelley's body. "Just drive where I tell you."

Fighting to keep his composure, Kelley drove on Oleta Drive, then turned onto a smaller road as he thought he'd been told. But he had misunderstood, and the concrete yielded to gravel.

"What in the hell are you doing?" the abductor said. "Can't you drive this automobile?"

Kelley put the car in reverse and returned to the paved road.

Kelley was six feet two inches tall and a muscular two hundred pounds. He was not easily intimidated; he had seen combat as a captain in the Army Medical Corps during the Great War, and he had once gotten into a fistfight with a man over a parking space. Still, he had to fight to keep calm as his captor steered him over bumpy roads.

Kelley was wearing his favorite diamond ring. Surreptitiously, he slipped it off and tucked it between a cushion and the car seat. His wallet might be emptied, but he wouldn't lose his ring!

"What the hell are you doing?" the gunman said. "Keep your hands on the wheel."

Kelley also tried to remove his tie pin.

"I said, keep your hands on the wheel!" his captor said. He ordered Kelley to turn this way and that—to the east and then north, he thought— then announced, "We're going to hold you for ransom."

Which was just what Kelley had concluded.

"Stop," the gunman ordered at last. "Now get out."

Kelley did as he'd been ordered. Standing on trembling legs in the dark amid the wind and rain, he was almost relieved when a blindfold was placed over his eyes and he heard other voices. His captors pushed him into another car and drove off. From the vehicle's lurches and occasional stops, Kelley knew that he was being taken on a circuitous route. Finally, the car stopped, and he was pulled out. It was quiet all around; he sensed he was in a country setting. After a brief walk in the rain, with his captors steering him, he heard a door being opened. Then he was told to walk ahead.

The door had a rickety sound, not at all sturdy. *I'm in some kind of shack*, Kelley thought. Then he was led up a set of stairs, his minders taking care not to let him fall. Once upstairs, he was spun around and told to sit. He did, landing on a cot.

So quiet outside, he thought. *I'm in a shack on a farm. God knows where.*

He heard the abductors whispering. Now and then, the voices rose above whispers. Three voices...no, four. One man had an oddly pleasant, almost musical voice. Another had a decidedly foreign accent.

Kelley thought how worried his wife must be. Time began to blur. He wasn't really comfortable on the cot, but he felt exhaustion overtaking him. He began to sleep, off and on. No one had told him he couldn't sleep.

He heard an airplane—a Ford trimotor, he could tell from the sound. And then it was morning again. He could tell it was morning even with a hood over his head.

"You're going to write a letter," one of the men told him. "You're going to tell your family that you're all right—which you will be, as long as you do as you're told."

The hood was removed, and Kelley was given pen, ink, and paper. The men holding him stood behind him. He heard metallic clicking noises; he recognized the sound of weapons being cocked and uncocked. *Trying to make an impression on me*, he thought.

He didn't turn his head to get a look at the men. He just wrote a terse note to his wife, assuring her he was well and would see her soon—though he didn't know if he would.

One of the men took the pen and paper away, and then a plate was put on the cot. Meat, overcooked by the looks of it. Bread too. Kelley given a bottle of milk. He noted that the bottle was imprinted with the words "St. Charles Dairy Co." St. Charles, a city in the county of the same name, is a suburb northwest of St. Louis.

"Eat," a man said. "Then we're going for a ride. Don't worry. You'll get a chance to use the bathroom."

Again, Kelley heard the sound of a Ford trimotor overhead. He thought one of his captors said something about "the mail ship."

Kelley strained to hear every voice, every sound, on the chance he'd pick up a clue that might be useful later. He thought he heard someone mumble the name "Goldie."

A little later, Kelley had the sensation of a big rubber band being slipped over his head. Then he felt pressure around his eyes, and suddenly, he couldn't see. *Goggles*, he thought. *I'm wearing goggles with black tape on them.*

Not too roughly, Kelley was pulled to his feet and led back down the stairs. Then he was outside, in the fresh air. He heard a car door open, then his abductors pushed him inside the vehicle. Kelley could tell he was in the rear seat. He heard a driver get in, then someone entered the front passenger door. The engine started.

"Lie down," one of the men commanded.

Kelley knew from the sway of the vehicle that it was making frequent turns. At first, he felt the car going over bumps. The bumps subsided. After a while, the car was on a smooth straightaway. Kelley waited to feel the next turn. Instead, the car kept going straight.

We're on a long bridge, he thought. *They're taking me across the Mississippi to Illinois.*

———

Kathleen Kelley became distraught when her husband did not return late Monday night. Nor did he call. It simply wasn't like him. She phoned several relatives and friends, including William Orthwein, and they rushed to the Kelleys' house to offer succor.

The police were notified. Several detectives were assigned to the disappearance, which was not officially a kidnapping early on. But the discovery of the doctor's car, abandoned several miles from the address he had been lured to by Holmes, removed any doubt. There were oil stains and bits of gravel on the floors of the front passenger side and the rear seat.

The police quickly arranged to tap the Kelleys' telephone on the assumption that whoever had taken the doctor might call with a ransom demand.

As the night wore on without word, Kathleen was near collapse. Finally, she heeded the pleas of her family and took to her bed.

=====

As the St. Louis newspapers noted, there had been a number of other kidnappings in the region during the previous several months. Most had involved people who elicited little sympathy.

Two big-time bookmakers, William Rutstein and Herman Kohn, who worked together and ran at least five gambling dens, were among the targets. Alas for the would-be kidnappers, Rutstein and Kohn were no dunces with firearms. They shot it out with their assailants, killing one and routing the others.

And even as the fate of Dr. Isaac Kelley was unknown, it was disclosed that some people of means had been coerced by telephone or mail into paying what could be called "preventive ransoms," meaning they paid to avoid being kidnapped in the first place.

=====

Dr. Kelley's new place of captivity was no more comfortable than the first.

"Why don't you fellows let me read?" he suggested. "Just let me have a magazine or newspaper." His captors give him a newspaper in which he read about his own kidnapping. They gave him some detective magazines—not his usual reading fare. Then he was given a biography of Al Capone.

His captors also made him write a second letter to his wife, declaring that he would not be released until a ransom of $150,000 was paid.

Most of the time, he could not see, either because a hood was draped over his head or goggles were in place. His emotional state swung from anxiety to boredom. Occasionally, he heard the rumble of a train not far away.

The food did not improve. He slept fitfully. He was beginning to feel the lack of a shower and change of linen, and his socks were clammy. His feet were cold, too, as his captors often removed his shoes. To prevent him from fleeing, Kelley assumed.

He told himself that the police must be doing all they could to find him.

═══════

Ace reporter John T. Rogers of the *St. Louis Post-Dispatch* had been covering the Kelley kidnapping. He had been working long hours, shuttling between the newspaper office, the police station, and the Kelley home, mostly waiting for something to happen.[15]

Around 1:30 on the morning of Tuesday, April 28, Rogers arrived home after another tiring day. His wife said a man who wouldn't identify himself had called several times, saying he wanted to speak to the reporter.

The phone rang again. This time, Rogers picked up.

"Have you got your clothes on?" a man asked.

"Yes," said Rogers, who wanted dearly to get out of his clothes and dive into bed.

The caller said Rogers should go to North Grant Boulevard and Finney Avenue, park, and blink his headlights because "a friend of yours wants to see you."

Rogers was jump-started out of fatigue by adrenaline and his reporter's instincts, which seldom failed him. Fifty years old in April

1931, Rogers had written extensively about major crimes, including murders committed by the Ku Klux Klan. In 1927, he won a Pulitzer Prize for leading the *Post-Dispatch*'s inquiry into a corrupt federal judge and forcing the judge's resignation.

Rogers got back into his car, hurried to the designated spot, blinked his lights, and waited. Before long, the passenger side door was yanked open, and a man got in. "Don't get nervous," the man said.

Don't get nervous? The newcomer had a pistol in each hand!

"Is this going to lead anywhere?" the shaken reporter managed to say.

"Yes."

Rogers was ordered to drive to a bridge and cross the Mississippi to East St. Louis, Illinois. Once across the river, he was directed onto a dark road, which led north into a rural section of St. Clair County. Soon, the car went by an abandoned service station.

"Turn around," the gun-toting passenger commanded. He told Rogers to drive into the gas station lot as he would if the station were still open for business, then go right back onto the road. Rogers did as he was ordered.

———

Kelley sensed that his time in captivity was ending. His keepers were behaving differently, their whispers telling him they must be trying to figure out how to let him go without being caught.

And there was a moment when he saw one of his captors standing in a doorway, lovingly caressing a Thompson submachine gun. "If you do any talking, you'll be smeared with this," the kidnapper said.

Possibly because he'd experienced combat in the Great War, Kelley was able to think more clearly than other men would have in the same circumstances. Why would his keepers warn him not to talk too much? *Because they're going to free me*, he reasoned.

Sure enough, late on the night of Monday, April 27, exactly a week after he'd been taken, Kelley was hustled outside and pushed into a car, the taped goggles over his eyes. As the car sped off, he detected the sound of another vehicle close by.

Kelley felt the car turning this way and that, describing a route he wouldn't be able to reconstruct. He heard no big-city noises. *We're still out in the country somewhere*, he thought.

Suddenly, the car came to an abrupt stop. The rear door opened, and Kelley was pulled out.

"Just wait here," a man said.

Then he was alone in the chill of the night. The surface beneath his feet was hard, and a faint odor of gasoline and oil was in the air. He could hear two car engines idling.

───────

When Rogers had driven about a hundred yards past the abandoned gas station, his armed passenger ordered him to pull off the road and stop. Rogers waited in the dark. After a few minutes, two sets of headlights approached. The man with Rogers reached over and flicked the switch to blink the headlights. The approaching headlights blinked in reply as the cars went by.

"Make a U-turn and follow those cars," the man ordered. As Rogers did so, he saw that the two cars had stopped next to the station. He was ordered to stop behind them.

"There's your friend," the passenger said. "He's waiting for you."

"What friend?" the bewildered reporter asked.

"Dr. Kelley," the man said as he got out and ran to one of the waiting vehicles.

As the two cars sped off, Rogers spotted a man standing in the station lot. Slowly, Rogers drove toward him. As the man was illuminated in the headlights, Rogers saw him take off a pair of goggles.

"Is this Dr. Kelley?" Rogers asked as he got out of his car.

"Yes!"

After Rogers introduced himself and shook Kelley's hand, the doctor said, "My God, this was an experience! I'm glad to be back in the hands of my friends."

At which point, the newly freed Kelley got into Rogers's car. Then, in a development that seems astonishing today, Kelley was driven not to his own home to be reunited with his family but to the home of the reporter. There, in the middle of the night, Kelley told his story to the exhausted but exhilarated Rogers in minute detail. A photographer took a picture of Kelley wearing the goggles the kidnappers had put on him.

Finally, as dawn was approaching, Rogers drove Kelley home, where he was reunited with his wife and had a shower, a change of clothes, and a nap.

Rogers had a big exclusive, and he had revenge over his archrival Brundidge for his exclusive on Charles Abernathy.

―――――

"My experience convinced me that the kidnappers were experts and had planned my abduction for weeks," Dr. Kelley said. When asked why he thought he had been singled out, he replied, "I have no idea."[16]

Oh, but he did. Surely, the motive was money. If the kidnappers were such experts, a reporter suggested, they must have obtained a ransom, right?

"That's a tough question," Kelley replied.

A tough question? Well, the reporter pressed, was a ransom paid or not?

"I can't answer that positively," Kelley said. "I was informed that no ransom was paid."

William D. Orthwein, the lawyer and cousin of Buppie Orthwein, said he *could* answer positively. "I can tell you frankly and honestly that not a dime has been paid," he told newsmen.[17]

The police believed that Kelley had been held initially in a rural area of St. Charles County, Missouri. They deduced that much from the label on the milk bottle Kelley had been given and his recollection of the airplane overhead, most likely flying a mail route between St. Louis and Kansas City, Missouri. And so what? The police could hardly check every farmhouse, every barn, every shack in St. Charles County.

Questions persisted. Denials notwithstanding, had a ransom been paid? No, William Orthwein and the Kelley family continued to insist. If not, why was Kelley not held until a ransom *was* paid? Why didn't the kidnappers just telephone the Kelley residence and make arrangements? Perhaps they suspected—correctly—that the Kelley phone was tapped.

"Kidnapping certainly has become one of our leading occupations," Kelley remarked the day of his release. "I wonder who's next on the list."[18]

———

The kidnapping of Dr. Isaac Kelley was shelved, at least for the time being, but not before persuading Missouri politicians that it was time— no, well past time—for the federal government to get involved in stamping out the scourge of people-snatching for ransom.

Questions surrounding the Kelley case would be left unanswered for three years until a former justice of the peace who owned a tavern and pool hall and was having money troubles sold a sensational account to the *Post-Dispatch*.

The story he told involved a woman of high society, two doctors (one her husband and the other her lover), and a shady lawyer. As the drama played out, in court and in the newspapers, many in the city's social elite were humiliated, perhaps to the pleasure of the less well-to-do.

But that's a story for later.

CHAPTER FOUR

A DRESSMAKER
WITH A VISION

Kansas City, Missouri
Wednesday, December 16, 1931

Nell Donnelly had a dream: "I want to make women look pretty when they are washing dishes."

How absurd! How impractical! Didn't she know a woman's proper place? No, actually. Nell Donnelly was not just a skilled seamstress; she was a force not to be denied. So she started her own dressmaking company. By her early forties, she was rich.

She was born Ellen Quinlan, the twelfth of thirteen children of a couple from County Cork, Ireland, on March 6, 1889, and grew up in Parsons, Kansas, after the family came to America in search of better things. She was just sixteen when she married Paul Donnelly, a representative for a shoe company, and moved with him to Kansas City.

To be sure, she *was* a skilled seamstress, but working with needle and thread or sitting at a pedal-powered sewing machine was not enough for her. Nell Donnelly had a vision and a will that would not be denied.

She envisioned house dresses with added ruffles and other frills that would appeal to the typical housewife of that time: a stay-at-home mother whose family couldn't afford much extravagance. The ruffles and frills would make her dresses a bit more expensive than the plain cotton dresses women were used to wearing while doing chores. But a woman wouldn't have to have a truly *rich* husband to buy the dresses designed by Donnelly, and she felt sure there was a market out there.

Was there ever! By 1930, the Donnelly Garment Company, which she started with her husband's help in Kansas City early in the twentieth century, employed a thousand people and sold stylish yet affordable house dresses across the country under the Nelly Don label.

On Wednesday, December 16, 1931, as Donnelly was arriving home in her chauffeur-driven Lincoln convertible, four gunmen hijacked the car in the driveway. Then they drove Donnelly and her young chauffeur, George Blair, about twenty miles west and imprisoned them in a farmhouse.

The next day, a lawyer for the Donnellys, James E. Taylor, got a letter addressed to Paul Donnelly and demanding $75,000 for Nell's freedom. Taylor knew just whom to call: his law partner, James A. Reed, a neighbor and friend of Nell Donnelly. Reed, who was in court in Jefferson City at the time, immediately raced to Kansas City to take charge.

———

James Alexander Reed had just turned seventy, and he was as well connected as a man could be. He was close to Thomas J. Pendergast, the Democratic political boss who ran Kansas City at the time and who had helped Reed become Kansas City mayor from 1900 to 1903 and later a U.S. senator for three terms.

Handsome, with wavy hair and dark, deep-set eyes, Reed looked like an aristocrat. In fact, he had grown up poor, one of six children born to farm parents in Ohio. The family moved to Iowa when Reed was a young boy, and his father died when Reed was eight. He attended high school irregularly yet managed to become a lawyer by studying law books he bought from the sale of a horse.

He started a law practice in Kansas City in his late twenties and was appointed Jackson County counselor in 1896. Two years later, he was elected county prosecutor. Reed served in that post for just two years before the Pendergast machine tapped him to run for mayor in 1900. (Perhaps Pendergast thought it safer not to have Reed in the prosecutor's office, where he had won convictions in all but two of the 287 cases he brought to trial.)

Reed served a term as mayor and was elected to the Senate in 1910. He was briefly a candidate for president in 1924 and again in 1928, when he decided not to run for a fourth term in the Senate.

———

In his years in Washington, Reed never forgot the folks back home. He wrote dozens of letters of recommendation for people seeking patronage jobs in the Pendergast operation. Inevitably, then, he knew people who were frowned upon by good-government purists.

One of Reed's acquaintances was a man named John Lazia. With his glasses, receding hairline, and prominent jowls, "Brother John" Lazia, as he was sometimes called, might have passed for a school principal or perhaps an accountant or an insurance salesman.

The appearance was misleading. Having fled the boredom of school in the eighth grade, Lazia became a street thug. While still a young man, he was sentenced to twelve years in prison for armed robbery. But Tom Pendergast had an eye for talent and helped Lazia obtain parole after less than a year. In return, the authorities wanted Lazia to join the army.

But Pendergast wanted Lazia in *his* army. Lazia became a Pendergast loyalist and by his early thirties was a bootlegger, owner of a soft drink company and a bail bond company, and operator of several gambling resorts. (Pendergast also used his influence to get lenient treatment for Lazia on tax-evasion charges.)

"Brother John" was head of the city's Northside Democratic Club and acted as a "get out the vote" organizer in Italian neighborhoods for Pendergast-machine candidates. Lazia also had influence over hiring and firing in the Kansas City Police Department.

After Nell Donnelly was kidnapped, Reed wasted no time phoning John Lazia, with whom he was well acquainted. We can never know exactly what Reed said, but we can be sure of the gist of it: "Nell has been kidnapped, and I need the help of your gangsters to find her and bring her home. And don't worry about the police." With the police on the sidelines, Lazia dispatched search parties. Within hours, his men had found a restaurateur they suspected had knowledge of the kidnappers. The Lazia men used their considerable powers of persuasion on the restaurant operator and were soon on their way to the farmhouse where Nell Donnelly and her chauffeur were being held.

Guns at the ready, Lazia's men barged into the farmhouse, found Donnelly, and informed her out-of-town captors that they had made a big, big mistake. Perhaps acting on orders, Lazia's men exercised compassion and did not kill the abductors.

Donnelly and her chauffeur were driven to Kansas City, where they were dropped off. They had coffee at an all-night café before making their way home. Their ordeal had lasted a day and a half, and they had been freed with no ransom having been paid.

Before long, several suspects were arrested, likely with tips provided by Lazia's operatives. Two men were convicted and given life sentences; a third got thirty-five years.

So the kidnapping of Nell Donnelly had a happy ending (except for the kidnappers). And yet there was an unsettling message. James A. Reed, former U.S. senator, former Kansas City mayor, former *prosecutor*, hadn't called the police in the moment of crisis. Instead, he had called on a known mobster.

Would the relatives of other kidnapping victims be tempted to do the same? The kidnapping and rescue of Nell Donnelly had gotten a lot of press coverage. What kind of message did the episode convey? Nothing very good.

By this time, in Kansas City and other big cities, gangsters were becoming a second arm of government—helping the political parties select candidates, helping the police hire, fire, and promote. They acted as unofficial chambers of commerce in some places, welcoming gangsters visiting from other cities as long as the visitors paid deference and sometimes tribute.

How had all this come about? Machine politics had sprouted and thrived in many cities, in part because clubhouse politicians offered jobs and services to immigrants. Then came Prohibition. Millions of law-abiding Americans still wanted to drink and not always in speakeasies. If an honest American wanted a steady supply of top-shelf liquor and wine to sip in the living room or serve to dinner guests, he couldn't rely only on the neighborhood druggist. He needed a reliably civilized distributor or salesman, preferably someone who was friendly and nonthreatening.

And if an honest American wanted to gamble in an area where gambling was officially illegal, that was another recreation provided by gangsters—another "service," as it were. Inevitably, with so much cash sloshing around, some of it flowed to city hall and the precinct house. The pols and the police, after all, felt entitled to their "licensing fees." And where was the harm, really, as long as everyone got along, especially if more violent and vulgar out-of-town criminal elements were kept a safe distance away?

Honest Americans wanted goods and services that only criminals provided—that was the basic, contradictory fact of life in America at the time. The gangsters were not only corrupt. They were corrupting.

CHAPTER FIVE

BELOVED INNOCENT

Hopewell, New Jersey
Tuesday, March 1, 1932

Charles and Anne Lindbergh had finished dinner and were relaxing in the living room of their new home. They could hear gusts rattling the tree branches on this cold and rainy night.

Here, in a wooded and hilly region of western New Jersey, Lindbergh had the privacy he so needed. He had found something close to happiness. "Colonel Lindbergh," as he was formally known, had become quite well-to-do, his celebrity having opened various boardroom doors for him. Yet though he was acquainted with titans of business and industry, he had few close relationships outside his family.

Adorable Charles Jr., not quite two years old, was asleep in his upstairs room as nurse Betty Gow peeked in on him around 8:30. She was relieved to see the baby blissfully somnolent in his night robe. He had a cold, for which he had been given medicine.

Around 9:10 or 9:15, Lindbergh heard a noise that sounded to him (as he would testify later) like pieces of wood clattering.

"What is that?" he said to his wife, who answered with a shrug.*

The Lindberghs were not concerned enough to get up and check. They had a playful little terrier that was known to get into things. There was a crate of oranges in the kitchen; perhaps it had fallen off a counter. Or maybe it was the wind.

Around 10:00 p.m., Gow went to look in on the baby once more—and got the shock of her life. The crib was empty. There were muddy footprints on the floor, leading from the crib to a nearby window, which appeared to have been pried open. On the window sill was an envelope containing a note demanding $50,000 in twenty-, ten-, and five-dollar bills. It was signed with a symbol of two overlapping rings in blue ink and a smaller center circle in red.

The nurse raced downstairs. "The baby's been kidnapped!" she shouted.

Lindbergh and his wife rushed up to see for themselves. Then Lindbergh called the Hopewell police chief, Charles Williamson, who called state police headquarters in Trenton, then drove to the Lindbergh home with another officer.

Philadelphia police were notified, as were New York City police. Special guards were posted at the Holland Tunnel, ferry terminals, and the George Washington Bridge, which had opened just the previous summer.

Meanwhile, Lindbergh and a bevy of police officers searched the grounds of his property. Two sets of footprints and marks from a ladder were found under the nursery window. A chisel lay nearby. Soon, a makeshift wooden ladder was found about seventy feet from the house.

---

*   The scene and dialogue are derived from the testimony in the trial of the suspected kidnapper, which began on January 2, 1935, and was exhaustively covered by the *New York Times* (www.nytimes.com).

It was broken in the middle. Later, Lindbergh would speculate that the wood-clatter sound he thought had come from the kitchen was really the sound of a ladder falling outside the house.

The ransom note contained the word *were* when obviously *where* was meant. It said the child was "in gute care." And it warned Lindbergh "for making anyding public or for notify the police."[19] It seemed clear that the author was either a foreigner or pretending to be one. Or if he was an American, he was not an educated person.

———

Just after 11:00 p.m. on March 1, the night supervisor at the FBI called J. Edgar Hoover at home to tell him that a police teletype had just reported the kidnapping of the Lindbergh baby. Hoover knew that the FBI had no jurisdiction in the case, since kidnapping was not a federal offense. Still, he ordered that he be kept informed of any developments. He was called again about two hours later with the information that a ransom note had been found at the crime scene.

At once, Hoover summoned his driver and went to bureau headquarters. Most of his aides were already there. It was quickly decided that the bureau would offer "unofficial" assistance to Charles and Anne Lindbergh. A special squad of about twenty men was set up for that purpose.

No doubt, Hoover felt sympathy for the parents. Nor could he have failed to realize that if the FBI could help recover the child, the prestige of the agency would increase enormously.[20]

———

The *New York Times* devoted four front-page stories to the kidnapping the next day. The main story noted that a woman was believed to be involved, since some footprints below the window were considerably smaller than others. The police in New Jersey and nearby states were told to be on the alert for suspicious-looking couples, especially any who may have asked for directions to the Lindbergh home.

The police theorized early on that the kidnapper or kidnappers would have used a stolen car. The license plate numbers of sixteen cars stolen in New Jersey between noon and midnight were transmitted to police in several states.

A front-page story in the *Times* reported the reaction of Senator Patterson of Missouri, cosponsor of the federal kidnapping law pending on Capitol Hill. "It is a shock to me to hear of this outrage," he said. "I hope the child will soon be returned... This filthy act will aid us in passing the needed legislation."[21]

That prediction turned out to be right, of course. But some initial "facts" were quickly shot down. The smaller footprints beneath the window were indeed those of a woman—Anne Lindbergh. So perhaps there was only *one* kidnapper.

———

On the very back page of the *New York Times* of March 2, 1932, was a seemingly routine article. It told of a dinner the night before at the Waldorf-Astoria where more than sixteen hundred alumni of New York University had celebrated their alma mater's centennial. Thirty-four alumni received the newly created meritorious service award from Chancellor Elmer Ellsworth Brown, the *Times* reported. The article listed several people who spoke at the dinner.

But the most important fact about the dinner concerned someone who was expected to be there but did not appear: Charles A. Lindbergh. Curiously, the article did not note the famous aviator's absence. Perhaps the reporter simply did not know Lindbergh was supposed to be there, even though his anticipated appearance had been well publicized. Perhaps a cub reporter was assigned to the event and didn't think Lindbergh's absence was such a big deal.

It's certain that with the news of the kidnapping breaking on the same night, the editors weren't much concerned with the NYU dinner. Soon, it would be reported that Chancellor Brown was to blame for Lindbergh's failure to attend. In a note to Lindbergh before the dinner, the chancellor had apparently said the event was to be on the *fourth* of March, not the first. So Lindbergh innocently dined at home on March 1, the night his son was taken from his crib.

For conspiracy theorists, the seeds of suspicion had been planted.

———

Three days after the kidnapping, Hoover went to Hopewell, New Jersey, to offer his assistance to Charles and Anne Lindbergh. They declined to see him. Hoover then conferred with Colonel Herbert Norman Schwarzkopf, head of the New Jersey State Police, who told the FBI boss that his people could manage things by themselves. Schwarzkopf was leery of federal men parachuting into his cases (although the Treasury Department would play a vital role as it recorded the serial numbers on the ransom currency), and he would soon have plenty of turf battles without having to worry about Hoover.

But Hoover craved a role in the case, even hoping he might be put in charge overall despite the absence of an officially defined role for the FBI. U.S. attorney general Homer Cummings even wrote to Governor A. Harry Moore of New Jersey that "a coordinator of tested ability was available in the person of J. Edgar Hoover."[22]

The governor ignored the suggestion, which had undoubtedly been inspired by Hoover himself. As the investigation lurched on, it became clear that Hoover, glory hound that he was, had precisely the organizational skills that were sorely needed.

CHAPTER SIX

THE BOY IN THE WALL

Niles, Ohio
Wednesday, March 2, 1932

As Americans were waking up to the horrible news about the Lindbergh baby being kidnapped the night before, they worried about their own children: Were they *really* safe playing in the streets or in the fields? Were they safe in their own homes?

James DeJute Jr., the eleven-year-old son of a contractor in Niles, a small city in northeastern Ohio, had been fighting a cold, but he was well enough to go to Lincoln School. Jimmy, as he was called by just about everyone, happened to be wearing his Lindbergh-style pilot's cap.

It was no secret that Jimmy's father, James Sr., prospered as a contractor. But the DeJute family was hardly famous, and it was the opposite of high society. An outsider might have assumed that the DeJutes were descended from French aristocracy. In fact, the name "DeJute" was invented, shortened from the Italian "DeGuido."

This morning, Jimmy was accompanied by his cousin, Anna. As

they took a shortcut through the grounds of St. Luke's Episcopal Church, they saw a brown coupe parked by the curb. The hood was up, and two men seemed to be looking at the engine.

"Hey, little boy, come here!" one of the men called out, as Anna would recall later.

Jimmy approached the men. When he got close, they grabbed him. He yelled and struggled and broke away for a moment, but the men caught him and put him in the car in front of his screaming cousin. Then the car sped away.

Other schoolboys noted the license plate number. But the license number was useless: the plate was soon found behind a church, where it had been tossed. It had been on a *black* coupe stolen in Niles in early January.

———

Jimmy had a brother, Anthony, who was several years younger—just a toddler, really. Anthony was too young to comprehend what was happening in his parents' house. All he knew was that his mother and father were afraid. They went from room to room, whispering to each other, and his mother's eyes were red from crying. Now and then, the phone rang. His father whispered into it.

My brother is gone, Anthony thought. *And maybe they think it's my fault.*

For Anthony had wished that his older brother would go away. From the time he first had feelings, Anthony sensed that his parents liked Jimmy better. Now, Anthony's wish had come true. His brother was *gone*. Anthony wished that Jimmy would come back. He prayed as hard as he could before falling asleep.*

———

* Here, I am indebted to David Anthony DeJute, Anthony's son, for sharing his father's recollections.

The agonizing wait went on until Saturday, March 5, when a veteran Trumbull County detective, W. J. Harrison, who had sources on both sides of the law, got a cryptic phone call. "Go to Scotty's place, and you will find that DeJute kid from Niles," the caller said.

Lawmen in the region were familiar with "Scotty's place," a recently abandoned gambling den that stood behind a barbecue joint and a filling station on a road on the outskirts of Youngstown, Ohio. The previous year, a woman who ran a house of pleasure had been kidnapped and held at Scotty's until she arranged for a ransom to be paid.

Deputies from Trumbull and Mahoning Counties staked out Scotty's place, which was supposedly vacant. So why was smoke coming from a chimney? The lawmen rushed the building and kicked in the door.

There was no one there. The interior was devoid of furniture, though there were rugs on the floor along with an old mattress and a couple of pillows. A fire was burning in the kitchen stove, and a partially eaten loaf of bread lay in a corner.

Then Detective Harrison spotted a math textbook on the floor. On the flyleaf was written "James DeJute, 327 Robbins Avenue, Niles, Ohio, grade 5A, Lincoln School."

For a moment, a sickening silence enveloped the investigators. The kidnappers must have found out, somehow, that the law was coming. They had fled with their captive.

But a rifle and pistol were visible in one corner. The kidnappers wouldn't have left their weapons behind, would they?

"Jimmy!" an officer shouted in desperation.

"Yes, sir! Yes, sir, here I am!" came a boy's voice from behind a wall.[23]

A couple of lawmen kicked at the wall, which was only plasterboard covered with wallpaper. And there stood James DeJute Jr., shivering and pale, between two young men. One of the men held a revolver, but he surrendered it at once.

"Take me home, please, to my father and mother," the boy pleaded, breaking into tears.

Home Jimmy went, in a police car with siren screaming, to a joyful reunion with his parents. Neighbors and hundreds of other well-wishers swarmed over the DeJutes' property.

Outside of seizing him in the first place, the abductors had treated him kindly, the boy said. "They were good to me and told me I could call them both 'Mister.'" Most of the time, he was kept in a dark closet, the boy said. He was given soft-boiled eggs and was promised that he'd go free as soon as his father paid money.

A special grand jury was to convene the following Monday to indict the culprits, identified as John Demarco, thirty, and Dowell Hargraves, twenty-seven. "Both are habitués of Youngstown pool rooms and speakeasies, with questionable records," the Times reported.

Hargraves waived his right to a trial by jury, perhaps fearing that ordinary people not well versed in the law would be eager to find him guilty, especially with the Lindbergh kidnapping the talk of the land. He put his fate in the hands of an Ohio state court judge, who promptly found him guilty of kidnapping and sentenced him to life in prison.

Demarco, too, would be convicted and sentenced to life in prison, as would a third man, Anthony Lauri, thirty-seven, of Youngstown.

In sentencing Hargraves on March 16, 1932, the judge said kidnapping was a crime that "strikes a blow at the tenderest and most sacred affections of human blood" and was becoming all too common.[24]

And there was a chilling footnote to the DeJute case. According to a March 4 report in the New York Times, Jimmy's father had received a note the day after his son's abduction. The note demanded a ransom of

$10,000; otherwise, the boy would be returned "in installments." And just so there would be no misunderstanding, at the top of the note were the words "Remember Marion Parker."[*]

---

[*]   "Kidnappers Demand $10,000 for Return of Ohio Boy," *New York Times*, March 4, 1932.

CHAPTER SEVEN

THE YOUNGER TWIN

Los Angeles
Thursday, December 15, 1927

Marion and Marjorie Parker were identical twins, but they were by no means the same. By the time they turned twelve, on October 11, 1927, their distinctive personalities had emerged. Marion was more of a tomboy, and she was happier playing with toy trains than with dolls, which Marjorie preferred.

And Marjorie was content helping her mother, Geraldine, around the house, while Marion liked to accompany her father, Perry, to the First National Trust and Savings Bank, where he was a mid-level officer.

Their personality differences notwithstanding, the girls loved each other's company, and both adored their brother, also named Perry, who was eight years older. (Marion had been given her first name, instead of the more common "Marian" for a girl, after her father's middle name.)

On this Thursday, which was chilly by Southern California standards, the girls were happy as they rode the streetcar to Mount

Vernon Junior High School. Part of the day was to be devoted to Christmas parties in each classroom.

Around noon, a wavy-haired young man walked into the school office, where he was met by Mary Holt, the teacher in charge of attendance and registration. "I need to see the Parker girl," the man announced. "I work with Mr. Perry Parker at the bank. Mr. Parker has been in an accident and is calling for his daughter."[25]

Holt was confused. "We have *two* Parker girls at our school," she said.

"He wants the younger one," the man replied.

The *younger* one? In fact, Marjorie was the younger twin by a few minutes, but she was slightly larger than Marion. So the girls occasionally joked that Marion, not Marjorie, was the younger sister.

"Do you mean Marion?" Holt asked the stranger.

"Yes, ma'am, that is her name." Sensing that Holt was uneasy, the visitor urged her to call the bank to confirm his account.

Holt was a seasoned administrator, a stickler for rules and procedures, which was why she was acting school administrator on this Thursday when Principal Cora Freeman happened to be away for several hours. She was known to be protective of the children and cautious about strangers in the building. She would sometimes call the parents before releasing a child to someone else.

Which is why what Mary Holt did—or did *not* do—next was so strange and heartbreaking.

The young man had such a friendly, self-assured manner that Holt decided there was no need to check out his story, even though she should have found it implausible on its face. So she summoned Marion from the Christmas party.

And here was another fateful what-if moment. Marion knew that her father was staying home from the bank on this day to celebrate his birthday with his wife. Yet she apparently did not ask details about the "accident" that had befallen him. Perhaps she was too stunned by the news to think clearly, or perhaps she was charmed by the cheerful stranger. Perhaps she felt comfortable with the man after meeting him in the company of a trusted authority figure, Mary Holt. For whatever reasons, Marion left the school with him.

Later that afternoon, Principal Freeman returned. Holt told her Perry Parker had been in an accident and that a family friend had fetched Marion. Freeman was not alarmed; she was familiar with Holt's habitual caution and had confidence in her judgment.

Yet oddly—bafflingly, really—Freeman did not ask if *Marjorie* Parker had been notified of her father's mishap or if anyone in authority had even talked to her. Nor, apparently, did the principal press for a clearer explanation on why the "family friend" had not picked up both twins.

Marjorie Parker waited outside the school for her sister so they could catch a streetcar home together. That was their usual routine. When Marion did not emerge, Marjorie thought she must have stayed late to help a teacher clean up after a party. Marjorie, not wanting to miss the next streetcar, went home alone.

Perry and Geraldine Parker were not alarmed when Marjorie appeared without her sister. The idea that Marion had stayed to help a teacher seemed quite in character. But after a while, Perry Parker decided he'd better drive over to the school to get Marion. He thought she might be nervous traveling home in the dark, which was fast descending.

So Parker called the school, was put through to Mary Holt, and identified himself.

"How are you feeling?" she asked.

"I feel fine, Mrs. Holt. Thank you for asking. Is Marion still at school?"

Why no, Holt said. Marion left hours before with "the man you sent to pick her up" because of the accident.

Parker was flabbergasted. "I was not in any accident, and I did not send anyone to pick up Marion from school!"

Parker hung up in dread and was about to call the police when the doorbell rang. A telegram had arrived: "Do absolutely nothing till you receive special delivery."[26]

A short time later, another telegram: "Marion secure. Use good judgment. Interference with my plans dangerous. George Fox."

George Fox? The Parkers did not recognize the name.

Through the night, the parents agonized. By morning, they could wait no longer. They phoned the police. Detectives hurried to the house. They told the Parkers that several other young people had gone missing recently.

As the detectives were taking statements from Perry and Geraldine Parker on Friday morning, a special delivery arrived. It had been mailed at six o'clock Thursday evening. It was addressed to "P. M. Parker" and demanded $1,500, in the form of seventy-five twenty-dollar gold certificates. The letter ordered Parker to "go about your daily business as usual" and not to call the police. It promised that further instructions would be coming. "Failure to comply with these requests means no one will ever see the girl again except the angels in heaven." The letter was signed "Fate."

Even more chillingly, there was an accompanying note, written in Marion's hand. "Dear Daddy and Mother: I wish I could come home. I think I'll die if I have to be like this much longer. Won't someone tell me why this had to happen to me? Daddy please do what this man tells you or he'll kill me if you don't."

The police were puzzled by the demand for only $1,500. To be sure, that was a fair sum at the time, but a ransom demand was typically for a far larger amount. Perhaps the kidnapper (or kidnappers) knew that the Parkers, while comfortable enough, were far from wealthy.

———————

Somehow, Perry Parker held himself together as he went to work at the bank that Friday. As instructed, he got $1,500 from his personal account—and recorded the serial number for each bill. Meanwhile, the police went to Mount Vernon Junior High School to question Mary Holt. Emotionally shattered, she described the man who had spirited Marion away: twenty-five to thirty years old, about five feet eight inches tall, brown wavy hair, brownish-gray overcoat, and a dark gray hat. Spoke good English, seemed to be well educated.

When Parker arrived home on Friday afternoon, there had been no further word from the kidnapper. Around eight o'clock, the phone rang. "Mr. Parker, do you have the money?" a man said.

"Yes, I have it. Is Marion all right?"

"I'll call back in five minutes."

But a full half hour went by. Finally, the man called again and told Parker to drive alone to a certain section of Gramercy Street and wait there. Parker did as ordered. He waited in the dark for hours. Shortly before midnight, he drove home. There, he learned that the police had followed him, hoping to catch the kidnapper. Parker feared that the kidnapper had sensed this.

He had. "Mr. Parker, I am ashamed of you!" the abductor wrote in another special delivery letter on Saturday. "You'll never know how you disappointed your daughter... Pray to God for forgiveness for your mistake last night." But at least the kidnapper, who signed the letter "Fate-Fox," said he'd give new instructions by Saturday evening.[27]

And there was another plaintive note from Marion, begging her father to follow the kidnapper's instructions.

Two more warning letters arrived that Saturday. The first was signed "Fox-Fate." The second said: "Fox is my name. Very sly you know. Set no traps. I'll watch for them. Get this straight! Remember that life hangs by a thread. I have a Gillette [razor] ready and able to handle the situation." It was signed "Fate."[28]

By this time, the Parkers and the police wondered what kind of lunatic or monster they were dealing with. Just after seven in the evening, the kidnapper called and specified a circuitous route that Parker should take to a particular street corner. Parker left immediately with the money, the police having promised not to follow.

This time, he did not have to wait long. In his rearview mirror, he saw another car approaching. The vehicle stopped with the passenger side alongside Parker's car. The driver, whose face was partly covered by a bandanna, leaned out the window and pointed a sawed-off shotgun at Parker. "You see this gun?"

"I see it."

The kidnapper demanded the money. But Parker, after all he and his family had been through, demanded to know where his daughter was.

The abductor held up a blanket-wrapped form. For a moment, Parker saw the face of his daughter. The cheeks were bright. Were her eyes open...?

"Marion?"

"She's sleeping," the kidnapper said.

Parker handed over the money.

"Wait here just a minute," the kidnapper said. With that, he slowly drove off. After a moment, Parker began to follow, trying to make out the license plate number. But the plate had been bent to obscure the digits.

After a block or so, the car slowed, and Marion was pushed out, falling to the curb. Parker braked and rushed to his blanket-wrapped daughter, kneeling next to her. Her eyes *were* open!

"Marion?"

No response.

Parker embraced his daughter, sensing instantly that the form was too small. With shaking hands, he unwrapped the blanket and screamed.

Marion Parker was dead, a wire wrapped tightly around her neck. Her death-glazed eyes had been sewn open. Makeup had been applied to her face to make her appear alive. Her legs had been cut off and her arms severed at the elbows. Only part of her torso was there, wrapped in towels. Her intestines had been cut out and her body stuffed with rags.

The father's screams had prompted someone to call the police. Hardened detectives wept at the scene. Parker was driven home in a police car; another officer followed, driving Parker's car.

Parker told his wife, son, and surviving daughter that Marion was dead. For the moment, he kept the more horrifying details to himself.

Around that time, the kidnapper stopped at a Los Angeles café for a bite to eat. He paid with one of the bills from the ransom and smirked at the pretty young cashier, saying, "You'd be surprised if you knew who I was."[29]

The next day, Sunday, December 18, six separate bundles containing parts of Marion's body were found along roads in the Elysian Park section of Los Angeles. The car used by the kidnapper, a new gray Chrysler coupe, was found in a parking garage. It had been stolen in Kansas City a month before.

The doctor who performed the autopsy said he could not be certain if Marion had been alive for any of the desecration inflicted on her body.

Mary Holt was desolate, even though Principal Freeman said she herself might have let Marion go with the charming stranger had she been there. Or perhaps Freeman was just trying to comfort her colleague and friend. It was no use. Holt was inconsolable. She broke down while testifying at a coroner's inquest the Monday after the slaying and had to be helped out of the room by her husband. Soon, she stopped working at the school. Her hair turned prematurely white. She would be haunted by her terrible mistake for the rest of her life.

Thousands of police officers from San Diego to San Francisco and little towns in between were looking for the killer. Anyone remotely suspicious was questioned. The case was covered sensationally in papers from coast to coast.

One of the towels used to wrap Marion's body bore the label of the Bellevue Arms Apartments northwest of downtown Los Angeles. The manager recalled renting an apartment the previous month to a man who fit the description of the man who had taken Marion from her school. The man had given his name as Donald Evans and had asked for a quiet room in the rear. He had left a couple of days before. Perhaps because Evans's apartment was vacant, the police did not immediately search it.

Meanwhile, the Los Angeles Police Department had a fingerprint expert, Howard Barlow. Given the science of that time, his contribution seems all the more remarkable: he managed to lift prints from the stolen car the kidnapper had used. The smirking, arrogant criminal had neglected to wipe the car's interior before abandoning it.

The fingerprints in the car matched those on the ransom messages sent to the Parker house. They also matched prints from an old bank-forgery case that had been handled in juvenile court because of the tender age of the offender, William Edward Hickman. He was nineteen when police concluded that Donald Evans and Hickman were one and the same and that he was the kidnapper.

The police returned to the Bellevue Arms Apartments to search the apartment that "Donald Evans" had vacated. Inside, they found bloodstains, copies of newspaper accounts of the kidnapping, and, in a wastebasket, half a hazelnut. Someone recalled that half a hazelnut had been found in the wrappings around Marion's body. The two halves were found to fit perfectly.

Some Gillette razor blades were found. And on a sugar bowl, there was a thumbprint that matched Hickman's.

Hickman had once been a messenger at the bank where Perry Parker worked. After being fired for forging checks worth several hundred dollars, Hickman had been given probation in juvenile court, but he could not get his bank job back. The police speculated he may have blamed Parker for that and wanted to hurt him—and make some money—by kidnapping his daughter, whom he had likely seen at the bank. (Parker had had nothing to do with his hiring or firing.)

An increasingly frail Mary Holt was shown a photo of Hickman and identified him as the man who had taken Marion away.

But some people in Kansas City, where he had grown up, refused to believe Hickman could be such a monster.

"It can't be so; my boy could not do a thing like that," Hickman's mother, Eva, said in Kansas City. "My boy is a good clean boy."[30] Some former teachers echoed those sentiments.

Hickman was born on February 1, 1908, in Hartford, Arkansas, one of several children of William and Eva Hickman. The father was a philanderer, and his wife was mentally unstable, spending time in the State Lunatic Asylum (as the mental hospital was then called) in Little Rock. The marriage broke up, and in 1921, Eva Hickman moved to Kansas City.

Young William (or Edward, as he often called himself) made friends easily. He was a good student at Central High School in Kansas City:

class vice president, honor society member, student council member, yearbook editor, a fine public speaker, a star on the debate team, a member of a church Sunday school basketball team.

Then he changed. When he had to settle for honorable mention in a couple of speaking contests, he seethed in anger. He abandoned his friends, quit extracurricular activities, neglected his schoolwork. He managed to graduate and enrolled at a junior college—where he lasted for nine days. Aimless, he worked at odd jobs.

A different and sinister personality now resided in the body of William Edward Hickman. Or had that personality been dormant in him for years? The "new" Hickman had no conscience, no empathy, no real concept of shame or remorse. He was a psychopath.

The new Hickman dreamed of going to Hollywood and becoming a movie star. In one of his odd jobs, at a public library in Kansas City, he befriended a similarly restless youth named Welby Hunt, who was three years younger. In November 1926, the pair robbed a candy store, getting away with about $70. They headed to California, where they would live with Hunt's grandparents. Hickman still hoped to make it in the movies—the longest of long shots, since this was still the era of silent films. Hickman's speaking skills would be useless.

On Christmas Eve, the pair robbed a drugstore. During the heist, a police officer wandered in. There was a shootout, and the proprietor was fatally wounded. The police officer was wounded in the abdomen.

Hickman and Hunt stayed out of sight for a while, but eventually, they needed money. They got jobs as messengers at a local bank—fatefully, the bank where Perry Parker worked. Then, on May 24, 1927, the body of Hunt's grandfather was found beneath a bridge in Pasadena. The day before, he had withdrawn a large sum of money from his bank. The money was not found with the body, but five purported suicide notes were.

Under normal circumstances, the murder might have overshadowed all other events. But Charles Lindbergh had landed in Paris just three days earlier, and for a moment in time, his triumph dominated the news.

Los Angeles detectives were instantly suspicious of the "suicide." In their experience, *one* note was usually sufficient for someone about to commit suicide. Besides, the five notes found with Hunt's grandfather appeared to have been written by two different people.

In the autumn of 1927, after losing his bank messenger job and being placed on probation for the check forgeries, Hickman returned to Kansas City and got a job as an usher in a movie theater. But he spent too much time watching the screen and not enough time ushering, so he was fired. Then, he apparently got the urge to travel...and to kill.

He stole a car from a traveling salesman and drove to Chicago. Then he is believed to have moved on to Milwaukee, where on October 11, a young girl was strangled by a man fitting Hickman's description. On to Michigan and thence to Philadelphia. On October 29, a gas station attendant in Chester, Pennsylvania, was shot to death during a robbery by a man answering Hickman's description.

Then the intellectual side of Hickman's personality—or former personality—is believed to have resurfaced. He is believed to have driven to Gettysburg to tour the Civil War battlefield.

After more frenetic travel in the East, he drove to Ohio, robbing three stores in the space of a half hour. After several more robberies, he was back in Kansas City, there to abandon the car he'd stolen from the traveling salesman and ponder what to do next.

On the night of November 7, just as Dr. Herbert Mantz of Kansas City was starting his new gray Chrysler coupe, Hickman emerged from the dark, pointed a pistol at the doctor, and took his car. Eleven days later, having driven back to California, he robbed a drugstore, getting away with $30. Then he settled into the Bellevue Arms Apartments.

On November 23, Hickman drove to San Diego to see the sights. He picked up a young couple who needed a ride to Los Angeles. On the way, it became clear that Hickman and the young man had similar interests: they planned to meet three days hence to do some stickups.

Hickman and his new accomplice robbed a drugstore on November 27 and two more on December 5. The accomplice asked Hickman why he stole sleeping pills and chloroform as well as money. Because I have an idea to make some *real* money, Hickman explained: kidnapping a child for ransom.

———

In the days after the murder of Marion Parker, Hickman was so loathed that several men who bore a resemblance to him were set upon and beaten by mobs before they could prove that they were *not* Hickman.

The real Hickman had driven a stolen car to Seattle, where he bought gasoline. The station attendant thought he recognized him and called police. Quickly, it was determined that the twenty-dollar bill Hickman spent for gas was from the ransom. Acting on a hunch that Hickman might head south again, the police staked out a stretch of highway leading from Washington State into Oregon.

He was spotted three days before Christmas near the little town of Echo in northeastern Oregon. The police found about a thousand dollars of the ransom money, along with a sawed-off shotgun and an automatic pistol, in the car he was driving. Hickman was jailed in nearby Pendleton, Oregon, for the time being.

———

The article on the arrest of William Edward Hickman was displayed on the front page of the *New York Times* on Friday, December 23, 1927.

The editors of the *Times* thought their readers deserved something more cheerful on page 1 for the start of the Christmas weekend. "A flying mother joined her more famous flying son here today," an article from Mexico City began.[31]

The article, in the center at the top of the front page, told of Mrs. Evangeline Lindbergh's flight to Mexico City to meet her son, Charles, who was visiting the capital for a few days, and Ambassador Dwight Morrow, his father-in-law.

In an uncharacteristic display of emotion, Charles went up in his plane, the *Spirit of St. Louis*, to greet the aircraft carrying his mother, but because of clouds, they didn't see each other until both were on the ground. A luncheon was held in their honor, and Colonel Lindbergh was unusually effusive. "I have never spent a more enjoyable time," he said. "I wish to thank you all for the reception you have given me here today, and I assure you that it is one of those which I shall never forget."

The heart of the Lone Eagle soared on wings of joy as the year of his epic triumph was coming to an end.

CHAPTER EIGHT

SANE OR INSANE?

Pendleton, Oregon
Early 1928

"Kidnappings and savage murders are the worst of America's crimes and everything should be done to prevent anyone interfering in any way with the liberty and life of American citizens," a letter to newspapers across the country declared. "Young men and college students should consider the Parker case as a typical crime of the worst that can happen when a young man gradually loses interest in family, friends, and his own honesty."[32]

The author of this sage advice for young people knew what he was talking about. His name was William Edward Hickman.

"I put my own life in a mess and the way out is dark," he wrote as he awaited trial. "Think it over, see my mistake. Be honest and upright. Respect the law. If you do these things you will be happier in the end and you will have gained much more from your life."

How had Hickman become a monster? He had been born prematurely. Was there a problem—oxygen deprivation, say—as he came into the world? He came from a broken home, but so do many children.

Regardless of his early problems, he was clearly intelligent enough to have made his way in the world by honest means.

Psychiatrists who examined Hickman found him lucid and clear-headed, quite able to understand what he had done. They declared, in essence, that he was not insane. Just evil.

In his brief jail stay in Oregon, Hickman was interviewed by an editor and reporter for the *Pendleton East Oregonian* newspaper. He told them he had indeed traveled to Chicago at one point, but he denied killing the young woman in Milwaukee in October, so that crime remained unsolved, at least officially.

Most importantly, Hickman claimed that he had had a partner in the kidnapping and murder of Marion Parker and that the partner had done the actual killing. Investigators soon debunked that claim.

Hickman had trouble sleeping in the Oregon jail, as he was taunted by other prisoners. Then as now, many criminals, even the most incorrigible, despise men who prey on children. No doubt, Hickman was relieved when Los Angeles police officers arrived to take him back to California on a train. It was Christmas Eve.

On the train, Hickman wrote a confession of sorts. He also talked freely, the words trickling out of his mouth like drops of sewage. He insisted he had not violated Marion sexually. He said they had enjoyed going to the movies together. He conceded that she had become anxious and tearful and wanted to go home. He said he strangled her by surprise to spare her fear beforehand.

Yes, Hickman conceded, he had acted alone in abducting, killing, and dismembering the twelve-year-old. (Later, he recalled that, while he was cutting up her body in his bathtub, he became hungry. So he took a break to snack on crackers and sardines.)

"I would like to say I have had no bad personal habits," the killer wrote on the train. "I have never been drunk or taken any intoxicating drinks. I do not gamble."[33]

―――――――――

Hickman's mother retained a prominent Kansas City lawyer, Jerome K. Walsh, to defend her son. Walsh was joined by a Los Angeles lawyer, Richard Cantillon.

During the trial in early 1928, the lawyers tried what was a novel defense at the time: Hickman pleaded not guilty by reason of insanity. Basically, the lawyers' assertion went like this: Hickman must be insane, because no *sane* person would do something as horrible as he had done. Therefore, Hickman's life should be spared.

The jurors heard from Hickman's parents about their boy's troubled childhood. The jurors did not hear from Hickman himself, since his lawyers persuaded him that testifying on his own behalf would not be wise.

Of course, no one knows what the jurors said to one another during deliberations, but they must have focused on the basic weakness in the defense position. Taken to its logical conclusion, the lawyers' argument seemed to be the more horrible the crime, the more likely that the criminal is insane, and therefore he should not be punished as a sane person would be.

After deliberating for only forty-three minutes, the jurors convicted Hickman of murder. On Saturday, February 11, the judge decreed that he should hang on April 27—a date with death that no one expected Hickman to keep, since his lawyers were planning appeals.

By this time, the killing of the druggist during the robbery that Hickman and Welby Hunt committed on Christmas Eve 1926 had been all but forgotten. But the law had to take its course. Soon after the trial in the Parker case, Hickman and Hunt were convicted of murder in the drugstore heist. The verdict didn't really matter as far as Hickman was concerned; he could only hang once. And Hunt would not hang at all, since he was only sixteen at the time of the crime. He was sentenced to life in prison.

***

As he languished on death row in San Quentin prison, Hickman explored his spiritual self. He pronounced himself a convert to Catholicism. He discovered new depths of compassion in his personality, writing a letter to the widow of the slain druggist in which he addressed her as "Dear friend" and apologized for causing her "any past grief."[34]

Hickman told his guards he would meet his fate—and his maker— like a man. His rendezvous with death was now set for Friday, October 19, 1928.

That morning, he breakfasted on eggs, prunes, coffee, and a roll. Natty in a new black suit, he was led from his cell by a priest and the prison warden shortly before ten in the morning. Walking was hard, since his ankles were chained and his arms bound to his sides, but he had two big guards for support. And he only had to walk about forty feet to the gallows in a room nearby. On the way, he mumbled in response to the prayers offered by the priest.

Alas, the child killer had overestimated his newfound manliness. His legs buckled on the ninth step of the gallows, and he had to be dragged the final four steps to the top. As the black hood was placed over his head and the noose was adjusted, Hickman started to collapse again. Eager to get things over with, the hangman signaled for the trap door to be sprung. Because Hickman was slumping over, he bumped against the gallows instead of falling neatly through the opening. Without a clean drop that would have broken his neck and brought instant death, Hickman jerked and twitched as he strangled at the end of the rope.

A dozen or so officials and reporters watched. A few of the witnesses toppled off their wooden chairs in a faint. After fifteen minutes, a prison doctor climbed a stepladder, put a stethoscope to the chest of the condemned, and pronounced him dead. (Perry Parker did not watch the execution, though he could have. He had had enough of death.)

William Edward Hickman was gone from this world at the age of twenty, not much pitied for having endured a slow death and not greatly mourned.

CHAPTER NINE

A CASE LIKE NO OTHER

Hopewell, New Jersey
Early March 1932

Cars full of sightseers clogged the previously little-traveled road past the Lindbergh estate. Thousands of investigators from various police agencies joined the hunt for the child and his abductor. Motorists with small children in their cars were pulled over and checked.

Lindbergh let it be known he was ready to pay a ransom once he was given delivery instructions. Anne Lindbergh pleaded on the radio for her baby's return. She gave details of his diet and feeding schedule in the hope that the kidnapper or kidnappers would hear and heed.

On Friday, March 4, the Lindberghs received a second note with the same circle symbols as the first. In the same fractured English, the note said that because the police had been called, the ransom was being raised to $70,000, and that it might be necessary for the baby to be kept for a longer time.

Various people, cranks and otherwise, offered to help find the infant. Al Capone, newly ensconced in federal prison for income tax evasion, said he was sure he knew the gang responsible for the abduction and that he could negotiate with the culprits and obtain the release of the child. Of course, Capone added, he would have to be let out of prison to offer his help. (His offer was declined.)

Without consulting the police, Lindbergh himself managed to contact some underworld figures. Talk to people in your line of work, he asked them. Find out what happened to my son.

Somehow, a Norfolk, Virginia, man convinced a prominent clergyman and a retired navy admiral that he knew the child's abductors. Word of the Norfolk man's claims reached Lindbergh, who asked the man to negotiate for the release of the child. The Norfolk man knew nothing; there were no negotiations.

Reporters swarmed around the Lindbergh property in Hopewell. Scores of newspapermen took over a garage on the estate, sometimes literally rubbing shoulders with investigators. Showing remarkable restraint, Lindbergh asked the horde of reporters if they could thin their ranks, at least temporarily, to relieve the strain on the telephone and telegraph lines in the region. For days, telephone operators in Hopewell screened calls to the property, putting them through only when they were satisfied that the callers were well-meaning and not deranged.

The police assigned to the case deferred to Lindbergh. He was allowed to take over some avenues of the probe—to interfere, really—in a way an ordinary man would not have been.

———

From the start, it was clear to Colonel Herbert Norman Schwarzkopf, the first superintendent of the New Jersey State Police, that he had a problem. Schwarzkopf was thirty-six at the time and hardly a pushover. He had graduated early from West Point in 1917 and had seen combat in the Great War, where he had endured a mustard gas attack that caused him to have respiratory problems for the rest of his life.

Due to his leadership ability and his fluency in German (he was the son of German immigrants), he rose quickly in the army. In 1921, having attained the rank of colonel, he accepted an offer from Governor Edward I. Edwards of New Jersey to head the newly formed state police force, which he divided into two troops. The northern troop would ride motorcycles and combat gambling, narcotics trafficking, whiskey running, and other mob-related activities, especially in the suburbs of New York City. The southern troop would be on horseback and go after the many moonshine rings that flourished in the woods and hills where the Garden State was still lightly developed.

Schwarzkopf personally trained the first contingent of twenty-five troopers, so at the time of the Lindbergh kidnapping, he was used to being in command. Yet even he found himself overwhelmed by Lindbergh's controlling personality and even more by his fame.

Amid this circus atmosphere, investigators tried to be sensible and methodical. The workmen who had built the Lindberghs' house were questioned and their backgrounds checked. All were cleared. For a time, a boyfriend of nursemaid Betty Gow was under suspicion. He, too, was cleared eventually.

There were early clues that seemed promising. A waitress in Pennington, New Jersey, called the state police to say that on the Friday before the kidnapping, she served three men who asked for directions to the Lindbergh estate. The three men were tracked down. They were newsreel photographers who had been at Valley Forge, Pennsylvania, for a celebration honoring George Washington. They had simply decided to film the Lindbergh property as long as they were in the area.

As for the chisel found on the ground, it was the kind of tool that could be found in countless garages and basements. A man familiar with lumber studied the ladder pieces found beneath the window. He detected nothing remarkable but, as would be revealed later, he didn't look closely enough.

———————

Politicians in New Jersey and elsewhere said that kidnapping should be punishable by death, as it already was under state law in Illinois and Missouri where, of course, kidnappings were becoming alarmingly frequent.

Under state law in New Jersey at the time, kidnapping by itself was only a misdemeanor, a fact that suddenly seemed startling and that would call for prosecutors to engage in some legal gymnastics later on. For the moment, Lindbergh asked that there be no change in New Jersey law. Not until his son was returned safely, he said. Some police officials argued that the death penalty would just encourage kidnappers to kill their victims. After all, what would the kidnappers have to lose? On March 8, a week after the infant was taken away, Major Charles Schoeffel, deputy superintendent of the state police, announced vaguely that there had been "progress."[35] The next day, his boss was more reassuring. "We have every reason to believe that the baby is alive and well," Colonel Schwarzkopf said on March 9.[36] His remarks seemed to suggest that negotiations for the child's return were underway.

Within a week of the abduction, there was a report—false, as it turned out—that the president of Princeton University, Dr. John Grier Hibben, was acting as a liaison between the Lindberghs and whoever had stolen their son.

Meanwhile, the kidnapping was generating a volume of newspaper coverage more commonly devoted to wars or assassinations of heads of state. For eleven straight days, an article about the kidnapping was in the upper right corner of page 1 of the *New York Times*.

As the remarks of Colonel Schwarzkopf and Major Schoeffel had hinted, there were signs of hope that the Lindbergh infant might be returned alive and well. For negotiations *were* taking place, and they involved a man who was the strangest person to wiggle his way into the investigation— and would be one of the most important.

John F. Condon was a retired school principal and teacher who lived in the Bronx. He was seventy-two years old in 1932 and something of a community activist. He had a bushy mustache and a dramatic shock of white hair.

Moved by the plight of the Lindberghs, he wrote a letter to a small newspaper in the Bronx in which he offered up his entire life savings of about $1,000 for the safe return of the child. He offered to act as an intermediary, using newspaper ads to communicate with the kidnapper. The ads would be signed "Jafsie," the nickname he coined from his initials.

The letter was printed in the Bronx newspaper on March 8. The very next day, Condon got a letter at his home. It purported to be from the kidnapper, who said Condon would be acceptable as a go-between. Within the envelope was another envelope, containing a message to Lindbergh reiterating the ransom demand, raised to $70,000 from the original $50,000. It was signed with interlocking circles, just like the original message left on the window sill. The interlocking circles on the notes, along with the exact wording the kidnapper had used, were known only to a very few investigators.

At once, Lindbergh said he wanted Condon to act as his liaison. All right, Schwarzkopf said, but we're going to tap Condon's phone. Lindbergh overruled him, fearing that somehow the kidnapper would find out. Lindbergh's lawyer, Henry Breckinridge, moved into Condon's home to keep track of events. He would stay there for two months.

There followed much back-and-forth between Condon and the kidnapper over the next several days, with Condon using newspaper ads on his end. A meeting was arranged in Woodlawn Cemetery in the Bronx for Saturday, March 12.

That night, Condon was driven to the rendezvous by his friend Al Reich, a one-time prizefighter. Reich parked a few blocks from the cemetery. Nervously, Condon approached the entrance. He saw a slim figure emerge from the gloom inside the gate and climb over.

Here, what actually happened can never be known. Condon later claimed that he pursued the man and eventually caught him. But some people involved in the case were immediately skeptical. Condon, after all, seemed to be a blowhard, and he was seventy-two years old.

In any event, Condon and the man from the cemetery sat on a bench in Van Cortlandt Park. "Call me John," the stranger said.

As Condon recalled it, the man wore a topcoat and a hat, which he kept low over his forehead. Condon was bigger than the other man and understandably nervous. Yet he managed to say that the Lindberghs wanted proof that he really had the baby before they paid any ransom.

There ensued a rambling conversation, the exact words of which can never be known, as Condon was prone to embellish the facts (or invent ones) whenever he recounted his role in the Lindbergh case, which he did often.

But if Condon was to be believed, "Cemetery John" described himself as "only a go-between." Then he said something chilling: "Would I burn if the baby was dead?"[37]

Finally, John said that he and the people he was working for would provide proof that they had the child.

Then he stood up and melted into the dark.

On Wednesday, March 16, a package containing a baby's sleeping suit arrived at Condon's house. The Lindberghs confirmed it was the one worn by the baby at the time of the kidnapping. They saw that the garment had been laundered. What did that mean?

Finally, a meeting was arranged for delivery of the ransom. This time, the meeting between Jafsie and the shadowy figure would be in St. Raymond's Cemetery in the Bronx. It was set for the night of April 2, a Saturday.

<hr/>

To say that "life goes on" seems heartless, even all these years later, when one contemplates the anguish of Charles and Anne Lindbergh that March. But life *did* go on as always.

On March 10, the *Times* analyzed the approaching elections in Germany, where Paul von Hindenburg seemed to have an excellent chance of being reelected president of the Weimar Republic. The report was heartening, especially because of the anti-Semitism that was brewing in the country and the presence of a fiery orator who was tapping into the passions and resentments of ordinary Germans. But, as the *Times* noted reassuringly, "Among those whose opinions are worthwhile because they know Germany best, the chance of a victory for Adolf Hitler is calculated at a small percentage indeed."[38]

Just as heartening, the *Times* noted that while anti-Semitism was prevalent in the rank and file of the Nazi party, the party leadership appeared not to be encouraging such feelings. Indeed, party leaders seemed to be *dis*couraging such sentiment and saying nothing that would commit themselves to "definite drastic measures" should their dreams of power come to pass.

<hr/>

There was no outside world for Charles and Anne Lindbergh, secluded in their big but suddenly empty house in Hopewell, New Jersey. Inevitably, there was speculation that whoever took the baby might have had help from within. "From the mass of confusing detail that piled up, one fact stood forth clearly," the *Times* declared on March 3. "That was that the kidnappers must have been familiar with the plan of the house and with Colonel Lindbergh's plans as well. Not only did they place a ladder against a window of the nursery which Mrs. Lindbergh had tried unsuccessfully to lock, but they chose a night for the crime which the aviator had announced he would spend in New York attending a New York University dinner. His attendance at the dinner had been widely advertised and it was only because he had his dates mixed up that Colonel Lindbergh happened to be at home."[39]

There was something else: it was the Lindberghs' routine at the time to spend weekends in Hopewell, then return to Englewood to stay with Anne's mother, whose husband, Dwight, had died unexpectedly the previous October 5. But because of the baby's cold, they decided to stay in Hopewell for a few days after the weekend of February 27 and 28—a fact known only to people in the household.

The impression was growing that the kidnapping simply couldn't have been the work of one person.

———————

"Kidnapping: A Rising Menace to the Nation" was the headline of a very long *Times* article the Sunday after the Lindbergh baby vanished. "No conceivable event, unless it were an invasion of the White House itself, could have so dramatized the crime of kidnapping as did the carrying off, last Tuesday night, of the infant son of Colonel Charles A. Lindbergh."[40]

The article recounted some cases of the distant and not-so-distant past. Most poignantly, the article was accompanied by a photograph of a comely girl of ten. The photo showed intelligent eyes and a smile mature and dignified for someone so young. The photo caption stated that she "was kidnapped in New York in 1928 and never heard from again." Her name was Grace Budd.

CHAPTER TEN

A FRIENDLY FARMER

New York City
Sunday, May 27, 1928

"Young man, 18, wishes position in the country," read the advertisement placed by Edward Budd in the Sunday *New York World Telegram*.[41]

Indeed, Eddie Budd was eager for work. His father, Albert Budd, was a low-paid doorman at an insurance company and had a glass eye. Albert's wife, Delia, was obese and could not read. The glitter and seeming prosperity of the twenties was a galaxy away from the lives of the Budds.

They had three other children: Albert Jr., Grace, and Beatrice, the baby of the family, who was five. The family lived in a cramped apartment in the Chelsea section of Lower Manhattan.

Eddie wanted to help out financially. Besides, the family apartment at 406 West Fifteenth Street could be sweltering in the summertime, which was just beginning.* Fit and energetic, Eddie wanted to try country living, away from the heat, noise, and smells of the city.

On Monday afternoon, a small, tweedy-looking man of late middle age knocked on the door, introduced himself as Frank Howard, and declared, "I am looking for a young fellow named Edward Budd. I read his ad in yesterday's paper."

"I'm his mother," Delia Budd said, inviting the visitor to come in (Delia's husband was still at work). She explained that Eddie was nearby with his best friend. Then she told Beatrice to run and fetch her brother.

"You remind me of my granddaughter," Howard said, handing the girl a nickel as she was on her way out.

The newcomer had a gray beard and mustache, and his suit was rather worn. He looked more like a farmer than a city slicker.

While they were waiting for Eddie to appear, the visitor explained his situation. He had a farm in Farmingdale, Long Island. The farm had three hundred chickens and six milk cows. The twenty-acre spread was a cornucopia of fruits and vegetables.

The farmer said he already employed several hands but he needed one more, maybe two. He wasn't getting any younger, and his wife was no longer around. They had been happy in their old life when he was an interior decorator in Washington, DC. Then his eyesight had begun to fail, and he'd had to find something new. He'd always dreamed of having a farm, and he'd put away enough money to make his dream come true. Trouble was, his wife hadn't liked life on the farm, he went on in his sad, quiet voice. So she had left him a decade or so before, leaving him to raise their six children alone.

---

*   It would be a furnace-like summer. On one day alone, July 6, six New Yorkers died from the heat, the *New York Times* reported.

Delia was relieved when Eddie appeared with his sister Beatrice. Eddie's best friend, Willie Korman, had also come to the Budds' apartment.

The conversation turned much more cheerful. The visitor said he was proud of his children, who had all turned out well. "One of my boys is a cadet at West Point," he boasted.

Then he got down to business: he would pay $15 a week for as long as Eddie could work on the farm. How did that sound?

It sounded wonderful to Eddie and his mother. Then Eddie spoke up for Willie: maybe there was a spot for him on the farm too?

Sure! There was never a shortage of work on a farm, Howard said. And Willie was healthy and had big shoulders, like his friend Eddie.

Fine then, Howard said. He would return with a car on Sunday, June 3, and take the young men to the farm for a summer of wholesome outdoor labor. He told them to pack their oldest clothes.

"I must be on my way," Howard announced, looking at his watch. "I have a business engagement in New Jersey." With brisk but friendly goodbyes, the farmer left.

Eddie and Willie exulted in their good fortune. All week long, they looked forward to the trip. On Saturday, they sat in the Budds' apartment, duffel bags packed. Hours went by. Then, late in the afternoon, a knock on the door. A Western Union delivery boy handed Eddie a handwritten note: "Been over in New Jersey. Call in morning. Frank Howard."

―――――――

At midday Sunday, a smiling Frank Howard appeared. He came bearing gifts: a pot of cheese and a basket of strawberries—from his farm, he said.

Albert Budd, who had been at work when Howard made his first visit, was introduced and took an immediate liking to the Long Island farmer, who explained that he'd been in New Jersey to buy horses. "Oh, about the message I sent yesterday. Is it still here?"

"On the mantel there," Albert said.

Howard went to the mantel, picked up the message, and casually put it in a pocket. Albert thought the action rather odd but didn't think much about it.

The Budds invited the visitor to stay for a potluck lunch. Eddie and his brother, Albert Jr., were outside at play, but they had promised to come home in time to eat.

As people were seating themselves at the kitchen table, they heard the front door opening, followed by light steps in the hallway. A girl was humming a cheerful tune.

"That'll be Gracie," Delia said.

Standing in the doorway, ten-year-old Grace Budd was flower-pretty, still wearing the white dress she'd put on for the family's weekly visit to church.

"Come here, child," said the clearly enchanted Howard, beckoning the girl to sit on his lap.

Grace did, briefly. Then Howard gave her a few coins and told her to go buy candy for herself and her little sister. As the girls were hurrying out, their mother told Grace to tell Eddie to come home for lunch.

In no time, Eddie and Willie appeared, breathless from running.

And out of the blue, Howard announced that they weren't going to the farm right away. He had just heard from his sister that she was giving a birthday party for one of her children that very afternoon. After the party, Howard said, he'd come to get Eddie and Willie. Howard gave the young men $2 to go to the movies in the meantime.

Then the friendly farmer had an inspiration: perhaps Grace would like to attend the party! She was just the right age and would fit in.

Delia was hesitant, more so than her husband. Well, where would the party be, the parents wanted to know. In a very nice building at

137th Street and Columbus Avenue, Howard replied. He promised to have the girl back by nine that night.

So it was settled. Delia helped Grace into her dress-up spring coat, and off she went, still wearing the white dress she'd had on for church, holding the hand of the friendly farmer from Long Island. Delia watched them disappear around a corner.

As dusk yielded to darkness with no sign of their daughter, Albert and Delia Budd tried not to worry. Maybe the party was running late—although it was getting *very* late for a children's party to still be going on. Maybe Grace was staying overnight at the home of Frank Howard's sister.

The night brought no sleep for the parents. Early Monday morning, they sent Eddie to the nearest police station to report Grace's absence. Very soon, Lieutenant Samuel Dribben and three detectives arrived at the Budds' apartment. The cops were very concerned; several unsolved child murders had occurred in the city in the past few years.

What about this "party," the cops wanted to know. Where was it?

In a building at 137th and Columbus Avenue, Grace's parents said.

As gently as he could, Lieutenant Dribben told them there was no such place, that Columbus ended at 110th Street. Albert and Delia Budd seemed numb with guilt and dread.

Dribben told two detectives to check rooming houses. Another detective took Eddie and his friend Willie to the police station to look at pictures in the hope they would recognize the man who had taken Grace away.

Quickly, two more detectives were put on the case. One would search the records of the Motor Vehicles Bureau for information about Frank Howard. The other detective was to trace the Western Union message the friendly old man had sent the previous Saturday—the message he'd plucked off the mantelpiece and casually put in his pocket.

Several detectives were sent to Nassau County on Long Island to look for a farmer named Frank Howard in Farmingdale. As the name of the community suggested, there were a number of farms around Farmingdale. But there was no farmer named Frank Howard.

But investigators found that, years before, there had been a Frank Howard who owned a farm in Farmingdale, *New Jersey*. What was more, his general description fit that of the Frank Howard who had taken Grace Budd. But it was soon confirmed that the Frank Howard in New Jersey had sold his farm and moved to Chicago years before—and had since died.

In the days after Grace's disappearance, the police publicized their search for the origin of the Western Union message that had been sent to the Budds. Telegraphers and clerks sifted through tens of thousands of message duplicates. Finally, the source was found: the message had been sent from the Western Union office at Third Avenue and 103rd Street in Manhattan.

Detectives figured that the cheese and strawberries given to the Budds had probably been purchased near the Western Union office. Sure enough, the police located a nearby deli selling the type of cheese Howard had brought to the Budds. And a peddler in the neighborhood recognized the price scrawled on the strawberry container as from his own hand. But no one at the deli recalled who had bought the cheese, and the peddler remembered nothing about the man who had bought the strawberries.

The locations of the Western Union office, the deli, and the pushcart peddler suggested to detectives that the man they were hunting lived in East Harlem or at least spent time there. But where exactly, and who the hell was he?

And something else: unlike nearly all kidnappings of the era, there had been no demand for ransom. Not that it would have mattered: the Budds had no extra money. Every dollar they brought in went to pay for rent, food, and modest clothing (when the hand-me-downs were finally too threadbare to wear).

———————

For Grace's parents, the brutally hot summer was a season of torture. They hoped—or tried to hope—that their beloved daughter was still alive, that whoever had taken her would not... They couldn't stand to dwell on the possibilities.

No doubt, some newspaper readers and some detectives wondered at the gullibility of people who would let their daughter go off with a man who was little more than a stranger. What kind of parents would do such a thing?

Albert and Delia Budd had not been given much in life. Delia was obese and illiterate. Albert had one good eye, along with a strange-looking glass eye. Every day, he opened doors for people who dressed better than he did, were better educated than he was, and earned far more money than he ever would. Sometimes, they thanked him; often, they ignored him.

The world of Albert and Delia, like their apartment, was a small, cramped place. That was why they didn't know that Columbus Avenue ended at 110th Street. That was why they had been duped by the seemingly friendly man, the prosperous farmer, who had treated them with respect and brought them gifts.

On the very Sunday that Grace disappeared, the *New York Times* was stuffed with ads meant for people whose lives were a galaxy away from the world of the Budds. Macy's offered a forty-three-piece porcelain dinner set "with border of rose and black" for only $18.74. Readers were reminded that "travel is that most delightful of diversions if one is properly equipped with the right luggage and clothes." Maine, Cape Cod, Havana, and Bermuda beckoned.

The glitter and glamour that lucky people partook of in the late 1920s would never touch the lives of Albert and Delia Budd. They knew that, and they did the best they could.

What kind of parents were they? They were parents who loved their children and took them to church on Sunday. They raised a sturdy son, Eddie, who by the age of eighteen was eager for a good day's pay for a hard day's work.

And until June 3, 1928, they were raising a lovely young girl who, by all appearances, would grow up to be a lovely woman. Albert and Delia Budd, who had never had much, had lost their priceless jewel.

Then, just days after Grace vanished, came a tiny flicker of hope.

———

"I have Grace. She is safe and sound. She is happy in her new home and not at all homesick. I will see to it that Grace has proper schooling. She has been given an Angora cat and a pet canary. She calls the canary Bill..."[42]

An Angora cat and a canary named Bill? A ten-year-old girl spirited away but not homesick in her new life? Some detectives thought the letter was from a crank. They were right. Nothing came of the letter, just as nothing came of various messages and phone tips right after Grace vanished.

Over the next two and a half years, the patience of Detective William King was tested in ways so bizarre, they would have been funny had he not been engaged in a deadly serious investigation. A prison warden in Florida thought one of his recent inmates, an inveterate liar and con man who had once posed as a doctor and recruited young girls to pose as his daughters, might be the man King was looking for. Delia Budd identified the new suspect as the beast who had taken her daughter. That was enough for a grand jury to indict him.

Then a seemingly better suspect was dragged into the investigation, this one the estranged husband of a bitter wife who claimed in September 1930 that she had seen him in Perth Amboy, New Jersey, with a lovely little girl on June 3, 1928, the very Sunday that Grace Budd had walked out of her parents' lives.

But why had she waited so long to come forward? "I was sick at the time," she explained. "By the time I got better, I had forgotten. Then something made me remember..."

Delia Budd identified *him* with the same certainty she had shown with the Florida ex-con. He, too, was indicted and even went to trial— for one day. Then the judge saw that the evidence wasn't just flimsy. Given Delia Budd's unreliability, it was virtually nonexistent.

The judge threw out the case. The indictment against the Florida ex-con was also dismissed. The investigation was back where it had started.

———

William King had joined the police force in 1907, left to fight in the Great War, then rejoined the department in 1926. He had been around long enough to see the awful things that people could do to one another. And he had built a reputation as an investigator with bottomless patience, an iron resolve, really. It would be tested as never before, but he would never lose it.

CHAPTER ELEVEN

ANOTHER DOCTOR TAKEN

Peoria, Illinois
Monday, March 14, 1932

Had the Lindbergh case not been dominating the news that spring, a kidnapping in Peoria, Illinois, might have gotten more attention.

On this Monday night, Dr. James W. Parker was kidnapped from the driveway at his home in Peoria while he was about to drive to his club. Or perhaps he was seized while he was arriving home *from* his club. Contemporary news reports differed on that point.

What is known is that the doctor's wife, Donna, who was also a physician, got a telephone call late that night from a man who introduced himself as "Double X." The caller told her that her husband wouldn't be coming home on this night but that she would hear from him in the morning. His car could be found near a city golf course, Double X said. Donna Parker was warned not to contact the police.

It is also known that Dr. James W. Parker became an unwilling passenger in his own car after it was commandeered by two men. We can also be sure that Dr. Parker hoped a quick agreement with his captors would bring his early release. But that was not to be; his ordeal would last eighteen days.

In the first minutes, Parker was taken to a remote location in Peoria where he was blindfolded and transferred to another car—one that had followed the doctor's own, it would be revealed later. Then it was on to a farmhouse near Manito, in Mason County, about thirty miles from Peoria.

———

At the time Donna Parker was talking on the phone to Double X, an alert security guard at the Pere Marquette Hotel in Peoria saw something suspicious. The guard, Edward Ohl, saw a man enter a phone booth in the hotel lobby while another man stood outside as though he was a lookout. The man in the phone booth, it would be learned, was James W. Betson, a former police officer, though that description hardly does justice to his resume. The apparent lookout was Arlo Stoops, who had a brother named Raymond, who had leased the farmhouse that became James Parker's new quarters.

Parker was told he would be well treated. He was also told to write letters to relatives and friends saying that his captors wanted $50,000, an enormous sum for the Parkers, who were well off but not wealthy.

In captivity, Parker was guarded by the Stoops brothers and several other men who took turns watching over him. Days went by, and Parker had no idea how long he would be held.

As would be revealed later, negotiations were going on. Soon, the abductors reduced their demand to $10,000—a sign that they knew their negotiating position was poor, or that they were panicking, or both.

The kidnappers were right to be nervous, for the law was in fact closing in.

On the night of Friday, April 1, the captive was bundled into a car, blindfolded, taken for a lengthy ride, and finally tossed out of the vehicle, unharmed. Almost at once, two men were arrested and charged with being part of the plot. Soon afterward, a third man was arrested.

Not long after Dr. Parker's release, it was reported that his wife and other relatives had decided immediately after the kidnapping to seek the help of the Chicago Secret Six, a crime-fighting organization created by prominent businessmen. Officially, it was the Citizens' Committee for the Prevention and Punishment of Crime. Since it was reputed to have half a dozen members, a reporter dubbed it "the Secret Six." And so it became in Chicago lore.

The Secret Six was created in 1930 by a blend of civic pride and self-interest. Robert Isham Randolph, a consulting engineer who was one of the group's organizers, was president of the Chicagoland Chamber of Commerce. He and other prominent business figures were looking forward to the world's fair to be held in the Windy City in 1933.

With Chicago's reputation as a gangland hub well established and with some police officials and rank-and-file cops believed to be corrupt, the businessmen were desperate to avoid further blemishes on the city's image. The memory of the St. Valentine's Day massacre of 1929, in which seven gangsters were shot to death in a garage, was still fresh.

Enter Alexander Jamie, chief investigator for the Prohibition-enforcement unit of the Department of Justice and the brother-in-law of Eliot Ness of "the Untouchables" fame. Jamie became the chief investigator for the Secret Six, which got funding from the group's wealthy founders.

A shrewd and seasoned investigator, Jamie knew that information was everything, and he did not flinch at using unconventional methods to obtain it. Thus, the Secret Six opened its own speakeasy in the Chicago suburb of Cicero to eavesdrop on liquor-fueled underworld gossip.

Right after Dr. Parker was abducted, operatives of the Secret Six, along with the Illinois State Police and Peoria police, zeroed in on the three men who would become the case's major defendants: Joseph H. Pursifull, James W. Betson, and Claude "Red" Evans. Evans had already done serious prison time and had been jailed yet again, on a safe-cracking charge, days after Dr. Parker was released.

But Pursifull and Betson were the ones with the truly remarkable backgrounds. Pursifull was a Peoria lawyer and former candidate for state's attorney. An ex-Sunday school teacher, he had written a book dispensing advice on love and marriage. As for Betson, he was described in the press as a former detective and Ku Klux Klan leader who had once aspired to be Peoria's mayor. He was arrested in the campaign headquarters of the notoriously corrupt Lennington "Len" Small, a former Illinois governor who was trying (unsuccessfully, it would turn out) to win that office once again in 1932.

———————

Eventually, nine men and one woman were implicated in the abduction of James Parker. Besides Pursifull, Betson, and Evans, they included Raymond Stoops; his wife, Bessie; their son, Dean; and Raymond's brother, Arlo, a Peoria bond salesman. Raymond and Bessie Stoops owned the farmhouse in the hamlet of Banner, fifty miles south of Peoria, where Parker had been held.

Eight defendants were convicted. Betson, Evans, and two other men considered the leaders of the kidnapping ring got twenty-five years in prison. Other defendants got shorter sentences, including Pursifull, identified as a mere go-between, who got five years. (Bessie Stoops, her son, and a worker on their farm were acquitted.)

Law enforcement officials in Illinois were pleased that the James Parker kidnapping case was one in which the victim's family had cooperated fully—unlike, say, the kidnapping of dressmaker Nell Donnelly, in which gangsters were conscripted to act as police officers. The law enforcement people were saying, in effect, "You should trust us more than you trust kidnappers and other criminals."

Perhaps the lawmen were thinking of Nell Donnelly, the wealthy dressmaker who had been kidnapped and freed with the help of gangsters while the police remained on the sidelines. Or perhaps they were thinking of the Lindbergh case. Surely, they knew that Lindbergh had reached out to gangsters—to no avail, it appeared.

CHAPTER TWELVE

HOPE AND HEARTBREAK

New York City
Saturday, April 2, 1932

His time had come. John F. Condon, retired educator, was embarking on the greatest adventure of his life. It was no secret to anyone who knew him that he loved the limelight. Now, he was basking in it, and he might be able to render a great service as well.

They waited in Condon's home: Condon himself, Charles Lindbergh, and Lindbergh's attorney, Henry Breckinridge. Around eight in the evening, the doorbell rang. A note had been left by a cab driver, who walked away into the dark, forever unidentified. The note instructed Condon to go to a greenhouse on East Tremont Avenue and look for a message on a table outside the entrance.

Lindbergh drove as he and Condon left the house in Al Reich's car. Reich's car had been used for the first meeting, and Lindbergh and Condon speculated that the kidnapper might be wary if another vehicle appeared. On the way, Condon glanced over just as Lindbergh's lapel was open for a moment. The famous flyer was carrying a pistol in a shoulder holster.

Lindbergh parked not far from the greenhouse. Condon got out, relieved that Lindbergh stayed in the car. He walked to the greenhouse, found the table, and saw the message, held down by a stone. It was too dark for him to read, so he took the message to the car.

By the dashboard lights, Condon and Lindbergh read the message: "Cross the street and walk to the next corner and follow Whittemore Ave," it began.* It ordered Condon to come alone and bring the ransom money.

Lindbergh wanted to accompany Condon, but Condon persuaded him to stay in the car. The two men decided to defy the kidnapper up to a point: Condon would not give the kidnapper the money until after they had met.

In the cold, Condon walked the route specified by Cemetery John. The path took him along the edge of St. Raymond's Cemetery. It was very dark, and Condon felt vulnerable. Would the kidnapper be furious that Condon didn't have the money with him? On the other hand, *not* having the money might be good, because the kidnapper would have to—

"Ay, Doctor!" The shout was in a heavily accented voice. It came from the dark, among the tombstones. "Over here! Over here!"

Condon found himself on a dirt road next to the cemetery with the man inside walking parallel to him. Then the man scaled a small fence and crouched behind a hedge. Condon approached him. Yes, it was Cemetery John. He asked Condon if he had brought the $70,000.

Condon said the money was in a nearby car with Lindbergh. The exact words that were uttered next are forever unknown, but as Condon

---

*   Cahill, Robert T. Jr. *Hauptmann's Ladder, a Step-by-Step Analysis of the Lindbergh Kidnapping.* (Kent, OH: Kent State University Press, 2014), 77.

told the story, he complained to the kidnapper about the ransom being increased to $70,000 from the original $50,000.

Whereupon, in Condon's telling, the kidnapper said, "Well, I suppose that we will be satisfied to take the fifty thousand."

Cemetery John agreed to provide a note with directions to find the baby—but only after the money had been handed over. What's more, the note was not to be read for six hours.

Condon returned to the car, told Lindbergh what had happened, and got the entire $70,000, just in case the man in the cemetery changed his mind about accepting only $50,000. Crucially, the $50,000 was packed in a wooden box, while the remaining $20,000 was in a separate packet.

Condon went back to the hedge where he'd last seen Cemetery John and waited in the dark. After thirteen minutes, according to Condon's watch, John reappeared. Condon handed over the box with the $50,000 and got an envelope in return.

Then Cemetery John vanished among the graves, and Condon felt a moment of pride that he had saved Lindbergh the $20,000 in the separate packet.

(The FBI squad assigned by Hoover to keep tabs on the Lindbergh case had learned in advance that a ransom was to be paid on the night of April 2. Though some of its members were eager to follow Condon and stake out the drop site, Hoover had instructed his agents that under no circumstances should they intervene until the child was safely recovered.)[43]

In the car, Lindbergh was cautious and resisted the impulse to tear open the envelope. If John had specified that the note inside was not to be read for six hours, then so be it. Lindbergh feared that the kidnappers—if indeed there was more than one—might be watching his every move, even in the dark.

Lindbergh intended to drive Condon home with the envelope still sealed. But within minutes, the aviator who had seemed to have ice water for blood could wait no longer. So Condon told him to drive to a small house, vacant for the time being, that he owned about a mile from St. Raymond's Cemetery.

With privacy guaranteed, they opened the envelope. The note inside lacked the familiar signature symbol the kidnapper had been using, but the handwriting was the same. The note said the child was being cared for by two "innosent" persons on the twenty-eight foot "Boad Nelly" located "between Horseneck Beach and Gay Head near Elizabeth Island."[44] The allusion was apparently to the island of Martha's Vineyard.

───────

Somewhat surprisingly, the serial numbers of all the bills in the ransom had been recorded only after Frank J. Wilson, a special agent in the intelligence unit of the Internal Revenue Service, discovered that that little detail had been overlooked. Recording the numbers was no small task in those pre-Xerox days, but it was vital.

The $50,000 portion of the ransom was in twenties, tens, and fives, with a good portion of the money in gold notes. While still legal tender, gold notes were being withdrawn from circulation. Increasingly, they attracted attention when used for everyday transactions.

And the Treasury Department had been especially clever with the $20,000 in the separate packet. That money was in the form of four hundred gold certificates of $50 each. The gold fifties were much less common than the twenties, tens, and fives and were sure to attract the attention of clerks or bank tellers and be the easiest to trace should the kidnapper or kidnappers spend them.

Of course, because Condon had talked Cemetery John out of taking the extra $20,000, the ploy with the gold fifties had been spoiled.

It seemed that no one in the know had bothered to tell Condon about it. He learned of it just after the cemetery rendezvous as he boasted to an IRS agent about saving Lindbergh some money.

Desperate to recover his son, Lindbergh arranged to borrow a seaplane from the navy. In the middle of the night, he drove to an airport in Connecticut. He was accompanied by Breckinridge, a man from the IRS, Reich, and Condon. It was agreed that Reich would stay on the ground and drive Lindbergh's car to an airport on Long Island so he could pick up the searchers when they landed. (Why was Condon along? Perhaps Lindbergh thought an extra set of eyes couldn't hurt, even the eyes of an old man. Anyhow, Condon had already shown his ability to insinuate himself into just about any situation.)

By dawn's early light, Lindbergh took the navy plane into the air. It flew over Cape Cod and circled Martha's Vineyard, sometimes dipping to within a few feet of fishing boats. After several hours, Lindbergh landed near Cuttyhunk Island and taxied to a dock—where a gaggle of reporters awaited. Lindbergh and his companions pushed their way through the scrum, had lunch, and took off again. They searched until dark, seeing nothing that looked like a twenty-eight-foot boat named *Nelly*. Lindbergh flew the plane to Long Island, where Reich met them and drove the party to New York City. Then a tired Lindbergh drove to his home.

The next morning, Lindbergh took off again, this time in a plane of his own and alone. He flew over the water off New England, then as far south as Virginia, looking for a boat named *Nelly*. He must have been as tired as he'd been while flying across the Atlantic. But this time, there was no prize. He returned to his home without his son or any clue where he might be.

CHAPTER THIRTEEN

CHASING THE MONEY

New York City
April 1932

On Wednesday, April 6, 1932, David Isaacs, a retired clothing merchant in Upper Manhattan, withdrew $47 in interest that he had accrued from a savings account at the Ninety-Sixth Street branch of the East River Savings Bank. The withdrawal was in the form of two twenty-dollar bills, a five-dollar bill, and two one-dollar bills.

On April 13, Isaacs stopped at a branch of the Corn Exchange Bank at Broadway and Ninety-First Street to exchange one of the twenties for smaller currency. By this time, banks across the country had been given circulars listing the serial numbers of the Lindbergh ransom money. But the human element was all-important. Considering all the money they handled in a given day, would clerks and tellers be alert enough to spot a ransom bill?

Yes. A Corn Exchange Bank teller checked the circular and saw that the twenty that Isaacs wanted to exchange was from the ransom.

At once, the teller and Isaacs notified the Secret Service. Isaacs said the bill had been in his wallet for a full week. Officials at the East River Savings Bank branch said the bill probably was included with some sixteen hundred deposits made on April 4 and 5. Several detectives were assigned to try to track down the depositors, though it seemed a virtually impossible task.

But at least someone out there was spending the money.

Yet the manhunt was hampered by bureaucratic and jurisdictional issues. New Jersey police were investigating the kidnapping itself. New York police were investigating the extortion committed when the man in the Bronx cemetery got Lindbergh's money. The two police factions cooperated only half-heartedly. They were engaged in the kind of turf battle not uncommon between police agencies. And there was precious little state-to-state coordination among the lawmen—a problem that the federal anti-kidnapping statute, which was still working its way through Congress, was supposed to correct.

―――――――――

Meanwhile, efforts went on behind the scenes to reconnect with the kidnapper or kidnappers. Condon continued to place ads in the Bronx paper. "What is wrong?" an ad on April 6 began. "Have you crossed me? Please better directions. Jafsie."[45]

Major Schoeffel, the deputy commander of the New Jersey State Police, booked passage for England, there to confer with Scotland Yard and pursue a rumor that the child had been taken overseas just after being abducted.

Maryland State Police searched isolated areas of both shores of the Chesapeake Bay after hearing that the baby might be on a boat in the region.

On April 14, Lindbergh declared that it was of "the utmost

importance" that neither he nor his wife "nor our representatives" be followed by reporters for fear of ruining negotiations with whoever had the baby.[46]

Colonel Schwarzkopf tried to head off any questions about negotiations. It was clear from the Lindberghs' language and Schwarzkopf's reticence that the legendary aviator trusted himself more than the police to get his son back.

———————

Lieutenant Detective James Finn of the New York City police watched the developments in New Jersey with frustration and, more and more, a sense of foreboding.

Finn, in charge of the New York City facet of the investigation, had never bought into the theory that the baby had been taken by professional criminals. Gang members wouldn't be stupid enough to steal the child of a national hero, Finn thought. Such a crime would bring way too much heat. Besides, there were many targets with more money than Charles Lindbergh, notwithstanding the advantages the aviator's fame had brought him.

Thus, Finn thought, Lindbergh's early attempts to recruit organized crime figures in the search for his child were useless. Most likely, the kidnapper was an amateur with no ties whatsoever to gangsters.

Finn felt left out of the overall investigation. Colonel Schwarzkopf, perhaps eager to keep as much personal authority as possible over the investigation, even refused at first to let Finn see copies of the ransom notes—despite the fact that the notes had all been mailed from New York.

As for Finn's growing sense of foreboding, it was triggered in part by a long conversation Finn had had with a psychiatrist.

CHAPTER FOURTEEN

THE PROFILER

New York City
April 1932

Dr. Dudley D. Shoenfeld knew that, even in the twentieth century, there were people who viewed his field of psychiatry as no more scientific than astrology or voodoo. And sadly, there were people who might benefit from visiting him but were embarrassed at the thought of seeing a psychiatrist.

Which was a shame, really, because Shoenfeld was the least threatening of men and not just because he was only five feet four inches tall. He smiled easily, had many friends, and enjoyed parties. Now and then, he rested his formidable intellect by going to Yonkers Raceway, where he loved to bet on the trotters, sometimes after trading hot tips with the elevator operator in his Midtown Manhattan apartment building.

Shoenfeld had been drawn to the study of the mind while a navy physician during the Great War, after his graduation from New York University and its medical school. Besides maintaining a private practice, he worked at Mount Sinai Hospital and was a consultant at the Hebrew Orphan Asylum. He was a charter member of the New York Psychoanalytic Society.

He was no worshipper of the Lone Eagle, for he had heard that Lindbergh was an anti-Semite, like many Americans at that time. But Shoenfeld could empathize with the ordeal of the Lindberghs, since he and his wife, Helen, had a young son, Richard.

Shoenfeld, who had turned thirty-nine on March 24, had been following the Lindbergh case with interest and, increasingly, with dismay. He couldn't understand why some investigators theorized in public that the kidnapping must have been committed by an organized gang. Shoenfeld thought gang involvement was almost inconceivable, given the firestorm that a crime against the Lindbergh family would set off.

"No gang would have undertaken so hazardous an enterprise for the ridiculous sum of $50,000," Shoenfeld would write later. And if a gang had been reckless enough to undertake the kidnapping, "the ransom demand would have been much higher."[*]

But Lindbergh subscribed to the organized gang theory and wanted the New Jersey State Police to walk a tightrope. Above all, of course, he wanted them to recover his son unharmed. If they could do that *and* track down the kidnappers, fine.

Shoenfeld thought the police were deferring to Lindbergh too much, that Lindbergh's interference had "placed the troopers in the roles of estate guards and messenger boys" whose main task "was the sorting of crank clues."

Shoenfeld also knew, from his contacts in the realms of science and

---

[*]   The direct quotes in this chapter and my paraphrasing of Shoenfeld's views are from his
       1936 book *The Crime and the Criminal: A Psychiatric Study of the Lindbergh Case*,
       as well as a memo he wrote after meeting with Finn. And I am indebted to Dr. Peter D.
       Byeff, whose late mother, Ruth Eile, was Shoenfeld's personal secretary for many years.
       Dr. Byeff was kind enough to share his own recollections of Shoenfeld.

medicine, that the New Jersey State Police had bungled a test for finger-prints on the kidnapper's ladder days after the baby was stolen.

Dr. Erastus Mead Hudson, a New York City physician who for years had been interested in fingerprinting, had volunteered his services just after the kidnapping. Of crucial importance, Hudson had been trying out a new method using silver nitrate in a chemical process that could lift prints that were otherwise indiscernible. Given a small section of the ladder, he was allowed to demonstrate his method to a group of troopers—who then tried to imitate the method themselves, hopelessly smudging whatever prints might have been discovered.

(Had someone had the good sense and exercised authority, the ladder might have been quarantined from the start until a fingerprint expert like Dr. Hudson was allowed to examine it. For that matter, the FBI might have been valuable early on in this aspect of the case. The bureau's laboratory was being set up in 1932, and FBI technicians were gaining expertise in the art and science of fingerprint analysis.)

———————

Dudley Shoenfeld's specialty was not chemistry but psychiatry, and it was in that capacity that he became acquainted with Leigh Matteson, science editor of the International News Service. The journalist was seeking support for a theory that had been forming in his mind: that the Lindbergh crime was the work of one man, a man who might be considered insane but would function well enough to carry out the kidnapping.

Matteson had visited Dr. Lindsay R. Williams, secretary of the New York Academy of Medicine, who had referred him to Dr. Israel Strauss, chairman of the Committee on Medical Jurisprudence. Finally, Matteson was referred to Shoenfeld, who was secretary to the committee at the time.

Shoenfeld and Matteson traded opinions and hunches. Then

Matteson set up a meeting between the psychiatrist and Detective Finn. So Shoenfeld and the detective sat down one day in April 1932, just after Condon's mysterious night meetings with Cemetery John.

We can envision Finn, who was more open-minded than many cops about psychiatry, and Shoenfeld quietly discussing the most sensational crime of the era, with the psychiatrist smoking the "luxury cigarettes" he liked to buy from Nat Sherman's fashionable tobacco shop in Manhattan.

Finn said he had heard rumors that members of some gangs were eager to cooperate with lawmen, eager to convince them they'd had nothing to do with the kidnapping. If they could do that, they could resume their activities without distractions. Finn thought the gangsters' eagerness made it all the more likely that professional criminals had nothing to do with the crime.

Shoenfeld agreed. He told Finn that the behavior of Cemetery John in the meetings with Condon—talking to Condon at length, even negotiating at the last minute over the exact ransom amount and agreeing to accept less—was hardly the work of a slick intermediary working for professionals.

But could a lone amateur really have climbed a ladder to the Lindberghs' second-floor nursery, opened a window, and spirited the baby away without inside help? Some police investigators had declared that feat virtually impossible.

Shoenfeld disagreed. He pointed to a 1920 case in a small town in Pennsylvania. A mother and father lived in a private house with three children, the youngest just eighteen months old. One night, the mother heard a sound and awoke her husband to investigate. When the father entered the second-floor nursery, he found the two older children asleep and the nearby baby's crib empty. A ladder had been used to gain entry.

Ransom negotiations followed, the police set a trap, and a man was arrested as he picked up a package he thought held the ransom money. The man confessed and said he had accidentally smothered the infant while carrying it away. Then he'd weighted the body down and thrown it into a river. The body was never found. The man was sentenced to life in prison.

The Pennsylvania case showed that it *was* possible for a kidnapper to climb a ladder and remove a small child from a home and do it quietly enough to avoid detection, Shoenfeld said.

Implicitly, Shoenfeld was accusing investigators of a failure of imagination and of failing to do their homework. He was also engaging in—pioneering, really—a blend of science, art, common sense, and intuition that would one day be called criminal profiling.

The Lindbergh kidnapper was a German immigrant; that much seemed clear from the ransom messages. Shoenfeld told Finn he'd like to see them instead of just reading about them in the newspapers. Finn said he'd see what he could do.

Ominously, in Shoenfeld's view, none of the ransom notes had contained threats to the baby. Rather, they had said that the child was well. But Shoenfeld thought a kidnapper would more likely threaten harm to a victim rather than offer reassurances to spur quick payment of ransom—if the victim were still alive, that was.

Then there was Cemetery John's cryptic comment to Condon: "I'm only a go-between. Would I burn if the baby was dead?"

Shoenfeld told Finn the kidnapper had almost surely killed the baby just after taking him.

What kind of man would do such a thing? What was the key to catching him? In a sense, Shoenfeld theorized to Finn, the key might lie not in the kind of man the kidnapper was but in the kind of man *Lindbergh* was. Think of magnets, Shoenfeld said. Opposites attract; in a perverse sense, the kidnapper was drawn to Lindbergh.

After his 1927 flight, Lindbergh was—or appeared to be—virtually omnipotent. He soared above the world, this boyishly handsome man, seemingly indifferent to the adoration from below, which he attracted endlessly and effortlessly.

The kidnapper was the polar opposite, "inferior in the world of reality," and had probably had earlier brushes with the law, Shoenfeld said. Perhaps he had been incarcerated. Surely, he had delusions of grandeur along with a tremendous unconscious drive to be powerful.

To the kidnapper, Lindbergh was an enemy, everything the kidnapper wanted to be but never could. Taking the child meant the kidnapper had triumphed over the father, wounding him, as he himself had been wounded by life. How gratifying it was to force "the great man, Colonel Lindbergh" to bow before him by paying a ransom! But the money itself was not as important to the kidnapper as the power he had displayed in acquiring it. He had brought the Lone Eagle down to earth, where he himself felt so inferior.

If and when the kidnapper was caught, Shoenfeld predicted, he would not display fear or apprehension; indeed, he would not even *feel* those sensations, since he lacked the normal emotional development to do so.

The suspect would seem mild-mannered and would tell obvious lies yet not be able to feel how ridiculous he was being, Shoenfeld told Finn. But paradoxically, given his deep-seated feelings of inferiority, "he thinks he is capable of getting away with anything, merely by trying."

He would probably talk a lot but he would say essentially nothing, Shoenfeld went on. Physical violence wouldn't result in a confession because "he would enjoy playing the stoic and thus demonstrating his superiority."

But a questioner who feigned a sympathetic, simple-minded demeanor might—*might*—obtain a confession by leading the suspect on "from extravagance to extravagance" and thence to overconfidence and carelessness.

"None of your routine questioning methods, however, will serve to obtain that confession," Shoenfeld said. "Of this, I am certain."

One more thing, Shoenfeld said. If the police discovered who the kidnapper was, they should arrest him away from his home. If he was arrested *in* his home—well, who knows? Maybe he had hidden the ransom where the police would have a hard time finding it. But if they arrested him when he was away from home, he would have some of the ransom bills on his person. Even when he was not planning to spend them, Shoenfeld thought that he would like to carry them as little trophies from his great triumph.

After the meeting, Finn contacted Schwarzkopf, who agreed to let the psychiatrist see photostatic copies of the ransom notes. But Schwarzkopf, in another mind-boggling display of bureaucratic territoriality, said that Finn could *not* see them, that the New Jersey State Police did not need the assistance of the New York police, thank you very much.

By this time, Dudley Shoenfeld wasn't surprised at the turf battles between police forces. But at least Detective James Finn had listened to him. Maybe something good would come out of their session one day.

Many months would pass before Shoenfeld's theories about the kidnapper could be compared to the actual human being. Then the police would see that the psychiatrist had been remarkably perceptive.

CHAPTER FIFTEEN

TWO VICTIMS

Englewood, New Jersey
May and June 1932

The household help at the Lindberghs' home near Hopewell had been questioned and cleared, their whereabouts on March 1, the day of the kidnapping, accounted for. Then there was Violet Sharpe, a twenty-eight-year old maid at the Englewood estate of Anne Lindbergh's mother. Sharpe had left her native England two years before in search of a better life in the United States.

Questioned by the New Jersey State Police nine days after the baby was taken, she gave answers that were vague, even contradictory. She seemed defensive and surly.

Asked where she had been on March 1, she claimed at first that she had gone on a double date to a movie that night. But she said she couldn't recall the name of the man who had accompanied her, nor the names of the other couple, nor the title of the movie, nor even the location of the theater.

So, she was asked, how did you meet this guy who took you on a date and whose name you don't even remember?

Sharpe said she and her sister, Emily, were strolling on Lydecker Street in Englewood, not far from the Morrow estate, on Sunday, February 28, when a man waved from a car. For a moment, Sharpe said, she thought she knew him, so she waved back. As he stopped the car, she realized she didn't know him after all. But the man had a friendly way, and he asked her out, Sharpe politely declined, but the man was persistent. He got her phone number and said he would call. He did, early on the evening of March 1, saying he'd pick her up at the Morrow estate around eight o'clock.

Sharpe's story raised suspicions from the onset, yet the police did not question her again until April 13. This time, the police expressed their skepticism, and Sharpe admitted that she'd lied. She said the foursome had not gone to the movies; rather, they had gone to a roadhouse in Orangeburg, New York, just across the New Jersey border and a half hour drive from Englewood. Sharpe said she drank coffee while the other three drank beer. And this time, she remembered her date's first name: Ernie.

After some dancing to the radio, Sharpe said, the group left, and she was dropped off back in Englewood around eleven o'clock.

Sharpe's new account did not dispel the suspicions. For a young single woman to go to a roadhouse during Prohibition with a man she'd just met called her character into question, at least in the eyes of some people, even if she had drunk nothing stronger than coffee. Besides, she still couldn't remember her date's last name.

Investigators saw other reasons to focus on Sharpe. They discovered that she had $1,600 in her bank account. That was a lot of money, especially for a maid who was paid $100 a month. And her sister, Emily, had sailed for England just a few days after the ransom money was handed to Cemetery John.

Or should Sharpe have been given the benefit of the doubt about her bank account? After all, her job included board and lodging, and her expenses were not high. It would have been reasonable to conclude that she was simply a thrifty young woman.

But the stars seemed to be aligning against Sharpe. She had lost weight and was feeling ill. On May 11, she was admitted to a hospital in Englewood with a severe infection of her tonsils and adenoids. Her tonsils were removed, leaving her with a terrible sore throat.

The afternoon of Thursday, May 12, was cool and drizzly as a truck driver pulled off a road in a wooded area not quite five miles from the Lindbergh estate in Hopewell. He walked forty feet or so into the woods to relieve himself. A horrid stench was in the air. He spotted what looked like a baby's foot, then a skull, beneath leaves and brush. A closer look revealed the corpse of an infant, badly decomposed and half torn apart by animals. The search for the Lindbergh baby was over.

The search had extended over a wide region of the country and out to sea, yet it had ended not far from home and only seventy-five feet or so from the emergency phone lines set up by the police. Colonel Schwarzkopf quickly came under criticism from people who lived near the Lindbergh estate and had complained that the police hadn't searched the area closely enough.

An autopsy confirmed that the infant son of Charles and Anne Lindbergh had died of a skull fracture, almost certainly the night he was taken. The Lindberghs, fearing that a grave would attract ghoulish souvenir hunters, had their baby's remains cremated and scattered at sea.

Schwarzkopf said a group suspected of being behind the kidnapping was under surveillance. "Early arrests in the case were predicted," the *New York Times* reported.[47]

Soon after the discovery of the dead child, it was reported that Lindbergh had recently been on a boat off the New Jersey coast in a futile attempt to signal the kidnappers, who were supposedly on another boat.

Within a week after the baby was found, there were reports that the New Jersey State Police were closing in on five men and a woman as their main suspects.

John Condon viewed hundreds of photographs in police files in the hope that he would recognize "one of the men with whom he unsuccessfully negotiated," the *Times* reported.

Now, there was an assumption that more than one person must be involved in this, the new "crime of the century."

———————

News that the baby had been found dead affected Violet Sharpe profoundly. Already physically ailing, she sank into a black mood. After a few days in the hospital, she returned to the Morrow home in Englewood to recuperate. Unsympathetic and under growing pressure, Colonel Schwarzkopf pressed her for yet another interview.

Sharpe balked, contending that she was still too ill. A doctor supported her, telling the police that she had a fever and that it would be best for her if another session were not held immediately. But Schwarzkopf insisted, and another round of questioning was scheduled for the evening of Monday, May 23, in a study at the Morrow home. Present were Schwarzkopf, Inspector Harry Walsh of the Jersey City police, another New Jersey detective, and Charles Lindbergh.

Yet again, Sharpe was asked about the chance meeting with Ernie on Lydecker Street ("Are you in the habit of picking up strange men?") and her earlier lie about going to a movie. She was asked for further details about her trip to the Orangeburg roadhouse. Her answers seemed clipped and grudging.

But she volunteered one thing she'd neglected to mention before. Ernie had called her around one in the afternoon of March 1 as well as that evening before picking her up.

The timing was crucial. By the early afternoon of March 1, word had reached the Morrow estate that Charles and Anne Lindbergh and their baby would be staying overnight at Hopewell instead of coming to Englewood. Thus, the question: was this mysterious Ernie part of a kidnapping conspiracy, and had Sharpe given him information that would aid him? (But if so, why did she *voluntarily* mention the earlier phone call?)

When the May 23 interrogation was over and a tired Sharpe had left the room, Lindbergh said she had been acting like a person who was ill and despondent over the death of a child she had adored; he didn't think she was involved in the kidnapping. The police were not convinced. They intended to question her further.

―――――――

On June 7, Sharpe wrote to a friend in Britain, saying that she felt weak and weighed only one hundred pounds. She was homesick. "But I cannot leave the country, or they would think I knew something about the baby."[48] She confided that she felt that "life is getting so sad, I really don't think there is much to live for anymore."

On June 9, Inspector Walsh appeared at the Morrow home again, along with a secretary. Again, the inspector tried to pick Sharpe's story apart, only this time, he added something new. He showed her a photograph of Ernest Brinkert, who had owned a taxi company in White Plains, Westchester County, New York, and had a record for larceny and assault. Sharpe was apparently unaware that the police had surreptitiously searched her room and found a few business cards for the taxi company.

"So," Walsh demanded, "is this the Ernie you went on a date with?"

"Yes," Sharpe replied. "That's him."

"So," the inspector pressed, "why didn't you tell us before?"

Sharpe explained, again, that she hadn't recalled her date's *first* name early on, let alone his last name.

Walsh goaded Sharpe, putting her into a state so agitated that the police secretary took pity and summoned a doctor. The doctor arrived quickly, examined Sharpe, and announced that questioning must cease for the day. Her heart was racing, and her blood pressure was high. She was near hysteria.

The morning of the next day, Friday, June 10, Walsh called the Morrow estate and said he was sending an officer to bring Sharpe to his office for still more questioning, this time with a doctor looking on. When she learned that her ordeal was not over, Sharpe screamed and rushed upstairs. She grabbed a can of powdered silver polish, which contained cyanide. She mixed some of the powder with water, went to her room, and drank. Minutes later, she was dead.

Schwarzkopf and his detectives were dismayed. They had hoped to pressure Sharpe into telling them who else was involved in the kidnapping and murder—besides Ernest Brinkert, that is. The police dearly wanted to find him. In the best of all worlds, John Condon might even identify him as Cemetery John.

Finding Brinkert was surprisingly easy. Just hours after Sharpe's death, a White Plains detective went to the home of a man who had fielded Brinkert's calls for taxi service. Brinkert happened to call in on Friday night. He told the detective that he'd heard that he was wanted for questioning and would be happy to turn himself in.

The detective didn't want to wait. A trace had been put on the call, showing that it had come from New Rochelle, not far from White Plains. The detective rushed to the location and took Brinkert into custody late Friday night. By this time, Condon had been called to

Westchester County and shown a photograph of Brinkert. The photo wasn't that clear, and he couldn't say for sure if Brinkert was the man from the cemetery. Then, when he saw him in person that night, Condon *could* say for sure: he had never seen Ernest Brinkert in his life. Standing a mere five feet four, Brinkert was several inches shorter than Cemetery John.

Brinkert said he didn't know Violet Sharpe, that he couldn't account for the presence of the cards for his taxi service in her bedroom (there were probably a lot of his business cards floating around out there), and that he and his wife had been at the home of another couple in Bridgeport, Connecticut, the afternoon and evening of March 1, the date of the kidnapping.

The couple in Bridgeport readily confirmed Brinkert's account.

So perhaps the case against Sharpe was really *not* so strong. Perhaps there was no case at all. One has to wonder if Schwarzkopf and the New Jersey detectives went to bed that night with chills in their stomachs. But the real nightmare would come the following day, Saturday, June 11.

———————

The suicide of Violet Sharpe was the lead story in the *New York Times* that Saturday. It quoted Colonel Schwarzkopf as declaring that the death confirmed "the suspicion of the investigating authorities concerning her guilty knowledge of the crime against Charles A. Lindbergh Jr."[49]

The article went on in that vein as Schwarzkopf and Walsh recalled that she had lied about her whereabouts the night of the kidnapping and apparently lied about knowing Ernest Brinkert, who had very likely graduated from minor crime to kidnapping and murder, with Sharpe's inside help. At least, that was the obvious implication.

"Of all the 29 servants in the Lindbergh and Morrow homes that were questioned by us after the kidnapping, Miss Sharpe was the only one who could not tell a story that stood up," Walsh said. As for the money in Sharpe's savings account, he said, "I'd feel quite comfortable if I had as much."

———

Even as hundreds of thousands of people were reading the damning remarks of Schwarzkopf and Walsh in Saturday morning's newspapers, the terrible truth was emerging.

First, a butler at the Morrow estate remembered something. "The man you're looking for is Ernie *Miller*, not Ernest Brinkert," he told the police on Saturday. The butler had recalled that Sharpe was acquainted with a young man named Ernest Miller from Closter, another community in Bergen County, New Jersey, not far from Englewood. Sure enough, Ernest Miller was located on Saturday and said that he'd gone to the roadhouse with Sharpe the night of March 1.

Later Saturday, a young woman from Palisades Park in Bergen County told the police that she and a young man, also from Closter, had been the other couple on the March 1 outing. And no, a man named Ernest Brinkert had not been with them.

The recollections of Ernest Miller and the young woman from Palisades Park about the trip to the roadhouse coincided in every detail with the account that Sharpe had given.

What must Colonel Schwarzkopf and the detectives have felt as they realized that Sharpe, who had admittedly lied at first, had told the truth in the end? In their earlier comments, Schwarzkopf and his men had virtually convicted her. Now there would have to be another announcement, a humiliating one.

———

As Inspector Walsh put it in a Saturday evening news conference, "a chap named Ernie Miller" had indeed confirmed Sharpe's story "and says he cannot understand why she kept it from us."[50]

"This is a peculiar turn of events," Walsh said lamely. "It is no fault of ours... I cannot understand why this girl, if she had nothing to do with the kidnapping, preferred death to revealing Miller's name. I cannot understand it at all."

But in her June 7 letter to a friend in Britain, Sharpe had told of her poor health, her homesickness, the pressure she was under. Elizabeth Morrow, Anne Lindbergh's mother, was a woman with traditional attitudes, and Sharpe may have feared she would lose her job if Mrs. Morrow found out about the trip to the roadhouse. Perhaps that was why she lied about it.

In short, Violet Sharpe may have been on the verge of a nervous breakdown. How else to explain her mistake in looking at a photo of Ernest Brinkert and identifying him as her companion the night of March 1?

The *New York Times* reported in a front-page article on Sunday, June 12, that "a sudden twist" in the Lindbergh case tended to clear Sharpe. Her sister condemned the police. "Ever since the baby disappeared, Violet was badgered and questioned until she did not know what she was saying or doing," Emily Sharpe said. "She was driven nearly mad."

Yet Schwarzkopf, who had declared Sharpe guilty of *something*, still would not exonerate her. "The fact still remains that conflicting statements were made," he told reporters. He insisted that she had not been subjected to undue pressure. But how likely was it that New Jersey policemen of the 1930s, working on the biggest case of their careers, took pains to be kind and courteous to her? In fairness, they were under enormous stress. They were also unfettered by Supreme Court rulings that would be handed down three decades later, rulings that would offer some protection to unsophisticated people of modest means who panic under police scrutiny—people like Violet Sharpe.

Is it conceivable that Sharpe took her own life because she thought she had inadvertently given the kidnapper or kidnappers information about the Lindbergh household? Yes, it is conceivable. But all these decades later, no evidence to support that idea has surfaced. All she seems to have been guilty of was foolishly lying.

Violet Sharpe was buried in Brookside Cemetery in Englewood, which is also the resting place of Anne Lindbergh's father, Dwight Morrow. Colonel Schwarzkopf and his men had to shake off whatever guilt and embarrassment they felt. With bills from the ransom coming into banks sporadically, they had a money trail to follow. Were there any other clues, any avenues of investigation free of emotion and guided by pure science?

Yes.

CHAPTER SIXTEEN

THE MAN WHO LOVED TREES

Madison, Wisconsin
Early 1933

It was so fitting that Arthur Koehler had but one hobby: cabinetmaking.

From his boyhood in Manitowoc, Wisconsin, where he was born on June 4, 1885, Koehler was fascinated by trees. He loved the smell of a forest, loved the bark on trees, the rings inside them, the sap.

Indeed, he *revered* trees. "They carry in themselves the record of their history. They show with absolute fidelity the progress of the years, storms, droughts, floods, injuries, and any human touch. A tree never lies." Perhaps, he mused, "the ancients who believed in trees as gods were not so wrong."*

His father was a carpenter and taught his son the skills of his trade. Koehler was good with tools when he was still in elementary school.

---

*   This quote and others by Arthur Koehler are from his article "Who Made That Ladder?" in the *Saturday Evening Post* of April 20, 1935.

Koehler earned a bachelor of science degree in forestry from the University of Michigan and a master's in wood anatomy from the University of Wisconsin. By the early 1930s, he was head of the U.S. Forest Service's laboratory in Madison, Wisconsin. He was, arguably, the foremost authority on wood in the United States and perhaps in the world.

Koehler and his wife, Ethelyn, had three children. Later, Koehler would recall shuddering as he looked at their baby son and imagined the anguish the Lindberghs were feeling. He was eager to help them. Soon after the kidnapping, he wrote to Lindbergh, telling him it might be possible to trace the origins of the wood in the kidnapper's ladder.

Koehler was not surprised when Lindbergh didn't respond. The famous aviator was being inundated with advice, much of it well-meaning, some of it from cranks.

Colonel Schwarzkopf heard of Koehler's offer and sent small slivers from the ladder to Koehler's lab. Soon, Koehler sent back a report with his findings: the slivers were of ponderosa pine, a tree native to the western United States and Canada. Tiny fibers of wool were attached to the slivers. Could they be from the clothing of the man who had climbed the ladder?

No, it was soon determined. The fibers were from woolen blankets that New Jersey State Police officers had draped over the ladder at the crime scene for protection. Disappointed and probably a little embarrassed, Schwarzkopf shelved Koehler's report.

But in February 1933, Schwarzkopf decided to turn again to Koehler. After all, the investigation was nearly a year old and at a standstill. Nor had Schwarzkopf forgotten what Koehler had discerned just from studying slivers. What might the wood expert learn from studying the entire ladder? So Schwarzkopf invited Koehler to come to Hopewell, New Jersey, to see the ladder. The decision may have been the most important of Schwarzkopf's career.

Right away, Schwarzkopf was impressed with Koehler, a tall,

imposing man who looked like an outdoorsman. But he was a scientist first, and while he knew his task was daunting, he approached it with confidence. "The ladder was homemade, which meant that it contained individual characteristics," he wrote later.[51] "It was not one out of a thousand or ten thousand, all superficially alike; it was the only one like it and could be expected to reveal some of the peculiarities and associations of the man who made it."

Koehler determined that whoever built the ladder knew something about woodworking but was a "slovenly carpenter." He saw that the hand plane used by the ladder builder was dull. The three-quarter-inch chisel used to carve the recesses for the rungs—presumably the chisel found at the crime scene that had also been used to pry open the nursery window—was quite sharp, although the recesses had been carved in a sloppy fashion.

Later, the New England manufacturer of the chisel would determine it was about forty years old. It was perfectly ordinary, similar to tools found in countless basements, garages, and workshops. But as he reflected on what it had been used for and that it might have been wielded to smash a baby's skull, Koehler realized, "I could not touch it without a sense of horror."

Koehler urged Schwarzkopf to let him take the ladder to his lab for further study. The colonel agreed.

Back in Wisconsin, Koehler dismantled the ladder, which had eleven rungs and six boards that made up the side rails. Some of the side-rail boards were of North Carolina pine, which, despite the name, is grown in a number of Eastern states, especially along the Atlantic Coast. Other side rails were of Douglas fir, grown in the West. The dowel pins used to hold the ladder together were of birch, common in temperate regions. The rungs were from ponderosa pine, eight of the eleven from the same piece of wood.

Perhaps most significantly, one side-rail board from North Carolina pine had four holes where nails had been. Koehler speculated that whoever built the ladder may have run out of fresh wood and used secondhand wood to finish. Koehler also observed that two of the holes were made by square eight-penny nails, which were somewhat old-fashioned.

There were no rust marks around the nail holes, indicating that the board must have been used indoors originally, with no exposure to rain and snow. The lumber was of a low grade, not suitable for finishing but suitable for rough construction, as in a barn, garage, or attic.

The nails had been hammered in at different angles and depths, and the distances between the nails varied. Somewhere, Koehler knew, there must be another board or joist to which the rail board had been nailed. If that other board with corresponding nail holes were found, it could be invaluable evidence against the kidnapper, especially if it were found in his house or garage.

On March 8, 1933, Koehler stated his conclusions in a report to the New Jersey State Police. Then he asked if he could search the Lindbergh property and surrounding area for wood that matched the ladder. Schwarzkopf assigned two detectives to work with Koehler. For three months, they searched buildings, garages, outhouses, and shacks, not only around the Lindbergh tract but on properties of people with connections to the case, however slight. Nothing.

In early June, Koehler went back to Wisconsin to study the ladder pieces under a microscope and magnifying glass. In so doing, he discovered clues that would have eluded almost anyone else on the planet.

Koehler detected small grooves in the wide surfaces of the boards used to make the bottom two side rails. He recognized that the grooves, virtually invisible to the naked eye, had been made by an eight-bladed machine planer in a lumber mill. Moreover, Koehler was able to determine that one blade was slightly out of kilter with the others. He also found marks on the edges of the pieces of wood, marks that told him the side cutter was a six-bladed machine. Koehler thought the "eight-blade, six-blade" arrangement was unusual. Finally, he detected a defect in one blade of the side cutter.

Thus, Koehler could eliminate those mills that did not have certain types of planers. Last and most important, Koehler was able to determine from the intervals between the tiny marks on the wood and his familiarity with the speed of wood planers that the wood had been fed through the machines at a rate of 230 feet a minute. Koehler knew this speed was consistent with industrial wood planers used in the South.

So Koehler studied the *Southern Lumberman's Directory*, which told him that there were 1,598 machine-planing lumber mills between New York State and Alabama.

Visiting all the mills was not feasible—even if he managed to visit two mills a day *working seven days a week*, it would take him more than two years—so Koehler mailed requests to the mills for wood samples without mentioning that his query was in connection with the Lindbergh kidnapping.

Koehler learned that there were just two manufacturers of machine planers in the Eastern United States. He visited both, conferring with men who were intimately familiar with the devices. They told him that markings on the particular piece of wood from the ladder indicated that the machine that planed it had been fitted with a drive pulley of an unusual size. This was an invaluable fact.

Koehler learned that only twenty-five lumber mills using the kind of machinery that had cut the ladder pieces were operating in the region where Carolina pine grew. With his knowledge that the machine he was looking for left telltale marks from a blade that was defective and another that was out of kilter *and* that one of the machines had been fitted with an unusual drive pulley, Koehler was zeroing in on his target. He was also able to rule out those mills that did not produce one-by-four-inch boards like those used to build the ladder.

Eventually, Koehler received a wood sample that seemed promising. It was from the Dorn Company in McCormick, South Carolina. The sample had been processed in a machine with the eight-blade, six-blade setup. But the Dorn sample had no sign of the blade defects that had so intrigued Koehler. Still, he was not discouraged, reasoning that the blades had been sharpened or replaced.

Koehler contacted the company again, this time requesting samples of wood more than two years old. The company sent the wood Koehler had asked for, but the markings on the wood were not what Koehler had expected. He knew he'd have to journey some nine hundred miles from Madison, Wisconsin, to McCormick, South Carolina.

There, in that tiny, sleepy town on the edge of the Georgia border, he interviewed J. J. Dorn, the owner of the mill. Dorn recalled that a few years earlier, a factory-installed pulley had caused the wood to be fed into the planer too fast, so in September 1929, he'd bought a replacement pulley of a different size at a hardware store. The hardware store pulley was used off and on, depending on the particular job.

Koehler asked the mill owner to process a sample of wood with the hardware store pulley. Voilà! The wood came out with markings exactly like those on the ladder used in the kidnapping. "The Sherlock Holmes of the Forest Service," as he would one day be called, knew he had found the right lumber mill.

"I sniffed with gratitude the odor of pine sawdust, machine grease, and sweaty overalls," Koehler recalled.

But where had the mill sent the one-by-four-inch boards used in the ladder? Koehler knew he could rule out lumber processed before September 1929, when the hardware store pulley was installed, and he needn't bother with lumber sent out after March 1, 1932, the day of the kidnapping. Still, the Dorn mill had shipped a fair amount of lumber in the two and a half years that Koehler needed to focus on.

Koehler and Lewis Bornmann, the New Jersey State Police detective who had assisted him in the search around the Lindbergh property, set about tracking lumber shipped from the Dorn mill to yards in New Jersey, New York, Connecticut, and Massachusetts. More than forty carloads of wood had been sent to twenty-five different lumberyards in those states from September 1929 to March 1932.

Eighteen carloads had been shipped to places within twenty-five miles of Hopewell, New Jersey—but all had been unloaded at fenced-in factory sites where there were no retail sales. Thus, those sites could be ruled out.

One by one, Koehler and Bornmann visited the other yards. Weeks went by, then months. Finally, on Wednesday, November 29, 1933, they arrived at the National Millwork and Lumber Company on White Plains Road in the Bronx. There, the foreman confirmed that a shipment of pine from the Dorn mill had been received on December 1, 1931, three months to the day before the kidnapping.

But the entire shipment had been sold, the foreman said. There was no wood left for Koehler to examine. And the company did business on a cash-only basis, so it was virtually impossible to find the buyers.

Koehler was crestfallen.

Then the foreman recalled that a portion of the December 1, 1931, shipment had been used to build a storage shed right on the National Millwork and Lumber Company property. At Koehler's request, a section of a one-by-four-inch board was cut from the shed. With a magnifying glass, Koehler saw that the markings on the board matched those on the wood from the ladder.

We can only imagine the emotions Arthur Koehler felt that

Wednesday, the day before Thanksgiving.* His science had triumphed; *he* had triumphed. He had studied wood from the ladder and traced it to the region where the tree had been felled, then on to the mill where the bark had been stripped and the wood cut into boards, and finally to the Bronx lumberyard that had received the boards—and sold them for cash, without paperwork. Dead end. Or maybe not. Now, investigators were looking for a man of German descent, probably an immigrant, likely a carpenter, who had bought wood at the Bronx lumberyard and whose handwriting matched that in the ransom notes. And since the man had communicated with John Condon through a small newspaper in the Bronx, there was a good chance that he lived in that borough. The universe of possible suspects had been narrowed dramatically. And Koehler thought the ladder wood might yield still more clues.

---

*   The holiday was still celebrated then on the last Thursday in November, not the fourth Thursday.

CHAPTER SEVENTEEN

STRICTLY BUSINESS

St. Paul, Minnesota
Thursday, June 30, 1932

If he had time to look at the morning paper, young Haskell Bohn saw an abundance of news about politics.

Governor Franklin D. Roosevelt of New York had a plane standing by in Albany to fly him to Chicago, assuming he was nominated for president at the Democratic National Convention, as seemed likely. Roosevelt's aides said that, with stopovers, the flight would take some seven hours. If Roosevelt alighted looking cheerful and energetic, there ought to be no more whispers that he suffered from physical infirmities that would make it difficult for him to fulfill the duties of the presidency. One thing was already clear at the convention: there was overwhelming support among the delegates for repeal of Prohibition and, pending that, for legalizing the manufacture and sale of beer. Surely, that would boost sales of refrigerators, which was definitely good news for Haskell Bohn and the family-owned Bohn Refrigerator Company.

Haskell's grandfather, Gebhard Bohn, had come to America from Germany in the nineteenth century, lacking money, fluency in English, and social polish. But he was blessed with enormous drive, business and mechanical skills, and perhaps a touch of genius. He worked hard at menial jobs, tinkering to great effect in his spare time, and settled in St. Paul.

He and two brothers started a company that sold window parts, furniture, and other household goods. But Gebhard saw the future coming, and it was called refrigeration. Before his death in 1924, he had invented a refrigerator far more efficient than most others at the time, one that was eventually used in nearly all railroad dining cars in the country.

His son, Gebhard C. Bohn, was also a visionary, unlike some sons of business pioneers. The younger Gebhard decided that the company founded by his father should concentrate entirely on refrigeration. He saw that the old-fashioned kitchen ice box belonged to the past. Every family would want an electric *refrigerator*. Nor would the appliance be a luxury; after all, dining out was unaffordable for many families. It was essential that store-bought food last as long as possible.

Restaurants, country clubs, flower shops—all needed refrigeration. There was a huge and growing market, and the Bohn enterprise captured much of it. Having caught the wave of the future, having helped to create the wave, the Bohn family was very wealthy during the Great Depression.

———

There was another recent development that had been covered rather modestly in the newspapers, considering its importance. Eight days earlier, President Herbert Hoover had signed the federal anti-kidnapping law—the Lindbergh Law, as it came to be known. Its chief sponsors, Senator Roscoe Conkling Patterson, a Missouri Republican, and

Representative John Joseph Cochran, a Democrat from St. Louis, were understandably tired of the kidnappings in their state. The young Adolphus Busch Orthwein, the noted eye doctor Isaac Kelley, the daring dressmaker Nell Donnelly—those were only the most noteworthy victims in Missouri in recent months. There had been others not quite famous enough to get national attention.

And of course, the Lindbergh tragedy had made it impossible for Congress not to do *something* before fleeing the sweltering heat of the Washington summer.

There had been differences between the House and Senate versions of the law, with the House version providing for the death penalty for someone convicted of transporting a victim across state borders unless the jury recommended mercy.

Under the Senate version, the maximum punishment was life in prison. Supporters of the Senate version argued that subjecting a kidnapper to a death sentence could encourage him to kill his victim so the victim couldn't testify against him.

In the end, the Senate version won the day, with life in prison the maximum sentence for transporting a victim across state lines.* On June 17, the House unanimously approved the Senate version, which had been approved on June 8. (There was nothing in the final bill to prevent a kidnapper from being sentenced to death under *state* law if a victim was killed in a state that had the death penalty.)

Importantly, the law provided for a seven-day waiting period before federal investigators could enter a case; in other words, if a victim was not found within that time, he or she was presumed to have been taken across state borders.

---

* As will be seen, the issue of the death penalty in the federal law would be argued and reargued over the years.

Just before 9:00 a.m. on June 30, twenty-year-old Haskell Bohn emerged from his house to be driven to work at the refrigerator plant. It was a warm day; the temperature would climb into the upper eighties by late afternoon.

As he and the family chauffeur approached the garage behind the family home, Bohn's world turned upside down. Two men with pistols approached quickly, removed Bohn's glasses, wrapped tape over his eyes, and led him away after giving the chauffeur a note.

Bohn was steered into a nearby alley and shoved into a car where he lay on the floor, his eyes still taped. The whole operation had taken only moments. Bohn had had no time to react. The kidnappers had carried out their operation without a flaw.

And away they want, the kidnappers and their captive. Bohn had no way of knowing that the note left with the chauffeur demanded $35,000 ransom. He also did not know—and surely would not have cared—that he had just become the first ransom-kidnapping victim since the Lindbergh Law took effect with President Hoover's signature.

His captors drove for about an hour, then stopped in a building that smelled like a garage. For another three hours, Bohn sat in the car, wondering what his fate would be. Were the men holding him waiting for confederates to arrive? Making plans on the fly? Finally, a man yanked him from the car and steered him, still blindfolded, for what he estimated to be two hundred feet. Then it was into a building—a house, Bohn sensed—and down some steps. Bohn assumed he was in a basement.

He was guided a few feet, then told he could sit. He did, on a bed. He heard the voices of several men, then the voice of a woman. A man said he would get plenty of food and cigarettes and wouldn't be mistreated if his father cooperated.

Almost immediately after Haskell was seized, the Bohn family began to get letters from the kidnappers. In demanding full cooperation, they alluded darkly to the murder of Charles Lindbergh's baby. But Gebhard Bohn did not panic. He had the emotional support of his brother, William, who rushed from his home in Los Angeles to St. Paul to aid in negotiations.

The St. Paul police announced that they would not interfere. The stance of the police was not surprising in view of how government and law enforcement functioned—or didn't—in St. Paul.

Meanwhile, Haskell Bohn was in a twilight world. For much of the daytime in the basement, his eyes were taped shut. But when the tape was being changed, he caught glimpses of the men and the woman who were holding him. He thought he'd be able to identify them if he got the chance.

His jailers kept their promise. He was treated humanely. A woman cooked his meals; the food wasn't bad. But he wanted to go back to his real life. He wanted to eat food cooked in his own home, wanted to shower and change clothes.

At night, the tape was taken off, so he could stare into the dark before falling asleep. He welcomed the sleep; it brought freedom from the fear and monotony he had endured for...how many days?

On the evening of Wednesday, July 6, his eyes were bandaged and taped shut anew. He was told to stand up. He dared to hope.

Then up the steps, out the door into the night, and he was lying on the floor of a car again. The engine turned over, and the car moved. Bohn welcomed the sensation.

He guessed that an hour went by before the car stopped. He was pulled out of the car, not too roughly, and the tape and bandages were removed. The car sped off, and he was alone.

It was a clear, blue-black night, pleasantly warm. The sky was full of stars. He thought he smelled water, like a lake. But where was he? On a dirt road out in the country. No lights.

He walked. Very soon, his legs were sore from lack of exercise, but he didn't mind. He was free. After about a half hour, he saw the lights of a farmhouse. He knocked on the door. The farmer, Roy Bell, was surprised to see a well-dressed but disheveled young man who had obviously had a rough time. Happily, Roy Bell's house had a telephone.

Before police officers came to take him home, Bohn learned that he had been freed near Medicine Lake, several miles west of Minneapolis. Later, he learned that the negotiations over his release had gone smoothly. The kidnappers had settled on a much smaller ransom. Some reports put the amount at $12,000, while others put it as low as $5,000. Perhaps the kidnappers were rank amateurs. Or maybe they were cold professionals, happy to cash in quickly, risking little and moving on to the next opportunity.

In fact, Haskell Bohn and his family had just been victimized by a man who was trying to bring a businesslike approach to kidnapping, a man who would soon be suspected of taking part in the Lindbergh crime. His name was Verne Sankey.

CHAPTER EIGHTEEN

CRIMINAL AND FAMILY MAN

Verne Sankey lacked the swaggering corpulence and menace of Al Capone or the dashing good looks of the notorious bandit John Dillinger. Indeed, he was a short, bald, rather owlish-looking man. As far as we know, Sankey never killed anyone, although he was not allergic to gun smoke.

He was a family man, a loving husband and father. He was mild-mannered by gangster standards. While not an altogether honest man, he had a personal code of honor. His name may not be widely known in the twenty-first century, yet no history of crime in the 1930s is complete without his story.

Sankey was born in rural Iowa in 1891. When he was a boy, his family moved to Wilmot, South Dakota, where his father took up farming. As was the custom then, the father conscripted his three sons to work on the spread. For a time, Sankey's two older brothers were content with their fate or at least resigned to it.

But dawn-to-dusk toil in the fields and barn with cows and chickens for company held no appeal for Sankey. He yearned for big money and places to spend it. So he bade farewell to family and farm when he was nineteen and found work on a railroad. He worked hard, becoming an engineer after stints as a watchman and fireman. While life on the rails had its sweat and tedium, Sankey got to see much of the Upper Midwest and stretches of western Canada. He earned a respectable salary.

But Sankey preferred a fancy hotel room to a caboose, and he loved to gamble. With the coming of Prohibition in 1920, he established himself as a bootlegger, a career change made easier by his familiarity with Canada, where liquor could be bought legally. Soon, he was smuggling booze from Canada into the Upper Midwest of the United States.

By the mid-1920s, he and his wife, Fern, his childhood sweetheart from Wilmot, had settled in the little town of Melville, Saskatchewan. He became a Canadian citizen. His bootlegging enterprise thrived as he crossed the border easily with his young daughter, Echo, accompanying him on occasion. (He had sensed that her presence alleviated the suspicions of customs agents.)

By the late 1920s, Sankey had become a liquor supplier to members of the social elite of Denver. He was a trustworthy, gentlemanly bootlegger who sent Christmas cards to his customers. He was the kind of criminal with whom law-abiding people felt comfortable.

He and his wife moved from Melville to Regina, the provincial capital of Saskatchewan. Sankey supported amateur hockey, loved to bowl, and was a friendly neighbor.

But the dawn of the thirties threatened Sankey's prosperity. The Depression was deepening, and fewer Americans had money to spend on contraband liquor. Big criminal syndicates took more control of the remaining bootlegging business. Sankey didn't have platoons of gun-toting toughs to stand up to the syndicates. What could he do?

In February 1931, two masked gunmen robbed the Royal Bank in Regina, taking some $13,000. The locals, well aware of his bootlegging history, speculated that Sankey may have been one of the robbers. But he was never implicated officially, just as he was never charged with several other bank robberies in the region that he was suspected of around that time.

Weeks after the Regina bank heist, Verne and Fern Sankey returned to South Dakota. They rented a house in the little town of Kimball, in the south-central part of the state, where their daughter attended school. By this time, Verne and Fern had an infant son, Orville.

Soon, Sankey bought a few hundred acres of land about twenty miles northwest of Kimball, near the tiny hamlet of Gann Valley. He built a small house on the land and raised cattle, turkeys, and vegetables.

The Sankey spread was remote and hard to reach, even by the standards of that windswept, Dust Bowl era when paved roads were scarce far from the big cities. The Sankeys' nearest neighbor was three miles away. But Sankey did not isolate himself. He kept in touch with his neighbors, went to church with them, attended socials and festivals. And he made friends with the local sheriff and prosecutor.

Had Sankey, who had fled the farm in his youth, been drawn back to the joys of country living? Not really. In the summer of 1932, he and Fern relocated to a house in Minneapolis, the twin city of St. Paul. Around the Twin Cities, it was impossible not to be aware of the Bohns, who were a staple of local coverage.

By this time, Sankey was ready to get into kidnapping. He was convinced he could do it more efficiently than the kidnappers he knew from the true-crime magazines he loved to read.

———

Sankey kept in touch with friends he had made while working on the railroad in Canada. Among them were Ray Robinson and Gordon Alcorn, both Canadians, and Arthur Youngberg, a native of northern Minnesota.

All were a decade or so younger than Sankey. Alcorn, especially, was drawn to Sankey, for whom he had been a railroad fireman while Sankey was an engineer. As the Depression worsened, Robinson, Youngberg, and Alcorn had trouble finding and keeping steady jobs.

Robinson was a sometime guest at Sankey's isolated farm. Sankey and Robinson began to talk about snatching someone for ransom. The talk was hypothetical at first, then much less so as the focus turned to the Bohn family.

It would be revealed later that Haskell Bohn was not held captive in some remote country location but in the basement of the Minneapolis house where Sankey and his wife were staying. For months afterward, Sankey seemed to have gotten away with the caper. Bohn had been freed just before the seven-day waiting period, which would have authorized federal investigators to enter the case, had expired. Sankey figured the local cops didn't have a clue who had kidnapped Bohn. He was right, at least for the moment, and he was looking for other targets.

On to Denver!

CHAPTER NINETEEN

IN THE MILE HIGH CITY

Denver
Early 1933

Denver would not be the first location of many people seeking mild winter weather, but the city did offer relative relief from the razor cold of South Dakota and Saskatchewan. And Verne Sankey knew from his bootlegging days that some very rich people lived in the city and its suburbs.

So Verne and Fern Sankey rented a house in Denver, and Sankey began gathering information. From public records, he gleaned data on the wealth of about thirty "candidates" for his next caper. He pared the list to several prospects, including the beer magnate Adolph Coors and Charles Boettcher II, a member of one of Colorado's wealthiest families.

For weeks, Sankey drove around Denver to canvass the homes of the possible targets. He was accompanied by his friend Gordon Alcorn from the railroad days.

Finally, Sankey decided: the honor of being his next kidnapping victim should go to Charles Boettcher II.

"Charlie" Boettcher, as he was known to all, was thirty-one years old in early 1933. He had graduated from Yale and was married to a beauty queen from Montana named Anna Lou Piggott. The Boettchers lived in a twenty-one-room mansion in an exclusive Denver neighborhood. By early 1933, the couple had a five-year-old daughter, and Anna was expecting another child in March.

Charlie was an aviation enthusiast. Charles Lindbergh was a friend and had been a houseguest. The Boettchers worshipped the Protestant God and moved easily in Denver high society, Charlie more so than Anna.

Although Charlie had been born to great wealth, he had succeeded on his own, forming a successful brokerage firm with a friend. In the midst of the Great Depression, Charlie and Anna Boettcher lived a life so full of riches and seemingly free of cares as to be inconceivable to millions of Americans.

And yet Charlie Boettcher could never be entirely happy with who he was, what he was: the easygoing son of a man who needed to dominate everyone around him, Claude Boettcher.

Claude's father, Charles Boettcher Sr., was a man of amazing ability and iron determination. He had come from Germany in the nineteenth century and made a fortune selling hardware to miners. Then he had pioneered Colorado's sugar beet and cement industries, two sectors of the economy that seemingly had little in common. But Charles Boettcher Sr. had a genius for business.

A photograph of Charles Sr. in late middle age shows a handsome, confident-looking man with a slight smile beneath his mustache. One could imagine him in the uniform of a Prussian general. A photo of his son Claude seems to show a very different kind of man: stern eyes behind pince-nez and a humorless, disapproving face, as though someone had just broken wind at the dinner table.

Yet appearances notwithstanding, father and son were enough alike that Claude was not overshadowed by a powerful father as some sons are. Claude was hard-driving like his father and aggressively expanded the reaches and riches of the family enterprises, investing in mining, railroads, banking, real estate, and utilities as Charles Sr. crossed into his senior years.

It was the fate of the patriarch's *grand*son, Charlie, to be left out. He lacked the vision and grit of his father and grandfather and so was denied a seat in the most holy and sacred inner lodge of the family, whose membership consisted of Charles Sr. and Claude.

Or so young Charlie thought. The impression was reinforced when Claude bought a controlling interest in his son's brokerage firm, a move Charlie did not resist. But how could he, given Claude's emasculating generosity? After all, the twenty-one-room mansion where Charlie and Anna Lou lived had been built by Charlie's father as a wedding present.

Thus, Charlie played the role seemingly meant for him. He dressed well, partied enthusiastically, and gambled, sometimes too much. He drank, often too much. He did not always reject the affection of other women. His vices put strains on his marriage. But Charlie and Anna Lou were not recluses. They went to a social event on the night of Sunday, February 12, 1933.

It was near midnight when they arrived home after a pleasant evening that included a snack at a chili parlor. As they pulled into their driveway, two men with handkerchiefs on their faces emerged from the darkness near the garage.

"Come here, Charlie, and throw up your hands," a man said. "Do what you're told, and everything will be all right."

"Don't resist!" Anna Lou, still in the car, implored her husband.

The man reached into the car and handed Anna Lou an envelope. "Mrs. Boettcher, open that envelope, please."

As she did, a smaller envelope fell out.

"Now open that one," the man said as he retrieved the bigger envelope. "Good night."

The stunned wife saw the two men hustle Charlie off into the dark. When she had ceased trembling, she opened the smaller envelope and found a typed note.

The noted demanded $60,000 in old tens and twenties. The signal that the money was ready was to be an ad in the *Denver Post*. It was to read, "Ready to come home, Mabel."

"Do not notify the police," the note warned. "You know what happened to little Charles Lindbergh through his father calling the police. He would be alive today if his father had followed instructions given him."[52] That wasn't entirely accurate, of course, but the words were still chilling.

At once, Anna Lou called Charlie's father. She told him about the kidnappers' warning. But Claude Boettcher was not a man to take orders from criminals. Of course, he called the police, and within minutes, officers were questioning Anna Lou. She was able to describe one of the kidnappers accurately: a man in his forties, around five feet seven inches tall, solidly built.

The police thought the kidnapping was the work of well-rehearsed professionals. They had minimized the chances of leaving fingerprints with the double-envelope gimmick and by taking care not to touch the Boettchers' car. No doubt, the men had put Charlie in another car and were long gone.

———

It seemed to Charlie Boettcher that the ride went on forever. Many, many hours went by. For him, it was always night; his eyes were taped shut.

The car slowed to a stop. Charlie, blindfolded and with his wrists tied behind his back, was pulled out. Then the car started up again but stopped just a short distance away. Charlie was bewildered until he heard the sound of gasoline being pumped into the car by an attendant.

Charlie was put back in the car, and away they went. On and on, they drove. The car stopped a second time to refuel, with Charlie and one of the kidnappers stepping out as before. Then it was back on the road.

Now and then, his captors spoke to him. Their words were a mix of encouragement and threats. "Do what we say, and you'll be fine. Fight back, and things will be 'unfortunate' for you."

The car stopped yet again for fuel. Three stops for gas; that had to mean a lot of miles. But miles to *where?* Many, many hours. Charlie sensed that morning had come and gone and maybe the afternoon. Was it night again?

At long last, the car slowed to a stop. The car doors opened, and he was pulled out. It was colder than it was in Denver. Charlie didn't know it, but he was at Verne Sankey's ranch in South Dakota, almost six hundred miles from Denver.

Charlie was led through a door—into a house, he sensed.

"Take this fellow downstairs and put him in the little room," a man said.

"They'll have us all in jail," another man replied. His voice was different; Charlie sensed he was not one of the men who had abducted him.

"Don't worry," the first man said. "This is as safe as sitting in an armchair."

———

In Denver, Mayor George D. Begole immediately issued a proclamation urging law-abiding citizens everywhere to help in the apprehension of the kidnappers. Colorado Governor Edwin C. Johnson voiced similar sentiments. (Begole was a Republican and Johnson a Democrat, but the plight of Charlie Boettcher was a bipartisan concern.)

Several thousand volunteers from the American Legion and civic clubs joined police officers in searching the Denver area for any sign of Charlie Boettcher or the men who had kidnapped him.

Applications for pistol permits rose sharply, especially among the Denver elite. Some wealthy Denver residents looked for chauffeurs who were familiar with firearms as well as cars.

On Valentine's Day, forty-eight hours after Charlie Boettcher was seized, J. Edgar Hoover waded into the case, sending several FBI agents to Denver to...to...

To do what, exactly?

The seven-day waiting period for federal intervention was still in effect, but Hoover still sensed an opportunity to expand his agency's power. As the comments of Denver Mayor Begole and Governor Johnson had indicated, the Boettcher family had friends in politics. Franklin D. Roosevelt, who had routed President Hoover in the 1932 election, was to be inaugurated as president on March 4 and had let it be known that he was planning a nationwide anticrime campaign. J. Edgar Hoover envisioned a chance to solidify his position in the new administration and to carve a major role for the FBI.

It turned out that the FBI was largely on the sidelines and did not turn up a single significant clue as the Boettcher kidnapping was being investigated. But this would not stop Hoover from shamelessly issuing statements later that described his bureau's "vital role" in solving the case.[53]

As will be seen, the case would be solved in part because someone drank too much and talked too much.

―――――――

"Ready to come home, Mabel," read the ad placed in the *Denver Post* by Claude Boettcher as the kidnappers had demanded. Soon, Claude was exchanging letters with the kidnappers, with the Episcopal church the Boettchers attended acting as a go-between. Verne Sankey was making the exhausting commute from his South Dakota ranch to Denver to follow local developments.

Tension soon arose between the Denver police and the Boettcher family, with the police brass warning against capitulating to the kidnappers. To do so, the police argued, would encourage other would-be kidnappers. But Claude loved his son (perhaps more than Charlie realized) and would do anything to get him back.

Claude had friends in the highest realms of politics as well as finance and society. He had been a delegate to the 1928 Republican National Convention in Kansas City, Missouri, at which Herbert Hoover had been nominated. *Time* magazine had pronounced him one of the country's most influential men.

In short, Sankey, who had said that kidnapping Charlie Boettcher would be like sitting in an armchair, had wildly underestimated the Boettcher family's vast influence and the storm that kidnapping a member of the clan would set off.

From the start, the Denver police chief, Albert T. Clark, said gangsters in Chicago or Kansas City, Missouri, were probably behind the kidnapping. The chief professed optimism that the kidnappers would soon be caught and that Charlie Boettcher would be unharmed.

N. W. "Red" Mitchell, reputed to be linked to Kansas City bootleggers, was picked up. Mitchell had supposedly been spotted following Charlie and Anna Lou Boettcher from the chili parlor, and Chief Clark said Mitchell didn't have a good alibi for that fateful Sunday night. Unfortunately, Anna Lou could not identify him as one of the men who had confronted her and her husband.

No matter; there were plenty of suspects. Chief Clark said he wanted to talk to Louis "Diamond Jack" Alterie, often described in the press as a former Chicago gangster who had once been a lieutenant of Dean O'Banion, a one-time bootlegger and rival of Al Capone. (O'Banion was shot to death in 1924 in the flower shop he ran as a cover for his criminal activities.)

Initially, Alterie seemed to be a promising suspect: he had been tried in Chicago the previous June on a charge of kidnapping a bookmaker for ransom. Alterie was acquitted of actual kidnapping, but a conspiracy-to-kidnap charge remained against him in Chicago, prompting him to relocate to Glenwood Springs in Western Colorado. There, he ran what the press described as a dude ranch, surely an allusion to Glenwood Springs' reputation since frontier days as a haven for gambling dens and brothels.

Unfortunately, investigators had just missed their chance to interview Alterie. Having been convicted of assault in Glenwood Springs, he'd been given a choice by the law, one reminiscent of Colorado's Wild West days: go to prison or get out of Colorado for good. The deadline was February 1. Alterie checked out of the state a day early without leaving a forwarding address.

Meanwhile, the police in Chicago tried to help their Denver counterparts by hauling in several men with shady reputations, most intriguingly Mike "Bon Bon" Allegretti, a cousin of Al Capone. All were said to have traveled to Denver recently or to have talked on the phone with people in Denver, or both.

None of those leads panned out, nor did the arrests of a score of other suspects who, if not exactly innocent in their daily lives, were innocent of the Boettcher kidnapping. Investigators were further confounded when Joe Roma, a part-time grocer and full-time bootlegger who had offered to help track the kidnappers, was shot to death while playing the mandolin in his Denver home. He left a steaming pot of spaghetti on the stove. (It was soon determined that Roma had met his demise because of a dispute over liquor trafficking.)

━━━━━━━━

In his basement prison, Charlie occasionally managed to dislodge his blindfold enough to peek out and note his surroundings: cement floor, part of it covered by linoleum, part by a carpet. Two chairs, a table, a coal oil lamp.

He subsisted on sandwiches, soup, milk, coffee, and water. And he listened intently for sounds that might be clues to his whereabouts, should he ever get back home. He listened for airplanes, train engines, train whistles. Nothing.

Ironically, the very isolation of the Sankey ranch was becoming a danger for the kidnappers. When neighbors dropped by now and then, they were country-friendly and informal, apt to barge in without knocking, then call out names: "Hi, Fern... Hi, Verne... Hi, Gordon..."

Suppose some of the neighbors suspected that someone was being held for ransom at the Sankey ranch. They'd think he must be rich and that the family might be offering a reward. In fact, Claude Boettcher was offering a reward of $25,000 for his son's safe return.

Thus, another irony: although Charlie was the prisoner, Sankey wanted to be free of *him* as soon as possible—but not before being paid for his trouble. Yet getting the ransom money was proving to be a great deal of trouble. Claude was standing strong.

"I am going no place at no time to deliver money on their word to release my son later," he said. "Public opinion may condemn me as a heartless man... But I feel if I paid that money before I got my boy, I would be signing his death warrant. Men who will kidnap will murder."[54]

The father was not being callous; he had lost twenty pounds in the days following the kidnapping. He simply remembered the Lindbergh kidnapping a year before. Charles and Anne Lindbergh had complied with the ransom demand, and still their baby had been slain.

Further complicating things was an apparent disagreement between the Denver police and Claude, with the latter pressing for a free hand in negotiating with the people who held his son.

———————

Because he was blindfolded, the days and nights blurred for Charlie. When his body ached for sleep, he thought it must be night. He'd been counting the days. He thought it was February 28, which meant he'd been yanked out of his old life more than two weeks before.

"Stand up," a man said.

Charlie obeyed. Then he was pulled up the basement steps, out into the cold, and then he was in a car again. He dared to hope.

He sensed that there were two men in the car. "Keep that blindfold on," one commanded.

The hours and miles went by. *They must be taking me home*, Charlie thought. The view inside his blindfold was gray instead of pitch black. The change meant it was daylight.

His blindfold came loose a little, enough for him to spot a train station as the car went by it. A sign read "Torrington, Wyoming."

Torrington was a little town on the eastern side of Wyoming, north of Denver. So, Charlie figured, if he was being driven home, the car he was in was headed south. Which meant that when he'd been kidnapped, he'd been taken north. Pretty far north too. But then where?

At long last, the car stopped, and Charlie was pulled out. Walk, he was told. Count to 150 paces before you turn around.

He walked, realizing that he was more tired than he had ever been.

The night was mild; he really didn't need his overcoat. He heard the car speeding off. Not waiting to reach 150 paces, he wheeled around, took off his blindfold, saw the car melting into the blackness.

As his eyes adjusted, he realized he was in a quiet residential neighborhood. East Denver! Only a few miles from home! He walked a little more and saw that he was at Thirty-Fourth Street and York Avenue. There, on York, was a drugstore, only a block away.

It was just before 8:00 p.m. on March 1, 1933, coincidentally the first anniversary of the Lindbergh kidnapping. From the drugstore, Charlie phoned his father. Then he phoned a friend who lived not far away. Oddly, he did not call his wife.

The friend sent a car, and Charlie was driven to the friend's home. Exhausted, Charlie collapsed onto a bed. He lay there for a couple of hours, crossing between sleep and half-awake.

Finally, the friend roused Charlie and told him his father was eager to see him. The friend drove Charlie to Claude Boettcher's home, stopping in an alley so Charlie could hop a fence and enter his father's house out of sight of reporters and photographers.

After what must have been an emotional reunion, Claude talked briefly to the *New York Times* by telephone. He confirmed that his son was safely home but refused to divulge more details. Then Claude opened the front door of his house and waved a pistol at the throng of press people. "Stand back!" he said. "I'm sick and tired of being pestered."

Seemingly forgotten was Charlie's pregnant wife, Anna Lou. More than three hours elapsed between Charlie's release and his reunion with his wife and young daughter. It's unclear whether this lapse arose from the domineering, super-male personalities of Charlie's father and grandfather or pure neglect on Charlie's part, perhaps linked to pure exhaustion. Regardless, it would become clear one day that the long ordeal and her husband's actions immediately after his release had done terrible harm to their marriage…and to her.

———————

While there had been tension between the Boettcher family and the Denver police, there had also been a secret agreement: as soon as Charlie was back home safe, a posse of police officers would swarm the ransom-delivery location and nab the kidnappers.

Which was what almost happened. By prearrangement, the Boettcher family chauffeur, a family friend, and two private detectives had driven to a point north of Denver where one of the men tossed a package containing the ransom into a dry creek bed. It was dark as Sankey and Alcorn approached the pickup point. Sankey saw the delivery car and was alarmed when its headlights blinked. A signal to the police, Sankey thought. He was right. Just after Sankey scrambled down to the creek bed, picked up the ransom, and returned to his car, he saw the headlights of other cars coming at him, and fast. Cop cars, he thought. Right again!

Bullets smashed through the windows of Sankey's car, covering Sankey and Alcorn with pieces of glass. Sankey sped off, the souped-up V-8 engine in his car easily overmatching the horsepower of the police vehicles. And though Sankey didn't know it, because of a communication lapse within the Denver police department, not all roads into and out of the city had been blocked off.

Sankey and Alcorn drove on lightly trafficked country roads with their lights off, ending up in Greeley, Colorado, in the middle of the night. The distance between Denver and Greeley is a mere sixty miles, an easy hour's drive on Interstate 25 today. The circuitous route followed by Sankey and Alcorn required eight hours.

They had hoped to rest in Greeley, a quiet city of about thirteen thousand at the time (compared to just over one hundred thousand nowadays). But a car with shattered windows and no headlights was an attention-getter even for small-town cops. Sankey's car was spotted by officers in a squad car, and when Sankey made several turns with the cop car always in his rearview mirror, he knew he was being followed.

Finally, Sankey and Alcorn found themselves cornered on a road next to a warehouse. At the most inopportune moment, Sankey's car stalled. Alcorn got out and ran. Not Sankey. Using his car as a shield, he exchanged gunfire with the police. Then he realized to his horror that his car was rolling away from him; he had parked on a slope. He sprinted after the vehicle, scrambled in, and with deft moves of clutch and gas pedal, managed to restart the engine.

And away went Sankey, his car skidding and swerving, taking curves that made it teeter on two wheels until he was free of Greeley, out in the open country with darkness for company. He made it back to his ranch in South Dakota on March 2, to be reunited with Arthur Youngberg, his friend from the railroad days and a sometime accomplice in crime.

But where was Alcorn? As would be learned later, he walked a lot, across fields and dirt roads, after the gunfight in Greeley. Then he hopped a freight train to Cheyenne, Wyoming, then a bus to Nebraska after a rest in a cheap hotel, then on the road again. He arrived at the ranch two days after Sankey did.

There at the remote ranch, the three men thought they were safe. And they might have been, except for a veteran of the Great War named Carl Pearce.

———

Carl Pearce was a sad figure who had gotten to know Verne Sankey in Denver, where Pearce sold insurance for a time. He was good at it, at least to start with, earning several thousand dollars a year. But while he was fine with numbers, his sales pitch was increasingly hampered by his drooping eyelids and the often uncontrollable shaking of his head and hands.

Pearce had suffered shell shock during combat in France. Psychiatric treatment and hospital stays were to little avail, and his condition worsened over time. More and more, his voice cracked when he was with people, which made him more nervous, which caused his voice to crack more frequently. And so on.

He couldn't hold a job. His wife left him. He began to drink a little. Then he began to drink a lot. Not surprisingly, he became acquainted with bootleggers. He descended the social ladder by a rung or two. Ever short of money, he passed some bad checks. He was caught and went to jail for ninety days, emerging in the autumn of 1932, around the time Verne Sankey was evaluating candidates for a kidnapping.

Then Pearce's life changed for the better. He met Ruth Kohler, a widow and the sister of Sankey's wife, Fern. Pearce and Ruth fell in love. And when Pearce learned that Sankey was planning a kidnapping, he was happy to enlist in the plot for even a minor role.

———

As Sankey, Alcorn, and Youngberg were settling in at Sankey's South Dakota ranch, discussing how to divvy up the ransom money, Pearce was celebrating in Denver. His tongue loosened by strong drink, he told some acquaintances that he had played a part in the kidnapping of Charlie Boettcher and would soon be $2,000 richer for having typed the ransom messages to the Boettcher family.

Unfortunately, Pearce had talked in front of the wrong people. A woman who heard of his boasts was the wife of one of Pearce's bootlegger friends. She also happened to be a friend of a Denver cop. Soon, there was gossip aplenty, and Denver police and federal prosecutors in the Mile High City had gleaned enough information to haul people in for questioning.

On Sunday, March 5, Pearce, Fern Sankey, and her sister, Ruth Kohler, were interrogated. So was Ruth's teenage daughter. A search of the Sankey home in Denver turned up some $1,400 in cash and handwritten drafts of the ransom messages. What's more, the handwriting appeared to some investigators, at least at first glance, rather like the writing in the Lindbergh kidnapping notes.

Fern kept her mouth shut. Ruth denied taking part in the kidnapping but admitted that she had heard Verne Sankey and Pearce discussing the crime days before it was committed. The teenage girl was quickly cleared of any involvement.

Pearce folded when he heard that Ruth had implicated him. He gave his questioners the names of Gordon Alcorn and Arthur Youngberg and rough directions to Sankey's ranch. With remarkable speed, considering the relatively poor communications of that time, lawmen from Denver, Wyoming, and South Dakota were conscripted for a raid.

Meanwhile, Sankey, who was not yet aware that lawmen had brought in his wife and the others, hid his bullet-punctured car in a ravine near his ranch house. Looking at the machine, perhaps he reflected on the fact that he had crossed a Rubicon of sorts. Having seized a member of a family with friends in the highest of places, he was no longer a minor-league kidnapper. Plus, he had traded gunfire with cops. If he were cornered again, the cops might exercise their own swift justice.

———————

A small army of cops and sheriff's deputies was inching toward Sankey's ranch. "Inching" was the right word: a fierce blizzard had swept into the Dakota plains, forcing Sankey's hunters to abandon cars and make their way to the ranch on snowshoes as they navigated drifts up to four feet high.

On the night of March 6, the exhausted lawmen approached the area of Sankey's spread. To their pleasant surprise, they found Youngberg at the farm of one of Sankey's neighbors, where he was helping to butcher a steer. He surrendered meekly.

But there was no one at Sankey's ranch. Sankey and Alcorn had not felt as safe there as Youngberg had, so after burying some of the ransom money on the spread, they had persuaded Sankey's brother to drive them to the Twin Cities area. Sankey and Alcorn had outrun the blizzard and the law.

The FBI men whom Hoover had sent to Denver were not invited to join the party that stormed Sankey's ranch and arrested Youngberg. Nor were they involved in Denver arrests in connection with the case. But having boasted falsely, shamelessly, of the "vital role" the FBI had played, Hoover decided to exaggerate even more.

"The bureau's reputation of 'always getting its man,' regardless of obstacles, began to be demonstrated Wednesday in the countrywide manhunt now underway for the two other suspects, Verne Sankey and Gordon Elkhorn," a bureau press release boasted.[55] The comical misspelling of Alcorn's name was repeated in some news accounts. But the mistake was minor compared to the absurd assertion that the FBI had a reputation of "always getting its man."

Hoover had shown that he was willing, sometimes eager, to claim credit that rightly belonged to local law enforcement. And shrewd cynic that he was, he understood that many journalists of the day were far too willing to believe people in power.

———

Arthur Youngberg slashed his throat and wrists in jail in what may have been only a half-hearted suicide attempt. In any event, he survived. Soon, he was taken by train to Denver, where Charlie Boettcher identified him as one of his jailers. His ordeal still fresh in his mind, Charlie lunged at Youngberg and had to be pulled off him.

On March 9, police announced the discovery of Sankey's car in the creek bed near the ranch. Brought to the ranch, Charlie identified the basement as his place of detention.

By this time, Youngberg was telling all he knew about the Boettcher kidnapping. Sankey and Alcorn had made their way to Chicago, where they hid out separately. For some two weeks, lawmen stationed themselves at the Sankey ranch, hoping Sankey and Alcorn might return. They waited in vain.

One is tempted to feel some compassion for Verne Sankey, husband and father. His wife was in jail, and there was scant hope they could ever be together again, scant hope that there would ever again be a Sankey *family*. Perhaps, in his heart of hearts, he wished he had kept working on the railroads. Maybe he wondered what might have happened if he had become a truly legitimate businessman when his bootlegging and rum-running days were over.

And gambler that he was, he must have realized he had overplayed his hand by kidnapping Charlie Boettcher. Yet no one ever accused Sankey of lacking nerve. Would he dare to try his luck again?

CHAPTER TWENTY

A BREWER IS TAKEN

St. Paul, Minnesota
Thursday, June 15, 1933

William Hamm Jr. was one of the wealthiest men in St. Paul. He was president of the Hamm Brewing Company, founded by his grandfather Theodore Hamm, a German immigrant, in 1865. When Theodore Hamm died in 1903, his son William assumed control. And when William died in 1931, *his* son, William Jr., took charge.

Not unlike the Anheuser and Busch families in St. Louis, the Hamm family was part of city society's top tier, its members closely identified with St. Paul's growth and civic life.

And like the Anheuser-Busch company in St. Louis, the Hamm company had survived Prohibition by selling soft drinks and food products. With the end of the "noble experiment," the Hamm brewery was poised to prosper mightily, as it had invested in new equipment and repairs to help Americans quench their collective thirst.

Every weekday afternoon at 12:45, William Hamm Jr. walked the short distance from the brewery to his twenty-room redbrick mansion to have lunch. At thirty-nine and still a bachelor, Hamm might not have needed such a big house, but he was used to living large.

This Thursday, June 15, found the Upper Midwest in the grip of a heat wave. The temperature was in the high nineties, freakishly hot for Minnesota. Hamm was on his way home for lunch when a black sedan carrying three men pulled up beside him.

"You're Mr. Hamm, aren't you?" one of the men said as he engaged the brewer in a vigorous handshake.

Before Hamm could answer or even ponder why the car had stopped next to him, the men had alighted, seized and blindfolded him with a white hood, and shoved him into the car, forcing him to lie on the rear floor.

The brewery manager, William Dunn, was puzzled when Hamm didn't return from lunch. Then he got a phone call. "We have kidnapped Mr. Hamm," a voice said. "You will hear from us later."

===

Hamm had caught only a glimpse of the kidnappers, but he thought he recognized Verne Sankey from wanted posters.

He felt something sticking in his ribs; he assumed it was a gun. Hamm guessed they had gone about thirty miles when the car stopped. He heard the engine of another car, heard men in that car talking to the men who had seized him.

His blindfold was pulled off. Several pieces of paper were waved in front of his face, then placed on the car floor. A pen was placed in his hand.

"Sign them," a voice commanded. Hamm scrawled his signature. He expected the hood to be put over his head again. Instead, cotton-lined goggles were placed over his eyes. When the car stopped at long last, his goggles were removed. Because the summer solstice was approaching, there was still enough daylight for him to see a two-story house. The windows were boarded. *A farmhouse*, he thought. But where?

———

The next day, Friday, a taxi driver delivered a note to Dunn demanding $100,000 for Hamm's safe return. If the money was not forthcoming, the note said, Hamm would be killed. At the bottom of the note was Hamm's signature.

The taxi driver told police a man who had said his name was Gordon had given him $2 to deliver the message. Shown photographs of people known or suspected to be in the business of kidnapping, the cabbie picked out a photograph of Sankey.

There was speculation that Sankey had put together a new kidnapping organization to replace his friends from the railroading days, who had practically invited arrest with their carelessness. Carl Pearce had shot off his drunken mouth in front of the wrong people. And Ray Robinson, who had helped Sankey abduct Haskell Bohn, had stupidly deposited $10,000 in an account under his own name in a Winnipeg bank scarcely a week after Bohn was abducted.

Of course, that was an enormous deposit for a former railroad worker, and it aroused immediate suspicion. The police in Canada as well as the United States were aware of Robinson's ties to Sankey. On March 31, 1933, the Royal Canadian Mounted Police caught up with Robinson in a tiny village two hundred miles north of Winnipeg. Robinson readily admitted his own guilt in the Haskell Bohn affair. He also implicated Sankey's wife, recalling that she had cooked meals for Bohn during his captivity.

The capture of Robinson and his willingness to talk helped cause an odd coincidence that was part of a human drama. In June 1933, Fern Sankey was transported to St. Paul to stand trial in the Bohn kidnapping. The prosecution's case was fairly straightforward. It boiled down to a question: How could Fern Sankey *not* have been a willing participant in the crime when, in fact, Haskell Bohn was held in the basement of the Sankeys' home where Fern cooked for him?

But Robinson testified for the defense that Fern had not taken part in the kidnapping itself. What was more, he said, Fern had urged her husband to release Bohn early in his captivity.

A jury is not supposed to think badly of a defendant in a criminal trial if he or she does not testify. That, at least, is the theory and the law. In reality, many jurors want to hear the defendant say "I'm not guilty!" before giving him or her the benefit of the doubt.

Fern elected to tell her story: "I begged and pleaded with my husband to release the boy. I told him I had two brothers and how I would feel if one of them were in such a position. But he told me to mind my own business."[56] She said she was never present during negotiations.

The jurors surely knew that Fern had been separated from her two young children as well as her husband. She cried during part of her testimony. All in all, she was a sympathetic figure.

The jury got the case late on the afternoon of June 15, the very time when William Hamm Jr. was lying blindfolded on the floor of his kidnapper's car just after being snatched.

After deliberating for several hours, the jurors acquitted Fern Sankey of conspiring to kidnap Haskell Bohn. She slumped in her chair and said, "I am so glad."

But acquittal did not mean freedom. Fern was quickly rearrested to face federal charges in the Boettcher case.

Given the fact that a taxi driver had picked out a photo of Verne Sankey as the man who had paid him $2 to deliver a ransom message to William Dunn and considering that Fern Sankey had been on trial, it made perfect sense to conclude that Sankey was lurking in the Twin Cities area. Would he try to free his wife? After all, he had already shown he was willing to shoot it out with the police.

———————

"Turn your face to the wall."

Hamm soon got used to that command, issued each time one of the kidnappers entered the small, dimly lit room where he was being held. He never saw his captors' faces and could not tell from the voices how old they were. Hamm thought he detected five or six voices.

Except for the fact that he was being held very much against his will, he was not mistreated. At appropriate intervals, he was fed what he later recalled as decent, if rather plain, food. Nothing like the fare he was used to.

Now and then, Hamm was given progress reports. Things were moving along, he was told. In fact, the kidnappers were staying in touch by sending the notes pre-signed by Hamm to people who would deliver them to the family.

On the night of Saturday, June 17, a company beer truck left the Hamm Brewing headquarters, followed closely by a car carrying Dunn, a company lawyer, and several other men. Following them was still another car, driven by Chief Inspector Charles J. Tierney of the St. Paul police. Inside the beer truck was the ransom money, some from the Hamm family and some of it contributed by St. Paul businessmen.

The exact amount of the entire package was not revealed, but it was soon disclosed that the kidnappers had settled for less than their original demand of $100,000. That was another fact that pointed to Sankey. In both the Bohn and Boettcher cases, he had been willing to bargain down, to quit while he was ahead. It was the pragmatic, professional way to kidnap.

"Good news," one of his jailers told Hamm on the afternoon of Sunday, June 18. "The ransom's been paid, and you're going home."

The kidnappers waited until dark. Then they put the goggles over Hamm's eyes and put him in a car with three other men, including the driver. Then they were off on another long ride, one that Hamm was happy to be taking. The ride lasted most of the night.

_____

Shortly after 5:30 that morning, the car carrying Hamm came to a stop, and he was let out.

"If there is anything we can do to help you, Mr. Hamm, just let us know," a kidnapper said. [57]

The car sped off before he could reply—not that he would have asked for anything. He saw lights in a farmhouse. He was glad that farmers rose early and glad that the farmhouse, he soon discovered, had a phone.

The kidnappers had deposited Hamm near Wyoming, Minnesota. A St. Paul police officer came to fetch him. Hamm was back home around 8:30. His widowed mother collapsed in joy and relief.

For the time being, a key question remained: Where had Hamm been held? It would be a while before the question was answered.

_____

Back in his real world, Hamm recalled the moment when he was seized while on his way home for lunch. "I had only a fleeting impression of the two men's appearances, although one of them resembled Verne Sankey."

The *Minneapolis Tribune* jumped on Hamm's "partial identification" of Sankey, noting that federal officials had been pursuing a tip that Sankey and Alcorn had been hiding out not far from where the ransom was delivered and Hamm was released.

The *New York Times* had implicated Sankey from the start with its headline "Kidnappers Seize St. Paul Brewer...Hold William Hamm, 39, for $100,000 Ransom—Death Threat Made in Note...Sankey Linked to Gang—Fugitive in Bohn and Boettcher Abductions Is Identified as Sender of Missive."[58]

So Sankey had rolled the dice one more time! Or so it seemed.

But wait. Hamm said one of his kidnappers *resembled* Sankey. Was it possible that the headline in the *New York Times* and the report in the *Tribune* had gone too far in implicating Sankey? Could it be that Sankey had had nothing to do with kidnapping Hamm? And if he hadn't done it, who had?

Sifting through the events all these years later, one is tempted to ask why it took so long for lawmen to find the answers, since some avenues of investigation could hardly have been more obvious. Or perhaps law investigators *did* have suspects in mind but were loath to share their knowledge. For those looking for suspects and clues, they were there for the taking.

Elsewhere in the country, the summer of 1933 would be a busy one for criminals and those who followed their exploits, perhaps deriving vicarious pleasure in so doing. But let us first acquaint ourselves with St. Paul, Minnesota, and with some of the people who made that city so special.

CHAPTER TWENTY-ONE

DOTING MOTHER, DEVOTED SONS

The term *parenting skills* hadn't come into use in their lifetimes, but it is fair to say that Arizona Donnie Clark Barker and her farm laborer husband, George Barker, lacked them. It is fitting that she is far better known than he is, for she was the dominant personality in the household. She nurtured her four boys, all of whom would grow up to be criminals, and she tried to instill in each a sense of self-esteem. No wonder she was known as "Ma" Barker.

She was born in 1872 in southwestern Missouri, a rugged region where Civil War hatreds still smoldered, highwaymen roamed, and honest lawmen were scarce. The Barker boys, Herman, Lloyd, Arthur (later to be known as "Doc"), and Freddie, spent their boyhoods in tar paper–shack poverty. They were wild boys, for their passive father was too weak to be a disciplinarian, and their mother never tired of defending them, no matter how outrageous their behavior.

Around Webb City, Missouri, a mining town where the family settled, the conduct of the lads evolved from bratty to maliciously mischievous and on to criminal—petty at first, then less so. By the time the family moved to Tulsa, Oklahoma, the Barker boys (Freddie was the youngest and his mother's favorite) routinely engaged in robbery and thievery. But it was not what her boys did that bothered Ma Barker. It was how the law reacted to what they did. She was ever eager to defend her boys when the Webb City cops came after them for one crime or another, but she finally tired of the persecution. So the clan left for Oklahoma.

Ma Barker's blind devotion did not lessen as her sons morphed into hardened criminals who took up with men of the same ilk. The Barker boys surely sensed that they had no prospects for honest prosperity and social standing, and they didn't want their horizons in life defined by the ridges of the Ozarks. Soon, the Barker men were at ease with various Midwestern artists and thugs, including one Frank Nash, who in 1933 would unwillingly play a central role in one of the bloodiest incidents of the thirties. The Barker home in Tulsa became an occasional shelter for criminals on the run.

Ma Barker was never shackled to the social norms of the times. She tired of her milquetoast husband and left him for Arthur Dunlop, a shiftless drinker. Nor would Ma be limited by conventional notions of "a woman's place." She listened in on the household chatter about bank robberies, then began to take part in planning them, although she could hardly have been described as the "brains" of the outfit. Jigsaw puzzles took up much of her time.

Of course, Ma Barker envisioned starring criminal roles for her precious sons. The "bloody Barkers," as the sons came to be known, towered in infamy but they were slight of build. The tallest, Herman, stood only five feet five. He was the first son to die, shooting himself with his own pistol in 1927 when he was cornered and wounded by lawmen in Newton, Kansas, after robbing a store and killing a police officer. Herman was just thirty-four.

Meanwhile, Fred Barker was doing a stretch of five to ten years in the Kansas State Penitentiary for robbing a bank in Winfield, Kansas, in 1926. That crime, committed when Fred was twenty-four, could be called his first adult offense. He'd been arrested in his youth for vagrancy and relatively minor robberies—then released to the custody of his mother.

In prison, Fred became friends with Alvin Karpis, a son of Lithuanian immigrants, who was serving time for burglary and theft.

Fred and Karpis were released in 1931 and embarked upon a series of store burglaries. Surely, Arthur "Doc" Barker was eager to join them. But he was serving a life term in the Oklahoma state prison for killing a night watchman at a Tulsa hospital in 1918 while trying to steal a shipment of drugs.

Somehow, Doc won parole in September 1932 after serving thirteen years. The reunited Barker brothers, Fred and Doc, and Karpis made a natural team once Karpis was released. Soon, they were robbing banks, stores, and trains across the Midwest. (Sadly, Lloyd Barker could not be with them. He had been caught after robbing a post office in rural Oklahoma in 1922 and sent to federal prison for twenty-five years.[*])

Arthur Dunlop had a reputation for being a big-mouth drunk, which was why members of the gang did not trust him and probably explains why he was found shot to death near the town of Webster, Wisconsin, in 1932, just after gang members fled from their hideout in St. Paul, Minnesota, upon hearing that the police were on their trail. Rightly or wrongly, the gang members believed that Dunlop's loose tongue had revealed their location. Fortunately for them, they had only to pick up a phone and call St. Paul's police chief, Thomas "Big Tom" Brown, if they wanted to know what the cops were doing. And sometimes Brown would call them, as he probably did just before the gang left St. Paul in haste.

---

[*] The least gregarious of the brothers, Lloyd Barker was released in 1947 and married. He spent two years in the straight life as an assistant manager of a bar and grill in Denver before being shot dead by his wife in 1949.

Fred, considered the organizer of the outfit, and Karpis were careful planners. They also juggled the members of their gang, recruiting people with certain skills for particular heists, much as a pro football team acquires and sheds backup quarterbacks and placekickers as the needs arise. This technique brought in fresh blood and made it hard for pursuers to keep track of the gang.

Undeniably, reading about the exploits of Ma Barker and her sons and Alvin Karpis can be entertaining, especially since the people who suffered because of them are long gone. But a quick and perhaps incomplete summary of what the gang members did will dispel any temptation to glorify them. In addition to the night watchman killed by Doc and the Newton, Kansas, police officer slain by Herman, the gang's victims included a local sheriff slain during the robbery of a store in Mountain View, Missouri, in 1931; the police chief of Pocahontas, Arkansas, kidnapped in 1931 and driven to a field, where he was shot five times in the back; two Minneapolis policemen who were shot dead after a bank robbery in 1932; and a Minneapolis policeman who was slain during a post office robbery in 1933.

Perhaps the Barkers, Karpis, and other gang members grew weary of killing. Maybe they feared that their own blood would be spilled if they persisted in their violent ways. In any event, we can be sure that the kidnappings of Haskell Bohn of St. Paul, Minnesota, in 1932 and Charlie Boettcher of Denver in 1933 caught their attention, perhaps even inspired them. Verne Sankey had pulled off those operations with apparent ease. He had set a good example in a sense—one that members of the Barker-Karpis outfit were determined to follow.

But who would be their first kidnapping target? The Barker-Karpis members were open to suggestions. And there was no better place to find prospects than St. Paul.

St. Paul had a population of just over 270,000 as the thirties began, yet it was in a league with Chicago, Kansas City, and other bigger cities as a haven for bootleggers, bank robbers, and other kinds of gangsters, including kidnappers.

St. Paul's reputation as a sanctuary for criminals began at the turn of the century with what became known as the "layover agreement," an understanding between criminals and the police chief, John O'Connor. Simply put, when out-of-town gangsters visited St. Paul, they notified the St. Paul police. If the gangsters behaved themselves while in the city, they were unmolested and even tipped off about forthcoming FBI raids.

O'Connor's successors continued this arrangement, the intent of which was not just to keep crime down in St. Paul. In return for tolerating the criminals in their midst and warning them of impending federal raids, the police brass accepted payoffs, with some of the money trickling down to lowly patrolmen. And of course, some cash flowed into city hall.

Not surprisingly, alcohol was sold and consumed openly during Prohibition. There was a speakeasy in St. Paul called the Green Lantern where criminals gathered to see and be seen.* Bank robbers and other crooks from across the Midwest gathered there when they were in town. The notorious gangsters Harvey Bailey and Frank Nash were regulars. So was Verne Miller, a one-time South Dakota sheriff who found breaking the law more rewarding than enforcing it.

One reason gangsters felt at ease in the Green Lantern was the establishment's owner, Harry Sawyer (originally Sandlovich). Sawyer had inherited the Green Lantern, so to speak, after the car-bomb assassination of its proprietor, "Dapper Dan" Hogan, on December 4, 1928.

---

*   The Green Lantern still exists in St. Paul and boasts of its colorful past, as do many long-time restaurants and watering holes in cities where organized crime flourished.

Hogan, a money launderer, dealer in stolen goods, and all-around fixer who distributed turkeys to the needy at Christmas time, was perched comfortably on the bridge between St. Paul's criminal underworld and the city's compliant police force. He was known to encourage out-of-town mobsters to stay out of St. Paul unless they agreed to make their visits violence-free.

With Hogan's death, the Green Lantern was taken over by Sawyer, Hogan's top aide. The sixth of nine children, Sawyer was born in 1890 to an Orthodox Jewish butcher and his wife. Before landing in St. Paul and becoming Hogan's protégé, Sawyer lived in Nebraska, where he acquired the nickname "Omaha Harry" and compiled a record that included larceny, robbery, and auto theft. But he was never known to possess bomb-making skills, so people who believe that Sawyer was behind Hogan's assassination, which remains unsolved officially, are fairly certain that he hired outside talent to install the explosives beneath Hogan's car seat.

At the Green Lantern, Sawyer was a networker extraordinaire. If a visiting mobster confided that his gang needed a specialist—a burglar, say, or safecracker or getaway driver—Sawyer could find a candidate in no time. It might take a bit longer to find a reliable hit man, but he could do that too.

One can imagine a law-abiding citizen with a Walter Mitty complex, dropping in to the Green Lantern to quench his thirst after a routine day at his humdrum job, hoping to catch a glimpse of John Dillinger or Al Capone or the city's own Leon Gleckman, a bootlegger so successful he was known as the "Al Capone of St. Paul."

After a drink or two, a law-abiding citizen could go home and brag to his wife about standing at the bar near a lowlife mobster who might even be a cold-blooded killer but looked good in a double-breasted suit.

Gleckman had been kidnapped in September 1931 and held for

a week in a cabin in northern Wisconsin. The price for his freedom was originally $75,000, but the kidnappers settled for just over $5,000. The main negotiator with the kidnappers was Jack Peifer, owner of the Hollyhocks, another St. Paul nightclub where crooks were more than welcome.*

We don't know for sure if the FBI agents stationed in St. Paul ever dropped by the Green Lantern or the Hollyhocks, but they probably didn't. They wouldn't have gleaned much of value anyhow. The shady imbibers along the bar would have picked them out too easily.

For whatever reasons, intelligence gathering was not the FBI's strongest suit at the time. Had Hoover and his men been better at it, they might have realized that clues to the kidnapping of William Hamm were available amid the bar chatter and the clinking of cocktail glasses at the Green Lantern and Hollyhocks.

Hamm's sales manager, William Dunn, was reputed to be a middleman who delivered bribes to the police. Harry Sawyer knew Dunn, and Sawyer knew that Hamm (himself no stranger to mob people) followed the same routine every weekday, walking home from the brewery to have lunch at 12:45.

Regulars at the Green Lantern and Hollyhocks included members of the Barker-Karpis gang, along with other Midwestern lowlifes.

In the spring of 1933, Sawyer is believed to have approached Karpis and suggested that Hamm was an ideal kidnapping target.

The FBI ought to have learned all this earlier, but again, intelligence gathering wasn't their strong point. And in fairness, a lot more was going on in 1933.

---

* Five men were eventually arrested and imprisoned for the Gleckman kidnapping.

CHAPTER TWENTY-TWO

A SHERIFF TAKEN PRISONER

Bolivar, Missouri
Friday, June 16, 1933

Sheriff Jack Killingsworth and his wife, Bernice, were early risers. It was hard for them not to be, since their living quarters were in the same building as the Polk County jail. Nor did they mind getting up at sunrise; Jack liked to make his rounds in the cool part of the day.

The weather was promising on Friday, June 16. The temperature was in the mid-sixties at dawn, so it probably wouldn't go much above eighty during the afternoon. As they finished breakfast, Jack had a thought: maybe the couple's two-year-old son would like to come along.

"No," Bernice said. "Don't wake him. Let's just let him sleep."[59]

So the sheriff, who was thirty-six, set off alone on his daily tour. It was more about socializing than looking for trouble, since few bad things happened in Bolivar, about 120 miles southeast of Kansas City and at the time a community of just over two thousand. Jack Killingsworth knew a lot of people in town. Before being elected sheriff the previous year, he had been a salesman at Bitzer Chevrolet on the corner of Broadway and Missouri Avenue.

Of course, Jack Killingsworth liked cars, and he liked the people at Bitzer Chevy, so he usually started his patrol, if it could be called that, by hanging out there.

Just after 7:00 a.m., Killingsworth parked his car next to the Chevy dealership and walked into the garage section. Right away, he saw proprietor Ernest Bitzer sitting on a bench, talking to another man and looking very nervous. Several mechanics in coveralls were standing against a wall, also looking ill at ease.

Before Killingsworth could say hello, a man shouted, "There's the law!"

The sheriff recognized the man. He was Adam Richetti, a Bolivar native in his midtwenties who had moved away to embark on a career as a gunman and bank robber.

When the sheriff saw the face of the man sitting next to Ernest Bitzer, he was stunned. It was Charles "Pretty Boy" Floyd, whose image had been on wanted posters all over the Midwest. The cherubic, apple-cheeked features were misleading, for the twenty-nine-year-old Floyd was one of the most notorious killers and bandits in the country. Born in Georgia, raised in poverty on a farm in Oklahoma, he had turned early to crime. By the early 1930s, he was a celebrated bank robber, even seen as a hero by some Americans. There were stories, likely apocryphal, that he sometimes burned the mortgage documents in banks that he robbed, thus offering relief to debt-strained homeowners.

It took only a couple of seconds for the sheriff to note that Floyd and his friend Richetti were armed with a Thompson submachine gun and a pair of pistols. The sheriff was not armed, which may have been just as well. Had he been carrying a weapon and reached for it, he probably would have been killed.

There are conflicting accounts of what happened next, but it went something like this:

"Give me that machine gun," Richetti said to Floyd. "I'll kill him right now." He meant the sheriff. Then he added, "I'll kill everybody." It was clear that Richetti, a habitual drunk, had been imbibing heavily at an hour when normal people were having breakfast.

Floyd was a calming influence, an unusual role for him. So was Richetti's brother Joe, who was a mechanic in the garage.

Floyd and Adam Richetti had stolen a car in Oklahoma and driven into Missouri. They had robbed a bank in the town of Mexico, netting about $1,600, then headed toward Bolivar, about 170 miles to the southwest. On the way, the car broke down. Soon, a friendly farmer happened by in a truck and said he'd give the pair a ride and tow the car into Bolivar for repairs.

Had the farmer looked more closely at the stranded motorists, he might have recognized Floyd. But the farmer took no notice, which was probably lucky for him.

Once in Bolivar, Floyd and Richetti planned to get the stolen car fixed and get out of town. But the appearance of the sheriff forced a change in plans, so they gassed up Joe Richetti's new 1933 Chevy, transferred their arsenal to it, and ordered the sheriff to get in the back seat.

Then they sped out of Bolivar, with Floyd and Richetti taking turns behind the wheel. The bandits told the sheriff he'd be safe if he helped them elude pursuers. So Killingsworth steered the pair onto back roads throughout the region.

Richetti was drinking from a bottle for part of the trip, now and then talking in a slur about killing the sheriff. Floyd kept telling him to calm down and shut up.

Suddenly, the sound of a siren behind them. Get rid of them, Killingsworth was told. He waved his panama hat out the window, signaling the chasers to cease and desist. They did, to the relief of the sheriff. He was sure local cops would be no match for Floyd and Richetti, who had better weapons (and colder blood) than the pursuers.

Killingsworth tried small talk, volunteering the information that he had a wife and a little boy. Floyd said he too had a son, Jack Dempsey Floyd, who was eleven. Though the notorious bandit spoke fondly about his boy, he didn't seem like much of a family man. Floyd and Richetti talked about a couple of women they hoped to hook up with in Kansas City. Point us there, the sheriff was ordered.

Killingsworth obeyed, directing his captors north and west.

After a while, the duo decided to change cars to further frustrate anyone chasing them. The sheriff was ordered to get out and flag down a motorist.

Soon, a car approached. Seeing the sheriff's star, the driver stopped. Too late, he realized the situation. Move over, he was ordered. He complied.

Leaving Joe Richetti's car by the roadside, the bandits transferred their arsenal to the car they'd just seized and away they went, with two hostages now. At long last, Killingsworth and the other hostage were set free, unharmed, about twenty miles southeast of Kansas City, Missouri.

An embarrassing footnote had been added to Killingsworth's career. As for the motorist whose car had been commandeered, he had an adventure story to tell for the rest of his life. Not many honest men got to keep company with Pretty Boy Floyd and live.[*]

But the lingering question for lawmen as the sun set over Missouri that Friday, June 16, 1933, was: What kind of mischief might Pretty Boy Floyd be planning in these parts?

---

[*]   For information on the kidnapping of Jack Killingsworth, I am indebted to Larry Wood, author of *Murder and Mayhem in Missouri* (Charleston, SC: The History Press, 2013).

CHAPTER TWENTY-THREE

FROM HOT SPRINGS TO SLAUGHTER

Hot Springs, Arkansas
Friday, June 16, 1933

On the very day of Sheriff Killingsworth's misadventure, local cops and two FBI agents caught up with the fugitive named Frank Nash in Hot Springs, Arkansas, a playground for gangsters some four hundred miles southeast of Kansas City. Nash, who had escaped from Leavenworth federal prison in northeastern Kansas in 1930, was nabbed in a cigar store and pool hall run by Dick Galatas, gambling czar of Hot Springs.

In 1913, Nash was sentenced to life in prison in the state penitentiary in McAlester, Oklahoma, for murdering his accomplice in a robbery, presumably because he didn't want to share the loot. When America entered the Great War, Nash was granted early release so he could enlist in the army.

Nash fought in France, came home, and resumed his criminal career. In 1920, he was sentenced to twenty-five years for burglary with explosives—in other words, safecracking. Somehow, he became a trustee, which meant he could leave the walls now and then on errands, and was turned loose late in 1922. He joined a gang that robbed banks and trains. Captured in 1924 after taking part in a postal-train robbery in which a mail custodian was badly beaten, he was sentenced to twenty-five years in Leavenworth. Astoundingly, he charmed prison officials into making him a trustee again.

On October 19, 1930, he went on an errand and never returned. While at large, Nash managed to marry three times, with each of his wives apparently unaware of the other two. He robbed banks throughout the Midwest with a gang that included a Tennessee-born ex-bootlegger and robber formally named George Kelly Barnes. For some reason, Barnes dropped his surname and began to go by his mother's maiden name, Kelly. (Eventually, he became known as "Machine Gun" Kelly for his supposed acumen with that deadly weapon.)

At 8:30 on Friday evening, June 16, just hours after his capture, Nash was escorted onto a Missouri Pacific train in Fort Smith, Arkansas, by two FBI agents, Joe Lackey and Frank Smith, and Otto Reed, the forty-nine-year-old police chief of McAlester, Oklahoma, who was familiar with Nash from his earlier crimes and detested him.

The train arrived at Union Station in Kansas City, Missouri, at 7:15 Saturday morning, just a quarter of an hour behind schedule. Waiting were two young FBI agents, Reed Vetterli, in charge of the bureau's Kansas City office, and Ray Caffrey, plus two seasoned Kansas City detectives, Bill Grooms and Frank Hermanson.

The lawmen made an impressive-looking wedge formation as they led the handcuffed Nash through the station, which was teeming with travelers arriving and departing. FBI agents were not yet authorized to carry firearms, but this morning, Lackey was toting a short-barreled shotgun and a pistol. Smith carried two pistols and Caffrey one. Reed carried a short-barreled shotgun and a pistol. Both Kansas City detectives carried pistols, as usual. Vetterli was the only lawman who was unarmed.

The seven lawmen and their prisoner emerged from the station into the sunshine of the parking lot and walked to the two cars that were to transport Nash and his keepers to Leavenworth. Nash was put into the front seat of one car, positioned behind the steering wheel for a moment, so that the right passenger seat backrest could be folded forward to let Smith, Lackey, and Reed climb into the rear seat. The plan was to slide Nash over to the front passenger seat so the three lawmen in the rear could keep watch on him while Caffrey drove.

Meanwhile, several men were leaning casually against another vehicle parked nearby. Suddenly, the men were walking with deadly purpose toward the lawmen. Just as Caffrey was about to get into the car, the air exploded in "a rat-tat-tat of machine-gun fire," as the *New York Times* described it.[60]

"The sounds lasted only a few seconds," the *Times* account continued. "Mown down like grain in a field, the handcuffed prisoner and guards were all prostrate. The gunners leaped into their car and sped away, while the bystanders stood rooted to their places, horror-stricken."

Detectives Grooms and Hermanson lay dead on the pavement. Frank Nash was dead in the car, as was Otto Reed. Agent Ray Caffrey was mortally wounded and would die hours later. Lackey and Vetterli were wounded. Only Smith was unscathed.

The sickly sweet aromas of blood and gun smoke blended in the air. A crowd of sightseers, reporters, and news photographers swarmed over the scene, their feet slip-sliding through the gore. For dramatic effect in one photo, a lawman's bloody straw hat, with a hole blown through the front, was placed on the right front fender of the car that held the corpse of Frank Nash. Some people grabbed souvenirs. By the time police arrived, the crime scene had been hopelessly compromised.

The carnage would be known forevermore as the Kansas City Massacre or the Union Station Massacre. Although this book is primarily about kidnappings, the Union Station event demands to be explored—because of how the FBI bungled the transfer of Frank Nash, then covered up its mistakes, and because of a weird link to a kidnapping only days before.

Newspaper reporters occasionally refer to their craft as writing "the rough draft of history." Some drafts are rougher than others. Five men died at the train station. But what really *happened*?

The initial front-page account in the *New York Times* quoted Kansas City detective chief Thomas J. Higgins as stating confidently that the ambush was staged to free Frank Nash, who was killed accidentally by his would-be liberators.[61] Higgins noted that Nash was a friend of the notorious Harvey Bailey, who was serving a term of twenty years to life for murder and bank robbery when he and ten other prisoners escaped from the Kansas State Penitentiary on Memorial Day 1933 during a baseball game between two American Legion teams.

The Associated Press also quoted Higgins as saying that the station ambush was meant to free Nash. But the AP also observed cautiously that other officials "were divided as to whether the killings were the result of an effort to free Nash or to 'rub him out.'"[62]

The FBI at once asserted that Pretty Boy Floyd, who after all had kidnapped a Missouri sheriff only the day before, must be behind the slaughter. Thus, one of the most significant passages in the *Times* initial account was a reference to Higgins, who was said to "cast doubt on reports that Charles 'Pretty Boy' Floyd, the Oklahoma desperado, was involved" in the train station bloodshed.[63]

An AP account published in the *Times* under the headline "No Clue to Killers in Kansas City" also noted Higgins's doubts. It noted too that Sheriff Jack Killingsworth, who had been kidnapped by Floyd and Adam Richetti, was doubtful that Floyd was linked to the massacre.

Yet less than three weeks later, on July 7, 1933, a maddeningly brief AP report appeared deep inside the *Times* to the effect that Hoover had demanded the capture of Floyd (and several of the Kansas prison escapees) in connection with the train station slaughter.[64] The brief news report did not describe Floyd's exploits, but there was no need. By mid-1933, Floyd was wanted as a killer as well as a bank robber (his victims included several lawmen, along with rival criminals) and a prison escapee.

Reading the accounts these many years later, a journalist like myself wants to ask, "Did Higgins and Killingsworth say why they thought Floyd was *not* involved in the Kansas City violence? What reason did Hoover give for suddenly concluding that Floyd *was* involved? Why didn't someone in the *Times* Washington bureau question Hoover?"

But back then, the FBI chieftain did not submit to sharp questions from journalists. So was Floyd involved in the train station carnage? Maybe it doesn't matter now. Back then, it mattered a great deal, especially to Hoover.

In the summer of 1933, the Lindbergh kidnapping was still unsolved, and the FBI had largely been relegated to the sidelines in the case, despite Hoover's eagerness to help. Other kidnappings were being committed with dismaying frequency. Floyd was running and robbing amok. Perhaps most infuriating for Hoover, the notorious John Dillinger was cutting a dashing figure in the Midwest, sticking up banks and seemingly toying with FBI agents and local cops.

So the image of the FBI badly needed burnishing. If the Union Station slaughter could be pinned on Floyd and if FBI agents could catch him—or, preferably, kill him—then Hoover could claim a major triumph in his war on crime, and the FBI would have avenged the death of one of its own, agent Ray Caffrey.

Floyd made a convenient villain, even a credible one, since he had told Sheriff Killingsworth that he and his pal Richetti were on their way to Kansas City. Soon, another man was being mentioned as a likely accomplice of Floyd and Richetti: Verne Miller, the former sheriff from Huron, South Dakota, who had abandoned his law enforcement career to become a bank robber, bootlegger, and gunman.

But a different theory about the train station episode has persisted, and it is too plausible to be dismissed.* In this version, the Hot Springs gambling kingpin Dick Galatas contacted Kansas City crime boss John Lazia on Friday evening to tell him that Nash had been arrested. ("Brother John" Lazia, it will be remembered, was head of the muscle department for the Tom Pendergast political machine and had been instrumental in securing the release of the kidnapped millionaire dressmaker Nell Donnelly in December 1931.)

After hearing from Galatas, Lazia supposedly tapped into his extensive police sources and learned that a train carrying Nash was to arrive at Union Station on Saturday morning. On Friday night, Lazia is said to have met in a restaurant with Miller to discuss what to do.

Lazia apparently conscripted two of his most efficient gunmen, the brothers Homer and Maurice Denning, to help Miller on a mission—not to free Nash but to kill him so he couldn't tell what he knew about organized crime in Hot Springs or Kansas City or both.

---

* Here, I am indebted to the crime writer Jay Robert Nash (no relation to Frank) for his essay "Who Was Behind the Kansas City Massacre?" (http://www.annalsofcrime.com/index.htm#03–05).

The possibility that Miller was joined in the ambush by the Brothers Denning rather than Floyd and Richetti was given credence by a witness to the shooting, a gangster named James Henry "Blackie" Audett, who knew Floyd and Richetti by sight and who happened to be in the station parking lot that Saturday morning.

Years later, having left his life of crime, Audett recalled watching the train station bloodbath from less than fifty yards away and clearly seeing the killers. He insisted that they included the Dennings but *not* Floyd nor Richetti.

But why would the FBI insist that Floyd and Richetti were there? "The FBI had to solve the case fast because one of their own men got killed," Audett said, "so they pinned it on two guys who were already wanted and widely known."

———

There is another aspect of the Union Station Massacre that must be told. Early news accounts reported what seemed self-evident, namely that Nash and the four lawmen were slain by the ambushers armed with machine guns. Indeed, Grooms and Reed were both hit with machine-gun bullets, as was Lackey.

But the back of Nash's head was blown away, a massive wound characteristic of a shotgun blast from *behind* at point-blank range. Caffrey and Hermanson also suffered huge head wounds consistent with a shotgun fired at close range. The windshield glass of the car in which Nash was sitting was blown apart and out onto the hood, again suggesting a shotgun blast—from behind.

How to explain all this? The two lawmen who were carrying shotguns were the Oklahoma police chief, Otto Reed, and FBI agent Joe Lackey. Reed was known to be intimately familiar with shotguns. His favorite was a piece that he fitted with a short barrel for law enforcement and a longer barrel for small-game hunting. He even made his own ammunition for police work, cutting open the ends of shotgun shells, removing the standard pellets meant for birds and small game, and inserting ball bearings—the better to bring down human prey.

By contrast, Lackey seems to have been inept with shotguns. In a memo to Hoover after the shooting, he claimed that he had just borrowed a shotgun that morning from the Oklahoma City police department, that the weapon had "jammed" during the shootout, and that he couldn't get it to function at all.

But it seems far more likely that he was so unfamiliar with the weapon that he didn't know how to get it ready to fire, because as the lawmen and their prisoner were about to get off the train, Lackey mistakenly picked up Reed's personal shotgun, which functioned differently from the gun Lackey had borrowed. (Presumably, Reed quickly realized that Lackey had taken his weapon by mistake. So Reed carried the weapon that Lackey had borrowed.)

Most tellingly, ball bearings of the kind that Reed used in his custom-made ammunition were found at the massacre scene. But it seems unlikely that Reed took his own shotgun from Lackey in the car and then fired it. It seems much more likely that Lackey panicked, fumbled with Reed's gun, and when he finally did manage to pull the trigger with effect, fired wildly, first accidentally killing Nash, who was sitting in front of him, then Caffrey and Hermanson. (Apparently, Reed was killed before he could fire at all.)

For his 2005 book *The Union Station Massacre: The Original Sin of J. Edgar Hoover's FBI*, the Pulitzer Prize–winning journalist Robert Unger analyzed the ballistics evidence, the accounts of bystanders—one of whom saw Lackey fumbling with a shotgun—and the contradictory statements that Lackey gave.

Most significantly, Lackey changed his account of where he was sitting. Referring to himself in the third person in his initial memo to Hoover, he wrote, "Agent got in the backseat on the *left-hand* side [emphasis added]."[65] In another early internal memo, again in the third person, Lackey reinforced his recollection: "The agent was crouched down back of the driver's seat."[66]

But two years later, when Richetti was on trial for the train station shooting, Lackey changed his recollection again: "I was on the backseat on the *right* or west side [emphasis added]," he testified.[67]

The question of where Joe Lackey was sitting is all-important. If indeed he was sitting in the *left* rear, "crouched down back of the driver's seat," as he stated originally, he was sitting directly behind Nash, from which position he inadvertently blew off the back of the prisoner's head and, seconds later, accidentally killed Caffrey and Hermanson.

The contradictory accounts that Robert Unger unearthed are from the FBI's own files and were apparently unnoticed for decades, although some in the FBI's inner circle—Hoover and his sycophants—were aware of them. So, apparently, were some Kansas City FBI agents, who out of fear of the tyrannical director carried their dark secrets into retirement and to their graves.

One FBI man who was aware of what really happened at the train station confided later to Federal Judge William H. Becker of the Western District of Missouri. As Robert Unger recounts, the judge shared his recollection just before he retired in 1990. "Our agent sitting in the backseat pulled the trigger on Nash," the judge recalled the FBI man as saying. "That started it. The machine-gunners didn't shoot first. Our guy panicked."[68]

If the press of that era had closely probed what happened at the train station, Hoover might have been cashiered and forgotten, especially considering the embarrassments that lay ahead. But the director was able to control the narrative and portray his agents as heroes at the Union Station shooting—when, in fact, they were victims of their own incompetence.

Ingeniously, if cynically, Hoover was able to turn a debacle into a triumph and use public sentiment for his own ends. "The audacity of daylight slaughter in a city center could not be excused as the work of oppressed country boys in depressed times," as Unger put it. "Suddenly killers and thieves were judged as killers and thieves. And the public verdict was harsh."

"Demands for reform were heard in cities and towns all over the country, but the focus quickly settled on Hoover and his small bank of federal agents... The carnage in Kansas City embedded a Hoover versus Gangland image in the public mind. And if the country wanted a gangbuster, J. Edgar Hoover desperately wanted the job."[69]

And he wanted vengeance for the death of an FBI agent at Union Station. The people responsible, he declared, would be "exterminated, and exterminated by us."[70] Should the Kansas City police break the case before the FBI caught up with the killers, Hoover warned an aide, "it would spoil it for us."[71]

———

On that Saturday morning of the Union Station Massacre, Blackie Audett was sitting in a car with Mary McElroy, the strikingly pretty twenty-five-year-old daughter of city manager Henry McElroy.

Mary lived with her widowed father and was very close to him. A somewhat impetuous woman, she was attracted to danger and excitement. She had heard there would be plenty of both at the train station that morning and had persuaded Audett to accompany her there to watch.

Mary was acquainted with John Lazia and other gangsters, whose company she enjoyed and whose exploits she liked to hear about, so it is not hard to believe that she would have heard something in advance. What *is* hard to believe is that she would want to flirt with danger, considering the ordeal she had gone through just three weeks earlier.

CHAPTER TWENTY-FOUR

MARY'S ORDEAL

Kansas City, Missouri
Saturday, May 27, 1933

Mary McElroy was enjoying a bubble bath in the upstairs bathroom of her father's home, looking forward to going to the track later on. She liked betting on the horses, in moderation.

She heard a knock at the door, then heard the maid, Heda Christensen, answer. Mary couldn't hear what was said, but she sensed from the tone of Heda's voice that the maid was suspicious.

Mary found out later that there were two men. One of them explained that they were delivering cosmetics that Mary had ordered.

The men sure didn't look like cosmetics salesmen. When Heda balked and started to close the door, one of the men aimed a pistol at her. "Either open that door for us, or I'll shoot through it," he said.[72]

Both men barged in. One brandished a sawed-off shotgun. They went upstairs.

Mary had heard the ruckus below and was alarmed. "Who's there?" she said.

"We're kidnappers," a man answered. "We're going to take you away, and if you behave yourself, you won't get hurt. Hurry up and get dressed."

The men let her go to her bedroom unmolested to put on clothes. Then they ushered her downstairs and out the door after promising the maid they would be in touch.

The kidnappers drove across the state line into Kansas, stopping at a house and escorting their captive to a dingy basement room furnished with a bed, chairs, and a radio. The room had an unpleasant smell, not surprising as it had been used to keep chickens.

The kidnappers gave their prisoner detective magazines to read. They handcuffed one of her hands to a wall by the bed.

———

That night, Henry McElroy got a special delivery letter. It was a note from his daughter, stating that her captors wanted $60,000—or $100,000 if the police or newspapers were told that she'd been taken, in which case, Mary warned, "I may not be returned."[73]

And don't mark the bills in the ransom package, she warned. The kidnappers had threatened to harm her father or her brother, Henry Jr., if the bills were doctored.

When a kidnapper got in touch by phone, McElroy said he could come up with only $30,000, much of it raised by his friends.

The kidnapper hung up and called back two hours later to say that $30,000 would be acceptable. He assured McElroy that his daughter had not been harmed.

The next day, the kidnappers told McElroy to meet them on a lonely road in Wyandotte County, Kansas, just across the Missouri state line. McElroy and his son handed over a package with $30,000; in return, they were promised that Mary would be freed within two hours.

Sure enough, around four o'clock, Mary was blindfolded and driven to the entrance of a country club. She was put out of the car and given a small bunch of flowers. She removed her blindfold and saw the kidnappers driving off. She waved to them. They waved back.

After her father picked her up, she emphasized that she had not been harmed and described her abductors as gentlemanly.

Mary said she had almost enjoyed her time in captivity as a break in her daily routine. She said she joked with the kidnappers over the initial ransom demand of $60,000. "I'm worth more than that," she recalled telling them. "That's not as much as they got for Mike Katz!"

Mike Katz was a Kansas City, Missouri, druggist who was kidnapped in 1930 and reportedly paid a ransom of $100,000 to gain his freedom.

Speaking to reporters shortly after her release, Mary said her kidnappers had "treated me with such consideration, I have no malice toward them. They were just businessmen."[74]

Was it odd that Mary McElroy, who had been handcuffed to a basement wall and whose life had been threatened, described her kidnappers as almost chivalrous? She talked so sympathetically about them that those close to her feared she was having a nervous breakdown.

———

Since the ransom money had been delivered in Kansas, it appeared that Mary might have been taken across a state line. So the FBI stepped in, using surveillance methods not available to the locals. They soon intercepted a telegram from a car dealer in Amarillo, Texas, to a junk dealer in Leavenworth, Kansas. The telegram mentioned a W. H. McGee who wanted to trade in a 1932 Oldsmobile, which he said he had bought from the junk dealer. Would the junk dealer please verify?

There was nothing damning in itself about the telegram, but the agents asked themselves why anyone who had bought a car in Kansas would be trading it in in Texas. What's more, the Amarillo car dealer said W. H. McGee and several friends had arrived at his dealership on the morning of Saturday, June 3, in a car with a burned-out bearing. The travelers looked as though they'd been driving all night, pushing their car to the limits.

The Kansas City police chief called the police in Amarillo, who tracked down Walter H. McGee, a thirty-seven-year-old ex-convict who had served time in Oregon. He had in his possession $9,000 in cash—including bills that friends of the McElroy family had contributed toward Mary's ransom after first writing down the serial numbers.

At first, McGee denied taking part in the kidnapping. Brought to Kansas City for more intensive questioning, he was confronted by Henry McElroy, who recognized him as one of the men who had accepted the ransom money.

"We've met before," McElroy said.

"I want to tell you everything and get it over with," McGee said amid sobs.

He admitted his crime, implicating his younger brother, George, as well, plus Clarence Click, owner of the house in Shawnee, Kansas, where Mary had been held. A fourth man suspected of having a role in the kidnapping was never caught.

Not surprisingly, the plot to kidnap Mary had been thought up while the men were drinking beer. As McGee told it, they were inspired in part by the kidnapping of Charlie Boettcher in Denver.

In 1933, courts functioned at a speed that seems inconceivable today. Within two months of the kidnapping, the McGee brothers and Clarence Click were on trial in state court in Kansas City, with an assistant U.S. attorney general aiding Missouri prosecutors.

By then, it was clear that the kidnapping had indeed been an ordeal for Mary, despite her initial description of it as a bit of a lark. Escorted to the house in Kansas where she had been held, she collapsed and wept when she saw the basement room.

In questioning the victim's father during the trial, a defense lawyer tried to create the impression that Mary hadn't really been harmed.

"Yes, my daughter was injured," Henry McElroy testified. "To the extent that I fear she will never get over it."

The McGee brothers and Click were all convicted. George McGee was sentenced to life in prison, and Click got eight years. But Walter McGee, whom prosecutors portrayed as the ringleader, was sentenced to hang, despite the fact that Mary had not been harmed physically. The judge said kidnapping was a scourge that had to be stamped out.

Walter McGee appealed his sentence, to no avail. But he had gained a seemingly unlikely ally: Mary McElroy.

"Walter McGee's sentence has hung as heavily over me as over him. Through punishing a guilty man, his victim will be made to suffer equally," she wrote to Governor Guy Park in April 1935. "He will have this advantage—he would not have to think about his execution afterward. In pleading for Walter McGee's life, I am pleading for my own peace of mind."[75]

The governor heeded her plea and commuted McGee's sentence to life.

But there was no emotional relief for Mary, whose behavior became increasingly erratic. In one incident, she disappeared from her home and was found eleven hours later in Normal, Illinois. Brought back to Kansas City, she offered vague explanations for her absence and insisted that she held "no personal hard feelings" toward her kidnappers.[76]

Oddly, she added, "I am sure they do not hold hard feelings against me... I have nightmares about these men and the fates they brought upon themselves. I was part of the drama that fixed their destiny."

She even visited the McGee brothers in prison occasionally. "Something drives me to do this," she explained. "I cannot let them go."

Her behavior may have been a reflection of what would later be called Stockholm syndrome. The condition takes its name from a bungled 1973 bank robbery in Sweden's capital. Two bandits held four bank employees hostage in a vault for six days, threatening them with nooses and sticks of dynamite to keep them submissive. The siege ended when the police used gas, capturing the bandits and freeing the captives. The authorities were startled when the four hostages expressed concern, even sympathy, for the pair who had brutalized them.

Psychologists who have studied the Stockholm syndrome believe a bond is created when a captor threatens to kill or harm a captive, then relents—creating a feeling in the captive not only of relief but of grati-tude. Little acts of kindness in awful circumstances are interpreted as good treatment—which is what Mary insisted she had been given, despite being chased from her bath, taken from her home, and handcuffed to a wall in a basement room that smelled of chicken droppings.

The years after the kidnapping were unkind to Mary. The power of the Pendergast machine, which had enabled her father to live large despite a modest official salary, was ebbing. The 1933 train station bloodshed had outraged good-government idealists. Tom Pendergast sensed that his muscleman, John Lazia, who was rumored to have helped plan the ambush, was becoming a liability, so Pendergast began to distance himself.

Lazia, facing vicious new competition from other gangsters and without Pendergast's support, was assassinated by men with subma-chine guns and shotguns on July 10, 1934, after a night inspecting his nightclubs and gambling dens with his wife. He was thirty-seven.

In 1934, a reform-minded federal prosecutor, Maurice Milligan, became the U.S. attorney for the Western District of Missouri and set his sights on Pendergast and his cronies. President Roosevelt's treasury secretary, Henry Morgenthau Jr., marshalled his bureaucracy against the Kansas City machine.

In April 1939, Tom Pendergast was indicted for tax evasion.* Days later, Henry McElroy resigned as city manager. On May 5, the body of Edward L. Schneider, a bookkeeper for the Pendergast organization, was found in the Missouri River. Suicide notes were found in his car.

An investigation revealed that millions of dollars in city money had evaporated while Henry McElroy was city manager. On June 29, 1939, he was indicted by a county grand jury on embezzlement and fraud charges. Meanwhile, federal agents were picking over his tax returns. Knowing that he would soon face federal tax-evasion charges, McElroy sank into despondency. He died of a heart attack on September 15, 1939, at the age of seventy-four.

Mary was devastated by the disgrace and death of her beloved father. She was occasionally pestered by reporters who wanted her to tell the "real story" about the kidnapping.

On the morning of January 21, 1940, she wrote a note that said: "My four kidnappers are probably the only people on earth who don't consider me an utter fool. You have your death penalty now so—please— give them a chance." Perhaps not even she knew just what she meant.

After writing the note, she went into a sunroom, held a pistol near her right ear, and pulled the trigger. Mary McElroy was dead at thirty-two.

When notified of her death, the McGee brothers seemed heartbroken. "I wouldn't have felt the loss of my own sister more," Walter said.[77] He died in prison in 1949, two years before he would have been eligible for parole. His brother, George, was paroled in 1947. Clarence Click completed his sentence in 1938.

---

* Pendergast was convicted on tax charges and served fifteen months in prison. He died on January 26, 1945, at seventy-two.

CHAPTER TWENTY-FIVE

"JAKE THE BARBER"

Chicago
Saturday, July 1, 1933

John "Jake the Barber" Factor was described in the *New York Times* as a "suave, curly haired speculator" and "a bizarre figure in the world of international finance." He was also a man with "friends in all strata of society on both sides of the Atlantic," the newspaper noted.[78] He had plenty of enemies too.

Calling him "a bizarre figure" hardly did justice to Factor. He was a man who might have become wealthy by legitimate means, if only he had devoted his agile mind and considerable talents to honest endeavors.** But he preferred to separate gullible people from their money.

Born Iakov Faktorowicz in London on October 8, 1892, the son of a rabbi, he was raised in Poland. He moved to the United States with

---

** As did Jack's half brother, Max Factor, who was a Hollywood makeup man and founded a cosmetics empire.

his parents in 1904. He had little schooling and perhaps little need for it. He knew what he wanted: to climb out of immigrant poverty any way he could.

In 1926, he persuaded Al Capone and Arnold Rothstein, the New York City gambler most infamous for rigging the 1919 World Series, to stake him in a swindling adventure in Britain, where Factor published a tip sheet that touted stocks of dubious value in Rhodesian gold mines among other offerings. The promised returns seemed too good to be true (which, of course, they were), but hordes of investors, reportedly including members of the royal family, entrusted their money to the fast-talking American.

Pursued by British regulators, Factor fled to France, where he made another bundle by forming a syndicate that rigged the gaming tables at Monte Carlo. Then he sailed back to the United States, where he counted on the Capone outfit to protect him.

But Al Capone's influence did not extend to British diplomats and courts, which demanded that Factor be extradited to Britain to face trial on swindling charges. Factor fought extradition as long as he could, taking his case all the way to the Supreme Court, which seemed likely to find against him, given the strength of the evidence from London.

The Factor family seemed to be especially unlucky when it came to kidnapping. The previous April, John Factor's nineteen-year-old son, Jerome, a student at Northwestern University, had apparently been abducted and held for eight days.

The elder Factor had taken a suite in Chicago's Morrison Hotel, supposedly to negotiate for his son's release, ignoring the police and reaching out to his well-connected friends on the nightclub circuit and to Murray Humphreys, a labor racketeer and friend of the Capone organization. A ransom of $50,000 had reportedly been demanded for Jerome's freedom, but his father was supposedly telling close friends that he had tricked the kidnappers into freeing the young man for no ransom at all.

Later, there would be speculation that the "kidnapping" of Factor's son was a phony drama, meant to scare off the British, who might appear to be heartless by trying to extradite the father of a kidnapping victim.

As Friday night melted into Saturday and June yielded to July, Factor was plucked from his car while returning from a party he had given at a roadhouse just west of the Chicago suburb of Evanston. Those traveling with him, including his second wife, Rella, told police the kidnappers meant business: there were nine of them altogether, traveling in two cars and armed with shotguns and machine guns.

This time, it was Jerome Factor who was ensconced in a suite at the Morrison Hotel, trying to orchestrate the release of his father. And Jerome seemed to be using the tactics his father had relied upon, as the *New York Times* observed, "There were noted around the corridors several mysterious characters, recognized as hoodlums who, presumably, were endeavoring to make contact with the kidnappers."[79]

Perhaps not surprisingly, some lawmen in Chicago speculated right away that Verne Sankey, the family man, kidnapper and robber, and his bunch were responsible for grabbing Factor. Sankey was such a logical suspect. But he had nothing to do with the kidnapping of John Factor—if indeed there had even been a kidnapping.

Shortly before midnight on Wednesday, July 12, 1933, a street cop in La Grange, Illinois, a Chicago suburb, was walking his beat when an unshaven man in a rumpled white suit approached him. "I'm Jake Factor," the man said. "Please notify my wife I'm safe."[80]

Factor said he had just been tossed out of a car by his kidnappers, who had kept a hood over his head until the moment of his release. The cop took him to the La Grange police station, just a few blocks away, where Factor threw himself onto a cot.

No, he said, he didn't know how much ransom had been paid for his freedom, didn't know if any money at all had changed hands.

Some newspapermen were more certain. Without saying where the information had come from, the *New York Times* reported on July 13 that the kidnappers had accepted "anywhere between $75,000 and $200,000."

Wait, cancel that! On July 14, when Factor was "shaved and refreshed by alcohol rubdowns and a night's rest," as the *Times* put it, he changed his story.[81] He said a down payment of $50,000 had been conveyed to the kidnappers, with the promise that another $150,000 would be forthcoming. In return for the full amount, the kidnappers had pledged not to harm Jerome or Factor's seven-year-old son, Alvin.

Factor said he had been blindfolded for much of his captivity and that he had been kept in an upstairs bedroom of a house during the negotiations.

But the British authorities had never believed a bit of Factor's story. Well before Factor turned up in La Grange, the British lawyer leading the extradition campaign, Franklin Overmyer, asserted that the entire "kidnapping" was a hoax, as the *Times* dutifully noted at the end of its July 13 article.[82]

The very next day, however, there was a new theory, as the *Times* reported at the bottom of its article on July 14. "Convinced that the Touhy gang kidnapped Factor, police began a round-up of as many members of the gang as possible."[83]

To many Americans, the name Touhy was probably not as familiar as, say, Dillinger or Capone. But people in and around Chicago knew the name well.

CHAPTER TWENTY-SIX

ROGER "THE TERRIBLE"

Chicago
Summer 1933

No question about it: Roger "the Terrible" Touhy was an ideal suspect for just about any crime. He was a tough, shrewd Chicago bootlegger who was acquainted with loan sharks, gamblers, and various musclemen for hire. Remarkably, he had never been afraid to stand up to Al Capone, with whom he had a symbiotic relationship for a while.

Not quite thirty-five years old in the summer of 1933, Touhy had survived a childhood best described as short. He was the youngest of five sons of James Touhy, a Chicago policeman, and his wife, Mary, who died in a house fire when Roger was ten.

James struggled to raise his sons and two daughters, but he seems to have been overwhelmed. One son was shot dead by a Chicago policeman in 1917 while attempting a robbery. Another son was killed a decade later, reportedly by gunmen in Al Capone's gang, and another son was shot dead two years after that, again presumably by Capone men.

After dropping out of school in the eighth grade, Roger Touhy had several unglamorous but honest jobs. He served in the navy during the Great War. After the war, he married. He and a brother started a trucking company. By this time, Prohibition was in effect. Much of the cargo in the Touhy trucks consisted of beer and liquor. By the late 1920s, Touhy had broadened his business interests to gambling and slot machines, which he installed in many Chicago-area saloons.

Capone was buying hundreds of barrels of beer each week from Touhy. It was high-quality beer, made in a brewery run by Touhy and his associates and shipped in wooden barrels also made by Touhy and his men.

The Touhy gang was rumored to number as many as eighty men. So it seemed reasonable when Daniel Gilbert, the chief investigator for the Cook County (Chicago) state's attorney's office, announced that the Touhy gang was most likely responsible for the kidnapping of both John Factor *and* William Hamm.

As it happened, Touhy and several associates were then in Elkhorn, Wisconsin, recuperating from injuries they'd suffered when their car hit a telephone pole.

Melvin Purvis, the head of the Chicago FBI office, took his cue from Gilbert, ordering several FBI agents to accompany Gilbert to Wisconsin to bring Touhy and his associates to Chicago for interrogation.

The car crash was doubly unfortunate for Touhy and friends. Not only had they been shaken up, but a small arsenal of weapons was found in the vehicle by police investigating the smashup. The car was also found to be equipped with a special, large-capacity fuel tank—ideal for kidnappers, who could drive as long as they could stay awake without having to gas up.

In Chicago, Purvis himself questioned Touhy, who laughingly dismissed the suggestion that he'd had anything to do with kidnapping

Hamm. And when Hamm himself viewed Touhy and his several associates through a one-way mirror, he was far from sure they were the men
who had grabbed him. After all, Hamm had initially thought one of his
captors looked like Verne Sankey.*

But Purvis was persuaded by Gilbert's assertion of Touhy's guilt.
Though the historical record is murky on this point, Purvis's belief seems
to have been reinforced by another witness, who said he was confident
that Touhy had abducted Hamm.

A native of South Carolina and a lawyer, Purvis was twenty-nine
years old that summer of 1933 and still a bachelor. He was discreet,
serious, loyal, not given to easy smiling. His taste in suits ran from dark
to *really* dark. In other words, he personified Hoover's idea of the ideal
FBI agent.

Before he was assigned to Chicago, Purvis was an agent in
Birmingham, Alabama; Oklahoma City; and Cincinnati. Yet however
well-traveled he was and despite his schooling, he seems to have had all
the street smarts of a cloistered monk. His willingness to rely on Gilbert
was astounding, given the kind of man Gilbert was.

"Tubbo," as the portly, thick-necked Gilbert was known, joined
the Chicago police force in 1918, soon made sergeant, and was a captain
by 1927. His meteoric rise came at a time when Al Capone controlled
much of Chicago's underworld, and city hall and the police department
were corrupt. Perched happily atop the political dung heap for much of
the era was Mayor William "Big Bill" Hale Thompson, a Republican
who was in office from 1915 to 1923 and from 1927 to 1931 and who
was friendly with Capone.

---

* It is not uncommon for crime victims to misidentify suspects. I know of a case in which
two young men in New York City were mistakenly identified by women who had been
sexually assaulted during burglaries. When the culprit was finally caught, his picture
ran in the *New York Times* alongside those of the two innocent men. The three men
resembled one another, to be sure, but they could hardly have been mistaken for triplets.

After Thompson was defeated by Democrat Anton Cermak in the mayoral election of April 7, 1931, the *Chicago Daily Tribune* declared that Thompson's reign had brought "filth, corruption, obscenity, idiocy and bankruptcy" to Chicago and made it "a byword for the collapse of American civilization."[84] In the same editorial, the *Tribune* boasted of its condemnation of Thompson over the years: "It is unpleasant business to eject a skunk, but someone has to do it."*

If Melvin Purvis had had an ounce of shrewdness, he would have wondered how Gilbert rocketed from patrolman to captain in nine years, after which he became head investigator for the Cook County prosecutor's office.

Purvis might have wondered, too, if it was proper for Gilbert to be secretary-treasurer of a Teamsters union local while he was a young police officer. And Purvis ought to have wondered how Gilbert gained control of half a dozen Chicago Teamsters locals by the mid-1930s.

Purvis was remarkably careless and naïve in taking Gilbert's word that Touhy was behind the kidnappings of Hamm and Factor. Nevertheless, he was sufficiently persuaded to announce that the FBI had no doubt about Touhy's guilt, and would prove it in court.

And that was exactly what Hoover wanted to hear. He wrote Purvis to praise his diligence and that of the entire Chicago office of the FBI.

What Purvis and, of course, Hoover should have known was that Gilbert was working with Capone's organization to eliminate competition from Touhy and his associates, a goal that could be neatly accomplished if Touhy were sent to prison.**

There is more, much more, to tell about the life of Daniel "Tubbo"

---

* Thompson was the last Republican to serve as mayor of Chicago. Cermak was shot in Miami on February 15, 1933, by a man trying to assassinate President-elect Franklin D. Roosevelt and died on March 6.
** Capone himself had been sent to prison in May 1932 after being convicted of income tax evasion.

Gilbert, for it was such an American story, such a Chicago story. For now, let us stay with the summer of 1933.

On July 24, Touhy and three associates, Willie Sharkey, Edward "Father Tom" McFadden, and Gustav "Gloomy Gus" Schaefer, were jailed in Milwaukee to await arraignment and a hearing on whether they would be sent to St. Paul to stand trial for kidnapping William Hamm.

The authorities were confident. "We will have from four to six witnesses to identify the Illinois gangsters as those who engineered the Hamm plot," Thomas E. Dahill, the St. Paul police chief, promised.[85]

"We have a very good case against these men," L. L. Drill, the U.S. attorney in St. Paul, said.

The defendants' lawyer, William Scott Stewart of Chicago, said the charges against his clients were preposterous.

No one paid much attention to the defense lawyer at first. Languishing in jail to await trial, Touhy and his associates were all but forgotten for a while—and no wonder, given the smorgasbord of crime news that summer.

CHAPTER TWENTY-SEVEN

A PRINCE OF ALBANY

Albany, New York
Friday, July 7, 1933

Ah, the Great Empire State! Some of the men who lived in the governor's mansion in New York State's capital, Albany, became figures on the world stage: Franklin D. Roosevelt, Averell Harriman, Nelson A. Rockefeller. Two other New York governors, Alfred E. Smith and Thomas E. Dewey, captured their party's presidential nominations but missed the big prize. Nonetheless, their places in history are secure because of their fine public service.

But there has always been a shabbier Albany, one in which tawdry scandals bubble up occasionally like cesspool gas. Bribes for liquor licenses, do-nothing jobs, bloated contracts for public projects, backslapping, and backstabbing—all have been part of the political circus of Albany. One kidnapping in particular offered a glimpse of some of these goings-on.

The car was found in front of his father's house, the driver's side door open and the engine still warm, early in the morning. The vehicle belonged to John J. O'Connell Jr., a prince of a powerful political clan. Twenty-four years old, "Butch" O'Connell, as he was known, was mature, sensible. He wouldn't have left his car with the door open. Other young men might be stupid enough to get drunk and just stumble off, but not Butch.

So where the hell was he?

His uncles, the brothers Daniel P., known as "Big Dan," and Edward J. O'Connell, were bosses of the Albany County Democratic machine. Big Dan was the big boss of the family. He was born in 1885 in Albany, son of a tavern owner, and dropped out of high school. As a brash thirtysomething, he ran for city assessor and won. His victory surprised everyone in city politics, as the Republican city organization had been considered invincible. But Dan and his brothers worked tirelessly, and within three years, they were in command of a Democratic organization that controlled both city and county government.

Butch O'Connell's father was widely known as "Solly" O'Connell, and he was also active in politics. Solly's brother Edward was chairman of the Albany County Democratic Party.

Butch was expected to maintain the family's power in the capital of the Empire State. Sadly, a death in the clan, that of another uncle, Patrick O'Connell, just a few weeks before had created a possible stepping stone for Butch. Patrick had been clerk of the state senate, and there was speculation that Butch might succeed him.

Nor need Butch have worried about his future outside politics. His uncles were stockholders in the Hedrick Brewery, and Butch was learning all about the beer business. He would prosper, no doubt about that. Then as now, Albany politicians knew how to use their connections to succeed in business.

Though not particularly handsome, Butch was impressive looking in a square-jawed Irish way, and he looked good in a uniform, which he often wore as a lieutenant in the National Guard. He was still single, but his status was expected to change soon. He had a steady girlfriend, Mary Fahey.

Relatives and a few trusted friends gathered in Butch's home on Putnam Street in a quiet residential section of Albany. On Friday afternoon, the phone rang. It was picked up by George Myers, a family friend. "Tell Ed we have his nephew, and if he wants to see him alive again, tell him not to call the police."[86] Samuel Aronowitz, Edward O'Connell's law partner, got a similar call on Friday.

On Saturday morning, there was a third phone call, this one for Daniel O'Connell: "Look in your mailbox at the post office."

The mailbox contained a letter, hand-printed and with Butch O'Connell's signature, demanding $250,000 for Butch's safe return. Soon, there was another letter, this one instructing the family to insert an ad in the *Knickerbocker Press* on Sunday, listing men who would be trustworthy intermediaries.* The list was to be in code, using numbers for letters: 1 for *A*, 2 for *B*, and so on.

When the list was compiled, it was inserted in the newspaper by Walter V. Johnson, a friend of the O'Connells and the Democratic leader of neighboring Rensselaer County. This list showed a preponderance of Irish names whose bearers were familiar figures around Albany sporting venues.

The kidnappers found the list unsatisfactory and demanded a fresh list of possible intermediaries. This second list was also printed in code, although in the *Albany Times Union*. How the O'Connells came up with the new names or whether the kidnappers offered hints isn't known. In

---

* The *Knickerbocker Press* was one of several daily newspapers in Albany during that period. It was merged with another newspaper in 1937, and that combined paper eventually folded.

any event, as the *New York Times* put it, several men on the list "were members of or in direct contact with the Albany underworld."[87]

Despite the kidnappers' warnings, the O'Connells had notified the Albany police early on. Governor Herbert Lehman pledged "every resource of the state" to recover the young man. But very quickly, the O'Connells let it be known that they didn't want the police or federal agents in the way, that they wanted to negotiate for Butch's release.

Five New York City detectives were sent north to aid their Albany counterparts, stirring speculation that the kidnapping had been carried out by a New York City gang. But another, more plausible theory was that the kidnapping had been conceived and carried out by upstate enemies of the O'Connells, perhaps by beer distributors who had been chased out of Albany and supplanted by the O'Connell family's beer business.

Five days after the kidnapping, there were signs that the victim was about to be set free. There were rumors that the family had raised between $75,000 and $100,000 (the original demand of $250,000 was out of the family's reach), and several automobiles stood ready in the driveway of the home of Solly O'Connell in the Catskills for a possible rendezvous with the kidnappers.

Deep in a *New York Times* account of the episode there was this telling passage, which reflected the state of the battle against the crime of kidnapping: "In the meantime state troopers, federal agents and the New York City detectives, keeping out of sight, were carrying on their investigations, each group working independently."

Adding to the confusion was a demand from the kidnappers to see a third list of possible go-betweens.

———

The press coverage took on a tone that was remarkably cynical and, it seems, properly so. In case any reader had missed earlier allusions, the *Times* noted that for the most part the agreed-upon intermediaries between the kidnappers and the family "have no social standing except in the Albany underworld."[88]

One of the men on the list, Sylvester Hess, was a celebrant at a party given by gangster Jack "Legs" Diamond just before Diamond was shot to death on December 18, 1931. Diamond had been staying in an Albany rooming house while on trial in Troy, New York, for kidnapping a driver for a rival bootlegger. The party on December 18 was to celebrate Diamond's acquittal, but the joy lasted only until he was shot to death in the rooming house. Hess was one of those questioned in connection with the hit, though he was never charged. As for who actually killed Diamond, speculation focused on gangster Dutch Schultz, the brothers John and Francis Oley, well-known Albany area thugs (about whom more later), and even members of the Albany police department.[*]

Another name on the third list was Manning "Manny" Strewl, described in press accounts as a former bootlegger "whose occupation is hard to classify."[89] Strewl soon established himself as the chief negotiator between the O'Connell family and whoever was holding Butch.

As the days went by, the collective fear increased. Those who knew Butch personally worried that he might endanger himself by getting combative with his captors. He was, after all, a six-footer and weighed well over two hundred pounds, and he had played football in high school. He was not used to being pushed around.

Until the night he was taken, that is. As would be revealed later, he had been knocked into semiconsciousness, possibly drugged to further immobilize him, then put into a crate before he was transported to New York City.

---

[*]   In a sad sequel, Diamond's widow, Alice, was shot to death in her Brooklyn apartment a week before the kidnapping of Butch O'Connell, probably to ensure that she would be forever silent on what she knew about her husband's dealings. Unfortunately for her, she had a habit of talking too much when she drank.

On Friday, July 28, things began to move. The kidnappers had sent word that they would accept $40,000, a relative pittance compared to the original demand. Louis Snyder, a lawyer for Manny Strewl, picked up the money at the O'Connells' home in the Catskills and drove to New York City, where he had been told that Butch would be found safe.

On Sunday, July 30, after he had been held captive for twenty-three days, Butch was set free in the Bronx. Snyder and Strewl went to New York where Strewl made several telephone calls and took various taxi rides, as instructed by the kidnappers. He was blindfolded much of the time. After he handed over the money, he was dropped off at his own car, which by prearrangement had been parked at Broadway and 220th Street in the Bronx.

And there, in Strewl's car, sat Butch, blindfolded and gagged. Strewl freed the young man from his inconveniences and drove to pick up Snyder, who had been waiting a short distance away. Then it was on to Albany for a joyous family reunion.

Strewl quickly came under suspicion. He had seemed to wiggle his way all too easily onto the list of intermediaries who might be acceptable to the kidnappers, and then he had been chosen. Also, known samples of his handwriting resembled that in the notes sent to the family by the kidnappers.

On August 1, District Attorney John T. Delaney made a statement that seems astounding, at least by today's standards of conduct by prosecutors. Reporters, who knew that Strewl was being interrogated, asked Delaney if Strewl would be charged. "Oh, eventually, I suppose so," the prosecutor replied. "You can't act as a go-between in cases like this without being charged with something. But just now he is helping and has been helping… No one has been offered any protection. If they're in, they're in."[90]

With his seemingly casual remarks, the prosecutor had made it clear that the border between good citizens and criminals in Albany was easily crossed, if there was in fact a border.

No one who had followed the case and knew the nature of Albany was surprised when Strewl was indicted on charges of kidnapping. Others who were indicted included the thug brothers John and Francis Oley, an ex-con named Percy "Angel Face" Geary, and several others who were nowhere to be found at first. All were well known to local lawmen.

Strewl was convicted in a New York State court in March 1934 and sentenced to fifty years in prison. The Oleys and Geary remained at large, but they were not idle.

On the morning of August 21, 1934, the Oley brothers and Geary were part of a gang that held up an armored car at a Brooklyn ice house, then commandeered a boat to effect their getaway with more than $400,000. Unfortunately, a shotgun was accidentally discharged on the boat, mangling the leg of one robber so badly that he soon died despite the efforts of a shady surgeon who had been summoned to try to save him.

Francis Oley was eventually tracked to Denver, where he was arrested in 1937. He soon hanged himself in his cell. John Oley and Geary were also captured in 1937. On November 15, 1937, John Oley, Geary, and another prisoner escaped from the Onondaga County Penitentiary in Jamesville, New York, where they had been housed to await transfer to federal prison. They were soon recaptured and sent to that most dreaded of federal prisons, Alcatraz.

Oley and Strewl served some time on the island in San Francisco Bay and were probably grateful to be transferred to an easier federal prison in Atlanta. Strewl was released in 1958 and Oley the following year. But Geary adjusted so well to prison that he feared a return to the "real world," whatever that term meant to him. He begged prison officials to let him stay, but they declined. Three days before he was to be turned loose after serving twenty years, Geary ended his life by throwing himself under a moving truck in the Atlanta prison in 1959.

═══════════

John J. O'Connell Jr. lived up to the expectations of the clan's elders, becoming Albany County Democratic chairman in 1940 at the age of thirty. He served until 1946, when he relinquished the post to his uncle, Dan O'Connell, who until his death in 1977 was the real party chieftain in the county, whether he held the formal title or not.

Butch also became vice president and general manager of the family-owned brewing company, which profited from the O'Connells' ability to deny liquor licenses to establishments that dared to think about buying beer elsewhere. At least, that was the complaint of the O'Connells' enemies.

Butch O'Connell died on September 4, 1954, at the age of forty-four, a year after the death of his father. The strapping former football player had suffered a stroke the week before. He and his wife, Mary, had four children. No one suggested a direct link between his death and the ordeal he had undergone in 1933.

As for Manny Strewl, his life served as a reminder that no justice is certain this side of heaven. Released from the Atlanta federal prison in 1958, he lived another four decades, dying in 1998 at the age of ninety-five.

The ransom money in the O'Connell kidnapping was never found.

CHAPTER TWENTY-EIGHT

A BANKER WITH A HEART

Alton, Illinois
Monday, July 10, 1933

On the evening of Monday, July 10, 1933, a wealthy banker named August Luer and his wife of fifty-six years, Helena, were spending a quiet evening at home in Alton, Illinois, a small town on the Mississippi River about fifteen miles north of St. Louis.

The Luers had had a pleasant day, going for a car ride with one of their three grown sons. It was not really late on this Monday night, but the Luers were about to retire. Early to bed, early to rise was their habit. That way of life had served August Luer well in his seventy-seven years. He was president of the Alton Banking and Trust Company. He was also the retired president of a meatpacking company that he had founded.

Unlike some bankers of that time, August Luer was liked and trusted. While other banks in the region were going under, Luer pledged that his would never fail, that his personal wealth was behind the institution. It was just the message the Depression-weary people of Alton needed.

Around 9:00 p.m., the bell rang. Two neatly dressed men and a woman in a flowered dress were standing at the front door.

"We are trying to get in touch with Henry Busse," one of the men said. "We are strangers here. Can you help us?"

Luer was happy to invite the trio into his house. He knew Henry Busse, who lived just a few blocks away, and he said he'd be glad to phone him.

Luer had just lifted the phone receiver from its hook when one of the men and the woman grabbed him. The second man grabbed Luer's wife, started to choke her, and shoved her into a hallway, where she fainted. Luer struggled in vain as the two men lifted him and carried him out the front door. His bedroom slippers dropped onto the driveway before he was pushed into a car, where yet another man sat in the driver's seat. The car raced off.

Helena Luer had revived and run outside, screaming that her husband had been taken. She was terribly worried; her husband was suffering from heart disease and took medication.

The police immediately speculated that the kidnappers might be from a gang that operated out of East St. Louis, Illinois, about twenty-four miles south of Alton on the Mississippi River.

———

August Luer was blindfolded and exhausted when the car finally stopped. He guessed that he had been in the car, lying on the floor, for three hours. He needed to keep his heart rate as low as he could, for he had no medication with him. Panic was a luxury he could not afford.

Out of the car, he sensed that he was in the country, likely on a farm. The night was so quiet. He was led a short distance before his blindfold was removed. In the dark, he could discern the outlines of a toolshed. The structure was large enough to hold him in relative comfort.

But when the shed door was pulled open and a flashlight trained on the floor, he saw something that would terrify anyone with any tendency to be claustrophobic. In front of him was a freshly dug hole, roughly two feet square and four feet deep. And at the bottom of the hole was a narrow tunnel that led immediately into a pitch-black cave about seven feet long, three feet wide, and three and a half feet high. The walls and top of the cave were reinforced by wooden planks. The cave floor was dirt.

August Luer was given a sack filled with straw and feathers. He tried to tamp down the terror rising in his chest. He knew that the tunnel would be his "room" for as long as he was held captive. But he was not afraid just for himself; his wife was also in delicate health. He wondered if she could endure the ordeal of his absence.

He wondered how long he would be in this dark, awful place. His captors told him he'd be with them for several days as ransom negotiations took place. They told him they would bring him papers to sign. He wouldn't be able to read them, as he'd be blindfolded, but it didn't matter.

"Your only chance for freedom is to sign your name," one kidnapper told him.

On the first day, August Luer was given two ham sandwiches. He ate only part of one.

As time crawled by, he knew that night was becoming day, day was becoming night, night was turning into day, and...

Sleep came in spurts. He dared to ask for a car seat cushion. One was brought to him. He was given more ham sandwiches. They upset his stomach, so he asked for some medicine. The next day, he was given a dose of something in a glass of water. Then—praise God!—he was fed cantaloupes and oranges.

But what he craved more than anything was fresh air. He dared to ask if he could be let out for a few minutes. Not too roughly, one of his captors helped him out, led him upstairs, and sat with him on what felt like a sofa. Luer couldn't tell for sure; he was still blindfolded.

After a precious few minutes, it was back down to his dungeon.

———————

There is a reason for the term *usual suspects*. When a serious crime is committed, the police in a certain area are apt to focus initially on people who have committed crimes before, even if they have "paid their debt to society," as the cliché goes. So it made perfect sense for the police around Alton and East St. Louis, Illinois, to poke around in the usual flotsam and jetsam of society to see if they knew anyone who could be linked to the kidnapping of August Luer.

It was no surprise that Percy Michael Fitzgerald, who was thirty-nine in the summer of 1933, came under suspicion early on. His habit was to give his occupation as "paper hanger" whenever he was arrested, which was often. In truth, he didn't have time to hang paper, since he had been arrested about forty times in the previous two decades. He had been imprisoned for two years and eight months in Tennessee for safecracking and done six months in a Missouri workhouse for petty larceny, a charge that was reduced from a felony count of possessing burglary tools.

For reasons lost to history, criminals and other bottom-feeders around East St. Louis knew Fitzgerald as "the Dice Box Kid," a fact that was known to police, who suspected, not illogically, that anyone with a nickname like that had to be guilty of more wrongdoing than he had ever answered for.

So a photograph of Fitzgerald was among the two dozen likenesses of known criminals that were shown to Helena Luer right after her husband was taken away. Yes, she said. This looked like one of the men who had come into their home that night. (Nowadays, conscientious police officers show a victim of a crime or a witness numerous photographs in addition to the one they hope will be recognized. That way, investigators prevent accusations by defense lawyers that the identification has been tainted—i.e., that a witness or victim is automatically biased when shown only a photo or sketch that the police hope he or she will recognize. In the 1930s, the police were not bothered by such technicalities.)

In the summer of 1933, there was a finite number of hangouts that were frequented by lowlifes around East St. Louis and Alton. The police knew them all, and they knew which ones Fitzgerald liked. Federal agents and local cops kept tabs on Fitzgerald's haunts and grew increasingly suspicious when he was not seen in the usual places after Luer was seized.

———————

Half a dozen times, pieces of paper were held in front of him, and August Luer scrawled his signature on each one. He was sure they were messages to his family and others negotiating for his freedom. He remembered what he'd been told: *"Your only chance for freedom is to sign your name."*

Luer had counted his days in captivity. On Saturday, his captors pulled him out of the pit and told him they were taking him for a ride—and that he might be released. He dared to hope.

He was back in a car, blindfolded. Long minutes passed. Maybe the minutes became an hour. *Two* hours? He couldn't tell. Finally, the car stopped. He heard a train coming. *Dear God! Are they going to throw me in front of the train? No, no, that makes no sense. Does it?*

They rode on. One of his captors said, "We've been riding around in Missouri long enough. We had better get back to Illinois."

Were they trying to be clever, just saying that to deceive him on their real whereabouts? Did it matter? At long last, the car stopped again. Luer was helped out of the car and onto the roadside. He didn't know it, but Saturday night had just become Sunday morning.

"You can take the bandage off your eyes, and you'll see a red-and-blue sign," one of the captors said. "If you go to that place, you will find a telephone."

The car drove off. Luer waited cautiously, making sure they were gone for good. Then he removed the bandage that had covered his eyes, saw the sign in the distance, and walked. He went past the waterworks of Collinsville, Illinois, about thirty miles southeast of Alton and twelve miles east of St. Louis. Irrationally, perhaps because his mind was at the breaking point, he was afraid to stop at the waterworks because he thought a night watchman would mistake him for a tramp. In fact, he was unshaven, dirty, and in rumpled, soiled clothes and dust-covered shoes.

Finally, he came to the red-and-blue sign, which advertised a roadhouse. A small band was playing, and several couples were dancing. The moment he entered, the music and dancing stopped. The proprietor offered him a cup of coffee. No thanks, Luer said. "Please," he said. "Could I telephone my son? My family will be waiting to hear from me."[91]

In no time, police officers arrived, along with his sons, to take Luer home.

———

On the night of Monday, July 17, Fitzgerald turned up at one of his hangouts in Madison, Illinois, a little town near both Alton and East St. Louis, Illinois. Federal agents and a posse of local police arrested him without difficulty. Fitzgerald seemed almost relieved. "I'm right for this job," he told detectives. "You've got me hooked."[92]

The entire "job" had been a fiasco. The ransom notes that Luer had been forced to sign had never been delivered. Federal agents said no ransom was paid. It appeared that the kidnappers had simply grown weary of the frustrations and decided to free their hostage.

Fitzgerald quickly implicated three other men and two women in the enterprise. They were arrested in and around East St. Louis. Among the suspects were a husband and wife who lived on the farm in Madison County, Illinois, where Luer had been held.

If Fitzgerald was counting on his quick confession to gain him some leniency, he must have been disappointed. There were immediate cries of outrage over the treatment of a well-liked banker in his senior years and suffering from a heart condition. There was smoldering anger not just over what had happened but what *could* have happened.

"I can't conceive why they put that old man in the hole instead of in the shed above," one lawman commented. "Unless for this reason: Had he died, all they would have had to do would have been to fill in the hole. Then nobody on earth would ever have found his grave."[93]

Eight and a half decades later, it is impossible to measure the mood of the American people, but it is reasonable to assume that they were becoming increasingly disgusted, even horrified, at the plague of kidnappings.

In 1933, the killer of the Lindbergh baby was still at large. In Philadelphia in July, a real estate broker was fatally shot by would-be kidnappers as he tried to flee. And in the Midwest especially, the ordeal of August Luer, a man of integrity who was nothing like a stereotypical banker with cold eyes and a sharp pencil, stoked deep anger.

By the time detectives and prosecutors sorted out who should be charged with what in the Luer case, there were six defendants—five men and a woman. When they went to trial in late September in Edwardsville, Illinois, the Madison County seat, prosecutors said all should go to the electric chair. Assistant State's Attorney John F. McGinnis called the

J. Edgar Hoover in 1924.

Photo © Library of Congress

Charles Lindbergh
at the trial for Bruno
Richard Hauptmann.

Photo © Library of Congress

The Lindbergh
baby ransom note.

Photo © FBI

Charles Augustus Lindbergh Jr., whose kidnapping and
murder became known as "the crime of the century."

Photo © FBI

Charles Boettcher and his wife, Anne.

Photo © Stephen H. Hart Library,
Colorado Historical Society

**Charles Boettcher in his robe
the morning after he was freed
from his kidnappers.**

Photo © Stephen H. Hart Library,
Colorado Historical Society

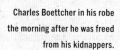

CHARLES BOETTCHER 2D

An exclusive picture of the kidnapped man as he appeared the morning following
his return home, after being held by an abduction gang for more than two weeks

Do not notify the authorities. If you want our captive returned to you alive and well, do exactly as we instruct you. Our terms are thirty five thousand dollars in exchange for our captive. You are to get the cash today in denominations as follows, 1000 five dollar bills, 1000 ten dollar bills, and 1000 twenty dollar bills. Get this money and have it at your home this evening and we will notify you just where and when to meet us. Have your car ready and go alone when delivering this money.

If you report this to the authorities we will not try to receive the money, nor will we return our captive to you. Remember, Lindy notified the authorities and you know what happened. We will not sign this note as there will be no necessity for any reply if you follow instructions.

If you do not follow instructions we will not try to contact you again. Get money in old bills. Have car with license No. B 54-480. ready and when you receive our message tonight, go alone with money and drive as told. Put these letters in with money in a club bag.

Verne Sankey, the man who kidnapped Charles Boettcher.

Photo © Stephen H. Hart Library, Colorado Historical Society

A portion of Charles Boettcher's ransom note.

Photo © Stephen H. Hart Library, Colorado Historical Society

An arsenal of weapons at Ma Barker's hideout.

Photo © FBI

Kate "Ma" Barker.

Photo © FBI

Frederick Barker, the youngest son of Ma Barker and one of the founders of the Barker-Karpis gang.

Photo © FBI

Arthur "Doc" Barker, the son of Ma Barker and a member of the Barker-Karpis gang.

Photo © FBI

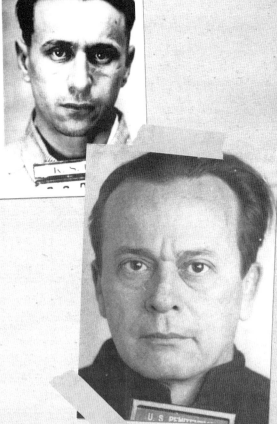

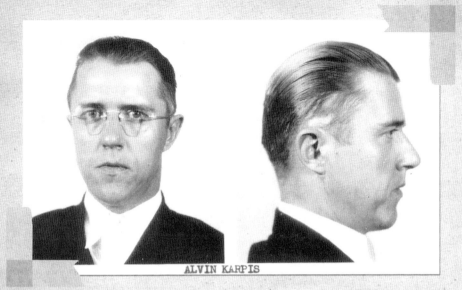

ALVIN KARPIS

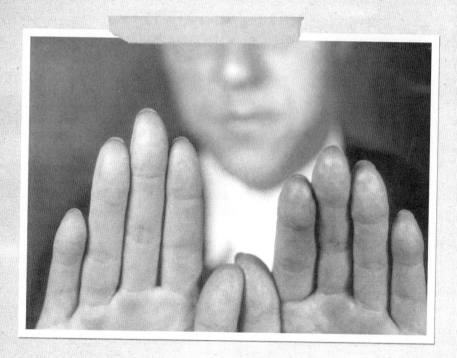

(Top) Depression-era gangster Alvin Karpis.

Photo © FBI

(Bottom) Alvin Karpis's fingerprints, which he had altered to avoid detection.

Photo © FBI

Kidnapping victim Haskell Bohn and his father.

Photo © Minnesota Historical Society

William Hamm (right) and his brewery manager, W. W. Dunn.

Photo © Minnesota Historical Society

Edward Bremer and his father, Adolph.

Photo © Minnesota Historical Society

CONFIDENTIAL

kidnapping "an atrocious crime" inflicted upon a "kindly old man" and urged jurors to "protect your home and fireside and children" by imposing the death penalty.[94] Were the prosecutor's remarks a bit extreme, considering that the victim had been freed by the kidnappers, albeit after an ordeal in a confined space? Again, the prosecutor was inviting the jury to imagine what *could* have happened. The judge must have been thinking along those lines too. In early October, after the six defendants were convicted, he imposed life terms on three of them, Percy Fitzgerald, Randall Norvell, and Lillian Chessen. Mike Musiala drew twenty years, and Christ Gitcho and Charles Chessen (Lillian's husband) got five years each.

Any Washington politician with decent political antennae could sense the deepening public anger at kidnappers or at least those kidnappers who preyed upon good citizens instead of fellow criminals. Joseph B. Keenan, the special assistant attorney general who was the spearhead of the federal government's drive to stamp out kidnapping, made it a point to sit in on the trial of Luer's abductors.

Keenan stayed in Edwardsville only a few days. Then he was off to Oklahoma City to check on the status of yet another sensational kidnapping.

CHAPTER TWENTY-NINE

THE OIL TYCOON

Oklahoma City
Saturday, July 22, 1933

Charles Urschel and his wife, Berenice, and friends Walter Jarrett and his wife, Kelly, were playing bridge on the sunporch at the rear of the Urschels' Heritage Hills mansion. The home was routinely described as "palatial," and in fact Charles Frederick Urschel was a fabulously rich oil tycoon, a billionaire if his fortune were converted to twenty-first century dollars. Jarrett, his friend and sometime business partner, had also been very successful in the oil fields.

Urschel, forty-four, was a powerfully built six-footer. He was occasionally called pompous, though not to his face. More charitably, he was described as forceful and dignified. He liked his privacy, didn't like to talk to strangers about his personal life, didn't like to read about himself in the newspapers. Who could blame him for that, really?

Besides, Urschel and his wife had good reason to be on their guard. The papers were full of lurid tales of kidnappings. Recently, the Urschels had read an article in *Time* magazine about the spread of the crime. It seemed that any family of means could be a target. Why, it was only last weekend that a banker in Alton, Illinois, was freed after being held for a week. He'd been taken right out of his home, and his wife had been roughed up! And as the foursome shuffled and dealt cards, the fate of John J. O'Connell Jr., the political prince of Albany, New York, was still unknown.

The Urschels' young daughter, Betty, had had a chilling experience just a few days earlier. While driving down from Tulsa, she'd spotted a blue car in her rearview mirror early on. She hadn't been alarmed at first, but the car, carrying two men, had stayed behind her all the way to Oklahoma City, more than a hundred miles to the southwest.

With loving firmness, Betty's parents told her to stay in the house. Maybe we'll hire a bodyguard if you absolutely have to go out, but otherwise, we want you to stay put, they said.

Dedicated bridge players, the Urschels and Jarretts stayed focused this Saturday night on spades, clubs, hearts, and diamonds. The weather had been in the nineties for a few days, hardly unusual for Oklahoma in July, but the night air on the screened-in porch was comfortable enough.

No doubt, the card players welcomed a respite from recent troubling economic events. Just three weeks earlier, on July 1, Albert R. Erskine, president of the Studebaker Corporation, was having breakfast with his family in their home in South Bend, Indiana, headquarters of the automaker. Studebaker was in deep financial trouble and had been placed in receivership, leaving Erskine president in name only. Rather abruptly, Erskine left the table, went to his study, and wrote a note: "I can't go on any longer." Then he picked up a revolver and fired a bullet into his chest, dying at age sixty-two.

And only four days before the bridge game, the stock market had reached its highest level of the year—only to plummet for three straight days, with Friday's trading the heaviest since October 30, 1929, when the economy had begun its spiral into the Great Depression.

It is likely that Charles Urschel and Walter Jarrett felt some sympathy for the thousands of speculators whose accounts had been emptied in Friday's trading. As oil men, Urschel and Jarrett knew what it meant to take big risks in business.

And there was disturbing news from abroad. Philip Zuckerman, a businessman who lived in New York City and traveled often to Leipzig, Germany, where he owned a business that imported furs from America, had been badly beaten a few days before by Nazi storm troopers. His wife had also been injured.

The Zuckermans and two relatives had been watching a parade of storm troopers when several marchers broke ranks and attacked, punching and trampling them. "One of my relatives wears a long beard, making it easy to pick him out as a Jew," Zuckerman said from his hospital bed in Berlin where he had gone for treatment.[95]

George S. Messersmith, the American consul general in Berlin, filed a protest with German government authorities, who promised "the most stringent action" against anyone found to have taken part in the assault. The Nazis, under Chancellor Adolf Hitler, had been in power less than six months, so perhaps it was too early to draw conclusions about them.

———

In the midst of the bridge game, Berenice Urschel thought she heard a car stop near the driveway. Moments later, as if in a dream, the door to the sunporch opened, and two men carrying machine guns entered. One was heavyset, the other more slender. The intruders were careful to stand in the edge of the light so their faces could not be seen clearly.

"Don't move or make a sound or we'll blow your heads off," the heavy intruder said. "Which one is Urschel?"[96]

Neither Urschel nor Jarrett replied. In their private lives, as in business and bridge, they had learned to hold their cards close to the vest.

"Well, come along," the heavy intruder said. "We'll take both of you."

The women watched in shock as their husbands were steered off the sunporch at gunpoint. The wives waited until they heard a car start and move away. Then they rushed to an upstairs bedroom, locked themselves in, and called the police.

Berenice recalled the *Time* article about kidnapping and that it had mentioned a new national hotline to call. She found the article and dialed the number: National 7117.

An operator answered, inviting her to go ahead. Understandably breathless, Mrs. Urschel said she needed to report a kidnapping. At that point, according to at least one account, a man's voice broke in. "This is J. Edgar Hoover, Mrs. Urschel. Give me every detail you can."[97]

———

The car had gone only a short distance when the driver said to his partner, "*Floyd*, give me a cigarette."

Jarrett had picked up the driver's extra emphasis on the name "Floyd."

A little farther on, the car stopped, and Jarrett was put out.

"If you want to help Urschel, don't tell anyone which way we're headed," one kidnapper said. "On your honor, if you have any honor."

Soon, Jarrett was able to hitch a ride back to Oklahoma City where he found Urschel's wife and daughter nervous but composed. There was nothing to do but wait for the kidnappers to name their price—and no one doubted that it would be steep.

"The ransom demand is expected to be one of the greatest ever made," a Texas newspaper, the *Austin American*, predicted two days after the kidnapping. "Few, if any, wealthier men have been held for ransom anywhere."[98] Not only were the Urschels wealthy, but their friends included some of the richest men in the oil industry, men who could be counted on to contribute toward Urschel's freedom.

The kidnappers probably didn't fully understand the kind of men Charles Urschel and Walter Jarrett were. Both had shrugged off losses and triumphed. They were tough, remarkably cool thinkers under pressure.

———————

Jarrett remembered what the kidnappers had said to each other: "*Floyd, give me a cigarette*," was one phrase. A few more times, the name "Floyd" was uttered, a bit louder than necessary.

Sure, Jarrett thought, smiling to himself. They're trying to put the blame for this latest kidnapping on Pretty Boy Floyd. His name had begun to surface in the Union Station Massacre, which had taken place only weeks before.

Jarrett had seen pictures of Floyd, and he was soon telling the police and reporters that neither of his captors looked a bit like him.

———————

For the rest of his life, Charles Urschel would remember the cold, empty feeling in his stomach as he lay on the floor of the sedan, his eyes taped shut. After a long while, the car stopped. From the smells, he thought he was in a garage. Then he heard faint metallic sounds. *They're changing license plates*, he thought.

He was put into another vehicle and told to lie down. After a few hours, the car stopped at a gas station. He was warned to keep quiet. He did and overheard a snatch of conversation.

"How are the farm conditions around here?" a kidnapper asked.

"The crops around here are burned up," a woman said as she pumped the gas.

Remember this, Urschel told himself. *The information may be useful.*

More hours went by. Finally, he was taken from the car and led through a gate into a house. He was placed on a cot. He heard one of his jailers lie down on a cot next to him. The prisoner heard the voices of a man and a woman. Then his ears were filled with cotton and taped over.

He was led to a second house and into a room where he was told to lie on some blankets in the corner. More voices, different from before. A handcuff was placed on one of his wrists, and the other hand was fastened to a chair. He slept fitfully.

━━━━━━━

In the morning, his jailers told Urschel to select a friend in Tulsa, write a letter to him, and say the ransom demand was $200,000—and there must be no funny business. Urschel chose J. G. Catlett, a wealthy oil man.

Urschel's handcuffs were fastened to a chain so he could move around a little. He was able to peek outside and saw chickens, hogs, and several cows. He was given a pair of pajamas to wear so his clothes could air out. He was fed canned tomatoes and beans. He was also given cigars—El Cheapo compared to what he was used to.

Days crawled by. He came to know the sound of the pulley used to haul buckets of water from the well. He mentally implanted the image of the old tin cup he was given to drink water from. He took care to leave his fingerprints on the cup and on surfaces in his little dwelling place.

He noted that each morning, a plane would go over around 9:45. Another would fly by around 5:45 in the evening. It rained very hard on the morning of Sunday, July 30, and no plane went over.

Urschel had vowed to remember each detail of his time as a kidnapping victim, from the moment he was abducted until—when? He wondered how his wife was bearing up, what his friends were doing to obtain his freedom. He wondered what was going on in the real world.

Two days after Urschel was taken, the FBI announced a time-out of sorts. It would suspend its investigation for twenty-four hours to give the kidnappers a chance to contact the Urschel family without interference. "Our only concern at this time is the safe return of Mr. Urschel," said R. H. Colvin, the agent in charge at Oklahoma City.[99] Local police, who had been guarding the Urschels, also agreed to step aside, for the moment, to put the kidnappers at ease.

By then, the crime was being investigated more intensely than any except the Lindbergh kidnapping. Hoover was so hungry to solve a high-profile case and polish his FBI's image that he pulled one of his top agents off the probe into the massacre at the Kansas City train station and assigned him to the Urschel case.

Hoover knew that Charles Urschel and President Franklin D. Roosevelt were friends.

On July 26, Urschel's friend J. G. Catlett got a Western Union package containing a letter from Urschel asking him to be an intermediary. There was also a letter from Urschel to his wife and a letter addressed to another friend of Urschel's, E. E. Kirkpatrick of Oklahoma City.

Kirkpatrick was instructed to obtain $200,000 in used twenty-dollar bills and to run an ad in the *Daily Oklahoman* reading: "FOR SALE—160 acres land, good five-room house, deep well. Also cows, tools, tractor, corn, and hay. $3750 for quick sale...TERMS...Box#_____"[100]

The kidnappers said they would be in touch after the ad had run—and they were true to their word. On July 28, the newspaper got a reply addressed to Kirkpatrick in Box H-807. It had been sent from Joplin, Missouri.

Kirkpatrick was told to pack the money in a light-colored leather bag. The next night, he was to board Train No. 28, "the Sooner," leaving Oklahoma City at 10:10 p.m. for Kansas City, Missouri. He was to sit in the observation platform and keep his eyes on the scenery in the direction the train was going. After a while, he would see a fire. That would be his cue to get ready to throw the bag off the train—which he was to do right after observing a *second* fire.

No tricks, the letter warned. No dummy package, no recording the serial numbers of the bills (the FBI did record the serial numbers despite the warning), no police involvement, or not only Urschel would be killed but "someone very near and dear to the Urschel family."

The letter said that, if the ransom drop-off went awry, Kirkpatrick was to proceed to Kansas City and register at the Muehlebach Hotel under the name E. E. Kincaid of Little Rock, Arkansas, and await further instructions.

Catlett and Kirkpatrick rode the train together, sitting in different sections of the observation car with identical leather bags—except that Catlett's contained the money, while Kirkpatrick's was filled with old magazines. Agents had decided on the dual-bag arrangement thinking it might somehow reduce the risk of a hijacking.

All night long, Catlett peered out the window into the darkness. Now and then, he saw lights from buildings and cars. But no fires.

In Kansas City, Kirkpatrick registered at the hotel under the name Kincaid and waited in his room. Soon, he got a telegram from Tulsa: "Owing to unavoidable incident unable to keep appointment. Will phone you about six. Signed, C. H. Moore."

Moore called around 5:30 p.m. Sunday, July 30, and told Kirkpatrick to take a taxi from the Muehlebach Hotel to the LaSalle Hotel, then walk west. After walking no more than half a block, Kirkpatrick was approached by a man who said, "Mr. Kinkaid, I will take that bag."

Bag in hand, Moore told Kirkpatrick to go back to the Muehlebach, that Charles Urschel would soon be released.

Kirkpatrick and Catlett checked out of the Muehlebach. Kirkpatrick returned to Oklahoma City, Catlett to Tulsa.

———————

"Well, Mr. Urschel, we are going to give you a shave and clean you up for a trip to town," one of the kidnappers said. It was Monday, July 31, and Urschel was very tired.

He was allowed to shave, then his eyes were taped shut once more, and then it was into a car, sprawled on the floor of a back seat again. But this time, Urschel dared to hope.

Another long, long ride. Then the car stopped. He was pulled out, and his eyes were untaped.

"You're just north of Norman," he was told. "Here's some money."

He could see the lights of the city. The car sped off into the night, and Urschel walked. After a while, he came to a hamburger stand, where he phoned for a cab. His captors had generously given him $10 for the fare. The taxi took him the twenty miles to his home in Oklahoma City.

Urschel rang the front door of his house. A man he didn't know opened the door, frowned at the dirty, unkempt visitor, then slammed the door.

"I got a big laugh out of being refused admission to my own house," Urschel recalled later. He made his way to the rear door, where the household help recognized him. How good it was to be home![101]

———————

Investigators checked airplane schedules within six hundred miles of Oklahoma City. American Airways had a flight that left Fort Worth, Texas, each morning at 9:15 for the 340-mile trip northwest to Amarillo, Texas, and a flight that left Amarillo for Fort Worth at 3:30 p.m.

Urschel had recalled hearing a plane for several days in a row at 9:45 a.m. and another at 5:45 p.m. But he had heard no plane on July 30, a day when there was pouring rain.

The airline people told investigators the Amarillo-bound plane was normally over Paradise, a somnolent little town in Wise County, Texas, some seventy miles northwest of Dallas, about 9:45 a.m. The Fort Worth–bound plane was normally over Paradise around 5:45 p.m. But the flight to Amarillo left Fort Worth two hours late on July 30 because of a storm and took a more northerly route—to avoid heavy rain in the Paradise vicinity.

Meteorological records showed the July 30 downpour was the Paradise area's first rain since May 20. The region had been so parched that the corn had begun to burn in June. What had Urschel heard the woman say at the gas station? "The crops around here are burned up."

So the Paradise area seemed a logical place to look for the kidnappers' lair. And since Urschel had seen cows, chickens, and pigs, it was a good bet he hadn't been held captive in "downtown" Paradise, to the extent there was one.

———————

On his farm several miles outside Paradise, Robert Green Shannon raised cattle until the grass withered during the Dust Bowl years. Then, like many other farmers, he struggled just to survive. As some other farmers did, he happily sheltered bank robbers and other criminals on the run. They typically gave him a few hundred dollars—big money, *precious* money—to let them hide out on his property for a few days.

Nothing had been easy for him. He was born in Arkansas in 1877, the sixth child of farming parents. Around the turn of the century, the family moved to Texas. Robert returned to Arkansas in 1904 to wed Mary Jackson, the daughter of a family friend, and the couple settled in Wise County, Texas. Mary died when she was only twenty-five, leaving Robert to raise their two young children. Soon, Robert went back to Arkansas and married his late wife's sister, Maude, who was just nineteen. They had three more children, and then Maude died in 1923.

In 1928, Shannon took up with a woman named Ora Brooks, a divorcée who had a daughter, Kathryn Brooks, from her first marriage. Ora's great-grandmother, a Cherokee Indian, had married a veteran of the War of 1812 who received land grants in Mississippi for his service. Thus, Ora and her three sisters were well educated by the standards of the time. After her marriage to Robert Shannon, Ora was said to have played the piano and taught Sunday school at churches in the Paradise area.

The family history is murky, but it is believed that Ora's daughter, Kathryn, married one Lonnie Fry in Oklahoma in 1918, when she was just fourteen. The next year, they had a daughter, Pauline, and apparently divorced not long afterward. Kathryn was briefly married for a second time, then divorced and proceeded to marry a Texas farmer and bootlegger named Charles Thorne when she was twenty-nine.

Charles Thorne soon died under puzzling circumstances, puzzling because he supposedly took his own life, leaving behind a perfectly typed suicide note that was grammatically correct—even though he was reputed to be illiterate.

Emerging from grief, Kathryn had a gangster boyfriend before meeting and eloping with George Francis Barnes Jr. Barnes was born in Tennessee on July 17, 1897. He went to school for a while, then tried being a salesman. He found that work unrewarding. Bootlegging was more exciting...and lucrative. He dropped the surname Barnes and went by Kelly, his mother's maiden name, or sometimes Kelley, perhaps to confuse lawmen when they were chasing him, which was often, as he liked to rob banks.

Years before, Kelly had married a teenage girl, had two children with her, then abandoned his family after realizing he wasn't cut out for domestic life. By the time he was in his early thirties, he had been arrested for liquor violations in Santa Fe, New Mexico, and Tulsa, where he was also charged with vagrancy. He did time in New Mexico State Prison and in federal prison at Leavenworth, Kansas, for selling bootleg liquor on an Indian reservation.

Upon getting out, he made up for his spartan existence behind bars. He loved fancy cars and other luxuries but didn't like the humdrum of a nine-to-five job. Luckily for him, he had a like-minded wife and friends, including the gangster and prison escapee Harvey Bailey, who was known for meticulously planning his bank heists.

Kathryn was handy with firearms and, according to legend, wanted to enhance her husband's masculine image. So she obtained a Thompson submachine gun from a pawnbroker and encouraged Kelly to practice with it on the ranch. Again, according to legend, Kelly supposedly got so handy with the weapon that he could write his name with bullet holes on the side of a barn. Thus he became known as "Machine Gun" Kelly, although it is unlikely that he was ever that accomplished with the Thompson.

Around this time, Kelly and Harvey Bailey were holding up banks with some frequency across the South and Midwest. Typically, they would head to Mexico after a heist, split up, and lie low for a few weeks, then hook up again to plan another job. Kathryn became an enthusiastic participant, taking part in the planning and helping to switch cars to stymie pursuers.

Surely, Kelly and his wife were shocked by the Union Station blood-bath on June 17, 1933. Just as surely, they had followed the exploits, real and imagined, of Verne Sankey, who had graduated from bank robbery to kidnapping.

Kathryn studied the society pages of several newspapers in the region, convinced that any of the "swells" who appeared in them must have money to spare. The oil baron Charles Urschel of Oklahoma City, about 185 miles due north of Paradise, was mentioned now and then.

So the stage was set for the events that began on the night of Saturday, July 22, 1933, as Urschel and his wife and their friends the Jarretts were playing bridge.

———

After Urschel was released and lawmen zeroed in on Paradise, Texas, and the surrounding area, they reasoned that an isolated ranch of several hundred acres just might have been the place where Urschel was held captive. Surveillance of the spread revealed that a conspicuous number of high-powered cars entered and left the ranch with some frequency.

Early on Saturday, August 12, 1933, a dozen lawmen from the FBI and the Dallas and Fort Worth police forces raided the ranch. They had expected to nab George Kelly, but he wasn't there. But to the lawmen's delight, they found Harvey Bailey asleep on a cot in the backyard, a machine gun and pistol by his side, other guns on the porch, and a powerful car poised for a getaway.

The man who had escaped so boldly from the Kansas State Penitentiary was prodded awake by the muzzle of a submachine gun and surrendered meekly. Perhaps he had lost some of his fighting spirit after being shot in the leg while robbing a bank in Kingfisher, Oklahoma, not long before. On his person was part of the Urschel ransom money, in marked twenty-dollar bills. Robert Shannon was arrested, as were several members of his extended family.

Urschel accompanied the lawmen on the raid. "Yes," he said after looking around the premises. "This is the room where I was held. There's the tin cup I drank from."

Urschel's fingerprints, which he had taken care to leave on as many surfaces as possible, confirmed his recollection.

Around the time of the raid, Albert Bates, a career criminal soon to be established as Kelly's partner in the Urschel kidnapping, was arrested in Denver. He, too, had some of the ransom money on him. Various other racketeers were swept up in St. Paul, Minnesota.

But where was Kelly? Had the roads been better in that era, he might have been just about anywhere, from Alaska to Miami or Boston to San Diego, considering that he drove a Cadillac with sixteen cylinders.

Weeks later, the Kellys were tracked to Memphis, where they had been put up by the brother of George's first wife. They were arrested early on the morning of September 26. Machine Gun Kelly never got to show his supposed expertise with the weapon that had given him his sobriquet. Instead, he surrendered his pistol as a tough Memphis police sergeant thrust the muzzle of a shotgun against his stomach.

And how disheartened Kelly must have been when his wife immediately pronounced herself relieved to be rid of the man who had lured her into wrongdoing: her husband!

Within months, more than a dozen people were convicted of taking part in the Urschel kidnapping, including several in St. Paul, Minnesota, where some of the ransom money had appeared. Besides the main players, George Kelly and Albert Bates, they included Kelly's newly unhappy wife and various people accused of secondary or even peripheral roles in the Urschel kidnapping.

One unfortunate soul was the brother of Kelly's first wife, the man who sheltered the Kellys in Memphis and who had run errands for them. There have been questions in the ensuing years as to whether the young man was even aware that his long-lost, one-time brother-in-law, whom he had known as George Barnes, was the wanted desperado Machine Gun Kelly. The young man had recently passed the Tennessee bar exam, but his aspirations for practicing law were dashed. He lost his law license and served time in prison for his marginal role, intentional or not, in helping the fugitive Kellys.

But Hoover was not overly concerned with legal niceties or collateral damage in his pursuit of bank robbers and kidnappers, or "sewer rats," as he described them. Nor did many reporters seem much interested in digging into possible miscarriages of injustice. On the contrary; newspapers were full of praise for the FBI, after Hoover boasted that his agents had secured the convictions or guilty pleas of twenty-one men and women in the Urschel case, with six of those people getting life sentences and others being sent away for years.

A movie newsreel was also unctuous. "Uncle Sam rolled up his sleeves and dealt gangland a swift, decisive blow," the newsreel narrator declared. "They are going for rides, and with the federal government at the wheel," the narrator said as the defendants were herded into a police van.[102]

In fairness, there was a lot of crime for editors and reporters to keep up with. On the weekend that Harvey Bailey was arrested at the Shannon ranch, a white mob in Alabama seized three young black men who were charged with murdering a young white woman. The prisoners were being transported by sheriff's deputies, their supposed protectors, from Tuscaloosa to Birmingham for safekeeping when they were ambushed on a dark country road.

Not long after they were spirited away, two of the men were found shot to death. The third was also shot but survived. Governor Benjamin Miller ordered an inquiry into how such a thing could have happened. Tuscaloosa County Sheriff R. L. Shamblin said he already knew: the International Labor Defense, a far-left group with communist links, had stirred up local feelings by assigning three lawyers to represent the defendants.

No inquiry was promised nor any comment offered on another

fatal shooting that weekend, that of a black man killed by the police near Tuscaloosa while swinging a club as he was resisting arrest for stealing chickens.

―――――

Harvey Bailey, who had escaped from the Kansas State Penitentiary the previous Memorial Day, the traditional start of the summer season, chose the official end of the season, Labor Day, to escape again, this time from the Dallas jail where he was being held while awaiting trial. On the morning of September 4, 1933, he sawed three bars from his tenth-floor jail cell and fled, armed with a revolver.

A reasonable person might have asked how one of the most wanted bandits in the country, a man who had already escaped from prison once, could break out again. Simple. A crooked deputy had smuggled hacksaw blades and the revolver into the jail and given them to Bailey. The fugitive was recaptured Labor Day afternoon in Norman, Oklahoma.

The deputy and an accomplice who had bought the blades were soon found out. The deputy was sentenced to two years in prison and his accomplice to fourteen months. The deputy's perfidy was a reminder, if any were needed, of the corruption that infected many police forces and sheriff's offices in that era.

―――――

The happy outcome of the Urschel kidnapping was a gift for Hoover, for even though he enjoyed wide support among the American people and seemed to be a master at shaping his own image, there were a few brave critics in the press corps. One was Ray Tucker, the Washington bureau chief of *Collier's* magazine, who wrote in the issue of August 19, 1933, that Hoover's agents were less competent than the director portrayed them to be, that Hoover kept them in "fear and awe by firing and shifting them at whim," and that Hoover was a publicity hound who walked with a "mincing step."[103]

That last was a veiled but hard-to-miss allusion to the fact that Hoover, then thirty-eight, was single and was never seen in the company of a woman except his mother, with whom he still lived. That attack on his masculinity had to smart.

———

Bailey was convicted just weeks later in federal court and sentenced to life for kidnapping. He was briefly confined to Leavenworth, but federal prison officials were not inclined to let him escape a *third* time. In September 1934, he was sent to a newly opened federal institution that was deemed to be escape-proof, perched as it was on a rocky island in San Francisco Bay: Alcatraz.

Machine Gun Kelly was also sent to Alcatraz in September 1934, presumably to live out his days there. Albert Bates had been sent to the dismal island months earlier.

Kelly's by now estranged wife was sentenced to life in the Women's Federal Prison at Alderson, West Virginia. Ranch owner Robert Shannon and his wife drew shorter but still substantial sentences.

The quick solution to the Urschel case, Hoover's well-publicized obsession with stamping out kidnapping, *and* the draconian sentences imposed on the defendants—would all those factors be enough to end kidnapping for ransom so that wealthy Americans could feel safe in their homes again? Hardly. At least not yet.

But a former deputy police commissioner of New York City was sure that *he* knew a way to stamp out kidnapping: make it a crime to pay ransom.

"After all, payment of ransom is accessory after the fact," Dr. Carleton Simon told the convention of the International Association of

Police Chiefs on August 1, 1933. "Kidnapping and all crimes would cease to be active when not lucrative and when the incentive is not there."[104]

Dr. Simon had become a criminologist for the New York Association of Chiefs of Police when he spoke those words, which showed no sympathy for someone who would pay money to get a kidnapped relative back.

"To my mind, the man who pays a ransom is a selfish individual endangering the lives of untold numbers," he went on boldly, if heartlessly. "He perpetuates and continues this nefarious traffic... This is a war against all crimes, and anyone who gives solace or information or contributes to the well-being of the criminal is as guilty as a traitor in actual warfare."

So, then, any parents whose child was kidnapped and who begged kidnappers to return the child unharmed and promised to pay money to see the child alive again—these people were traitors and selfish accomplices to crime. Far better, Dr. Simon seemed to say, for the parents to stand fast and refuse to pay a nickel. And if the child's corpse was found by a roadside, well, it was for the greater good.

Not surprisingly, Dr. Simon's coldhearted proposal went nowhere.

CHAPTER THIRTY

A MOMENTOUS MONTH

November 1933

As Thanksgiving Day* drew near, President Roosevelt expressed a hope: "May we on that day in our churches and in our homes give humble thanks for the blessings bestowed upon us during the year past by Almighty God... May we be grateful for the passing of dark days; for the new spirit of dependence one on another; for the closer unity of all parts of our wide land."[105]

But the "dark days" were far from over. For many Americans, a Thanksgiving Day feast with a golden turkey as the centerpiece was a vision hopelessly beyond reach. They would have to scrape to put any decent food on the table.

And events oceans away were casting ominous shadows. Although most Americans wanted to avoid getting swept up in another war, it was

---

* Again, the holiday was still celebrated on the last Thursday of November, not the fourth. In 1933, Thanksgiving Day fell on November 30.

getting harder to ignore what was happening in Germany. The assault on the American businessman Philip Zuckerman, who had been badly beaten by Nazi storm troopers in Leipzig in July, was looking less like an isolated occurrence and more like an ugly pattern.

So warned Samuel Untermyer, president of the World Jewish Economic Federation, at a September dinner in his honor in New York City. "A once proud and cultivated nation has been converted into a den of savage beasts of prey," he lamented, saying that the new regime was "bent upon the starvation and extermination of their own citizens."[106]

But former New York Governor Alfred E. Smith, who also spoke at the dinner, was less alarmed. The people in power in Berlin were so thuggish as to invite ridicule, he said, and "it is impossible for them to survive any length of time under ridicule."

Around that time half a world away, events in Japan seemed to portend an era of peace with the United States—or at least that was the opinion expressed in an interview in New York City with Count M. Soyeshima, described as "an outstanding Japanese liberal" who was an insurance executive in private life and was intimately familiar with the workings of his country's government. He declared that war between the United States and Japan was "unthinkable and impossible" and predicted that the Japanese army's influence in Tokyo would soon fade.[107]

———

Surely Arthur Koehler, the man who loved trees, had reason to feel blessed. On Thanksgiving Eve, as he stood in a lumberyard, he learned that his tireless work over many months had traced the wood used by the Lindbergh kidnapper from a South Carolina sawmill all the way to the Bronx.

And Chicago tough guy Roger Touhy and his lawyers could give thanks, at least for the moment. During a three-week trial, the basic weakness of the government's case against Touhy for the kidnapping of William Hamm became obvious. The several reliable witnesses that prosecutors had promised to produce turned out not to be so reliable.

Worst of all for the prosecutors, Hamm acknowledged on the witness stand, as he had earlier, that he wasn't really sure he could identify the men who had abducted him.

On Tuesday, November 28, the jurors deliberated several hours before acquitting the defendants. Afterward, some jurors made it clear that they considered the defendants to be unsavory characters, but that Hamm's shaky identification of his kidnappers was a fatal flaw in the government's case. "That, to my mind, was the climax of the case, even though it happened on the first day of the trial, when Mr. Hamm was on the stand," one juror said.[108]

"I think most of us would have preferred to have found them guilty," the jury foreman, T.O. Sundry, told reporters, "but we couldn't do it on the evidence the government placed before us."

The chief prosecutor, Joseph B. Keenan, who was in charge of Washington's war on racketeering in general and kidnapping in particular, was less than gracious in reacting to the federal government's first defeat in cases tried under the Lindbergh Law. "If a jury of citizens decides to turn these men loose upon the community, there is nothing we can do about it," he said, asserting that the Justice Department was still convinced the defendants were guilty.[109]

But perhaps not everyone in the DOJ was convinced. On its website today, the FBI proudly recalls how it eventually solved the Hamm kidnapping. "Using a then state-of-the-art technology now called latent fingerprint identification, the FBI Laboratory raised incriminating fingerprints from surfaces that couldn't be dusted for prints. Alvin Karpis, 'Doc' Barker, Charles Fitzgerald [another gang member], and the other members of the gang had gotten away, but they'd left their fingerprints behind—all over the ransom notes... The silver nitrate method and its application in the Hamm kidnapping was the first time it was used successfully to extract latent prints from forensic evidence," the bureau declares with pride, explaining how the silver nitrate solution reacted with leftover perspiration to form silver chloride and thus made the prints visible.[*110] "There they were: hard evidence that the Karpis gang was behind the kidnapping."

What a stellar example of the scientific approach to law enforcement that the FBI was pioneering and promoting!

But wait. The FBI says the prints were lifted on September 6, 1933. If so, Hoover and the lab officials knew two months before Touhy and his pals *even went on trial* that they had nothing to do with the Hamm kidnapping. Yet Keenan, the prosecutor, seems not to have known about the lab's finding, or why would he have said afterward that the Justice Department was still convinced Touhy and his associates were guilty?

If the FBI website is correct that the fingerprints of William Hamm's kidnappers were lifted on September 6, 1933, then Hoover and his top aides withheld that all-important information from prosecutors and let a trial proceed, knowing all the while that the defendants were not guilty.

But there was more. On May 6, 1935, more than a year and a half after the fingerprint discovery, the *Chicago Tribune* carried a brief report noting that $65,000 of the ransom in the Hamm case had been found in the Chicago Federal Reserve Bank, having flowed there from various cities, including Chicago, Cleveland, and Toledo, Ohio. The finding, the *Tribune* said, was "new evidence pointing to the Barker-Karpis gang as the kidnappers of William Hamm."[111] Remarkably, at least in my opinion, the newspaper did not bother to point out that the

---

*   Hoover recognized the potential of fingerprint analysis early on. From the mid-1920s, the FBI had been collecting prints from local law enforcement agencies. By the time the FBI laboratory was established in 1932, the bureau had a collection of several million fingerprints.

finding was further evidence, if any was needed, that Roger Touhy and his bunch had had nothing to do with kidnapping Hamm.

All this suggests that Hoover and a select few in the FBI concealed for many months their knowledge that the Karpis-Barker bunch were the real culprits in the Hamm case. But why the secrecy? If Hoover hid the knowledge so as not to tip off the Karpis-Barker gang that the FBI was on to them, Touhy and his associates still should not have been subjected to a trial. Again, the suspicion arises that Hoover just thought Touhy et al. belonged behind bars for…something.

Would the director have been so ruthless? Knowing what has been revealed about him since the 1930s—how he rewarded sycophants and rooted out critics, how he tried to crush people he perceived as his enemies—we can only conclude that he would have done almost anything to cling to power.

By this time, Hoover had established the FBI as his own fiefdom, answerable only in theory to the heads of the Justice Department. The attorney general at the time, Homer Cummings, who headed the DOJ from 1933 to 1939, was no friend of Hoover. In fact, when Cummings took office after Franklin D. Roosevelt's inauguration, he planned to oust Hoover and replace him with a former department official named Wallace Foster. Fortunately for Hoover, Foster died before Hoover could be jettisoned.

Then, just over three months into FDR's first term, came the Union Station Massacre, prompting the president to begin a much-publicized campaign on bank robbers, kidnappers, and killers who seemed to roam at will, especially in the Midwest. In those dark days of the 1930s, journalists had access to far less information than they do today. Government agencies and the police could dole out information—or withhold it—as they chose.

Still, by that time—no, long before—sharp journalists should have been saying to one another, "The Justice Department contradicts itself from one month to the next. It sounds like Hoover is the keeper of the secrets, cherry-picking the information he's willing to share, even with his so-called bosses. Who's really running the show?"

The fast-changing and conflicting accounts given by various officials, especially Hoover, were succulent, low-hanging fruit, ripe for picking by industrious reporters, not just for their own glory but for the public good. Instead, Hoover and his bureau got coverage best described as idolatry.

Occasionally, the journalists of the day became near contortionists in portraying the FBI as triumphant. Debacles were transformed into momentary setbacks that only inspired the bureau to go ever higher and further in pursuit of the truth. A reprise of the Hamm kidnapping, published in the *New York Daily News* on August 16, 1936, after the Justice Department had cleared up its own mess, called the eventual solution of the case "a brilliant victory—more brilliant, in a way, than any other triumph in the drive on the snatch racket, for at one time in this case the Government appeared to have been counted out... But we know now that the federal forces kept right on fighting. Their comeback bout has been a masterly one."[112]

But what about the ordeal of Touhy and his friends, who were no doubt guilty of a lot of things but were innocent of the kidnapping?

"This was not a defeat for American Justice," the article went on. "As a matter of fact, it was a magnificent triumph, for time was to prove that the Touhy mobsters had nothing whatever to do with the kidnapping of William Hamm."

If the Touhy acquittal was a "magnificent triumph," it was not because of the FBI. It was because of the conscientious Minnesota farmer who served as jury foreman and his fellow jurors. *They* saw through the government's case. If the FBI really did manage to lift the fingerprints of Alvin Karpis and his accomplices two months before Touhy even went on trial—and the FBI boasts that it did—justice was done not because of the FBI but despite it.

CHAPTER THIRTY-ONE

THE PEOPLE'S FURY
UNLEASHED

San Jose, California
November 1933

In the first half of the twentieth century, San Jose, California, was a small city in Santa Clara County near the southern end of San Francisco Bay. The city's population was a tiny fraction of what it would become in the twenty-first century, when it would surpass a million people.

In small-town San Jose, the wealthy Hart family was royalty. The Harts were well liked, for they were civic-minded, philanthropic, and friendly.

The patriarch, Leopold Hart, came to the United States from his native Alsace-Lorraine in the middle of the nineteenth century, eventually settling in San Jose and opening a dry goods and clothing store in 1866. In 1902, he started the L. Hart & Son Department Store in downtown San Jose. By 1920, it was the biggest department store between San Francisco and Los Angeles.

Leopold and his wife, Hortense, had a son, Alexander, and five daughters. Alexander, or Alex, as he was often called, gradually took over control of the store as his father aged and assumed full command when Leopold died in 1904. And Alex's son Brooke was groomed to take over from *his* father. On Thursday, November 9, 1933, Alex was expecting Brooke, who was twenty-two, to drive him to a meeting at his club; Alex himself didn't drive. The designated meeting time, 6:00 p.m., passed with no sign of Brooke. But the father was not alarmed, figuring that Brooke may have had car trouble—although Brooke's car was a new Studebaker roadster. If indeed the car had broken down, the Studebaker company would have some explaining to do!

Alex got a ride to his meeting, then a ride to the family's palatial home. He discovered that his wife, Nettie, hadn't heard from Brooke, nor had Brooke's younger brother, Alex Jr., nor had their sisters, Aleese and Miriam.

Around 8:00 p.m., Alex called the police, asking if his son had been in an accident. No, he had not, was the reply. "Then my son is missing," Alex said.

At once, the police arranged to intercept phone calls to the Hart's home. Around ten o'clock, a call came in. Pay $40,000 "if you want to see your boy alive again," a man told Alex, warning him not to call the police.[113]

But since a tap was already in place, the call was immediately traced to a public phone booth in the lobby of the Whitcomb Hotel in San Francisco. There was nothing Brooke's family could do except wait for instructions.

The next morning, Brooke's roadster was found on a remote stretch of road some twenty-five miles northeast of San Jose. The lights were still on.

At once, newspapers speculated that a big kidnapping ring from the East had come to the West to find fresh victims. The papers also feasted on rumors that Charles "Pretty Boy" Floyd, the gangster with several killings and robberies to his credit, was in the area. Soon, he was reported to be a prime suspect in the abduction of Brooke Hart. There were numerous abandoned silver-mining shafts and deserted cabins around San Jose that would make good hiding places. But searches turned up nothing.

Still, Brooke's father expressed optimism, noting that his son was strong and athletic.

Then, an apparent breakthrough. On Friday, Brooke's wallet was found on the guard rail of an oil tanker ship that had serviced the ocean liner *Lurline* in San Francisco harbor. Had the kidnappers dragged Brooke onto the *Lurline*, then thrown away his wallet? Or had Brooke himself managed to throw his wallet onto the tanker ship to aid searchers?

By the time the wallet was discovered, the *Lurline* was sailing overnight from San Francisco to Los Angeles on its way to Hawaii. When the vessel docked in Los Angeles on Saturday morning, the passengers were scrutinized, one by one. Now, investigators were checking a report that two stowaways might have boarded the ship. Were they the kidnappers?

Brooke Hart was not on the *Lurline*, nor was anyone who seemed a likely kidnapper.

But Brooke's family was heartened when two letters arrived at the Hart home over the weekend, one from Sacramento, the other from San Jose. Your son is all right, the letters said.

On Monday, November 13, investigators announced that telephone calls to the Hart house would no longer be intercepted. The announcement was meant to encourage the kidnappers to communicate instructions for Brooke's release. The next morning, federal and state investigators withdrew from the home entirely to further encourage the abductors.

A kidnapper called on Wednesday, November 15. Put $40,000 in a satchel, take the Malibu highway south toward Los Angeles, and look for a guy standing on the running board of a car, a man told Brooke's father. Give him the money, and he'll tell you where to find your son.

The call was traced to a nearby garage.* Sheriff William Emig and Police Chief J. N. Black raced there and arrested Thomas Thurmond just as he was hanging up. Thurmond, who was single and twenty-eight, directed the lawmen to a hotel, where they arrested John Holmes, whom Thurmond identified as his partner. Holmes, twenty-nine, was married and had two young children, although his marriage was strained because of his philandering.

Holmes had recently lost his job. Thurmond operated a San Jose gas station with his father. The suspects were interrogated separately for hours on end. When they finally cracked, they told what they had done.

They had become familiar with Brooke Hart's habits and travel and had talked about seizing him for ransom. Finally, as the young man was leaving a parking lot near the department store on November 9, Thurmond and Holmes were ready to act.

Holmes jumped into Brooke's car, pointed a pistol, and told him to drive. Thurmond followed in a separate car. Some miles away, Holmes told Brooke to stop. Then Brooke was forced into Thurmond's car. According to the kidnappers, he tried to hide his fear with a joke, something about it being the first time he had ever been kidnapped.

The kidnappers drove their captive to a point on the San Mateo-Hayward Bridge over San Francisco Bay and stopped.

---

* It is not clear from news accounts at the time if investigators were misleading the kidnappers when they announced on November 13 that they would no longer intercept calls to the Hart home or if they knew from earlier intercepts that the latest call must be coming from the garage.

By now, it was dark. The kidnappers forced Brooke from the car and put a pillowcase over his head. Holmes struck him on the head with a brick. The young man cried out, and Holmes hit him on the head again, rendering him semiconscious.

"They were pretty good blows, and he didn't give us much trouble after that," Thurmond recalled.

Then the kidnappers wrapped their victim with baling wire, tied two cement bricks to his body, lifted him over the bridge railing, and dropped him into the bay.

The shock of the cold water revived Brooke, and he called for help. Thurmond fired several shots at the body, and all was quiet.

"We thought it would be easier with him out of the way," one of the kidnappers explained matter-of-factly, according to a Justice Department official. "We didn't want to bother with lugging him around the countryside, and we didn't want to take the chance of his escaping and giving us away. So we just bumped him off."[114]

Before binding Hart and throwing him off the bridge, the kidnappers took his wallet. They split the money inside, pocketing $7.50 each. Then they drove to San Francisco, stopped at a speakeasy for drinks, and tried to phone the Hart home. They couldn't get a good connection, so they drove to the Whitcomb Hotel to use the phone booth there. Then it was back to San Jose.

So how did Brooke Hart's wallet wind up on the guard rail of the oil tanker? For some reason, Thurmond had kept the wallet. Then he thought it was best to get rid of it, so he decided to take a ferry across San Francisco Bay the night of the kidnapping and drop the wallet overboard. But instead of boarding the ferry, he had an impulse to throw the wallet off a pier. By the freakiest of chances, the wallet landed on the tanker guard rail and stayed there.

Thus, the ugly truth: Brooke Hart had not been kidnapped and slain by "professional" kidnappers from the East but by two unremark-able local men looking for quick and easy money. They could have had it, too, and without harming their captive, since Brooke's father would have given anything to have his son back.

Was jealousy a motive too? Brooke Hart had been born to privi-lege. Photographs of him showed a confident young man with wavy hair and an aristocratic bearing. He looked at ease in expensive clothes. He was everything Holmes and Thurmond were not.

On November 26, two duck hunters in a boat discovered Brooke's body floating in five feet of water half a mile south of the bridge. Alex Hart and his wife, Nettie, who had recently undergone surgery, collapsed upon hearing that their son was dead.

By this time, the press had reported that the confessions of Thurmond and Holmes did not jibe in every respect. Could the discrep-ancies help one or both of the killers avoid conviction and a trip to the gallows? There was also uncertainty as to who had jurisdiction. Was it Santa Clara County, since the victim had been kidnapped in San Jose? Or was it San Mateo County, since the victim had apparently been thrown off the bridge on the San Mateo side? But since the body was found near the bay shore of Alameda County, maybe Alameda should take charge.

When viewed without emotion (which was impossible for the people to do), these were not difficult questions. The issue of which county should have jurisdiction could have been resolved with friendly discussions among prosecutors.

But that would have taken time. The savagery of the killers, the nonchalant way they recounted their crime, had enraged the people of San Jose. They wanted *quick* justice. Talk of a lynching was in the air days before Brooke Hart's body was found. And Governor James Rolph said he had no intention of calling in the National Guard to protect a couple of lowlifes.

On the night of November 26, a crowd began to gather outside the San Jose jail. The crowd grew, morphing into a full-throated mob and lusting for blood.

Several times that night, jail officers hurled tear gas grenades to drive back the people. Then some men ripped two sections of heavy pipe, each some thirty feet long, from the construction site of a new post office next to the jail. Using the pipes as battering rams, the vigilantes surged into the jail, beating the sheriff and a deputy. The invaders seized the jailhouse keys and opened the cells that held Thurmond and Holmes.

The terrified prisoners were dragged to a park in front of the Santa Clara County courthouse, facing the jail. They saw ropes being hurled over tree limbs, to the accompaniment of whoops and cheers. Knowing the fate that awaited them, did Thurmond and Holmes, who had been unmoved by the terror and suffering of their victim, finally feel empathy for Brooke Hart?

Thurmond was first. Almost in a faint, he did not resist. Thousands cheered as his body was hoisted. But Holmes was powerful, over six feet tall and weighing more than two hundred pounds. He fought fiercely as the noose was tightened around his neck. Finally, he, too, was pulled up, writhing in the beams of flashlights as the mob howled.

———

The next day, Governor Rolph expressed his delight at the pioneer justice, calling the lynchings "a fine lesson to the whole nation."[115]

"With all the sorrows we have had, why should we add the sorrows of kidnapping?" he said. "It is about time the people should have comfort in their homes. This kidnapping business has become so bad that mothers and fathers are afraid to let their children out of their homes.

"Look at the Lindbergh case. Kidnappers have taken little children, killed them, and then jockeyed for huge sums of money. Now they have taken to kidnapping men and women for the purpose of extracting money from their distracted relatives."

Making clear that he had given considerable thought to his statement and that he meant exactly what he said, Rolph said he had checked to see how many California prison inmates were behind bars for kidnapping. He suggested that kidnappers be turned over to "those fine, patriotic San Jose citizens."

Rolph declared that no kidnapper would be released from prison while he was governor—and that he would pardon anyone arrested for lynching a kidnapper.

No doubt, many people felt as the governor did. Some said so publicly. "Congratulations on your attitude toward the Hart case," a minister from Redlands, California, wired Rolph. A former judge in Kansas City, Missouri, praised Rolph and the people of California "for their noble example in dealing with criminals."

But many people deplored the mob violence and Rolph's praise of it. "The very spirit of government has been violated and the state has been disgraced in the eyes of the world by a brutal outburst of primitive lust for vengeance," read a statement issued by the San Francisco Chamber of Commerce and signed by several prominent Californians, including former President Herbert Hoover, a Republican like Rolph. "A horrible crime had been committed which deeply moved every citizen, but lynching is unjustifiable and subversive of all government. It was mob violence, marked by the most degrading brutality."[116]

———

Two nights after the San Jose lynching, a mob estimated at seven thousand to nine thousand people broke into the jail in St. Joseph, Missouri, where Lloyd Warner, a nineteen-year-old black youth, was held on charges of sexually assaulting and beating a young white woman.

Warner had declared that he was ready to plead guilty; months earlier, he had escaped prosecution for attacking a black woman.

Police officers, jail guards, and several dozen National Guard troops tried to hold back the mob. Army tanks chugged to the jail. One tank driver was yanked out of his machine, putting it out of action. The mob dragged Warner to the courthouse lawn and hanged him from a giant elm tree. Then several people in the mob splashed gasoline on the corpse and set it afire.

Meanwhile, a lynching case in Maryland was playing out differently. In Salisbury, on the eastern shore of Chesapeake Bay, a mob gathered on November 28 with the collective purpose of freeing several white men who were suspected of taking part in the lynching of a black man several weeks earlier in Princess Anne, Maryland.

Local prosecutors had shown no urgency in investigating the lynching of George Armwood, twenty-four, who was suspected of attacking an elderly white woman on a country road. Nor had area residents pressed for prosecution. So Governor Albert Ritchie called up a contingent of three hundred Maryland national guardsmen to round up the suspects.

A mob estimated at three thousand people congregated outside the National Guard armory in Salisbury, railing against the governor and state Attorney General William Preston Lane Jr., who was in Salisbury that day. Some in the mob shouted their approval of California Governor Rolph's glee at the San Jose lynching. Shouts of "Lynch him!" were directed toward Lane, who wisely left town.

After holding back the mob with tear gas and bayonets, the guardsmen took the suspects to Baltimore to be jailed. But on November 29, just a day after the confrontation in Salisbury, a state judge in Princess Anne ordered the four suspects released, finding that the arrests had been improper. Outside the courthouse, a raucous celebration was punctuated by blaring car horns.

On the same day, Governor Rolph of California made it clear that he had not softened his vigilante attitude toward lynching. "No price is too high to pay if we can drive these fiendish kidnappers out of our state and nation," he declared. "When we consider the agony to which Brooke Hart, a fine sample of American manhood, was subjected, and when we think of the innocent Lindbergh baby wrested from the security of his very bed and murdered, can we blame the people for becoming aroused?"[117]

The violent events in late November 1933 and the extraordinary spectacle of a California governor applauding vigilante justice were treated by print reporters like the big stories they were. Had television and the Internet existed back then, there might have been serious debate on whether the country was changing in fundamental and deeply frightening ways.

Verne Miller, who had found his duties as a South Dakota sheriff too confining and so had turned to crime, was found dead in a ditch outside Detroit on November 29, 1933. He had been beaten and strangled. The FBI said it had information that he was killed in retaliation for shooting a mobster from Newark, New Jersey.

It seemed that the sunny prediction of former New York governor Alfred E. Smith that Adolf Hitler and his crew were too stupid to remain in power had been mistaken. On the contrary, Hitler now seemed firmly in control of Germany. It seemed that the very foundations of German society were crumbling. For one thing, a movement was underway to unite all Christians, Catholic and Protestant, under a new religion. "Together with Chancellor Hitler, we will build a new German church," Protestant bishop Ludwig Müller of Königsberg proclaimed in late November.[118]

Several other Protestant leaders, uneasy over Müller's ties to the Nazi regime, declared that they would have nothing to do with the movement, which embraced anti-Semitism. Nevertheless, Müller's statement illustrated how Nazism was affecting every aspect of German life.*

And while Americans shuddered at the thought of another war, there was a warning that, if one came, the U.S. Army would be ill prepared—unless drastic improvements were made. For the moment, the army was woefully below strength in numbers and equipment given "the obvious state of unrest now prevailing throughout the world," warned General Douglas MacArthur, the army's chief of staff.

But if Europe was in turmoil, there was at least some heartening news from the other side of the world. In a statement coinciding with the eve of Thanksgiving in America, the foreign ministry of Japan said it was hopeful that talks with the United States could head off any naval competition between the countries and thus preserve peace in the Pacific.

---

* The politically naïve Müller had been an obscure clergyman until his fervent Nazi beliefs caught the eye of Hitler, who had him installed as a bishop. Müller's movement never succeeded, and he committed suicide in 1945 in despair over Germany's defeat.

CHAPTER THIRTY-TWO

TOUHY'S TORMENT CONTINUES

Chicago
Monday, December 4, 1933

"With repeal less than 48 hours away, federal officials worked throughout today to put in running order the government's machinery for controlling the flow of legal liquor in wet states and protecting the dry."[119] So began a front page article in the *Chicago Tribune* trumpeting the end of the noble experiment, effective the next day, Tuesday, December 5. Utah had just become the necessary thirty-sixth state to ratify the Twenty-First Amendment, thus repealing the Eighteenth Amendment, which had established Prohibition. All across the country, people who liked an adult beverage or two (or four or five) now and then prepared to celebrate.

But it was a gloomy time for Roger Touhy, who had prospered by running illegal alcohol during Prohibition. Then there was Dan "Tubbo" Gilbert, the Cook County prosecutor, who was nothing if not persistent. With the acquittal of Touhy and his associates ("Touhyites," the Chicago papers called them) in the kidnapping of William Hamm, Gilbert was determined not to let Touhy escape his clutches. This time, he would try to get them for the kidnapping of "Jake the Barber" Factor (if indeed Factor had really been kidnapped).

On December 4, 1933, at Gilbert's request, Governor Henry Horner of Illinois signed warrants for the extradition from Minnesota to Chicago of Touhy and his associates Edward McFadden and Gus Schaefer. They had remained in jail in St. Paul on the authorities' assumption that Gilbert would want them sent to Chicago.

Another "Touhyite," Albert Kator, who had not been accused in the Hamm kidnapping, was also named a suspect in the Factor case. Yet another Touhy ally, Willie Sharkey, who had been a defendant in the Hamm case, had found the ordeal too much to bear. Emotionally undone despite being acquitted, he hanged himself in his jail cell in St. Paul.

In a coincidence that seemed remarkable but that Chicago journalists seemed not to have underlined, on the very day that Governor Horner signed the extradition order, the U.S. Supreme Court ruled that Factor should be extradited to Britain to stand trial in a stock-swindling scheme he had been accused of engineering, causing the loss of millions of dollars among people of means, including members of the royal family.

By the time of the Supreme Court ruling, the suspicions of British authorities—that Factor had faked his "kidnapping" to avoid extradition—had been well publicized, raising serious questions about whether Factor was a man who could be trusted to tell the truth about anything.

But Thomas J. Courtney, the Cook County prosecutor who worked closely with Gilbert, insisted that Factor should be allowed to stay and help bring Touhy and friends to justice.

Washington officials found Courtney's arguments persuasive, so Factor was allowed to remain stateside and to testify against Touhy and his codefendants. The first trial didn't go well for the prosecution— one juror admitted to lying under questioning during the jury-selection process, and another juror tried to get himself excused halfway through the trial—so a mistrial was declared.

Gilbert and Courtney weren't giving up. The defendants were soon put on trial again, and this time, all were found guilty. Immediately, each man was sentenced to ninety-nine years in prison—a compromise decided upon by the jurors, six of whom wanted to send the defendants to the electric chair.

"The jury had written 'finis' to the so-called terrible Touhys," a *Tribune* reporter declared.[120] The scribe indulged in some cruel sport, noting that Touhy appeared to become ill when the verdict was read, "gagging and coughing, his handkerchief held to his face." Schaefer was "white-faced." And Kator, "known as a cold-blooded gunman and killer, managed a last scornful grimace" as he was led from the courtroom.

But there was still more fun to be had. A few weeks later, Basil "the Owl" Banghart, a "machine gunner of the Touhy gang," as the *Tribune* put it, was tried separately for the Factor kidnapping.[121] Convicted on March 13, 1934, "the Owl," who it will be recalled was known for his big, slow-moving eyes and his wisdom, was immediately packed off to the penitentiary for ninety-nine years.

The *Tribune* writer had rich material indeed. Hours before Banghart was found guilty, "forces outside the law had disposed of Charles 'Ice Wagon' Connors, another Touhyite who had been identified as one of those involved in the Factor abduction...."

"His body, bullet-riddled, with his false teeth missing and a penny clutched in one rigid hand, was found beside 107th Street and a half-mile east of Archer Avenue," the reporter wrote. "It was the theory of the police that the copper coin had been left by the killers as a sardonic message to indicate that the notoriously stingy Connors had refused to contribute to the defense fund for his erstwhile companions," the writer explained.

There was such good sport to be had in the ordeal of Touhy and his fellow gangsters! And they *were* gangsters, if bootleggers and their henchmen qualified as such, though Touhy seems not to have been cut from the same cloth as some of the psychopathic killers of his era.

But from the vantage point of eight decades on, one cannot escape the feeling that something wasn't right about the verdict. Did none of the journalists know of Gilbert's ties to Touhy's rivals, the Capone organization? Did it occur to them to spotlight the fact that Factor was untrustworthy? Should they have dug a bit deeper?

The impression persists that Touhy and his gang were convicted, in effect, of being gangsters, that Gilbert and the jurors thought they belonged behind bars, if not for the "kidnapping" of Factor, then for... something. Maybe for being Touhy's rivals.

Anyhow, by early 1934, it seemed that Touhy was confined to obscurity forever. Nothing could have been further from the truth.

CHAPTER THIRTY-THREE

BREWER, BANKER, VICTIM

St. Paul, Minnesota
Wednesday, January 17, 1934

As summer morphed into autumn in the Upper Midwest, turning the leaves on the trees into a watercolorist's delight, there seemed to be no progress in the investigation of the kidnapping of William Hamm or at least none that the public was being told about. And suddenly, too suddenly for those who didn't ski or ice-skate or build snowmen, the trees were bare. It was winter again.

Edward G. Bremer had heard a rumor, which had been circulating among St. Paul's organized crime figures for months. The rumor was that he was the next likely kidnapping target.

Bremer was a prominent banker in a mob-infested city *and* an heir to a beer fortune. Inevitably, then, he occasionally did business with mob members or with people who knew mob figures. So it was no surprise Bremer was a target and that a kidnapping *that hadn't even happened yet* was grist for gossip.

Perhaps it said something about Bremer, or "Eddie," as he was known to relatives and friends, that he finally tired of having a bodyguard. So in November, out of arrogance or courage or both, he had told the bodyguard his services were no longer needed.

He wanted to live a normal life, or as normal a life as a wealthy man like him could live. Bremer was the president and owner of the Commercial State Bank. His father, Adolph, was majority stockholder in the Joseph Schmidt beer company. Adolph Bremer was also a personal friend of President Roosevelt and Minnesota Governor Floyd Olson.

On this cold Wednesday morning, Bremer, thirty-seven, left his eight-year-old daughter, Betty, at the Summit School. Then he started driving to his bank.

A short time later, a milk truck driver saw Bremer's car stop at an intersection and another car suddenly pull in front of it. The milk truck driver stopped to let some children cross the street. He turned to wave to the schoolchildren. When he turned his eyes to the traffic again, he saw Bremer's car driving away behind the car that had pulled in front of it.

When Bremer's car was found abandoned a short time later at the edge of the city, there were bloodstains on the front and rear seat cushions, so much blood that police immediately feared that Bremer was dead or dying.

Soon, a friend of Bremer, a wealthy contractor named Walter Magee, received a ransom note to forward to the family. It demanded $200,000 in used small bills and threatened death to Bremer if the demand was not met. Bremer himself had been forced to sign the note. His signature was shaky, nothing like his usual graceful penmanship, leading relatives to conclude that he must have been in great distress or in great pain when he signed his name.

Adolph Bremer had contacted the police right after his son was taken. A federal agent who had worked on the Urschel kidnapping immediately flew from Dallas to St. Paul. Other federal agents joined him. Phones at the Bremer home were tapped.

"Please don't make any move that will endanger Eddie's safety," the elder Bremer begged the police publicly.[122] The old man made it clear he wanted federal, state, and city lawmen to do virtually nothing while he and family representatives tried to recover Edward.

Hamstrung by the father's pleas, the police and federal agents agreed to stand down to await further word from the kidnappers. The kidnappers assumed that phone lines to the Bremer home were tapped, so they communicated via written messages. The kidnappers were not fools, after all. More importantly, given the nature of the St. Paul police department, it was likely that information about the investigation was being leaked to the kidnappers or to people in contact with them.

As the kidnappers had instructed, the Bremer family placed an ad in the *Minneapolis Tribune*, indicating a willingness to cooperate. "We are ready. Alice," the ad read.

Then, three days after the kidnapping, there was devastating news. The postmaster of Minneapolis, W. C. Robertson, announced the receipt of an anonymous letter addressed to him but meant to be read by "a Federal officer," according to the writer.

"Very sorry, but Edward Bremer is now resting in peace," the letter declared. "Was by accident bumped off. Body near Anoka, Minn. Will not be found until after the snow thaws. Contact all off. Please forgive us. All a mistake by one of our gang being drunk."[123]

Investigators who conferred with the postmaster concluded that the letter was probably from a crank. But the letter couldn't be ignored, especially since on the lower left corner, there appeared to be a rough diagram of three roads and a curved line. Did the curved line depict a section of the Mississippi River? Platoons of investigators searched both banks of the river, paying special attention to irregularities in the snow.

Nothing.

Then Joseph B. Keenan, the assistant attorney general spearheading Washington's drive to combat kidnapping, made an especially tactless remark that deepened the family's ordeal: "In the Bremer case we may have the misfortune of experiencing another Lindbergh situation."[124]

Magee, who had become the intermediary between the kidnappers and the Bremer family, pledged publicly that the family would let the kidnappers have a free hand—if only they would release their victim unharmed.

<hr>

Edward Bremer had been thoroughly traumatized. The men who'd seized him had pistol-whipped and punched him repeatedly. They had slammed a car door on his legs when he'd tried to break away. He'd been pushed down under the dashboard of the kidnappers' car for a time as he was driven hundreds of miles.

Somewhat reluctantly and emphasizing that he wouldn't have been roughed up if he hadn't resisted, his captors let Bremer clean himself up. Then they put mercurochrome on his wounds. Bandages were applied, some over his cuts, others over his eyes to blindfold him. Cotton was stuffed into his ears.

He was forced to sit on a bed facing the wall in a gloomy room. He was determined to remember as much as he could. He concentrated on the pattern of the wallpaper. He listened to the voices in the house, up to a dozen different ones at one time or another. He heard dogs barking. He heard cars outside occasionally—but no streetcars. *So*, he reasoned, *I'm not way out in the country, but I'm not in the heart of a city either.*

Most intriguingly, Bremer heard chimes from a church—not bells, but chimes. Twice a day, they played the "Angelus," a song he recalled from his youth. He tried to remember all the sounds. He hoped they would be useful if he were freed. And concentrating on something, *anything*, was a way to keep from going mad with terror.

He wrote a dozen notes to his family, trying to be reassuring. But in a note specifically to his father, he made it clear that captivity was an ordeal, and he asked for quick action to free him.

The kidnappers, in messages accompanying Bremer's notes, warned that the ransom demand would be raised to $500,000 if the initial $200,000 demand were not paid quickly. In fact, the family was eager to pay up to get Bremer back. Early on, Magee was instructed to take the $200,000 to a hotel in Des Moines, Iowa. He was to travel by bus. Unfortunately, the money was in a bank vault at the time, secured by a time lock, so the bus trip had to be canceled.

Finally, an arrangement was made. Magee would rendezvous at night with one or more of the kidnappers at a point on a road near Zumbrota, Minnesota, a little town fifty miles south of St. Paul. On the designated night, Magee drove for miles into the darkness until he saw blinking headlights and four red lantern-like lights by the road—the signal. He stopped, encountered two men, and gave them two cardboard packages with the money.

The kidnappers had let Bremer know that they were honorable people, in a sense. They told him that a rival gang had offered to "buy" him so they could extort money from the Bremer family. But don't worry, the kidnappers told Bremer with perverse pride. We'll keep our word.

On the night of Wednesday, February 7, 1934, Bremer was stuffed into a car in the company of three kidnappers. He dared to hope that his ordeal was ending. By this point, time and distance had lost all meaning for him. After traveling on a paved highway, the car pulled onto a gravel road. Two of the kidnappers got out, removed cans full of gasoline, and refueled the car. Then they drove back to the paved highway to continue the journey.

Finally, Bremer was put out of the car at Rochester, Minnesota, about eighty-five miles south of St. Paul. He made his way home by train and bus, still bruised and dazed. Given the hours that Bremer had spent in the kidnappers' car after he was seized, investigators speculated that he might have been driven to Kansas City, Missouri, some 440 miles due south of St. Paul. After all, Kansas City had a vibrant mob presence, and the kidnappers surely could have found accommodations there.

But they would have been welcome in Sioux City, Iowa, as well. Some 280 miles southwest of St. Paul, Sioux City had a population of about eighty-five thousand and was known informally as "Little Chicago" because of its thriving beer businesses during Prohibition.

But what about the chimes Bremer recalled hearing during his captivity? How many Catholic churches were there within a radius, say, of three hundred or four hundred miles of St. Paul that chimed out the "Angelus" twice a day? Maybe that was an angle worth pursuing.

Only hours after Bremer returned safely to his home, agents had more concrete clues to go on. The clues had practically been gift-wrapped for them—and their discovery made it clear that while the kidnappers of Edward Bremer were nasty, violent men, they were not particularly intelligent.

In retracing the route taken by Magee to rendezvous with the kidnappers, agents found four flashlights fitted with red lenses next to the road several miles south of Zumbrota, Minnesota. The flashlights bore the trademark "Merit Product." Checking the outlets where flashlights of that type were sold, the agents found that one outlet was the F. & W. Grand Silver Store in St. Paul.

Meanwhile, on February 10, a farmer near Portage, Wisconsin, found four empty gasoline cans and a tin funnel by the side of a road near his spread. He turned them over to the local sheriff, who turned them over to FBI agents, who immediately sent them to Washington for testing.

A clerk at the Grand Silver Store was shown a photograph of a man whose criminal exploits throughout the region were well known. Yes, she said. That was the man who bought the flashlights. His name was Alvin Karpis. His nickname was "Creepy," perhaps because of his eyes, which glittered with malevolence, and his pouty, mean lips.

The kidnappers' carelessness in leaving the flashlights and red lenses at the ransom-drop site was a big break for investigators. Had the kidnappers taken the flashlights and lenses with them, it probably would have taken much longer to trace the purchase to the Grand Silver Store.

And back came the results from the FBI laboratory in Washington. Its vaunted fingerprint unit had lifted a latent print from one of the gasoline cans. It had been made by the right index finger of one Arthur "Doc" Barker, whose fingerprints were in the FBI's collection because of his earlier arrests.

Feeling intense heat, members of the Barker-Karpis gang began darting hither and yon across the country, occasionally recruiting quack doctors to perform makeshift plastic surgery. Some gang members ventured as far as Cuba. The big showdown would come in a remote rural part of Florida where people coexisted with alligators and coral snakes.

But before that happened, a veritable feast of crime news (and entertainment!) would be served up almost daily.

CHAPTER THIRTY-FOUR

A GAMBLER FOLDS
HIS HAND

Chicago
Early 1934

Verne Sankey knew all the clichés of gambling; he *lived* by them. You have to play the hand you're dealt; you have to know when to hold and when to fold. It was neither fair nor unfair if you were dealt three bad hands in a row—or three good ones. It was what it was.

But there was one gambling cliché he failed to heed: quit while you're ahead.

He had pulled off the kidnapping of Haskell Bohn, the son of a refrigerator tycoon, in St. Paul, Minnesota, the previous summer. No one had been hurt, and the operation had netted a decent profit. He probably should have bowed out of the kidnapping racket right then.

But no. He had gone to Denver and masterminded the kidnapping of Charlie Boettcher in February 1933. The Boettcher family was wealthier and more influential than the Bohns, so it should not have come as a surprise that the Denver kidnapping generated much more heat. Plus, the operation was accompanied by a shootout with the police.

Sankey had become a trophy for ambitious lawmen. But it wasn't all his doing! He'd had nothing to do with the kidnapping of William Hamm, even though the newspapers had all but declared him guilty in that snatch. And the fact that Charlie Boettcher and Charles Lindbergh were friends had stirred whispers that Sankey might even be involved in the Lindbergh kidnapping. Yes, he was a gambler, bootlegger, robber, and kidnapper, but he was no killer. The very idea that he could have killed a *child* must have wounded him deeply, for he was a husband and father, a family man.

All right, he was not a *perfect* family man. He'd fled to Chicago to lie low, and he'd been lonely. So he'd taken up with another woman. After all, he didn't know when he'd be reunited with his wife, Fern, if ever. He tried to build a new life for himself in the Windy City.

———

Sankey had read newspaper reports about himself, in particular articles describing three prominent moles on his face. So one day in January 1934, he had a doctor remove them with an electric needle. Then he grew a beard, as the removal of the moles had made him unable to shave. By this time, he had become a regular at John Mueller's barbershop at 4823 North Damen Avenue in the city.

A sharp-eyed Chicago woman who lived in the neighborhood had spotted him on the street more than once, entering or leaving the barbershop. She remembered Sankey's photographs in the newspapers and called the FBI's Chicago office. This time, the occasionally dense Melvin Purvis listened alertly. He visited the barbershop and showed a photo of Sankey to the proprietor. "Yes," Mueller said. "That's one of my regulars. His name's W. E. Clark."

"No, it isn't," Purvis told the barber. "It's Verne Sankey. We'll be watching for him."

Purvis assigned several agents and handpicked Chicago cops to stake out the shop. This they did, day after frigid Chicago day. Nor did night guarantee a respite. There was a funeral parlor next door to the barbershop, and some agents slept in coffins so they could awake refreshed and in time to watch the barbershop from the moment its doors opened.

On Wednesday, January 31, Sankey entered the barbershop, looking uncharacteristically sloppy in a baggy suit. He wanted a haircut. As he sat nestled in the chair with a sheet around him, three federal agents and three Chicago detectives walked in. Two detectives approached Sankey, one on each side, and pressed the muzzles of their handguns against his head.

"Don't move, Verne," said Sergeant Thomas Curtain. "We're police officers. You're under arrest."[125]

Sankey surrendered meekly. When investigators searched the apartment where he had been living, not far from Wrigley Field, they found some $3,500 in cash, a shotgun, two pistols, and a supply of ammunition.

Under questioning, Sankey—who had somewhat improbably been pronounced "Public Enemy No. 1" by the Justice Department, largely because of the speculation linking him to several unsolved kidnappings—readily admitted to having snatched Haskell Bohn and Charles Boettcher, but he denied any part in the kidnapping of Edward Bremer. And he became indignant at the merest suggestion he might have been involved in the Lindbergh kidnapping: "I am a man. I would kidnap a man. I would never kidnap a child."[126]

<hr />

The Justice Department seized jurisdiction and made plans to ship Sankey to Sioux Falls, South Dakota, to have him answer first of all for the kidnapping of Charles Boettcher, who had been transported across state lines, giving Washington jurisdiction in the case. Sankey's wife was already jailed in Sioux Falls awaiting trial for conspiracy in the Boettcher case (she had been acquitted earlier in the Haskell Bohn kidnapping).

Manacled and escorted by several agents, Sankey made the journey to Sioux Falls by train. People who knew Sankey were aware that he had vowed never to go to prison, that he could not stand the thought of his two children growing up with a jailbird for a father. Perhaps these people should have spoken up, should have told the authorities that Sankey had a personal code of honor.

On the night of February 8, 1934, Sankey freed himself from his captors. Careless jailers had failed to confiscate the two neckties he had with him in his cell. These Sankey fashioned into a noose, put the loop around his neck, fastened the other end of the ties to a crossbar, and stepped off his cot.

Sankey's new widow screamed for an hour after hearing of her husband's suicide.

Charlie O' Brien, a *Denver Post* reporter who had followed Sankey's career, injected no compassion into his writing. "While this notorious outlaw and kidnapper was running loose with a gun preying upon unarmed victims, he obtained the undeserved title of being a 'desperado with nerve and bravery.' Sankey took the easy way out—suicide— leaving his widow and two children, Echo, 15, and Orville 5, to make their way thru life alone."[127]

Two days after the suicide of Verne Sankey, one of his accomplices, Gordon Alcorn, began serving a life term in federal prison for the kidnapping of Charles Boettcher. On his way to Leavenworth, he offered advice to young people tempted to embark on a life of crime: "Look into the future first. Try to see the terrible consequence and then avoid what I am facing now."[128]

CHAPTER THIRTY-FIVE

WHAT MIGHT HAVE BEEN

The Bronx, New York
Wednesday, February 14, 1934

New York City was shivering in a cold wave. The previous Friday, February 9, the mercury had fallen to fifteen below zero in Central Park, the coldest reading ever in New York City. Now, on this Ash Wednesday and Saint Valentine's Day, there was some relief, relatively speaking. It was three degrees at 8:30 in the morning; the temperature would top out around twenty in midafternoon.

Arthur Koehler and New Jersey Detective Lewis Bornmann visited another Bronx lumberyard and building-supplies company, Cross, Austin & Ireland, hoping to trace the origin and sales history of the Douglas fir that the kidnapper of the Lindbergh baby had used to fashion some parts of his ladder.

This time, they seemed to be lucky. This lumberyard kept scrupulous records. Koehler and Bornmann asked to see information on transactions from the previous three months.

"Certainly," said Arthur Tinker, secretary of the company. "And let me say you're lucky you don't have to copy the list of what we sell when times are good."

Just then, something strange occurred. As Koehler and Bornmann sat waiting in the lumberyard office, two men entered. One offered a ten-dollar gold certificate to buy a forty-cent piece of plywood.

"Do you have anything smaller?" cashier Alice Murphy asked. She had been warned to be on the lookout for counterfeit gold bills. Genuine ones were being withdrawn from circulation and were therefore becoming scarce.

The man who wanted the plywood snatched back the gold certificate as Alice Murphy was scrutinizing it and pulled out a five-dollar bill. The cashier went to the rear, near the little cubbyhole where Koehler and Bornmann were sitting, to open the safe so she could change the five-dollar bill for five singles.

When the cashier returned to the counter, the second man said, "Never mind. I have the change." Whereupon he plunked down forty cents. Then the man who had wanted to buy the plywood took the five singles from the bookkeeper, and both men started to leave. There are conflicting accounts on whether they abandoned the plywood altogether or said they'd return to pick it up after it had been cut to a certain size.

Both the yard foreman and Alice Murphy thought the men's behavior odd, so much so that Alice Murphy wrote down the license number of the small green car in which they drove away: 4U-13–41. But neither the foreman, who recalled one of the men as a previous customer, nor Alice Murphy thought to mention the encounter to Detective Bornmann and Arthur Koehler. And why would they have? The investigators, guided perhaps by an excess of caution and discretion, had chosen not to tell the people at the lumberyard that they were investigating purchases in connection with the Lindbergh kidnapping.

Looking back on the incident months later, Koehler recalled that his Forest Service badge might have been visible beneath his overcoat. And Detective Bornmann—well, he might have looked like the cop that he was.

Had there been more communication, yard employees might have remarked to the investigators on the nervous departure of the men who had left the plywood behind, might have wondered aloud if the very presence of the investigators had scared the men away. Alice Murphy might have told the investigators that she'd written down the license number of the car.

If that had happened, the Lindbergh case might have been solved months earlier than it was. Reflecting later on that reality, Koehler wrote that the close encounter at the lumberyard "keeps me wondering at the endless repercussions of all men's acts, that in a Niagara of mysteries pour down upon us unperceived, not understood, each day."[129]

Koehler and Bornmann were never able to trace the path of the Douglas fir used in the kidnapper's ladder. As for the car for which Alice Murphy wrote down the license number, it belonged to a man who lived in the Bronx. His name was Bruno Richard Hauptmann.

CHAPTER THIRTY-SIX

A SORDID DENOUEMENT

St. Louis
February 1934

After almost three years, Dr. Isaac Kelley, St. Louis's leading ear, nose, and throat specialist, had put his kidnapping ordeal behind him. At least the doctor had a good story to tell.

So, it turned out, did one Adolph Fiedler, a man hard to describe in a few words. He had been a justice of the peace in Maplewood, Missouri, where he distinguished himself by being indicted several times for soliciting bribes, accepting illegal fees, and perjury, among other things. But he was never convicted, a fact that said much about the administration of justice in St. Louis at the time.

By early 1934, Fiedler had money troubles. He ran a "recreation parlor," consisting of a tavern, restaurant, pool hall, and dance floor, that was barely earning enough to keep food on his table. And Fiedler needed a lot of food, since his weight fluctuated from three hundred pounds or so to more than five hundred pounds.

Fiedler knew he had a story to tell, a story to *sell*. He recalled that John Rogers, the indefatigable reporter for the *St. Louis Post-Dispatch*, had had a role in the release of Dr. Kelley. So Fiedler contacted the newspaper and promised an exclusive that would make many ears among the city's elite burn with embarrassment.

———————————

Perhaps John Rogers thought he had seen and heard just about everything. He was wrong, as he discovered when balding, blimp-like Adolph Fiedler waddled into the newsroom of the *Post-Dispatch* and announced that he knew who had pulled off the kidnapping of Isaac Kelley.

The *Post-Dispatch* offered Fiedler $1,000 to start with, plus $50 a week as sort of a retainer. No reputable news organization would agree to such a story-for-money deal today, but back then, competition among newspapers was intense, and ethics were flexible.

"How do I know who kidnaped Dr. Kelley?"* Fiedler began his fantastic story.[130] "Because the men who did the job hung around my place...because I had their confidence, and because I sat in at their conferences and heard the telephone calls that took Dr. Kelley out of his home. The kidnapers knew me and talked freely to me, but I took no part in the job myself."

Fiedler had no trouble naming the kidnappers. Three were professional criminals who had been slain in a gang fight about a year after the kidnapping, according to Fiedler. They were Tommy "the Rock" Hayes, leader of the Cuckoo Gang of professional criminals, and two of his associates, "Willie G." Wilbert and Harry "Pretty Boy" Lechler.

Others involved in the Kelley kidnapping were still around, according to Fiedler. He identified them as Felix "Hoosier" McDonald, who

———————————

* The newspaper's style was to render the noun and verb "kidnaper" and "kidnaped."

was then in prison on an unrelated robbery charge; Bart Davit; Angelo John "the Dago" Rosegrant; Tommy Wilders, associated with a St. Louis gang; and John C. Johnson, "a Negro farmer," as he was described at the time, on whose Saint Charles County property McDonald and Davit operated a still. It was there, according to Fiedler, that Kelley spent his first night in captivity.

Most intriguingly, according to Fiedler, the inspiration and ringleader of the kidnapping was a woman described in the initial story as "Mrs. N———." Why her name was not spelled out at first is not clear, but it was soon revealed that she was Nellie Tipton Muench. She was the daughter of the Reverend William Ross Tipton, a prominent Baptist minister in Columbia, Missouri, and the wife of Dr. Ludwig Muench, a well-known physician who was also an accomplished cellist. Dr. and Mrs. Muench lived in the same fashionable neighborhood as Dr. Isaac Kelley and his wife and traveled in some of the same social circles.

There was one other thing: Muench was a sister of Justice Ernest Moss Tipton of the Missouri Supreme Court. So given her family and social status, was it conceivable that she had masterminded a kidnapping, that she was "the high priestess" of the entire enterprise, as Fiedler put it?

Muench ran a dress salon with a clientele that included wealthy and influential men buying gifts for their mistresses. On at least one occasion, she visited the Kelleys' home to alter a dress she had sold to Isaac Kelley's wife, Kathleen. While tugging and stitching, Muench asked her if the doctor ever made any professional visits at night. Occasionally, Kathleen Kelley said.

At the time, Muench's dress shop was in debt. Since she had had at least one prior brush with the law (in 1919, she was arrested for stealing jewelry from a guest at a St. Louis hotel), the idea of committing a crime was not inconceivable to her.

There was early talk about kidnapping a member of the Busch

family, but it was decided that snatching someone from the clan that headed the beer empire would bring too much heat. After all, the sensational kidnapping of young Adolphus "Buppie" Orthwein on New Year's Eve 1930 was still fresh in the civic memory.

To judge by the wealth of detail that he supplied to John Rogers, Fiedler listened acutely as Muench and her accomplices brazenly discussed how to go about grabbing Dr. Kelley. Muench and at least some of the other plotters infiltrated a birthday party given at a hotel for Kathleen Kelley in early April 1931, barely two weeks before the kidnapping, to size up their prey. In fact, William D. Orthwein, one of Buppie's cousins, was married to Kathleen Kelley's sister, and he later testified that Muench and a man he recognized as Rosegrant were dancing nearby and drifted near the birthday party gathering as if showing a special interest.

"Don't worry," Muench told her confederates at some point. "I'll figure out how to get the doctor out of his house at night." Eventually, she learned the name of a prominent Chicago doctor with whom Kelley was acquainted. Whichever kidnapper called Kelley the night he was to be kidnapped was to use the name of the Chicago physician to gain Kelley's trust.

Unfortunately, neither McDonald nor Davit, who were to pull off the actual abduction, bothered to write down the name of the Chicago doctor. So on the stormy night when they planned to grab Kelley, they first stopped at Fiedler's hangout, where one of them telephoned Muench and sheepishly asked her to say the name again. Ballinger, she reminded him.

Then McDonald, calling himself "Holmes," called the Kelley residence and pleaded for the doctor to come and minister to his sick nephew. When the doctor balked at first, McDonald waited a while and called him again, this time persuading him to embark on what he thought was an errand of mercy.

Then McDonald and Davit "examined their pistols and asked me to wish them luck," Fiedler recalled. And off they went to snatch the doctor.

In Fiedler's recollections, the kidnapping was a failure. Not only were the abductors unable to collect a ransom, but by April 29, when he saw McDonald and Davit, "they were tired of cooking" for their prisoner and wanted to give him back.

———

State prosecutors obtained indictments against Rosegrant, Johnson, McDonald, Wilders, and Muench in March 1934, although Wilders remained a fugitive. The defendants successfully petitioned to have separate trials, and prosecutors elected to try Rosegrant first. They announced that they would seek the death penalty.*

Rosegrant went on trial in late September 1934. A key witness against him was supposed to have been Johnson, the farmer in whose home Kelley was held initially. Johnson had pleaded guilty months before and agreed to testify against the other defendants in hopes of a lighter sentence. Alas, his own sentence was death—not imposed by the state but by assassins armed with machine guns and presumably bent upon obtaining his silence. They gunned him down on May 12, 1934, as he was sitting outside the garage of a sheriff's deputy to whose home he had been sent for safekeeping.**

Upon hearing of the slaying, Fiedler decided to go into hiding. "It

---

* Since the kidnapping had taken place more than a year before enactment of the Lindbergh Law, that federal statute did not apply to the case. But Missouri lawmakers had made kidnapping a capital crime under state law in response to the plague of abductions in their state.

** An account in the *St. Louis Post-Dispatch* the next day told much about the casual racism that was the accepted order of the day, in St. Louis and elsewhere. A front page photo of the victim identified him by race, and the main article noted that he was a "Negro farmer." The headline was "Machine Gunner Murders Negro Who Implicated Three in Kidnaping of Dr. Kelley."

might be a good idea for me to put a few miles between myself and St. Louis," he reportedly told a friend.[131] Soon, he was placed in the county jail where, presumably, he would be even safer than he would have been at the home of a deputy.

Fiedler probably made a wise decision. Initially, the St. Louis police thought they had promising clues to the slaying, as witnesses had noted the license plate number of the car carrying the assassins. But just two days after Johnson was shot to death, it was discovered that the plates had "mysteriously disappeared from the State Auto License Bureau" weeks before, and there was no record of their having been issued to anyone.[132]

During the trial, Dr. Kelley identified Rosegrant as one of his captors and McDonald as one of his abductors. He also testified that he recognized Johnson's house as the location where he had been held for about thirty hours.

Rosegrant was convicted on October 4 and sentenced to twenty years in prison. Soon afterward, prosecutor Charles Arthur Anderson was trailed by a carload of mobsters who ran him off the road and into a ditch. The crackup left Anderson with a badly broken leg that required weeks of hospital treatment.

But the prosecutor was not easily intimidated. With the testimony of Fiedler and Kelley, he managed to win the conviction of Felix McDonald early in 1935. Already a convicted robber in a separate case, McDonald was sentenced to sixty years for the Kelley kidnapping. As for Bart Davit, he was sentenced to life in prison in October 1935 for killing a grocer during a 1932 holdup, so he was never brought to trial for the kidnapping.

This left Nellie Muench, whose trial in October 1935 was held in

Mexico, Missouri, 120 miles west of St. Louis, because of the publicity in the latter city. At first, she seemed to be a sympathetic defendant, since she was not only an attractive woman but...a new mother! Yes, after twenty-three years of a childless marriage, she held a baby boy in her arms.

Muench took the stand to deny all the accusations against her. Her denials were enough to persuade the jurors, who acquitted her on October 5, 1935. The overjoyed defendant walked proudly out of the courtroom, proclaiming herself ready to embrace motherhood and grateful for God's gift in the form of a child. "I was not guilty," she said. "The jury vindicated me. I never had a doubt. That's all."[133]

Actually, it wasn't quite all. It was soon revealed that there was someone who loved the baby boy even more than Muench: the infant's *real* mother, an unwed servant girl named Anna Ware, who had come to St. Louis from Pennsylvania to give birth. Days after Muench was acquitted, Ware sued to recover the child she had at first given up.

The ensuing hearing on Ware's petition contained elements of sadness and low humor. Dr. Marsh Pitzman, a wealthy bachelor and colleague of Nellie's physician husband, had certified that Nellie Muench had indeed delivered the baby she claimed as her own, an assertion supported by Dr. Ludwig Muench.

It was soon disclosed that Nellie Muench had made an earlier attempt to pose as a mother, working with her lawyer, Wilfred Jones, to obtain the baby boy of an unwed Minneapolis waitress who gave birth in a St. Louis hospital. But soon after arriving in the Muench home, the infant became ill and was taken by Jones and a friend of Nellie's named Helen Berroyer to a hospital, where he died on July 16.

The presiding officer at the hearing, the distinguished lawyer Rush Limbaugh Sr. (grandfather of the present-day conservative commentator), was incensed by the sordid series of events. The entire fake-motherhood scheme was "a deliberate and consummate deception," he concluded on December 5, 1935, going on to call it "a sham and shallow pretense" concocted to gain sympathy from the jury at the kidnapping trial, and just maybe for other "ulterior reasons."[134]

Soon, Muench was back in court, along with her husband, Jones, and Berroyer. All were charged with conspiring to obtain Anna Ware's baby without court approval. For eight days, the trial offered the jury— "a panel of open-mouthed farmers," as the *Washington Post* put it—an entertaining glimpse at the seamier side of city society.

The entertainment ended on the ninth day, April 16, 1936, when the judge declared a mistrial after learning that one of the jurors had been offered a bribe of $100 to deadlock the jury. The retrial was scheduled for August. This time, the proceedings went smoothly, and the defendants were convicted and fined. In addition to a $450 fine, Nellie Muench was assessed a $25 contempt-of-court penalty for an outburst at one of the witnesses.

Case closed? Not yet. Soon, it emerged that Muench had not only convinced Dr. Pitzman that she had really given birth but had told him that he was the father—and that she would reveal that fact unless he paid her to keep quiet. Or she might just commit suicide on the doctor's front porch. Pitzman had, in fact, been her lover. To buy her silence, he gave her several thousand dollars.

Now, Muench and her codefendants faced federal mail-fraud charges, since blackmail letters had been sent to Pitzman. The defendants were convicted on December 20, 1936. The sentences were imposed the day after Christmas, with Nellie Muench drawing a ten-year prison term and $5,000 fine; her husband, Ludwig, eight years and $5,000 (despite Nellie's insistence that he was blameless); Jones a ten-year term; and Berroyer five years.

It had all begun with the kidnapping of a wealthy doctor in April 1931. Much later, a grotesquely obese former justice of the peace, in whose presence people felt free to plan crimes, had come forward with a story, not out of a sense of civic duty but because he was short of money. A prosecution witness had been slain while under protection *at the home of a sheriff's deputy.* Mysteriously, the information on the license plates of the assassins' car had vanished from a clerk's office. A prosecutor had been run off the road and nearly killed. And a juror had been offered a bribe.

It was all enough to make one wonder how far Missouri had come from the days of the Wild West.

<hr />

Rather uncharitably, newspapers noted that Nellie Muench had to surrender the mink coat she had worn to court and exchange it for a plain calico dress that she would wear when helping to scrub the toilets and jail floors before she was shipped off to prison.

While Muench was imprisoned, her husband divorced her. She was released in 1944 and died in a Kansas City rooming house in 1982 at the age of ninety-one.[*]

---

[*] In recounting the denouement of the Isaac Kelley kidnapping case, I relied not only on contemporary accounts in the *St. Louis Post-Dispatch* but on Barry Cushman, "Headline Kidnappings and the Origins of the Lindbergh Law," *Saint Louis University Law School Journal,* 2011, *https://scholarship.law.nd.edu/law_faculty_scholarship/268Saint Louis University.*

CHAPTER THIRTY-SEVEN

EVIL RESURFACES

New York City
Wednesday, May 30, 1934

Scores of warships steamed into New York Harbor for a Memorial Day display of American naval might, a once-in-a-lifetime thrill for hundreds of thousands of men, women, and children. The fleet included battle-ships and aircraft carriers, whose planes ("the sky talons of the American fighting eagle," as the *Daily Mirror* put it) swooped and darted to the delight of the throngs below. President Franklin D. Roosevelt, who had been assistant secretary of the navy a decade before, beamed with pride.

The fleet would be anchored around New York for eighteen days. Its officers were celebrities, feted by Mayor Fiorello La Guardia and other politicians, while thousands of enlisted sailors swarmed into Times Square and Coney Island in search of good times in the big city. The friendly invasion got saturation coverage in the newspapers.

On Monday, June 4, the *Daily Mirror* ran a big photo spread of the festivities. A prominent photograph showed two smiling young sailors in the company of a pair of pretty teenage girls. A Brooklyn woman saw the face of one girl, a brunette, and was startled. The woman had followed the case of Grace Budd, the lovely young girl who had vanished in 1928 after a seemingly friendly old man said he wanted to take her to a birthday party.

The woman snipped out the photo, drew an arrow pointing to the brunette, and wrote, "This is the girl, Grace Budd." Then she mailed it to the Budds, whose address, 135 West Twenty-Fourth Street in Manhattan, had been in the papers occasionally. Still living in border-line poverty, the Budds had moved to a smaller apartment since Grace's disappearance.[135]

Delia Budd looked at the photograph and thought it looked like an older Grace. Several relatives and friends agreed. So the next day, Delia and her husband, Albert, took the photo to the police to show Detective Lieutenant William F. King of the missing persons bureau.

The detective understood the parents' desperate need to hold on to hope, but he was highly skeptical. Was it really possible that the pretty brunette was Grace Budd? If the girl in the photo *was* her, how to explain why she had not reached out to her parents? Was she being held against her will, with no chance to escape or to cry for help? Did she have amnesia?

Nevertheless, King did not discourage reporters from reviving the Budd case. Revisiting an unsolved crime, especially around its anniversary, was a staple of journalism then, as it is today. The anniversary of Grace's vanishing was on June 3. So the New York papers pounced on the chance to reprise the case, displaying the photo of the pretty girl and hinting that she just might be Grace Budd.

Not many days after the photo was published, a sixteen-year-old Bronx girl named Florence Swinney walked into a police station and identified herself as the brunette in the picture. She and a friend had been photographed with two nice sailors they had met in the city. End of story. End of a flicker of hope for Albert and Delia Budd.

But as sorry as he was for Grace's parents, Detective King was not displeased. The latest spate of stories had revived the public's interest in the Budd case. Some good might come of that, especially if that interest were rekindled at the right moment. King knew how to do that, but how would he know *when?* Instinct.

———

"I checked on the Grace Budd mystery," the enormously popular newspaper columnist Walter Winchell declared in the *Daily Mirror* in November 1934. "She was eight when she was kidnapped about six years ago. And it is safe to tell you that the Dep't of Missing Persons will break the case, or they expect to, in four weeks. They are holding a 'cokie' now at Randall's Island, who is said to know most about the crime. Grace is supposed to have been done away with in lime, but another legend is that her skeleton is buried in a local spot. More anon."[136]

Winchell's grammar and syntax ran off the rails, as usual, but so what? Winchell got Grace Budd's age wrong: she was ten, not eight, when she vanished in 1928. Again, so what? The error was minor by Winchell's standards, and the columnist wasn't paid for his graceful language. He was paid for dishing out juicy gossip, some of which even turned out to be true eventually.

But King knew that if anything in Winchell's latest column was true, it was pure chance. The police did not expect to break the Grace Budd case in four weeks. There was no jailed cocaine addict who knew anything about her disappearance.

Winchell had not "checked on" the Budd case, as he claimed. He had simply been fed a fictional tidbit by King. The detective had learned that doling out morsels about the Budd case to select journalists, sometimes coinciding with the anniversary of Grace's disappearance, always sparked letters and phone calls to the police. Some were from sincere people who thought they might have clues. Most were from screwballs.

King thought the filthy skunk who had stolen Grace probably looked at the papers now and then. Maybe he'd be tempted to get in touch, just to remind people he was still out there somewhere. You just never knew what might happen when you planted stuff in the papers.

King was willing to try just about anything. He was the very embodiment of tenacity, having traveled some fifty thousand miles by the autumn of 1934 to pursue possible clues, however far-fetched they seemed, to the fate of Grace Budd.

He had been the lead investigator in the Budd case early on and had seen how Grace's parents had been broken by their daughter's disappearance. He'd even postponed his retirement to pursue the case.

King figured that, if the creep who called himself Frank Howard *did* read the papers, he might have gotten a sick thrill over the false sighting of Grace over the Memorial Day weekend. Maybe the Winchell item would further stimulate him.

―――――――――

On the morning of Monday, November 12, a letter arrived at the Budds' apartment. It had been mailed the night before from the Grand Central Annex post office in Manhattan. It was addressed to Delia Budd, who couldn't read. She gave it to her son, Eddie, who had barely begun to read it before he bolted from the apartment and ran to a police station.

By midmorning, Detective King had the letter, which began "My dear Mrs. Budd." The writer said he had taken Grace to an abandoned house in Westchester County, killed and dismembered her, then eaten her flesh over the next nine days. He rhapsodized about the joys of cannibalism in general. As if to prove he was not making up his story, he mentioned bringing a gift of strawberries and pot cheese on his 1928 visit to the Budd apartment.

The writer did not sign the letter. Instead, he closed by emphasizing that he had not violated the girl sexually, "tho I could have had I wished."[137]

Hardened as he was by years of police work, Detective King realized he could still be shocked. Reading the letter was like bathing in sewage.

The strawberries and pot cheese? All right, those details had been in the newspapers, King recalled. But the letter writer had added a detail, declaring that around the time he took Grace away, he was living at 409 East One Hundredth Street in Manhattan. Why had he offered that clue? Or was it a clue? It could be that "Frank Howard" was playing games, that he had never lived at 409 East One Hundredth Street, just as he had never intended to take Grace to a birthday party at 137th Street and Columbus Avenue, a place that didn't exist.

But 409 East One Hundredth Street was a *real* address. And the handwriting in the letter to the Budd apartment looked like the writing in the message "Frank Howard" had sent on June 2, 1928, telling the Budds he'd been delayed in New Jersey and would come the next day.

The envelope the letter had come in had a preprinted return address on the back flap. The address had been crossed out with ink, but there remained an odd hexagonal emblem with a capital letter in each of the six sides, spelling out "NYPCBA."

What the hell is this? King wondered. *Some kind of weird religious organization?*

King looked more closely. Using a magnifying glass, he could see the return address the sender had crossed out but had not quite obliterated: 627 Lexington Avenue in Manhattan. Rushing to that address, he saw that it was not the home of a religious group; it was the headquarters of the New York Private Chauffeurs Benevolent Association.

King showed the organization's president, Arthur Ennis, the envelope with the logo and asked if a Frank Howard had ever been a member of the NYPCBA. No, Ennis said after checking his files.

Then King asked to see the personnel forms filled out by all of the association's active and retired members.

Ennis gave him a carton containing some four hundred forms. The detective took them back to his office to compare the handwriting on the forms to that on the revolting letter to the Budds. It wasn't far-fetched to imagine that the little gray man who had taken Grace was or had been a chauffeur. Driving all over the city, gleaning personal details from his customers while remaining anonymous...

But King was unable to find a match in the handwriting. So the next day, Tuesday, November 13, he went back to the office of the NYPCBA and asked Ennis to convene an emergency meeting of the association.

When the session was held the next day, King reminded the members about the disappearance of Grace Budd. He told them about the letter to Grace's mother in the envelope with the NYPCBA logo. He implored the chauffeurs: if anyone here knows who took some NYPCBA stationery from this office, come forward.

Just moments after the meeting adjourned, an embarrassed young man who was a part-time janitor and errand boy for the association came up to King and confessed to taking home some office stationery about six months before. The young man lived in a rooming house on Lexington Avenue, practically across the street from the office.

More optimistic than he had been in years, Detective King went at once to the rooming house—only to have his hopes dashed. There was no one living there who looked like "Frank Howard," nor did any handwriting on the sign-in register resemble that of the letter writer.

Quickly, King again contacted the young man who had pilfered the office stationery. Better try harder with your memory, King said.

Sheepishly, the young man recalled that when he took the stationery home, he was living in another rooming house, at 200 East Fifty-Second Street. Apartment 7. His memory refreshed, the young man recalled something else: he had only used one, maybe two, of the envelopes. The rest he had put on a shelf above his bed. He'd left them there when he moved out.

The detective hurried to the Fifty-Second Street rooming house and showed the landlady an old circular about Grace Budd's disappearance. The circular included a detailed description of "Frank Howard," and it drew an instant reaction. "My goodness, this sounds like the quiet little old man with a gray mustache who used to live in Apartment 7," she said. "He was here for only a couple of months. Left three days ago."*

King's heart sank.

She showed King the man's signature from when he'd moved in. King looked at the name: Albert H. Fish. A glance told him the signature and the handwriting on the letter to Delia Budd were a match. Had the snake managed to slither away?

"Tell me all you can about Mr. Fish," King pressed.

"Not much to tell," the landlady said. Then she uttered a matter-of-fact remark that stunned King. Mr. Fish had promised to return soon to get a check from his son in North Carolina, where he was working for the Civil Conservation Corps. Each month, the son sent his $25 check to his father to help support him. In fact, the landlady had cashed some of the checks for Mr. Fish. She knew the old man was expecting another one, which she had promised to hold for him.

By the end of that day, November 14, King had set his traps. He arranged for twenty-four-hour surveillance of the Fifty-Second Street rooming house. He called the headquarters of the North Carolina CCC

---

* This is an improvisation of dialogue for dramatic purposes.

camp and arranged for the finance officer to notify him when the next checks were sent out. He asked postal inspectors in New York City to be alert for any letters addressed to Albert Fish. And he asked Arthur Ennis of the chauffeurs association to notify him of any letters in association envelopes that were returned to his office as undeliverable.

———

In the third week of November, Ennis notified King that a letter mailed in a chauffeurs association envelope had been returned to the office because the addressee, a man in a Manhattan hotel, could not be located. The letter was in the same handwriting as the missive to Delia Budd. The writer said he was interested in joining a nudist club. He signed his name "James W. Pell."

King noted that the letter was dated November 11, as the note to Delia Budd had been. So, King reflected, the creep was in a writing mood that day.

More days passed. Thanksgiving went by. Still, King and his men kept the vigil.

———

A light rain was falling on New York City on Tuesday, December 4. The newspapers were full of Christmas shopping ads, at least for New Yorkers with money. On that day, King got a call from a postal inspector. A letter addressed to Albert Fish had just been intercepted at the Grand Central Annex post office.

King's hopes soared, then plummeted as more days ticked off and the weird old man failed to appear at the Fifty-Second Street rooming house.

On Wednesday, December 12, a cold spell hit its nadir with a low of eleven degrees in New York, a record for the date. Thursday dawned cloudy and much warmer. That afternoon, Detective King was at his desk when his phone rang.

"He's here," the landlady at the Fifty-Second Street rooming house said. "Albert Fish just came in and asked about his check."*

"Stall him," King said. "Anything to stall him. Offer him tea. Anything. I'm on my way."

The detective hopped into a squad car and raced uptown, praying that Albert Fish would still be there. He was, sipping tea at a wooden table in a furnished room. King entered and closed the door. "Albert Fish?" he said.[138]

The man looked up from his tea and nodded.

"I've got you now," King said.

"I'll tell you all about it," Fish said at police headquarters after some initial stalling. "I'm the man you want." The shabby but harmless-looking old man was ready to tell about killing Grace Budd.[139]

Early on, Fish was shown the chauffeurs association envelope that had contained the vile letter to the Budds. He acknowledged sending the letter (and the one expressing interest in a nudist camp) and explained that he had run out of regular envelopes.

But what had prompted him to use envelopes with the NYPCBA label?

A cockroach, Fish said. "I was sitting in a chair...and there was a roach on the wall, and I got up on the chair to kill the roach and saw the envelopes." He recalled seeing "a dozen or more" on a shelf where the mildly larcenous office assistant had left them.[140]

No doubt, King had acquired a sense of the bizarre in his years as

---

* This is an improvisation of dialogue for dramatic purposes.

a detective. Here was a moment to savor. For more than six years, he had spent endless hours investigating the disappearance of Grace Budd. He had drawn not only on his own bottomless patience but on all the investigative tools and techniques available to the police at the time.

Yet in the end, King had gotten his big break after planting a fictitious item in Walter Winchell's column. And he'd been given the priceless clue of the NYPCBA envelope thanks to a simple creature whose ancestors had dwelled among dinosaurs, eons before the birth of mankind. A cockroach.

————

It is difficult to describe Albert Fish without using superlatives. Hardened police officers, psychiatrists, and even Fish's own lawyer said the actions and words of the frail-looking little man were the most vile they had ever come across.**

Fish said he had taken Grace Budd on a train ride to Westchester County on June 3, 1928, after leaving the Budd family's apartment. Alighting from the train, the old man and young girl had walked to a deserted cottage. Seeing no one else in the vicinity, let alone the throng of happy children she had expected at a birthday party, Grace no doubt became frightened. Her fear did not last long, for Fish quickly strangled the girl—because of "my lust for blood," he explained.[141] Then he desecrated her body, carving it up and saving some pieces to indulge his cannibalistic obsessions. He scattered what was left around the grounds of the cottage.

Thus, even before her parents became alarmed enough to contact

————

** I choose not to dwell on Fish's legal journey from arrest to trial and beyond, which has been superbly told in *Deranged: The Shocking True Story of America's Most Fiendish Killer!*, Harold Schechter's book on the life, crimes, and death of Albert Fish. The book was invaluable to me.

the police and certainly well before the police began canvassing the neighborhood around the Budds' apartment, Grace was dead.

At first, Fish said, he had intended to make Eddie Budd his victim. But he changed his mind when he saw the sweet-featured Grace, the flower of the family.

Eddie was brought to the New York City missing persons bureau by Detective William King. "Go in there, Eddie," the detective said. "See if you can find the man who took your sister away—if he's in there."

A score or more of police officials and detectives were in the room, along with Albert Fish. At once, Eddie recognized Fish. "That's the man that took my sister away!" he screamed. The strapping young man in his midtwenties lunged at the little old man before he was restrained by detectives.

"That's Eddie," Fish said mildly.

Grace's father was brought in. "Don't you know me?" Albert Budd said, shaking with emotion.

"Yes, you're Mr. Budd," Fish said.

"And you're the man who came to my home as a guest and took my girl away," the father said before detectives gently led him away.

Willie Korman, the friend of Eddie Budd who had looked forward to joining Eddie in healthy work on a Long Island farm, also identified Fish.

The police took Fish to the abandoned cottage in Westchester. He pointed out the spots where he had disposed of some of Grace's remains. Officers dug, turning up bones and the young girl's skull.

"It makes my conscience feel better now that you have found her," Fish remarked to a police official. "I'm glad I told everything."

The abduction and slaying of Grace Budd was no isolated, spur-of-the-moment deed in the life of Albert Fish. Soon, he confessed to killing a seven-year-old boy on Staten Island in 1924 and a four-year-old boy in Queens in 1927. He also recalled abducting and torturing a young man in Wilmington, Delaware, in 1910 and torturing a boy near Washington, DC, although he didn't remember when. He cut them with knives, then fled, not knowing if his victims had died. He was also a prolific child molester.

The monster that thrived within Albert Fish was nurtured in an orphanage in Washington, DC, where he spent much of his childhood after he was abandoned by his parents. He recalled the institution as a place of sadistic discipline where whippings were routine. There, he learned not just to endure pain but to enjoy it—whether inflicting it on others or on himself.

The adult Albert Fish became a house painter and handyman. He married and had six children before his wife ran off with a boarder. He seems to have had mixed success as a parent. At least one daughter remained loyal to him even after he was arrested, while a son referred to him as "that old skunk."

While trying to preside over a household, Fish sometimes dined on raw meat, occasionally howled at the moon, and liked to spank himself with a nail-studded paddle. He was also given to shoving needles into his groin area for pleasure, self-punishment, or both.

Since there was no doubt about Fish's actual, factual guilt, his only chance to escape the electric chair was to plead insanity.

"This man is undoubtedly an abnormal individual," one psychiatrist concluded with remarkable understatement. Two other psychiatrists, or "alienists," as they were sometimes called at the time, ventured that Fish suffered from some "limited abnormalities."[142] Indeed.

But no, the two psychiatrists conceded, he was not "insane" in a legal sense. That is, he did not lack the capacity to understand that his actions were wrong.

So Detective William King had added to his understanding of the depths of human depravity, not that he needed any more insight. Even as he was stalking the killer of Grace Budd, he was following another ugly case, the disappearance of a six-year-old girl.

On September 19, 1934, Dorothy Ann Distelhurst vanished in Nashville, Tennessee, while walking home from kindergarten. Two days later, her father, Alfred E. Distelhurst, sales manager for a religious-book publisher, got a postcard saying information about her would follow. In another two days, he got a letter—mailed at Grand Central Terminal in Manhattan—demanding $5,000 and promising that instructions for delivery of the ransom would arrive soon.

A few days later, he got another letter from Manhattan, ordering him to come to New York and register in a hotel on Eighth Avenue. There, presumably, he would be contacted.

Instead of traveling to New York himself, Distelhurst sent a "friend" who registered in his name, the *New York Times* reported. After ten days in the hotel and with no contact from a kidnapper, the friend returned to Nashville. The friend was really an FBI agent. Distelhurst had informed the Department of Justice of his daughter's disappearance early on.

Meanwhile, the Nashville police learned that on the afternoon that Dorothy Ann vanished, a car with New York State license plates was seen near the Distelhurst home. The last two digits on the plates were 76. Plates with those digits were generally issued in Ulster County, north of New York City. But New York police were unable to find a car with 76 plates that had recently been in Nashville.

On October 12, Distelhurst got a third letter, also from New York City. The sender told Distelhurst to travel to Manhattan *himself* if he wanted his daughter back alive and to check into the hotel where he had been told to stay before. He was told to pace the hotel lobby at frequent intervals, day and night, to periodically stroll the streets near the hotel, and finally to take out a newspaper ad saying in part, "Dorothy, come home. Father in New York at same place…"

It seemed that the author of the ransom letters had not been fooled by the ruse of an FBI agent posing as a friend of Distelhurst. Perhaps Hoover's sober-dressing, unsmiling men still had not learned how to blend in.

Distelhurst came to New York City on November 7, paced in the hotel lobby, and strolled the streets as instructed. Nothing.

On November 12, he issued a statement begging the kidnapper or kidnappers to reach out to him. Distelhurst said details in the letters showed that the writer had "a complete knowledge of Nashville," including information about the Distelhursts' neighborhood.

The next day in Nashville, two groundskeepers for a tuberculosis hospital were digging flower beds in an isolated section of the hospital grounds when they discovered the nude body of a child under two inches of dirt. The remains had been there for weeks. Dental records soon confirmed that the body was that of Dorothy Ann Distelhurst. She had died of a skull fracture.

Either the kidnapper or kidnappers had killed the child, then tormented her father in a bid to get ransom, or some heartless chiseler who knew only that the girl was missing had tried to exploit the father's anguish. Whoever had written the letters to Dorothy Ann's father never got any money, suggesting that he had lost nerve in the end.

———————

As he sat on death row in Sing Sing prison, Albert Fish said he was looking forward to the exciting experience of the electric chair. "It will be the supreme thrill...the only one I haven't tried," he told his jailers.[143] His wish was fulfilled on the night of January 16, 1936. Just before he died at the age of sixty-five, he handed his lawyer a farewell statement.

"I shall never show it to anyone," the lawyer said after the current had passed through his client's body. "It was the most filthy string of obscenities that I have ever read."

CHAPTER THIRTY-EIGHT

IN GUN-BLAZING PURSUIT

Chicago
Early 1934

In following the travels of members of the Barker-Karpis gang and other bandits of the mid-1930s, one has to wonder: considering all they went through to evade the law, did they ever ask themselves whether it was worth it? But by the time they scattered in flight after the Bremer kidnapping in January 1934, it was much too late for soul-searching. The gang members had already crossed a Rubicon of blood.

On March 10, 1934, Alvin Karpis and Fred Barker underwent surgery in Chicago. The "operating room" was a hotel room, and the surgeon was Dr. Joseph Moran of Chicago, whose healing skills were blurred by alcoholism. Moran had done prison time for performing illegal abortions, and upon his release, he had no prospects of establishing a conventional practice. He did, however, manage to land an appointment as the physician for the Chicago Teamsters, Chauffeurs, Warehousemen, and Helpers Union. (Was it just coincidence that Dan

"Tubbo" Gilbert, Chicago investigator and pursuer of Roger Touhy, was a power in the Teamsters union at the time?)

Moran became noted for emergency stitching and bullet-removal work on wounded gangsters. Besides dabbling in plastic surgery, he was believed to help gangsters launder money now and then.

Karpis and Barker were in no position to look for an ideal doctor or to seek second opinions. They wanted to alter their faces and erase their fingerprints. The "surgery" by Dr. Moran was only partly successful, and the pain drove Fred Barker half-crazy for a time.

Then there was Fred Samuel Goetz, whose name somehow morphed into "Shotgun" George Ziegler. He was a gunman believed to have participated in the St. Valentine's Day Massacre of 1929.

Ziegler, then in his midthirties, had a personal profile unusual for a gangster. He was a graduate of the University of Illinois, where he earned respectable grades. He aspired to a degree of sophistication and was said to be a decent golfer. He had been an army aviator during the Great War, serving stateside and earning a commission as a second lieutenant.

But this officer was no gentleman.

He had a weakness for women—and girls, including those young enough to get him into trouble, especially if he forced himself on them, which he was not above doing. He was suspected in the attempted robbery of a Chicago doctor. The doctor was wounded, and his chauffeur was shot to death.

But the most impressive mark on his resume was his reputed role in the St. Valentine's Day Massacre of 1929, the bloodbath that left seven gangsters dead in a Chicago garage. And he was believed to have been one of several men who robbed a bank in Jefferson, Wisconsin, of $352,000 in cash and bonds in 1929.

Yet for all his crimes, he was able to avoid capture. Unfortunately for him, when discretion was called for, he sometimes chose to boast, typically after a few adult beverages. He unwisely bragged to gangster friends that he had planned the kidnapping of Edward Bremer. (He was exaggerating his role, though he *was* reputed to have helped plan the caper and to have taken part in ransom negotiations.)

Oddly enough, Ziegler appeared to have been trying to inject some boring domesticity into his life. In March 1934, he was reportedly living with a woman in an expensively furnished apartment on Chicago's South Shore Drive. The couple called themselves "Mr. and Mrs. George Seibert."

Late on the night of March 20, Ziegler was shot to death while emerging from Minerva's restaurant, a favorite hangout of his in suburban Cicero. His big mouth had apparently been his undoing. Appropriately enough, he was slain by shotgun—several blasts to his face, rendering him physically unrecognizable.

If the people who killed him were also Barker-Karpis gang members or alumni (a reasonable assumption), perhaps they should have lingered long enough to go through the dead man's pockets. As it was, lawmen found valuable information on Ziegler's corpse: slips of paper with names, aliases, addresses, and contact information for the Barker-Karpis bunch. One last item was added to Ziegler's resume, albeit posthumously. Chicago FBI agent Melvin Purvis said the bureau was looking into the possibility that Ziegler was one of the shooters in the Union Station Massacre in Kansas City the previous summer. And why not speculate about Ziegler? It couldn't be proven that he *wasn't* at the train station. And if people wanted to believe that he *was* there, it helped the FBI in its efforts to show that people who took part in the station slaughter were getting their just deserts, indirectly or otherwise.

———————

Meanwhile, life on the run was anything but easy for the Barker-Karpis folks. Arthur "Doc" Barker and an associate, Volney Davis, took their cues from Karpis and Doc's brother Fred and decided to have their appearances altered. This was done in Toledo, Ohio, in the spring of 1934, likely by the aforementioned Dr. Joseph Moran. After this ordeal, Davis decided he wanted a whole new life, so he and his girlfriend traveled to Buffalo, which had an underworld presence. There, they bought a truck and drove to Montana.

But they soon sensed that even the land under the Big Sky was not big enough. After picking up rumors that the law was on their trail in Montana, they traveled to Kansas City, Missouri, still a reliable sanctuary for those who had run afoul of the law.

Around this time, Karpis and his girlfriend had settled in Cleveland. Karpis just wanted to lie low. He had no interest in any "reunion" of the Barker-Karpis gang, which at full strength numbered in the dozens, if one included the supporting cast.

In the spring of 1934, the adventures of the Barker-Karpis desperadoes intersected with those of John Dillinger, the dashing bandit and escape artist. The confluence of events happened in part because Volney Davis was acquainted with people in both criminal camps.

On March 3, Dillinger escaped from the jail in Crown Point, Indiana, where he had been taken after being captured in Arizona. He was supposed to stand trial for the killing of a police officer during a bank robbery in East Chicago, Indiana. (The Dillinger gang had also been linked to the slaying of a Chicago police officer.)

In effecting his escape, Dillinger cowed jail guards with what was later thought to be a fake pistol whittled from a block of wood and blackened with shoe polish. The feat added to the bandit's dashing image. But Dillinger made a big mistake. He stole the sheriff's car and drove it across a state line, from Indiana into Illinois, on his way to

Chicago. Thus, he violated the recently passed National Motor Vehicle Theft Act, which made it a federal offense to transport a stolen motor vehicle across a state border.

The act had added to the responsibilities of the FBI, which Hoover welcomed. It had also put Dillinger squarely in the director's sights.

Then came one of the worst debacles in the history of the FBI.

The bureau got a tip that Dillinger, "Baby Face" Nelson, and several gangster companions had stopped at a remote vacation spot known as Little Bohemia Lodge in north Wisconsin for a rest. Hoover authorized his then-favorite agent, Melvin Purvis, to gather a posse and capture Dillinger—or maybe killing him would be better.

Purvis assembled some agents and secured some heavy weaponry, and the caravan headed to the northern reaches of Wisconsin. On the bitter cold Sunday night of April 22, 1934, the lawmen surrounded the cabins where Dillinger and friends were staying. After a while, the FBI men saw a car departing. The driver had the car radio on, so he probably did not hear orders to stop. The agents fired on the car and killed a thirty-five-year-old man who worked for the Civilian Conservation Corps. Two other men in the car, also innocent civilians, were wounded. The commotion aroused the bandits in the cabins, and in no time, the night was lit up with gunfire. An FBI agent was killed, and Dillinger and his crew escaped through the woods.

Trigger-happy agents had killed an innocent man, an agent had been slain—and the outlaws had escaped. It soon became clear that there had been inadequate coordination between the federal men and locals on where to put up roadblocks. The raid was a fiasco.

Even in that era of less aggressive reporters, the Little Bohemia Lodge disaster generated a lot of criticism of Hoover and his bureau.

A gibe from Will Rogers, a prominent humorist and commentator of the era, must have been especially stinging for the director: "Well, they had Dillinger surrounded and was all ready to shoot him when he came out, but another bunch of folks came out ahead, so they just shot them instead. Dillinger is going to accidentally get with some innocent bystanders some time, then he will get shot."[144]

And yet Little Bohemia may have created opportunity as well. As the *New York Times* reported two days after the shootout, "Aroused by the latest escapade of the bandit John Dillinger, President Roosevelt has requested early enactment by Congress of a sheaf of bills greatly enlarging the police powers of the Federal Government."[145]

The proposals, several of which found their way into law, made bank robbery a federal offense, made it a federal crime to kill an officer of the federal government, and in general lessened whatever protections criminals still enjoyed by crossing state lines. And it gave yet more responsibility to the FBI, which was becoming a national police force.

Was Hoover living a charmed life?

———

The not-so-subtle message that filtered down to FBI agents after Little Bohemia was simple: kill John Dillinger. There was scant sentiment among lawmen for capturing the bandit, who was known to be traipsing across the Midwest, and subjecting him to a "fair trial."

Not long after Little Bohemia, Volney Davis got a surprise visit at his home in Aurora, Illinois, near Chicago. Dillinger and a bandit pal, Homer Van Meter, had come to call, dragging along John "Red" Hamilton, another Dillinger confederate who had been gravely wounded in a gunfight in the flight from Little Bohemia Lodge.

Dr. Joseph Moran was summoned, but he refused to treat Hamilton, perhaps because he saw that Hamilton's wounds had turned gangrenous and were fatal. But Davis agreed to keep Hamilton in his house, caring for him as best he could until he passed away. When he did, Dillinger, Doc Barker, Van Meter, and Davis are said to have buried him in a gravel pit near Oswego, Illinois, though there are conflicting versions of this bit of gangster lore.

The last confirmed sighting of Dr. Moran alive was in a club in Toledo in July 1934. His drinking had gotten the best of him, and he was heard bragging to Doc Barker and a few associates about his value to the gang and the power he thought he had over them because of the tender care he provided.

Not long afterward, he left the club accompanied by some gang members and was never seen alive again. Later, Alvin Karpis claimed that Arthur and Fred Barker killed the doctor and buried him in a lime pit in Michigan. But Fred Barker reportedly offered a different clue in talking with other gang members: "He'll do no more operating. The fishes have probably eat him up by now."

His remark hinted at a more accepted version of Dr. Moran's fate: that Karpis himself and Fred Barker took the doctor for a boat ride on Lake Erie, killed him, and dumped him overboard. Fourteen months later, a badly decomposed, fish-nibbled body washed ashore on the shores of Crystal Beach, Ontario, minus hands and feet. The FBI said it identified the body through dental records as that of Dr. Moran.

Karpis claimed that the identification was wrong, but dental records were and are more reliable than the words of gangsters. So it seems that in death, the doctor rode the wind and currents across Lake Erie from Ohio to Canada, traveling through waters that had been there for eons, passing through stretches where the British fleet had sailed to meet the Americans in the Battle of Lake Erie in 1813. The doctor had come a long way.

And what of poor Harry Sawyer, the owner-host of St. Paul's Green Lantern hangout? He sensed that the new good-government spirit infecting St. Paul made it dangerous for him. So he left Minnesota and his beloved Green Lantern and moved to Las Vegas. But by April 1934, he still had not been paid for his help in setting up Edward Bremer for the kidnappers. So he wrote to Karpis in Cleveland and arranged to meet him there to get what was coming to him.

Sawyer reportedly hooked up with Karpis and friends in Cleveland that June, and plans were worked out for Sawyer and another gang member to take $100,000 or so of the Bremer ransom money to Miami in September for proper laundering. But here again, overindulgence disrupted plans. While Sawyer was away, his wife, Gladys, went to a hotel bar with some friends. They got so inebriated and vulgar that they were arrested on drunk-and-disorderly charges.

The FBI heard about the incident, but before agents could act, the Barker-Karpis folks decided it was time to leave Cleveland. One gang member flew to Havana to do some more money laundering. Fred Barker and Karpis went to Havana to relax, recuperate, and think.

———

Meanwhile, in their pursuit of John Dillinger, Purvis and his agents had picked up some good information—or perhaps they were finally acquiring the knack of gathering and sifting intelligence. Dillinger was in Chicago, staying with a woman who knew who he was but who was trusted by the outlaw regardless.

The woman, Anna Sage, was a woman of ill repute and sometime brothel owner who was terrified of being deported to her native Romania. She had one priceless piece of information to offer the federal government in return for being allowed to stay in the United States: she knew Dillinger's habits, and she could inform Purvis of his movements.

The story has been told a thousand times, but it is still riveting. On the night of Sunday, July 22, 1934, Dillinger took Sage to a movie, *Manhattan Melodrama*, a gangster flick starring Clark Gable and William Powell that was playing at the Biograph Theater on Chicago's North Side. Tipped off by Sage, Purvis and fifteen agents waited near the theater for the movie to end.

Purvis and his men waited breathlessly, then saw the moviegoers begin to stream out. Soon, they saw Sage, wearing a red or orange dress. She was walking with a man in gray slacks, a white shirt, and a boater hat. His once rusty-brown hair had been dyed coal black, and his face had been slightly altered, no longer bearing a scar that had adorned one cheek.

But Purvis recognized the man at once. He had spent too many hours staring at the face in wanted pictures, had thought of John Dillinger as he was trying to fall asleep, thought of the humiliations Dillinger had inflicted on the FBI, thought of how he had made his jailers and pursuers look like fools. Thought of the trail of blood and tears he had left across the Midwest.

Dillinger sensed the trap and tried for one last getaway, running into an alley near the theater. The lawmen blazed away. One bullet struck him in the head, another in the chest.

Two other bullets from federal guns hit two bystanders, both women. The women were not seriously wounded. Had one or both of the women died, could Hoover have survived? Could his bureau have survived and grown in influence, or would it have become a bureaucratic backwater?

But yet again, Hoover and his wild-shooting, occasionally trigger-happy agents were lucky. U.S. attorney general Homer Cummings, no fan of the FBI chief, called the news of Dillinger's slaying "gratifying as well as reassuring."[146] Hoover's stature and that of his bureau were more secure, in part because his agents had somehow avoided killing any innocent civilians while gunning down their target.*

———————

Not quite a month later, on Thursday, August 23, another Dillinger associate came to the end of his days in St. Paul, Minnesota. Homer Van Meter was confronted by four local cops, including Chief Frank Cullen, at a downtown street corner. Also among the lawmen was Tom Brown, once the city's mob-friendly police chief but more recently under investigation on charges that he had aided in the kidnapping of William Hamm and Edward Bremer.

The heavily armed cops maintained later that Van Meter ignored their order to stop and ran into a nearby alley, turning around to fire twice at his pursuers with a pistol. Within seconds, Van Meter's twenty-eight-year-old body was full of bullet holes. But it would have been hard to say that justice had been done. There was speculation that Van Meter had had a falling out with Baby Face Nelson, or Green Lantern proprietor Harry Sawyer and his friend Jack Peifer, who operated the Hollyhocks watering hole in St. Paul, or perhaps all of them. Later, there were rumors that Sawyer had set up Van Meter and that he and the four shooter cops split the money Van Meter had been carrying.

Friends of Van Meter said he should have had some $10,000 on his person, although his corpse yielded about a thousand dollars. In any event, there was nothing ennobling about the dispatch of Homer Van Meter. But then, there had been nothing very noble in how he lived.

———————

* In recounting the movements of the Barker-Karpis gang and John Dillinger's final journey, I summarized from accounts in the *Chicago Tribune*, the *New York Times*, and FBI files. And I am especially indebted to Bryan Burrough, whose riveting *Public Enemies: America's Greatest Crime Wave and the Birth of the FBI, 1933–1934* is essential reading for those seeking deeper understanding of that desperate time in American history.

Now, Hoover could devote himself to catching—better yet, killing—Charles "Pretty Boy" Floyd, whom he still blamed, at least officially, for the Union Station Massacre of 1933 and the death of an FBI agent.

CHAPTER THIRTY-NINE

VIGILANCE AT THE GAS PUMP

New York City
Friday, September 14, 1934

Walter Lyle met all kinds of people without going very far. That was the nature of being the day manager at a big service station in Upper Manhattan.

The week seemed to be ending on a good note. It was cloudy, and there might be light showers in the afternoon. But the temperatures promised to be in the high sixties, ideal for working outdoors, manning the pumps, checking oil, and cleaning windshields. The station was a busy one, taking up an entire block on the east side of Lexington between 127th and 128th streets.

Lyle, who was thirty-three, was happily married. He and his wife had a seven-year-old daughter. Life was good, especially considering the hardships that some Americans were enduring. Lyle knew he was fortunate to have steady employment. On this very Friday morning, newspapers were full of disturbing reports about strikes against textile factories from Rhode Island to the mid-Atlantic states and into the Deep South.

There had been numerous deaths and injuries. Only a week before, six strikers had been shot to death in Honea Path, South Carolina, in a pitched battle between pickets and workers who sided with management. Other incidents were almost as ugly, with governors in some states blaming the labor actions on Communists and other "red agitators" and calling up National Guardsmen to maintain order at bayonet point.

The violence was ugly enough to cause thoughtful Americans to wonder what was happening to their country.* Was the nation tearing itself apart?

—————————

Of course, Lyle knew that dealing with the enormous problems he read about in the newspapers was beyond his place. What he didn't know was that this day was to be one of the most important of his life.

Lyle and his assistants were on the lookout for counterfeit money, particularly gold certificates and bills of large denominations. The chain that owned the station wouldn't put up with being swindled. That's why Lyle and the other men who pumped gas were instructed to be alert, writing license-plate numbers on bills when customers didn't seem quite right.

Just lately, there had been some bad bills passed in the neighborhood, Lyle and his coworkers had been warned. The alert had gone out to all service stations in the area as well as retail merchants.

It was around 10:00 a.m. when a dark Dodge sedan pulled in.

Fill her up? Lyle asked the driver routinely.

—————————

* The textile strike, which began around Labor Day, had been years in the making, as manufacturers struggled with declining demand for goods after the end of the Great War as well as increased foreign competition. Industry leaders responded by increasing production demands and, particularly in the South, by resisting workers' attempts to unionize. The strike of 1934 subsided after three weeks, with workers achieving limited gains.

"Five gallons will be enough," the driver said.

"That'll be ninety-eight cents," Lyle told him.** Lyle had noticed that the man had a German accent. He pumped the gasoline and was surprised when the driver handed him a ten-dollar gold certificate. "You don't see many of these anymore," Lyle said.***147

"Ah, yes, you do," the motorist said a bit boastfully. "I've got a hundred of them left at home." After taking nine one-dollar bills and two pennies for his change, the driver started his engine and drove off—but not before Lyle wrote his license number on the ten-dollar gold certificate: 4U-13–41.

Then Lyle approached two station attendants, Joseph McCarthy and John Lyons, who were working nearby, and shared his suspicions about the motorist: Who the hell *brags* about having a bunch of gold notes at home? And why pay with a ten when you're buying less than a buck's worth of gas?

What Lyle and his coworkers did not know was that the general warning to watch out for suspicious money was not aimed just at counterfeiters. The warning had been issued because, after a lull, money from the Lindbergh ransom was appearing again in Upper Manhattan and the Bronx. In recent weeks, a twenty-dollar gold certificate from the ransom money had been used by a man buying a pair of shoes in the Fordham section of the Bronx.

On the morning of Monday, September 17, the deposits from the service station where Lyle worked were tallied at a branch of the Corn Exchange Bank at Park Avenue and 125th Street. A ten-dollar gold certificate bearing the notation "4U-13–41" was identified as being from

---

**   This is improvised dialogue, added for dramatic effect.
*** Again, for monetary reasons having to do with the Depression and certainly beyond the understanding of this writer, gold notes were being withdrawn from circulation and were therefore becoming scarce.

the Lindbergh ransom.* Bank officials notified the Justice Department, which in turn notified the police in New York City and New Jersey.

The New York motor vehicle agency quickly determined that the license-plate number was assigned to a car owned by Bruno Richard Hauptmann, who lived in a rented apartment at 1279 East 222nd Street in the Bronx with his wife, Anna, and their infant son, Manfred. A special squad was immediately assembled to track Hauptmann's whereabouts. Then several investigators called on Walter Lyle, who confirmed that he was the man who had jotted the license number on the bill.

Yes, Lyle remembered the guy who bragged about having a hundred of these notes. And, sure, he could describe him.**

The investigators noted that the general description offered by Lyle corresponded with that offered by John Condon, who more than two years earlier had come face-to-face with the man who took the ransom money.

Please keep quiet about this, the investigators urged Lyle. They had decided that, instead of arresting Hauptmann at once, they would follow him to see if he might lead them to accomplices. But by Tuesday night, the surveillance had produced no clues, and lawmen decided to arrest Hauptmann, lest he sense that he was being watched.

On the morning of Wednesday, September 19, about seventy-five police officers and federal agents were ready to ambush Hauptmann. Some surrounded the house where he lived, while others sat in cars in neighboring streets.

Hauptmann was seen emerging from his house and getting into his car. When he had gone about two blocks, he was pulled over by

---

* It will be recalled that an alert teller at another branch of the Corn Exchange Bank, at Broadway and Ninety-First Street, spotted a gold note from the ransom money in April 1932.
** This is improvised dialogue, added for dramatic effect.

plainclothes detectives. Without showing any nervousness or changing facial expression, he demanded to know why he'd been stopped.

Without answering, the detectives patted him down for weapons— there were none—and searched Hauptmann's pockets, finding a twenty-dollar gold note.

"Where'd you get this?" a detective asked.

Hauptmann replied that he'd been saving gold notes for years, thinking them protection against runaway inflation, which he'd experienced in his native Germany.

"What do you know about the Lindbergh kidnapping?"

"I? I know nothing at all about the Lindbergh kidnapping, gentlemen. I am a decent man. I live near here with my wife and child. I am a carpenter, gentlemen."

Hauptmann was taken back to his apartment, where investigators discovered the pair of shoes that had been bought recently at a store in Fordham. It was quickly determined that the twenty-dollar note found on his person was from the ransom money.

Hauptmann was taken to the Greenwich Street police station in Lower Manhattan. There, he underwent hours of relentless interrogation of the kind that would become unthinkable decades later when the Supreme Court decreed that a suspect had the right to keep his mouth shut and demand a lawyer. Hauptmann's wife was also questioned, although it is not clear what, if anything, her answers contributed. At the time and for the rest of her life, she insisted that her husband was innocent.

Investigators learned that Hauptmann hadn't worked for months, yet neighbors said he and his wife, who had quit her job as a waitress, seemed to live quite comfortably. Hauptmann said he had done well as an investor. Indeed, investigators learned that he had $24,000 or $25,000 in a brokerage account. But as details of his background emerged—Hauptmann had served prison time in Germany for robbery and theft before escaping and making his way to the United States illegally as a stowaway on a ship—investigators didn't believe he could have prospered on Wall Street, where so many sophisticated Americans had come to ruin.

Having noticed that Hauptmann had glanced uneasily out his apartment window toward his garage, investigators searched the structure—and found $13,500 in cash from the Lindbergh ransom. Hauptmann had a ready explanation: a friend and fellow German, Isidor Fisch, had given it to him. Hauptmann said he and Fisch had been partners in a fur-trading venture and that Fisch had entrusted him with the money before going back to Germany where, unfortunately, he died.

The money found in Hauptmann's garage had been wrapped in newspapers. Some of it was crammed into an old oil can, some of it secreted under the floorboards, and some of it concealed in the walls of the garage. Hauptmann offered no good explanation for these unorthodox business practices, yet he seemed unfazed when confronted by the absurdities in his story. In fact, he was behaving just as Dr. Dudley Shoenfeld, the psychiatrist and early criminal profiler, had predicted the kidnapper would if he were ever captured.

Well into the night of Wednesday, September 19, investigators dug and poked around Hauptmann's garage, toiling under the glare of spotlights. Incongruously, baby clothes for the Hauptmanns' infant son still hung on a clothesline, flapping softly in the breeze.

In the apartment, investigators found more of the ransom money in a shoe box in a closet. They also found a telephone number, scribbled on a closet door. It was the number of John Condon, who had acted as a liaison between Lindbergh and the kidnapper.

Inevitably, the commotion around the house and garage drew the attention of neighbors and soon of reporters, who picked up rumors that the New York police had a prisoner of great importance. So after wanting to keep the arrest secret for as long as possible, on Thursday, September 20, the authorities announced Hauptmann's capture.

Journalists were allowed to view him in the police station and noted that the "sullen and defiant" suspect had fought for the kaiser during the Great War. Police officers posed Hauptmann for the benefit of news photographers, with and without his hat, as the cameramen requested.

Oddly enough, John Condon was not absolutely sure that he recognized Hauptmann from the nighttime cemetery encounters. But other witnesses were more certain.

After Hauptmann's image was on the front page, a Manhattan storekeeper came forward to say he recognized Hauptmann as the man who had paid for a purchase with a ten-dollar gold certificate, later confirmed to be from the ransom, on March 1, 1933.

By early October, Hauptmann had been transferred to a jail in the Bronx, the borough where on April 2, 1932, the crime of extortion had taken place—i.e., the transfer of money from Condon to the mysterious man in St. Raymond's Cemetery. On October 3, 1934, at the request of investigators, a cashier at a movie theater in Lower Manhattan sat in a Bronx courtroom as Hauptmann made an appearance.

Yes, she said without hesitation. That was the man who bought a ticket to see a gangster movie (*Broadway Through a Keyhole*) on November 26, 1933. There was no doubt about the date: the very next day, Detective James Finn had visited her and revealed that the five-dollar Federal Reserve note the man had given her was from the Lindbergh ransom. The bill had been folded in eight parts so as to fit in a watch pocket, and the man hadn't so much handed her the bill as tossed it at her, rather rudely and arrogantly. (Finn recalled his conversation with Dr. Shoenfeld months before when the psychiatrist had predicted that the kidnapper would carry some of the ransom bills as trophies.)

The foreman and cashier at the Cross, Austin & Ireland lumberyard in the Bronx identified Hauptmann as the man who had intended to use a ten-dollar gold certificate to pay for a piece of plywood the previous February, then rushed out for no good reason.*

It also became known that Hauptmann had worked for a time at National Millwork and Lumber Company, the Bronx lumberyard where, it seemed all but certain, the kidnapper had obtained much of the wood used to construct his ladder.

Lewis Bornmann, the New Jersey detective who had worked with Arthur Koehler to trace the ladder wood, was checking the attic of the house where Hauptmann lived to see if there was yet more ransom money squirreled away. Bornmann found no more money—but he discovered what was probably the most damning evidence of all against Bruno Richard Hauptmann.

The attic flooring was incomplete, leaving sections of the beams, or joists, exposed. The partial flooring consisted of thirteen wooden planks nailed to the joists. Bornmann saw that one of the planks was shorter than the others. Looking more closely, he saw that about eight feet of the shorter plank had been sawed off, leaving a residue of sawdust and exposing four nail holes on the joists.

Arrangements were made to bring Koehler from Wisconsin to the Bronx to compare a section of the ladder made from "used" wood (containing old nail holes) with the shortened plank in the attic. Using a magnifying glass, Koehler determined that the grains in the ladder section and the plank were the same—meaning they had once been part of the same board.

Then came the real moment of truth. Koehler placed the ladder section on the joists and saw that the old nail holes on the ladder and

---

*   The man who was with Hauptmann at the time was never identified. He was not Isidor Fisch, since it was established that Fisch had died in Germany by then.

those on the joists lined up exactly. When he pushed nails through the holes of the ladder section, they slid perfectly into the joists.

We can only imagine the joy felt by Koehler, the man who loved wood, and Detective Bornmann. The journey from a South Carolina sawmill to a Bronx lumberyard had ended, at long last, in the attic of the man accused of one of the most sensational crimes of the twentieth century.

———

New York Police Commissioner John F. O'Ryan said the arrest of Hauptmann was the culmination of great cooperation among the New York Police Department, the Jersey troopers and the Department of Justice. New York Mayor Fiorello LaGuardia said he was pleased that his city's police were "cooperating so fully with other agencies."[148]

In reality, the two and a half years between the kidnapping and the arrest of Bruno Hauptmann had been marked by occasional jealousy and deliberate withholding of information between the police in New York and their counterparts in New Jersey. There had been the mistreatment of Violet Sharpe, the Morrow household maid who had been driven to suicide. And Hoover had been lurking on the sidelines, hoping to swing the spotlight onto his FBI.

New York prosecutors were ready to bring Hauptmann to trial for extortion.

No, don't bother, New Jersey prosecutors said in effect. We want to get this guy for kidnapping and murder and send him to the electric chair.

But that might not be as easy as the evidence suggested. Yes, there seemed to be plenty of evidence to prove that Hauptmann was the kidnapper. But it might not be possible to prove that he had intended to kill the baby. Maybe he had dropped the infant accidentally.

If kidnapping had been a felony in New Jersey at the time,

prosecutors would have been home free. That is, if they could prove that the baby died—accidentally or not—during the commission of a felony, then the kidnapper would be guilty of murder. But incredibly, given that the most famous kidnapping in American history had occurred in Hunterdon County, New Jersey, kidnapping in the Garden State was still a misdemeanor.* And an unintentional death that occurred during the commission of a misdemeanor would only have been manslaughter. In other words, prison for the kidnapper but not the electric chair.

Hauptmann might have spent the rest of his life behind bars had he been convicted of manslaughter in New Jersey, then convicted of extortion in New York State, and *then* convicted of entering the United States illegally as a stowaway. But that was not deemed enough.

Fortunately for prosecutors, larceny and common-law burglary (breaking into another's house at night with intent to commit a felony) *were* felonies in New Jersey at the time. So maybe prosecutors could show that Hauptmann committed a burglary, then committed larceny when he stole…the baby's clothes?

The rationale might have seemed a bit odd, but prosecutors were willing to thread any needles, jump through any hoops, to nail Hauptmann for murder. And while they didn't say so, they surely knew that the good people of the Garden State and their representatives on a grand jury wouldn't mind fancy semantics as long as the killer of the Lindbergh baby paid the ultimate penalty.**

---

*   In the aftermath of the Lindbergh crime, New Jersey lawmakers made kidnapping a felony. The law has been revised several times over the years and now provides for a maximum sentence of twenty-five years to life, depending on the age of the victim, whether he or she was harmed, etc. Since the death penalty was abolished by New Jersey legislators in 2007, the maximum sentence for murder in the state is life without parole. Thus, if a fatal kidnapping occurs in New Jersey at present, the kidnapper can be sentenced to life without parole.

**   Decades after the Lindbergh case, a well-known New York State judge commented that a prosecutor "could indict a ham sandwich" if he chose to. That was a bit of an exaggeration, but it reflected the power a prosecutor has.

The Hunterdon County prosecutor, Anthony Hauck, decided that he and the people in his office had enough to do without tackling the Lindbergh case. So he gave the mission to the New Jersey attorney general, a little dynamo of a man named David Wilentz.

As the American public absorbed the stunning news of the arrest of the suspected kidnapper of the Lindbergh infant, then followed the day-to-day procedures required to bring him before the bar of justice in New Jersey, Hoover was keeping track of sightings of Pretty Boy Floyd, whom he stubbornly blamed for the Union Station Massacre in Kansas City.

Hoover's prayers were answered in October 1934 when Floyd and his accomplice Adam Richetti were tracked into Ohio. On October 20, they traded shots with police near Wellsville. Floyd escaped, but Richetti was captured.

Two days later, Floyd stopped at a farm near East Liverpool, Ohio, to ask for something to eat. A farmhand notified the police, who swarmed onto the farm with federal agents, led by Melvin Purvis. While fleeing across a field, Floyd was cut down by machine gun and pistol fire.

Some accounts, including one in the *New York Times*, said that as he lay dying, with presumably nothing to lose in this world or the next, Floyd denied any role in the Kansas City carnage. Other accounts say Floyd was more ambiguous, refusing to say anything about the train station shooting but muttering his contempt for the law as he breathed his last.

A headline in the next day's *New York Times* declared, "Floyd Called Last of Massacre Gang. Justice Department Says All of Kansas City Killers Are Accounted for."[149]

But what of Purvis's remark the previous March that the FBI suspected "Shotgun" George Ziegler might have been among the train station shooters? Purvis made his comment after Ziegler had been blown away outside a restaurant in Cicero, Illinois. Perhaps it doesn't matter much in the history of the universe if Ziegler was involved. But for the sake of tidiness, it would have been good if the issue had been addressed after Floyd was slain.

Maybe the crime reporters of that time had enough to write about without worrying too much about what Purvis had said several months before Floyd was gunned down. Besides, Hoover and his people weren't much for engaging in question-and-answer sessions. They issued statements, and reporters dutifully wrote what they said.

———————

The killing of Pretty Boy Floyd so soon after the slaying of John Dillinger was a priceless opportunity for Hoover to rehabilitate his and his bureau's image. The clean-cut and youthful Purvis, who turned thirty-one two days after Floyd was slain, seemed to embody Hoover's vision of the ideal FBI agent (although Hoover reportedly referred to him as "Little Mel" because Purvis stood only five feet four inches).

After Floyd was hunted down and killed, Purvis was briefly idolized in the press, as though the debacle at Little Bohemia Lodge had never happened. By extension, the hero worship enhanced the image of the entire bureau. And Hoover could blame Floyd and Richetti for the Kansas City Massacre. Which the bureau does, to this day.*

Richetti was convicted of murder for the Kansas City Massacre. Proclaiming his innocence to the last, he was executed in the state's gas chamber on October 7, 1938.

———————

* Hoover became jealous of the attention Purvis was getting after Floyd was killed. Sensing that he had fallen out of favor, Purvis left the FBI in 1935 to practice law. Rumors persisted that Hoover was still undermining him—plotting to keep him from getting a judgeship, for instance. Purvis died in an apparent suicide in 1960.

Recall the account of James Henry "Blackie" Audett, the gangster who knew Floyd and Richetti and who witnessed the train station shooting. He insisted that neither Richetti nor Floyd was there. If Audett was right about what he saw, if he was telling the truth, it means that Richetti—a hardened criminal, to be sure—was put to death for something he didn't do.

CHAPTER FORTY

CLOSING THE RING

Miami

Late 1934

Perhaps the people in the Barker-Karpis gang dared to hope that the arrest of Bruno Hauptmann in the Lindbergh kidnapping, followed just weeks later by the killing of Charles "Pretty Boy" Floyd, would take them out of the spotlight. Perhaps the law would even forget about them for a while.

It was not to be. One day in Havana, Karpis saw a picture of himself in a local newspaper. For whatever reason, Karpis's survival instincts, which had served him well up to that time, told him he'd be safer in Miami than in Havana, so he and his girlfriend, Dolores Delaney, moved there in the fall of 1934 and took up residence as "Mr. and Mrs. S. A. Green."

Fred Barker was also getting homesick for the States. Luckily or not, he met someone in Havana who knew someone who had a cottage in Ocklawaha, Florida, near Lake Weir, a big freshwater lake in Central Florida. Ocklawaha was a little spot on the road that hardly deserved to be called a village, as it consisted of just a few houses and stores on Lake Weir, about a hundred miles southwest of Jacksonville. The community had one telephone. But the isolation was ideal for people wanting to get away from it all—or people running from something.

The man and woman rented the white nine-room summer house of the man who was president of the Biscayne Kennel Club of Miami. It didn't seem right to call the "Blackburns" a couple, since the woman was considerably older than the man who accompanied her. In fact, they were mother and son.

The region around Lake Weir offered terrific fishing and hunting. "Mr. Blackburn" had hired a guide to lead him to the best spots to catch bass and hunt deer. One day, he did manage to shoot a deer. When he rolled up his sleeves to clean it, a tattooed heart on one arm was exposed. The guide was startled; he recalled reading in a newspaper that one of the kidnappers of Edward Bremer, the St. Paul banker and beer tycoon, had a heart tattoo on one arm. Quickly, the guide notified the authorities.

Thus did federal agents learn that the "Blackburns" were really the Barkers—Kate or "Ma," still the spiritual leader of the family at fifty-five, and her tattooed son Fred, thirty-two. For a year, they had been hunted for their part in the kidnapping of Edward Bremer. The law had really started to close in on them in December, when Arthur "Doc" Barker and his girlfriend were tracked to a location in Chicago. Biding their time, agents arrested Doc on January 8, 1935, without trouble. In the apartment where he'd been staying, investigators found a Thompson submachine gun believed to have been used in a 1933 payroll robbery in St. Paul, Minnesota, in which a police officer was slain.

Later on the night of January 8, gang member Russell Gibson was also cornered in Chicago. He elected to try to shoot his way out of the jam and was mortally wounded. (He was soon buried, without pallbearers or ceremony, as cemetery workers hustled the casket to a waiting gash in the frozen earth, then sought indoor warmth.)

Searching the places where Doc and Gibson had stayed, agents found firearms and ammunition and a map of Florida—with Lake Weir circled.

———

Before surrounding the Lake Weir cottage on the morning of Wednesday, January 16, 1935, agents quietly warned nearby residents to get out of the area.

Daylight was breaking when the agent in charge, E. J. Connelly, shouted for the people in the cottage to surrender.

How rich must have been the emotions of mother and son in that moment! They had never wanted to be taken alive, and now they knew that the sun was rising on the last day of their lives. The moment to fulfill their destiny had arrived. All they had to do was reach out and grasp it—or bend their trigger fingers.

They replied to the surrender demand with a burst of machine gun fire. The dozen or so federal agents answered with their own machine guns, plus tear gas canisters.

"Rifles and machine guns would crack for 15 minutes, then there would be a lull, followed by a renewal of firing from both sides," the *New York Times* reported, quoting the Associated Press.[150] "Most of the firing from the besieged house came from upstairs."

After six hours of gunplay, during which agents fired some fifteen hundred rounds of ammunition, the house fell silent. "When the shooting ceased from the house around 11 o'clock, the agents sent a Negro cook, who had been working there, into the building. He returned saying, 'They are all dead.'"

True to herself to the very end, Ma Barker had died with a machine gun in her hand. A bullet to the head had killed her, perhaps after she saw her son fall. Fred Barker lay near his mother, three bullet holes in his head and eleven in one shoulder.

So Hoover's men had collected two more trophies, but the operation was hardly flawless. A mother and daughter whose home was nearby almost became casualties. Awakened by bullets crashing through their bedrooms and dining room, the women fled through a rear window.

"As we ran, some men yelled at us to stop," the older woman said later. "We did not stop. They began shooting at us. I learned later it was the federal men. We kept on running and they kept on yelling and shooting... They didn't know who we were. It was still a little dark."

The woman's account suggests that she and her daughter were nearly killed by agents. If one or both *had* been killed, the shootout on Lake Weir would have been a tragedy and debacle equal to or worse than the deadly fiasco at Little Bohemia Lodge, Wisconsin, less than a year earlier.

Maddeningly, there seems to have been little or no criticism in the press of the agents' performance or of the man at the top who was in charge of their training. Blessed with uncanny luck and astonishingly good public relations, Hoover had dodged another bullet.

———

Days before the Florida shootout that killed Ma Barker and her son, Alvin Karpis's girlfriend, Dolores Delaney, had begun to wonder just how safe the hideout really was. Acting on her instincts, she hopped a train to Atlantic City, New Jersey, with a friend, Winona Burdette, who also hung around with gangsters. Dolores had friends in Atlantic City, which she decided would be a good place to give birth. She was expecting a child by Alvin Karpis.

Karpis and another member of what was left of the gang, Harry

Campbell, stole a car in Florida and drove north to join the women in Atlantic City. But their new hiding place, a small hotel near the boardwalk, turned out to be no safer than the Florida location. An Atlantic City cop spotted the Florida plate of the stolen car in a garage. The police soon deduced that Karpis, Campbell, and the women were staying in the hotel next to the garage.

On the night of Sunday, January 20, several policemen gathered outside the hotel room. When the cops ordered them to come out with their hands up, the bandits replied with machine-gun fire. The police were not only outgunned but probably not as used to deadly gunplay as the men they wanted.

A detective was wounded, as was Dolores Delaney, who was caught in the line of fire and struck in the leg. Karpis and Campbell were such seasoned gunmen that they drove the lawmen back with machine-gun volleys even as they were putting on overcoats and stepping into slippers. They escaped from the hotel (Campbell was reportedly wearing only underwear beneath his coat) and stole another car. And off they went into a snowy night.

The fugitives drove into Pennsylvania. Near Allentown, they forced a motorist off the road, tied him up, put him in the back seat, and sped west. Some 350 miles and many hours later, they put him out of his car near Akron, Ohio, and drove off, leaving the motorist with an adventure story to tell for the rest of his days.

As for Karpis, the target on his back was bigger than ever. Charles "Baby Face" Nelson, notorious killer and robber who had been with John Dillinger in the battle at the Little Bohemia Lodge in Wisconsin, had been cornered and shot dead by federal agents at Barrington, Illinois, near Chicago, on November 27, 1934. But before he was slain, he managed to kill two agents. Since he had already been "credited" with killing one of Purvis's men at Little Bohemia, Nelson is believed to have killed more federal agents (three) than any other outlaw in United States history.

———————

It may be recalled that Volney Davis had friends in both the Dillinger and Barker-Karpis gangs. Davis was thirty-two years old in 1934. Born in Oklahoma, he was a rather handsome man with wavy hair.

Davis and his then-girlfriend, Edna Murray, were eventually suspected of taking part in the kidnapping of Edward Bremer, once the FBI figured out that the Barker-Karpis bunch (and not Verne Sankey or God only knew who else) had abducted the banker-brewer.

FBI agents caught up with Davis in St. Louis on Wednesday, February 6, 1935, and made arrangements to fly him to St. Paul to stand trial in the Bremer case. But on February 7, soon after the plane carrying him and two federal agents took off from Kansas City, it ran into bad weather and made an emergency landing on a farm near Yorkville, Illinois. Davis had been manacled while on the plane, but after the landing, his chains were removed as a farmer drove the prisoner and two agents to a hotel in Yorkville.

Incredibly, while one agent was telephoning Chicago for instructions, his partner took Davis to the hotel bar. "What'll you have?" the agent asked his prisoner and new drinking buddy.[151]

"I'll take beer," Davis replied. He held his stein just long enough to throw the contents into the face of the agent, whom he stunned with a punch. Then Davis plunged through the nearest window as the agent fired three shots at him. All missed. Davis quickly stole a car and motored off—to Chicago, fifty-eight miles to the northeast, it would be learned later.*

———————

* The account of Volney Davis's escape is taken from the *New York Times*, though it is not clear if the dispatch, written in Chicago, was by a regular *Times* correspondent or a freelance stringer.

Months afterward, Purvis would concede in the *Chicago Tribune* that the agents had bungled the handling of Davis, and indeed it cost them their jobs. Yet their flabbergasting incompetence seems to have set off little, if any, criticism of the bureau's leadership. Yet again, Hoover seemed almost immune.

Davis would remain at large until June 1, when he was caught in Chicago, this time for good. In his initial capture and before he fled after the plane made a forced landing, agents had found on him a piece of paper with a Chicago phone number. Agents staked out the address that matched the phone number and waited for Davis to show up—which he eventually did, no doubt much to the bureau's relief.

Davis sought to lessen his punishment by giving information on what was left of the Barker-Karpis gang and giving testimony against them. Still, he was convicted of taking part in the kidnapping of Edward Bremer and was sent off to Alcatraz to meditate for several decades.

By the spring of 1935, it was clear that the heyday of the Barker-Karpis gang was over and that the white heat generated by the kidnapping of Edward Bremer, which had once seemed such a tidy, professional job, had contributed to the gangsters' undoing.

On Saturday, May 3, Harry Sawyer was arrested in New Orleans, becoming the thirteenth person arrested in the Bremer case. He had been doing what he knew best: running a dance hall and gambling den on the Mississippi coast.* Altogether, some dozen people had been indicted for the Bremer kidnapping by this time. It was believed to be the first case in which the federal government went after not only the principals but virtually *everyone* involved in a kidnapping.

On Friday, May 17, 1935, five defendants were convicted in St.

---

* Sawyer would spend nearly twenty years in Leavenworth and Alcatraz. His wife divorced him. He was paroled in 1955 and soon died of cancer.

Paul of taking part in the Bremer crime. Two of them, Doc Barker and Oliver Berg, were immediately sentenced to life in prison for being among the ringleaders of the enterprise (though it probably didn't matter much to Berg, who was already serving a life term in Illinois state prison for murder).

But the biggest fish of all, Alvin Karpis, was still at large. Another suspect still missing was Dr. Joseph Moran, whose remains at that moment were floating across Lake Erie toward Canada. Another gang member, it was learned later, shared a weakness with Dr. Moran. He talked too much. His name was William Harrison, and it was discovered later that he had been lured to an abandoned barn in rural Illinois in early 1935 and shot to death. His body was incinerated.

And one mystery about the Bremer kidnapping remained. It will be recalled that during Bremer's captivity, he heard church chimes playing the "Angelus." Investigators set about trying to find the church, thinking it might lead them to the kidnappers' lair. But did it?

Not long after Edward Bremer was freed, the *New York Times* reported that FBI agents had zeroed in on the small village of Menominee, in northeastern Nebraska, where a Catholic church with chimes was found. But Bremer eventually identified his place of imprisonment as a house owned by one Harold Alderton in Bensenville, Illinois, not far from Chicago and well over five hundred miles east of Menominee, Nebraska.

On Hoover's orders, agents spent hundreds of man-hours "revisiting every town between Joliet and central Wisconsin in search of the right combination of trains, church bells, and factory whistles Bremer had heard while in custody. The agents churned out hundreds of reports but...found nothing."[152] One FBI official even floated the idea of enlisting boy scouts in the search.

What part the mysterious chimes played, if any, in leading

investigators to the kidnappers wasn't explained after the initial flurry of publicity at the time.*

———————

There was so much domestic crime news in the early months of 1935 that it may have been hard for some readers to keep up with international affairs. And no doubt about it, much of the news from abroad was depressing, particularly in Europe. Adolf Hitler seemed less and less willing to be friendly with Britain and France, who had fought Germany in the Great War, and more and more eager to reclaim his country's place on the world stage.

Chancellor Hitler was even uttering suspicious and hostile words toward the Soviet Union, complaining that the Land of the Tsars posed a security threat to Germany in the East. All in all, there was almost nothing conciliatory in what the German leader was saying. But upon reflection, a reader might find comfort. Surely, the German dictator would not go to war against Britain, France, *and* the Soviet Union. That would be an unimaginable conflagration.

———————

In the summer of 1935, Doc Barker was shipped to Alcatraz for what was supposed to be a long stay. (He would make his stay a relatively short one, as he was shot dead on January 13, 1939, during an escape attempt.)

But though the Barker-Karpis gang had been dismantled—all but destroyed, really—Hoover could not have been totally content. Alvin "Creepy" Karpis remained at large, traveling from Hot Springs,

---

* Yet the anecdote was too good to be abandoned. When Edward Bremer died in 1965 at the age of sixty-seven, some versions of his obituary reported that he had helped investigators by recalling the church chimes.

Arkansas, to New Orleans (or so it was rumored) and venturing north now and then to pull off another heist.

Hoover detested Karpis—detested the cold, defiant eyes, the insolent lips that looked as though a worm might crawl from between them. Given what we have learned about the director over the years, he may well have disliked the very *foreignness* of Karpis, né Karpowicz, born in Montreal to Lithuanian parents.

If his agents could capture Karpis, the last slimy vestiges of the gang would be eradicated forever. Then the bureau would finally get the full credit it deserved.

In the spring of 1936, the "war on crime" hadn't gone out of fashion, and Hoover and his men still enjoyed a good public image, mostly. So Hoover felt confident enough to seek a doubling of the FBI's budget for the next fiscal year.

But not everyone in law enforcement worshipped the FBI. Far from it. Lawmen in other agencies, federal as well as state and local, thought Hoover and his men hogged the credit for a notable arrest whenever possible. And despite his bureaucratic agility and his political in-fighting skills, Hoover made his share of enemies, sometimes because of pure pettiness.

So it was that on the morning of Friday, April 10, 1936, when Hoover walked into a Senate hearing room to push for his huge budget increase, he got a hostile reception. And small wonder: the budget subcommittee chairman was Senator Kenneth McKellar, Democrat of Tennessee, who despised the director. Hoover had ignited the senator's fury by refusing to hire a pair of Tennessee men backed by McKellar and, when the senator complained, by firing three agents from Tennessee out of spite.

Hoover came into the hearing armed with charts, graphs, statistics, and other data to convince the lawmakers that the bureau was accomplishing a lot—and could accomplish even more with a bigger budget.

But McKellar seemed not much interested in Hoover's dog-and-pony show. He began with some barbed questions about how the bureau generated publicity for itself. "It seems to me your department is just running wild, Mr. Hoover. With all the money in your hands, you are just extravagant."[153]

McKellar grilled Hoover on his qualifications to run the bureau. Hoover noted that he had been with the Justice Department for nineteen years.

"Did you ever make an arrest?" the senator asked.[154]

"No, sir," Hoover replied. "I have made investigations."

"How many *arrests* have you made, and who were they?"

Somewhat lamely, Hoover replied that arrests were made by "officers under my supervision."

Then the stinger: "I am talking about the actual arrests," McKellar said. "You never arrested them, actually?"*[155]

The silence was deafening. The director was being subjected to the kind of ear-burning humiliation he was used to dishing out but wasn't used to taking. When he got back to his inner sanctum, he issued an edict: find Alvin Karpis, and fast. And save him for *me*.

As it turned out, Karpis was relatively easy to find. By late April, he was in New Orleans, and the stage was set for the director's moment in the limelight.

When FBI agents, aided by postal inspectors, knew with near certainty where Karpis was holed up, Hoover was flown to New Orleans. On the evening of May 1, with Hoover waiting in the wings with a posse of his men, Karpis and an associate and the latter's girlfriend emerged from their hotel. Agents swarmed about them, and they were taken without resistance.

---

*   On this occasion, Hoover was, it could be argued, being treated unfairly. After all, the FBI had not even been given the power to make arrests until 1934. And Hoover was supposed to be an administrator, not a gumshoe street cop with handcuffs at the ready.

It has long been debated whether Hoover trained a gun on Karpis or just how close he was physically to the gangster, but no matter.

"Karpis Captured in New Orleans by Hoover Himself" read the headline in the *New York Times* the next day. "Another Man and Woman Are Also Seized by 15 Agents Under Federal Chief."[156]

All these years later, the episode conjures images of bwana sitting under a shade tree, sipping a gin and tonic and rifle at the ready, as bush beaters drive a trophy animal in his direction. But the headline and article beneath it conveyed none of that.

————————

Karpis was soon on a plane to St. Paul, Minnesota, where he was under federal indictment for the kidnappings of William Hamm and Edward Bremer. Perhaps hoping for leniency, he agreed just before trial to plead guilty to the Hamm kidnapping alone. But there was no mercy. By late summer, he was on his way to Alcatraz to serve a life sentence. The Barker-Karpis gang had passed into history, at long last.**

————————————

** The exchange between Senator McKellar and Hoover was recounted in Burrough, *Public Enemies*.

CHAPTER FORTY-ONE

IN THE WORLD'S SPOTLIGHT

Flemington, New Jersey
Wednesday, January 2, 1935

The spotlights of the nation and the world were trained on the quiet little borough of Flemington in Hunterdon County. It was there, in the century-old county courthouse, that Bruno Richard Hauptmann went on trial for the murder of the Lindbergh baby. Reporters, photographers, and movie-newsreel crews from around the globe were there to chronicle what will always rank as one of the most sensational criminal trials in American history.

Nowadays, many months might elapse between the arrest of a suspect in an infamous crime and the beginning of the trial. But Hauptmann was brought before the bar of justice just three and a half months after he gave the service station attendant the gold note that brought about his arrest.

Charles A. Lindbergh was there as jury selection began, sitting in front of the railing that separates the audience from those involved in the trial proceedings. The *New York Times* noted that he was only several seats away from the defendant. Astoundingly, Lindbergh was able to enter the courtroom while carrying a pistol in a shoulder holster, the weapon clearly visible when he leaned forward to talk to prosecutors. (The *Times* explained matter-of-factly that the colonel had carried a weapon for several years, since receiving death threats.)

With remarkable speed, eight men and four women were selected for the jury. Testimony began on January 3, after opening statements by the prosecutor, state attorney general David Wilentz, and the chief defense lawyer, Edward J. Reilly, who asserted that the crime was conceived and carried out entirely within the Lindbergh home—though not by anyone in the Lindbergh family. Was he trying to take advantage of the suicide of Violet Sharpe, who had come under suspicion early on?

Bizarrely, he said the defense would show that a gang of five people carried the baby from the house and that the ladder found at the scene had nothing to do with the crime. Nor, he insisted, did his client, whose connection with the ladder had seemingly been established, have anything to do with the crime.

"I have an awful lot of questions to ask Colonel Lindbergh, an awful lot of things I want answers to," the defense lawyer asserted cryptically in a radio interview. "An awful lot of questions."[157]

David Wilentz's position was far less mysterious. He said the state would show that Hauptmann used the ladder he had made to burglarize the Lindbergh home and that he took the baby and fell off his ladder on the way down, a plunge that killed the baby, whose corpse Hauptmann concealed a short distance away.*

Wilentz was disdainful of the defense notion that several people were

---

* If Wilentz could prove that Hauptmann committed the felony of burglary, then the defendant would be guilty of murder, since the baby died during the commission of that felony.

involved. The crime was a one-man job, he said, and that one man was Bruno Hauptmann, who should be convicted and sent to the electric chair.

Charles and Anne Lindbergh testified early on, with the colonel recalling the wood-clattering noise he and his wife heard the night of the kidnapping, how he remarked to his wife, "What is that?" He recalled how they dismissed the sound as possibly coming from a falling orange crate in the kitchen—or from the wind outside. The colonel spoke in a clear, seemingly unemotional voice, not betraying whether he reflected on the fact that the clattering noise might have coincided with the end of his firstborn's life.

Lindbergh recalled how, upon learning that the baby was not in his nursery, he picked up a phone, half expecting that that the phone line had been cut by whoever took the baby. But it hadn't been, so he called local police. Then he grabbed a rifle he kept in the house and went outside, walking on the road in front of the house for perhaps a hundred yards but seeing nothing.

"It was extremely dark that night," Lindbergh recalled. He said the ladder was discovered by the Hopewell police chief, Charles Williamson, one of the first lawmen to reach the scene, who shined his flashlight on the ground near the nursery window.

Before long, Lindbergh said, the grounds outside his home were swarming not only with lawmen of several jurisdictions but with members of the press, who were "absolutely out of control" as they tromped all over the grass.

His wife, though composed, was more soft-spoken. She kept her self-control even as she described taking a walk outside the house hours before the kidnapping. Knowing that nurse Betty Gow was with the baby, Mrs. Lindbergh recalled tossing a pebble against the nursery window to get the nurse's attention, "and then she held the baby up to the window to let him see me."[158]

She even maintained her calm in what must have been one of the most painful moments for her, when she identified the sleeping suit the infant had worn the night he vanished.

The defense lawyer, Edward Reilly, had the good sense not to cross-examine a grieving mother, who uttered a quiet "thank you" as she was told she could step down.

Reilly was rougher on Lindbergh himself. Was the colonel *really* certain that the voice he heard in St. Raymond's Cemetery the night he went there with John Condon was that of Bruno Hauptmann?

Yes, Lindbergh responded, recalling that the mysterious man in the cemetery called out to Condon "in a foreign accent, 'Hey, doctor.'"*

The heart of Reilly's cross-examination was the attempt to show that the household help at the Lindberghs' home had not been properly vetted. "Thundering at the witness, Mr. Reilly demanded whether he had not made any effort 'as a father' to 'find out the backgrounds of the people that were in the house the night your child was snatched away,'" the *New York Times* reported.

Lindbergh coolly replied that, of course, he had placed his "entire confidence" in the police, who offered suggestions on whom to hire.

"Well, Colonel, as a man of the world, you certainly must have known that some of the police are not infallible, did you not?"

"I think we have very good police," Lindbergh replied.

The *Times* reporter made it clear who he thought had won the courtroom duel and where his own sympathies lay, observing how "the heavily built and red-faced defense counsel strikingly contrasted in figure with the tall, slim boyish-looking aviator" and how whenever Lindbergh "scored a neat rapier thrust against the lawyer's bludgeon" the crowd

---

* It is not clear from the trial testimony when Lindbergh might have heard the voice again by way of comparison. Perhaps it was during the hearing on Hauptmann's extradition from New York City to New Jersey.

of several hundred people "burst into laughter at the lawyer's expense," finally prompting the judge, Thomas W. Trenchard, to admonish the audience.[159] (This was not the only instance in which the *Times* violated its standards of dispassionate objectivity. At another point in the trial, the newspaper noted that Hauptmann was dressed "as he had been every day in a suit, the color of which closely approximates the field gray of the German wartime uniform."[160]

The second week of the trial brought more damaging testimony against Hauptmann. A Bronx cab driver identified the defendant as the man who paid him a dollar one night in March 1932 to deliver a message to John Condon, the eccentric Bronx educator who had insinuated himself into the ransom negotiations. "You're a liar," Hauptmann muttered at the cab driver.[161]

And Amandus Hochmuth, who was eighty-seven and lived in Hopewell, swore that he saw Hauptmann the day of the kidnapping driving by his home and in the direction of the Lindbergh estate with a ladder sticking out of the car. After Hochmuth identified him, Hauptmann turned to his wife, Anna, seated a short distance away and said in German, "The old man is crazy."

If defense lawyers thought they could undermine John Condon, they were mistaken. Still vigorous at seventy-four, Condon was not unnerved at testifying before several hundred people in one of the most publicized trials in the nation's history. On the contrary, he obviously relished it.

Prosecutor David Wilentz asked him to whom he talked on the night of March 12, 1932, in Van Cortlandt Park and to whom he gave the ransom money on the night of April 2, 1932.

"It was John," the witness replied.

"And who is John?"

"John is Bruno Richard Hauptmann!" Condon boomed.[162]

The *Times* account had Condon remaining unshaken through cross-examination and even enjoying the back-and-forth with defense lawyer Reilly. That evening after court, Reilly insisted that Condon had been mistaken about his encounters with the man once dubbed "Cemetery John," that the phantom-like figure was not Hauptmann but Hauptmann's friend Isidor Fisch, who had returned to Germany, where he died. (Whatever Reilly asserted outside of court wasn't supposed to matter if the jurors were heeding the judge's instructions not to read or listen to news accounts of the trial.)

The prosecution produced eight handwriting experts to testify that there was no doubt at all that the ransom messages were written by Hauptmann. They based their conclusions on comparisons between the writing on the notes, handwriting samples that Hauptmann gave after he was arrested, and earlier specimens of the defendant's penmanship, like those submitted with his application for a driver's license.

On the twelfth day of the trial, FBI agent Thomas Sisk, whom Hoover had put in charge of the bureau's contingent assigned to the case, testified on how Hauptmann, as he was questioned in his apartment, glanced furtively out the window toward his garage where the money was hidden. Suddenly, Hauptmann leaped from his chair and shouted, "Mister, mister, you stop lying!"[163]

The next day, Anna Hauptmann echoed her husband's outburst as a former neighbor testified that a day or two after the kidnapping, Bruno Hauptmann was limping noticeably. Her testimony buttressed the state's contention that Hauptmann had fallen from his ladder after taking the baby.

"You're lying!" Anna Hauptmann shouted.[164]

The prosecution added to the growing mound of evidence against the defendant by introducing a closet door from Hauptmann's apartment on which the address and phone number of John Condon had been written in pencil. An investigator testified that Hauptmann had offered a lame explanation for writing down the number, saying that he did so simply because he'd been following the case with interest. Yet with everything seeming to go against him, Hauptmann issued a statement through one of his lawyers. He expected to be acquitted, he said, because "the state has failed to prove its case."[165]

"I have no fear of cross-examination," he said. "I will tell the truth." And after he was found not guilty, "I hope the world will forget all about me and that I will be allowed to live quietly with my family."

But Wilentz was about to call his final—and most devastating—witness. He was Arthur Koehler, head of the U.S. Forest Service's laboratory, who had traced the origins of the wood the kidnapper had used to fashion his ladder. Wilentz asked Koehler to relate how he had traced some of the wood to the lumber mill in South Carolina.

"It's a long story," the witness said.[166]

"Let's hear it," Wilentz said. "We want the long story."

Wilentz had assumed that the jurors would find the "long story" an enthralling one. He was apparently correct, as the jurors leaned forward in their chairs as Koehler told of finding the South Carolina mill with its telltale machinery that left distinctive, if nearly invisible, marks on the finished lumber—marks that were photographed and shown enlarged in the courtroom.

Hauptmann listened white-faced as Koehler explained how he had matched some boards in the ladder—those that had been used before, as shown by nail holes—with the boards in Hauptmann's attic and how the nail holes perfectly matched the holes in the attic joists.

The witness said the chisel found on the ground near the Lindberghs' home was from Hauptmann's own tools—and was the only tool missing from the set.

Just as damningly, he testified that an examination of Hauptmann's hand plane (a carpentry tool used to smooth edges on wood and to shave boards down to near-exact size) showed that it had been used to shave a board on the ladder.

"Have you the plane and will you give us a demonstration?" Wilentz asked.[167]

"Yes," Koehler said. "I employ a very simple method that I learned as a youngster. I used to put a piece of paper over a coin and rub a pencil back and forth over the paper and get an impression of the coin on the paper."

He explained that he could get the same kind of impression by putting a piece of paper on a board that had been planed, thus revealing the marks left by that particular tool.

Then Koehler asked the judge if he could set up a vise on his bench to demonstrate. The judge gave permission, whereupon Koehler used Hauptmann's plane to shave the side of a board, put a piece of paper on the planed surface, and rubbed it with a pencil—and obtained an impression that matched the hand plane marks on a section of the kidnapper's ladder.

The defense had tried early on to discredit Koehler's testimony, questioning at the start whether there was even such a thing as "a wood expert," as lawyer Frederick Pope put it. But clearly there was. His name was Arthur Koehler, and he proved to be unshakable on cross-examination. He had the science on his side. Not only that, but he was the son of a carpenter and was an accomplished carpenter himself.

Shrewdly, Wilentz had managed to place sixty-year-old Liscom Case on the jury. Case could appreciate and understand Koehler's testimony better than his fellow jurors, as he was a retired carpenter.

Taking the stand in his own defense, Hauptmann said that on the night of the kidnapping, he and his wife were drinking coffee in the Bronx bakery where she worked and where he often picked her up to take her home. And the night the ransom was paid, he said, he and his wife were entertaining friends.

But the defense was unable to produce witnesses who could testify with absolute certainty that Hauptmann was where he claimed to have been on those nights.

On cross-examination, Wilentz ripped into the defendant, forcing him to acknowledge his record of burglary and robbery in Germany, his escape from jail in his native country, and his illegal entry into the United States. The prosecutor brought up a particularly ugly crime from the defendant's past, when Hauptmann and another man robbed two women who were wheeling baby carriages.

"Everybody wheels baby carriages!" Hauptmann replied, heatedly and illogically.[168]

"'Everybody wheels baby carriages,'" Wilentz repeated scathingly. "And you and this man held up these two women wheeling baby carriages, didn't you?"

The defense objected, and the judge ruled that the fact of the defendant's conviction in Germany had been well established. But Hauptmann's temper display and his odd response—"Everybody wheels baby carriages!"—had surely discredited him in the eyes of the jurors.

As for the big stash of money found where Hauptmann lived (money that he had claimed must have been left there by his deceased friend and business associate Isidor Fisch), the defendant claimed it was his habit to squirrel away money rather than deposit it all in banks. But this explanation didn't quite square with his claims, never substantiated, that he was sophisticated enough to have made money with good investments.

Wilentz's cross-examination went on for many hours. The prosecutor got the defendant to acknowledge contradictions, even outright lies, contained in his earlier testimony during a hearing to have him extradited from New York to New Jersey. And Wilentz induced the defendant to sputter and display hostility several times.

But in the end, it may have been a few indisputable facts that doomed Bruno Hauptmann. Money from the Lindbergh ransom had been found on his premises and in his pockets. John Condon's address and phone number were written on a closet door in his apartment. And the ladder used to build the wood had been traced to him, thanks to the solid science and endless persistence of Arthur Koehler, the man who loved trees.

We can be fairly certain that Dr. Dudley Shoenfeld, a pioneer in what would come to be called criminal profiling, followed the trial. Surely, he took some satisfaction in reading that the defendant had behaved as he had predicted: arrogant and seemingly confident, at least at first, that he could talk his way out of anything, no matter how ludicrous he sounded, no matter how much the truth was against him.

———————————

"The lowest and vilest type of man," Wilentz branded Hauptmann during the prosecution's closing statement on Wednesday, February 13, 1935. "An animal" and "a cold-blooded child murderer" who deserved to be put to death.[169]

Wilentz added a late element to his case: the hypothesis that Hauptmann had struck the baby on the head with his chisel as he lay in the crib, thereby stunning him into silence as he was being spirited through the window. Perhaps the prosecutor was trying to extinguish any lingering doubt among the jurors that a kidnapper could have climbed into the nursery and taken the baby without causing him to cry out. Or was he trying to excise any sympathy the jurors might have felt if they thought Hauptmann had killed the child accidentally?

Shortly before noon, the jury began deliberating.

In a quaint small-town custom, a 125-year-old bell in the courthouse was rung to signal the community that a jury had reached a verdict. The bell tolled at 11:28 p.m. the night of February 13, 1935. The jurors found Hauptmann guilty of murder. They did not recommend mercy, so Hauptmann was immediately sentenced to death. Upon hearing the verdict and sentence, Hauptmann's face went "ashen white" with terror, the *Times* observed.*[170]

By the night of his execution, Friday, April 3, 1936, Bruno Richard Hauptmann seemed to have accepted his fate. "I am glad that my life in a world which has not understood me has ended," he said in a statement composed shortly before the execution. "I protest my innocence of the crime for which I was convicted. However, I die with no malice or hatred in my heart. The love of Christ has filled my soul and I am happy in Him."[171]

He walked calmly into the death chamber at Trenton State Prison accompanied by two ministers, one of whom read from the Bible in German. His face was impassive as his arms and legs were strapped and the electrodes were fixed. The current rushed through his body, and he was pronounced dead a few minutes later.

---

*   I am indebted to Richard T. Cahill Jr., whose fine book *Hauptmann's Ladder: A Step-by-Step Analysis of the Lindbergh Kidnapping* added to my understanding of the legal proceedings. I am also indebted to the bygone reporters, editors, printers, and pressmen of the *New York Times* who produced the magnificent coverage of the Hauptmann trial. Their work showed the *Times* at its best.

CHAPTER FORTY-TWO

HEIR TO A TIMBER EMPIRE

Tacoma, Washington
Friday, May 24, 1935

"You're just like other kids." That was the message that John Philip Weyerhaeuser Jr. tried daily to convey to his two daughters and two sons. He wanted them to be healthy, happy, normal children.

But most children of that time were not chauffeured to and from their exclusive private schools. They did not live, as the Weyerhaeuser family did, in a mansion that was on a par with those owned by people whose surnames were Rockefeller or Carnegie or Vanderbilt. Indeed, the Weyerhaeusers were royalty in the Pacific Northwest, fabulously wealthy because of the family patriarch, Friedrich Weyerhaeuser, a German immigrant with the drive and vision characteristic of the men who became industrial titans in America's Gilded Age.

Friedrich came to the United States in 1852 at the age of seventeen. At first, he planned to make a living (and perhaps a fortune one day) brewing beer. But according to one story, perhaps apocryphal, he was afraid that a brewer might become his own best customer. So he worked on a railroad in Illinois and later at a sawmill where he soon rose to a managerial position.

But he was at heart an *entrepreneur*, not an executive. He moved to the Northwest and saw the future—and it was wood. He jumped at the chance to invest his savings in timberland—some nine hundred thousand acres of it, which he bought from the Great Northern Railway at a bargain price.

John Philip Weyerhaeuser Jr. was the grandson of Friedrich. He had just returned from Illinois, where he had buried his father, John Sr., who had died on May 16.

John Jr.'s son George Hunt Weyerhaeuser was destined to rule over what was becoming, and what is today, one of the greatest timber empires in the world. But in the spring of 1935, he was a nine-year-old schoolboy. On this Friday, May 24, he followed his usual routine: when the students at his private school were set free for lunch, he walked to the nearby girls' school that his sister Ann, thirteen, attended. There, the family chauffeur generally drove both home for their midday meal. There were two other children, Philip, ten, and Elizabeth, who was just two.

But on this day, George's class had been let out earlier than normal, so he got to his sister's school with time to spare. Rather than wait for her, he began to walk home. On the way, he took a shortcut through some tennis courts, where he encountered a man who said he needed directions.

George was all set to be helpful, but the man didn't really want directions. He wanted George. The man and several accomplices had been tracking the boy's movements for weeks, waiting for their chance. When George took a shortcut alone, they had it.

The man grabbed George and carried him to a car parked across the street. George saw another man sitting in the front seat. Then he was put into the back seat and covered with a blanket. For the next hour or so, the nine-year-old endured the emotional agony common to kidnapping victims, a fear to freeze the heart of an adult, let alone a child. George was terrified, not knowing what would happen to him, when he would get to go home. Had he done something *wrong* that this should be happening to him?

The car stopped. The men removed the blanket, and George saw that they were by the side of a country road. He was given an envelope and a pencil. Write your name on the back, he was told. He did. Then he was pulled from the car, blindfolded, and picked up by one of the men. Soon, he heard the sound of rushing water close by, then the sound was louder and beneath him.

He's wading across the stream, George thought. "Are you going to drown me?" he asked.

"No, kid, you're worth more to us alive."

On dry land again, George was set down, then led by the hand. He felt bushes and trees bumping him. *We're in the woods*, he thought. After a long hike, they stopped. George's blindfold was taken off. The first thing he saw was a hole in the ground. His captors chained his right wrist and leg and put him inside, then covered the hole with a board.

The men stayed nearby. George could hear them talking. Darkness came.

―――――

When George didn't come home for lunch, his parents were alarmed. When the people at George's school said they didn't know where the boy was, the distraught parents called the police. John Jr.'s wife, Helen, George's mother, was reported to be in a state of near collapse.

That night, a special delivery letter arrived at the Weyerhaeuser home. It demanded $200,000 in unmarked twenty-, ten-, and five-dollar bills for

George's safe return. And no gold certificates, the kidnappers decreed. They were apparently aware that Bruno Hauptmann, convicted only a few months earlier for the kidnapping and slaying of the Lindbergh baby, had been caught after spending a gold certificate from the ransom money.

George's signature was on the back of the envelope. The kidnappers also specified that an advertisement, signed "Percy Minnie," be placed in the *Seattle Post-Intelligencer* to signal that the family would comply with the demands.

On Wednesday, May 29, John Weyerhaeuser got a letter from the kidnappers. Go to the Ambassador Hotel in Seattle, register as "James Paul Jones," and wait, the letter ordered. And thank God Almighty, enclosed with the letter was a note from George, saying that he was safe.

Weyerhaeuser checked in at the hotel. That night, a cab driver delivered another letter to him. It ordered him to drive out of the city to a certain point on a country road and look for two sticks driven into the ground with a piece of white cloth attached. Weyerhaeuser did as ordered and found the sticks and cloth, along with a message directing him to find another sticks-and-cloth site farther along the road.

Weyerhaeuser did as commanded, but when he got to the second site, there were no further orders. He waited for two hours before going back to the hotel. Was he able to sleep at all that night? We don't know.

The next morning, Weyerhaeuser got a phone call.

"You didn't follow instructions last night," the caller said.

"I did," Weyerhaeuser said. "There was no other note. I couldn't—"

Click.

It was Memorial Day. Those millions of Americans whose lives were still normal were celebrating the start of summer. For Weyerhaeuser, it was a day full of fear and frustration. All he could do was wait. And wait.

By this point, Weyerhaeuser was carrying $200,000 in cash. It had been marked, despite the kidnappers' orders. Gathering the money had been an effort. Of course, the Weyerhaeuser family was worth many times that much. But it was no small feat to amass that much in *cash*.

Shortly before ten that night, another phone call. The man on the line had a European accent, Weyerhaeuser thought. The man told him to go to an address where he would find a note in a tin can.

But this time, it was decided that Weyerhaeuser would stay home and one of George's uncles, F. Rodman Titcomb, would try to make the delivery.* Titcomb drove into the country, found the location and the tin can—only to be directed to another site, and still another. He understood the kidnappers' tactics. They were not just toying with him; they were making it all but impossible for lawmen to pursue them without giving themselves away.

But local and state police had already agreed to stand aside, at least for the time being. So had FBI agents, a small army of whom had gathered in the Seattle-Tacoma area.

Finally on that wearying night, Titcomb was steered to a site on a dirt road off the main highway between Seattle and Tacoma. There, he found a flag and a note. Wait five minutes with the inside light of your car on, the note said. Then go to yet *another* place on the same road and find a note. He did.

Leave your car engine on and leave the money, he was ordered. Walk back toward Seattle. If the money is all here, your son will soon be back with you.

Titcomb had walked about the length of a football field when he heard sounds behind him. He turned in time to see a man get in the car

---

* Some later accounts say that George's father drove into the country to effect delivery. But reports at the time, including direct quotes from Titcomb, make it all but certain that he undertook the mission.

and drive off with the money. Titcomb walked until he was able to hitch a ride back to Tacoma.

———

Cowering in the hole in the ground that first night away from home, George Weyerhaeuser thought he heard the two men talking about how the police might fight him. For whatever reason, they pulled him out of the ground, carried him back to the car, and put him in the trunk. In that pitch-black place, he felt the car bump and jostle on the way to—where?

After a while, George was yanked from the trunk and led through more dark woods. Finally, the men stopped and ordered him to wait by a tree. George did, hearing the sounds of shovels plunging into dirt. The men were digging another hole. Finally, he was put into the hole, along with a car seat and two blankets. He heard something being put across the hole (tar paper, it would be revealed later), and George was left alone in the inky darkness. He thought he heard things crawling in the ground.

To the nine-year-old, it seemed forever ago that he had been walking home to lunch. In fact, it was "only" two days after he was taken that the two men (accompanied now by a woman) put him in the car trunk again and drove. George had no way of knowing that they had crossed the state line into Idaho.

In the early morning, the boy was taken out of the trunk and handcuffed to a tree. He could see mountaintops over the trees. He was guarded until night came. He tried not to be afraid. He remembered what the man had said: "You're worth more to us alive."

———

"This looks like a 'big league' job," U.S. Marshal A. J. Chitty said in Seattle.[172] "There was talk at first that it was done locally, but we've assumed now that outsiders, some big shot gangsters from the East maybe, are mixed up in it." (Perhaps Chitty's remarks reflected a lingering prejudice that the younger West had not yet "caught up" with the more sophisticated East. After all, it was not until 1928, with the election of the Iowa-born Herbert Hoover, that the country chose as its president a man born west of the Mississippi River.)

There was also speculation that left-wing union members were behind the crime (the Weyerhaeuser company was having labor troubles at the time), but union leaders quickly dashed any such talk, expressing hopes for the child's quick, safe recovery. "This is something in which differences of social position are erased," Rowland Watson, Northwest representative of the American Federation of Labor, declared as he urged members to be on the lookout for the boy.[173]

By any standards, the kidnapping was a bold one. The name Weyerhaeuser carried as much clout in the Northwest as the Bremer name did in the Midwest and the name Urschel did in Oklahoma. And Washington State had passed a law making kidnapping punishable by death under some circumstances. Simple conspiracy to kidnap was a felony.

———————

George listened to the voices; he thought he counted six, including that of a woman.

His captors had taken him to a house and blindfolded him, but not before he saw that the structure had two gables. He heard some of the men call one another by name: Harry, Bill, Allen. Or was it *Alvin*, as in Alvin Karpis, the bandit whose sneering face and piercing eyes were familiar throughout the country from wanted posters?

Sometimes, they took his blindfold off. When they did, they wore Halloween masks. George thought they looked funny, but he didn't laugh.

And while homesick, he wasn't terrified. He recalled what one of

the men had said early on: "You're worth more to us alive." He knew
he was.

Finally came the moment he had yearned for. One of the kidnappers approached him and said, not unkindly, "Kid, you're going home."

It was cold and wet, very early on the morning of Saturday, June 1,
when three kidnappers put him in a car and drove. It was pitch-black,
and while George didn't know it, he was near Issaquah, a little city east of
Seattle and northeast of Tacoma when the car stopped and he was let out.
He was given two dirty blankets and a dollar bill, stuffed into a pocket.

"Your pa will pick you up," a kidnapper said just before the car
sped off.

But how will he find me? George wondered. Instead of waiting, he
walked. And walked. It would be determined later that he walked some
six miles in the cold and rain before coming to a farmhouse. He knocked
on the door, and Louis Bonifas, a chicken rancher with ten children,
opened the door.

"I'm the little boy who was kidnapped," George said.

Bonifas's wife, Willena, sat George down and gave him breakfast
and dry socks and shoes. Then her husband put George into his Model
T Ford and headed toward Tacoma. As daylight was breaking, he found
a gas station, called the Tacoma police, and said he was taking the boy
home.

Then a reporter insinuated himself into the events in a way that
would be hard to conceive today. John Dreher, a veteran reporter for the
Seattle Times, got wind that George had been freed and was on his way
to Tacoma. So Dreher commandeered a taxi in the hope of intercepting
the car bringing him home. Dreher figured there wouldn't be many cars
on the road so early on a Saturday morning, and he was right.

Dreher saw Bonifas's car with a little boy inside, flagged the car
down, and somehow convinced Bonifas to turn George over to *him*.

Dreher either presented himself as a police officer or at least did not discourage the misperception that he was a cop. So on the way to the Weyerhaeuser home in the taxi, Dreher got an exclusive interview with the nine-year-old kidnap victim.

———

"Tacoma Boy Free, $200,000 Is Paid: He Names Karpis."[174]

That was the lead headline in the *New York Times* of June 2, 1935. On the inside page where the article was continued, there were photographs of Karpis and Harry Campbell, who had escaped with Karpis in the Atlantic City shootout the previous January 20.

But did it really make sense that Karpis (perhaps accompanied by Campbell) had driven across the country to pull off what they surely knew would be another sensational kidnapping, one that would put hundreds of federal and local lawmen on their trail? Not really.

The car belonging to F. Rodman Titcomb, George's uncle, was soon found abandoned in the Chinatown section of Seattle. Very quickly, money from the ransom began to turn up. A twenty-dollar bill turned up in Huntington, Oregon, where a train station agent recalled that a man had used the bill to buy a ticket to Salt Lake City. Another twenty turned up in Spokane, where it had been used to buy a postal money order. By June 7, a score of twenty-dollar bills from the ransom had turned up in Salt Lake City. So the FBI and local police were sure the kidnappers were from the region, not adventurous Easterners who had come west to strike gold.

At the FBI's urging, Salt Lake City police stationed undercover officers in the cashier's cages of downtown department stores. They didn't have to wait long. On Saturday, June 8, a young woman appeared at the cashier's cage with a five-dollar bill to pay for a twenty-cent purchase. The bill was identified at once as being from the ransom, and the woman was arrested. Another bill from the ransom was found in her purse.

Her name was Margaret Waley. She was just nineteen and had been living in Salt Lake City for only a few days. She was a newly-wed. The police staked out her residence, and soon her new husband, Harmon Waley, twenty-four, showed up. He, too, had ransom bills on his person—and he had a story to tell.

In 1930, Waley was doing six months for vagrancy in the Idaho State Penitentiary. There, he met William Dainard, who was serving twenty years for bank robbery. Somehow, he obtained a pardon and was turned loose in mid-1933. He knocked around the Northwest, drifting to Salt Lake City, where he met his future wife and married her after a three-day courtship. They eked out an existence as Waley dabbled in burglary and robbery.

Fatefully, Waley happened to run into Dainard in Salt Lake City, and they decided to relocate to Spokane, where they rented a house. In mid-May, Margaret saw a newspaper obituary for John Philip Weyerhaeuser Sr., which described the family's vast holdings. So the kidnapping idea was born. They rented an apartment in Seattle and waited for a chance to grab a member of the Weyerhaeuser family. They got their chance when young George took a shortcut on his way home from school.

The Waleys gave signed confessions to the FBI. Upon learning that they had been nabbed, Dainard took off for Butte, Montana, where he was spotted by a cop who thought he looked suspicious loitering near a car with Utah plates. As the cop approached, Dainard vaulted an alley fence and disappeared. Inside the car was a suitcase with some $15,000 in ransom money.

Back in Salt Lake City, the Waleys told the FBI where they had buried their share of the ransom: in a canyon several miles outside the city. Agents found some $90,000 in a sack wrapped in oilcloth.

The law moved with remarkable dispatch. Officials elected to try the Waleys in federal court on kidnapping, conspiracy, and extortion charges. Perhaps hoping for mercy, Harmon Waley pleaded guilty to kidnapping and conspiracy and was sentenced to forty-five years. Off he went, in July 1935, to Alcatraz.

Margaret Waley, despite having signed a confession, went to trial. She was convicted of kidnapping and conspiracy and sentenced to twenty years. But where was William Dainard?

Early in 1936, Federal Reserve notes with altered serial numbers began to appear on the West Coast. The FBI lab determined that the notes were part of the ransom. On Wednesday, May 6, employees of two San Francisco banks reported that a man had exchanged altered bills for clean ones. They noticed the man's car and wrote down the license plate number. The vehicle was registered to one Bert E. Cole, who was living in a hotel—across the street from the Federal Building, of all places. Early the next morning, FBI agents located the vehicle, disabled it, and waited. Around noon, "Bert Cole," better known as William Dainard, appeared and checked under the hood when his car would not start. Thus preoccupied, he was an easy arrest. Just over $7,000 in ransom money was found in his pockets and $30,000 in the hotel where he'd been staying.

The fight had gone out of William Dainard. He declined to be represented by a court-appointed lawyer and pleaded guilty at once to kidnapping and conspiracy to kidnap. He was sentenced to sixty years in prison, a short part of which was spent at the federal penitentiary in Leavenworth, Kansas, and in a mental hospital in Missouri. Then it was off to Alcatraz.

The final suspect in the Weyerhaeuser kidnapping, one Edward

Fliss, was tracked down and arrested in San Francisco in October. He pleaded guilty to being an accessory—his main job had been to launder the ransom money—and was sentenced to ten years in prison.

About $157,000 in ransom money was recovered, the rest having been spent or lost. But the return of the money to the Weyerhaeuser family did not end the story.*

George's father, John P. Weyerhaeuser Jr., gave Louis Bonifas a lifetime job in a Washington State lumber mill owned by his company. He also gave Bonifas a monetary reward, big enough so the chicken rancher with ten children could buy several acres of land and build a house.

The Weyerhaeuser case gave Hoover a happy ending and good reason to be proud. The FBI laboratory, created under Hoover, had traced the ransom notes, contributing greatly to the solution of the case.

Hoover was in dire need of an ego boost in 1936. *American Agent*, an autobiography by ex-FBI man Melvin Purvis, whom Hoover had driven into exile, was a bestseller, no doubt to Hoover's chagrin. (Two years later, Hoover's own ghostwritten literary effort, *Persons in Hiding*, was a flop, critically and commercially. "It is time that Mr. Hoover gave his ghost some fresh material," a *New York Times* review said. "This book is washed over and dimmed by banalities."[175])

———————

Margaret Waley was released from prison in 1948 after serving two-thirds of her sentence. Divorced from Harmon Waley, she remarried and settled in Salt Lake City. She died in 1989 at the age of seventy-four.

Harmon Waley wrote to the Weyerhaeuser family several times while in prison. He apologized for his crime and asked if he could have

---

*   In reconstructing the Weyerhaeuser case, I relied on contemporary accounts in the *New York Times* and the *Seattle Times*.

a job with the company when he got out. He was released in 1963 after serving twenty-eight years. In an act of great kindness, the Weyerhaeusers did give him a job at one of their Oregon mills. Waley died in Salem, Oregon, in 1984 at the age of seventy-three.

William Dainard was eventually granted parole and died in Great Falls, Montana, in 1992 at the age of ninety.

Edward Fliss served most of his ten-year sentence. He was released in 1946 and disappeared into anonymity.

George Weyerhaeuser's father, John Philip Weyerhaeuser Jr., died of leukemia in 1956 at the age of fifty-six.

And George Hunt Weyerhaeuser, whose kidnapping captivated the nation, graduated from Yale, rose through the ranks of his family's company, becoming chief executive. At the time of this writing, he is ninety-three years old.

CHAPTER FORTY-THREE

DEVIL AT THE DOOR

Tacoma, Washington
Saturday, December 27, 1936

The glow of Christmas still filled the home of Dr. William W. Mattson and his wife, Hazel. They were away at a holiday party, sure that their children were safe in their house. How could they *not* be? Dr. Mattson was one of Tacoma's best known surgeons, and the family lived in an exclusive neighborhood overlooking Commencement Bay.

It was shortly before 9:00 p.m. and the Mattson children—William Jr., sixteen; Muriel, fourteen; and Charles, ten—were enjoying root beer and popcorn in the sun porch that adjoined the living room. With them was Muriel's friend Virginia Chatsfield, fifteen, from Seattle.

William Mattson and his wife had decorated three large pine trees for the season. The trees stood where their lights lit up the porch and living room. There were decorations in the windows too. The Christmas lights bathed the spacious lawn outside.

All in all, it was the kind of evening that creates memories for a lifetime, of home and hearth and childhood friendships. Then everything changed, suddenly and forever.

Someone knocked loudly on the French doors that led onto a terrace at the back of the house. Charles went to investigate, then ran back to the others, saying that he had seen a man wearing a mask standing in the courtyard.

The pounding on the door resumed. The man muttered gibberish, but the children could tell he wanted to come inside. Then he smashed some glass panes, reached in to unlatch the door, and stepped in. It was impossible to reconstruct exactly what the intruder did and said, since the only witnesses were terrified children, but in their collective recollection this is about how things unfolded:

"Don't you kids try to start anything, because I have a bullet-proof vest on," the intruder said. Then he said something that seemed to make no sense: "I've put a lot of money into this house and I want to get some of it back."[176]

William Jr. told the intruder it was not his parents' habit to keep large sums in the house. The man searched William's pockets, finding nothing. Then he looked at Charles. "I want you to come with me right away. You're worth money." The invader dropped a piece of paper on the floor, grabbed Charles by the arm, dragged him through the rear door, and warned the other children not to call the police, or he would come back and kill them. Then he was gone with his young captive.

William Jr. called the police, who were at the house within minutes, then called his parents. The kidnapper's mask had slipped partly off, and the children were able to describe him: dark hair, brown eyes, unshaven. He was about five feet seven and of medium build, maybe thirty-five to forty, wearing a dark-blue jacket and dark work trousers. Charles was wearing blue knickers, a gray sweater, and slippers.

Investigators discounted the possibility that the kidnapper had come and gone by boat, as the night of the abduction coincided with one of the lowest tides of the year.

The piece of paper left by the kidnapper was a ransom note, folded and appearing to have been carried in a pocket for some time. It demanded $28,000 in various denominations and in old bills. The family was instructed to place an ad in the *Seattle Times* ("Mabel— Please give us your address") to signal a willingness to cooperate. If the ad were not placed, the ransom demand would double, then double again, the note warned. "Dont fail & I wontt. The boy is safe. Tim."[177]

The note had been typed in an ink of unusual color, perhaps from a child's typewriter. How had the kidnapper (kidnappers?) arrived at the figure of $28,000? And why was the note not addressed specifically to the Mattson family? Perhaps, detectives theorized, the kidnapper had carried it in a pocket until he zeroed in on a target. There were several well-to-do families among the Mattsons' neighbors.

Hoover immediately sent nine agents to Tacoma to assist local police on the theory that the Lindbergh Law had been violated. Within a week, some forty more agents would be dispatched to Tacoma, led by FBI assistant director Harold Nathan.

The kidnapping was, of course, a sensational crime, made more so by the disgraceful behavior of newspaper reporters and photographers, newsreel cameramen, and radio reporters. Members of the Mattson family were followed, making it impossible for Mattson to deal directly with whoever had taken his son. Every new tidbit of "news," true or otherwise, was printed and broadcast.

Meanwhile, the police and FBI agents were staying more or less on the sidelines, giving Mattson every chance to negotiate privately with the kidnappers.

The situation became more chaotic. Other messages were sent to the Mattson home, apparently from people hoping to insinuate themselves into the negotiations and hijack the ransom money. On Tuesday, December 29, a special delivery letter arrived at the home. It declared that anyone could deliver the ransom money, once arrangements were made, as long as the courier was alone and driving a Ford. The letter was signed "Tim."

The Mattson family ran more newspaper ads, trying to convey the message that the way was clear for a deal and that lawmen were standing down, pending safe return of Charles.

Again, Mattson went public with a plea to the news media, practically begging reporters and photographers to stop following him and stop reporting supposedly "inside" information.

The first week of 1937 brought cold and snow to the Puget Sound region. Members of the Mattson family were sick with worry, as Charles had not been wearing outdoor clothing when he was spirited away.

Most alarmingly, Mattson *had* been in direct contact, by phone and letter, with the kidnapper but had found his responses increasingly confusing and contradictory. What in God's name did he have to do to get his son back? The only man who could answer Mattson's questions seemed nearly incoherent.

On Sunday, January 10, and Monday, January 11, the Mattsons ran one last ad in the *Seattle Times*, asking for specific instructions—and proof that Charles was still alive.

———

Around 9:00 p.m. on Sunday, Gordon Morrow thought his bulldog, Nick, was acting mighty strange. The beast was running from door to door, barking all the while, as if eager to get out of the house and explore—what? But Nick was not the only dog who seemed excited. Other canines belonging to the farm families in the vicinity were also baying.

Sorry, Nick, it's no night to be outdoors, Gordon thought. The nineteen-year-old thought he might go rabbit hunting the next day near his home in Snohomish County, several miles from Seattle. But for now, indoors was the place to be.

The next morning, snow covered the fields and woods near the Morrow house, but Gordon was still in the mood for hunting rabbits. Near a side road about a half mile west of the Pacific Highway, he saw a naked, doll-like form in the snow. Coming closer, Gordon saw that the form was the body of a young boy—the Mattson boy, he thought at once. He ran home to tell his father, Charles Morrow, then ran a half mile to a gas station to phone the Snohomish County sheriff's office.

A family friend and a relative identified the body as that of Charles. The boy had been treated cruelly, as evidenced by bruises and marks on his wrists indicating he had been tightly bound. He had been killed by blows to the head, possibly with a metal pipe. Grease marks, abrasions, and dirt on the skin indicated that his body had been in the trunk of a car.

Subfreezing temperatures made it impossible to determine a time of death. The boy could have been killed shortly after he was taken but probably no later than four days before the body was discovered, coroners concluded.

President Roosevelt issued a statement on January 12 declaring that the slaying "has shocked the nation" and was "renewed evidence of the need of sustained effort in dealing with the criminal menace."[178]

Hoover sent a large floral arrangement to the funeral service, held on Thursday, January 14. He pledged that his agency would use "all the resources at our command to apprehend and bring to justice the kidnapper and slayer of the Mattson boy."[179]

In a gesture of truly amazing grace, Dr. Mattson thanked members of the news media for finally heeding his pleas and leaving him alone while there was still hope for his son. But the Tacoma Chamber of

Commerce was unforgiving, issuing a statement condemning newsmen for their behavior in taking advantage of the tragedy.

———————

Investigators were optimistic at first. Whoever left the body in the field had left footprints, and his car had left tire marks in the snow. But those clues led to nothing.

Then, hope. On Friday, July 8, 1938, a man named Lester Mead was arrested on a farm near Ritzville, in southeast Washington State, after saying that he had killed someone. Since Mead, who was thirty-two, resembled the description of the Mattson kidnapper, he was taken to Tacoma for questioning. After three days of interrogation, he said he had kidnapped and killed Charles Mattson.

But it was soon revealed that Mead had escaped from a mental hospital *after* the kidnapping of Charles Mattson. "He is entirely harmless, but is given to fantastic theories that he is a big-time criminal," the hospital director told the *Seattle Times*.[180]

And that may have been the last time the Mattson kidnapping was big news—or news at all. The years went by, and various crackpots "confessed" to the crime, only to be proven innocent. The merciless, half-witted kidnapper—*"Don't you kids try to start anything, because I have a bullet-proof vest on"*—was never caught. No doubt he passed from the scene long ago. One can only hope he finally found himself in front of the highest court of all, an otherworldly tribunal from which there was no appeal.

CHAPTER FORTY-FOUR

AMBUSHED ON THE ROAD

Chicago
Saturday, September 25, 1937

"The car behind has been following us for some time and displaying unusually bright lights," Charles Ross commented to his former secretary and longtime friend, Florence Freihage. "I don't like the looks of this. I'll cut over to the side and let him pass."[181]

Ross's suspicions were correct. As he pulled his car over to the side of the road, his secretary recalled later, the car that had been following veered sharply in front of him, blocking any forward progress. And here came two men from that car, one with a revolver in hand.

The gunman yanked on the driver's side door, which was locked. Then he tapped on the door window with his revolver and told Ross to get out. Ross complied and was quickly searched and stuffed into the car of the kidnappers—for there seemed to be no doubt that the two ambushers were just that.

Freihage implored them not to hurt him, telling the kidnappers that Ross had a weak heart and high blood pressure. Ross was also seventy-two years old, and Freihage, who was forty-four, was afraid the sudden shock of events swirling beyond his control could do him great harm.

One of the abductors asked about her relationship with Ross.

When Freihage explained, the man seemed interested. "Oh, his *secretary*," he said. "Can he stand a touch for a quarter million?"[182]

"I don't...I don't think so." In a futile goodwill gesture, she offered the man her purse. He took $85 from it and told her to stay quiet in the car if she didn't want to be killed or want her ex-boss and friend to be killed.

Quickly, Freihage took inventory of the man: curly hair, pointy nose, sharp features in general.

"Don't call the police after we have gone, or we'll kill him," one of the kidnappers said.[183] And off they went with their new prisoner, Charles Sherman Ross, retired president of the George S. Carrington Company, printers of valentines and other greeting cards.

There was no doubt about it: Ross had a head for business. He was a former druggist who became an investor in real estate and building materials, where he made "a sizable fortune," as the *New York Times* put it, before becoming a partner in the Carrington company, from which he had retired in 1935.[184]

Yet he and his wife, May, were not *fabulously* wealthy like the Weyerhaeusers, Urschels, or Boettchers, families who had been victimized by kidnappers. Florence Freihage knew this, which may be why she voiced doubt that Ross and his family could come up with a quarter million dollars in a hurry.

Freihage was accustomed to conferring with her former boss every week or so. Ross kept up with company affairs and was in the midst of selling his interest in Carrington.

On this Saturday evening, Ross and his former secretary had dined at the Fargo Hotel in Sycamore, Illinois, and were heading back into Chicago proper when they were waylaid. Normally, Ross's wife would have dined with them, but she had been taken ill.

After she shook off her initial shock and fear, Freihage drove Ross's car to a nearby service station and called the local police, who in turn notified the Illinois State Police.

Then it was time to wait.

═══════

There was much going on in the wider world. Chancellor Hitler welcomed Benito Mussolini to Munich. The German dictator and his Italian counterpart seemed to be getting along famously. Dispatches from Germany reported, somewhat vaguely, that they would discuss how to preserve peace.

In the Orient, events were far more disturbing. Japanese bombers continued their attacks on the Chinese capital of Nanking. Hundreds of civilians were killed, and destruction was widespread. Other cities in China were also under attack, indicating that Japan was hoping to secure a quick victory in its war with China. The ruthless and relentless nature of the Japanese campaign could only make observers wonder how the Japanese would behave as conquerors.

═══════

As would be learned later, the kidnappers drove their captive into Wisconsin and across the state to Minnesota where, late on Sunday, they neared the hideout they had prepared near the community of Emily. The hideout was in the woods. It was a coffin-sized hole lined with wood chips.

═══════

On Thursday, September 30, five days after the abduction, a ransom-extortion letter was received by Harvey Brackett, a former business associate of Ross, in Green Bay, Wisconsin.

"Dear Dick," the letter began. "I am being held for ransom."[185] The "Dear Dick" was proof positive that the letter was from Ross, as "Dick" was his affectionate, if improbable, nickname for his wife.

"I have stated I am worth $100,000 including the G. S. Carrington Co. stock held in escrow by First National Bank," the letter went on. "Try and raise $50,000. Yours, Charles S. Ross." The letter concluded, "Contact Harvey S. Brackett. Say nothing to anyone except Harvey."

FBI agents deduced that the letter had been intended for May Ross but that the kidnappers had decided to send it directly to Harvey Brackett, along with another letter, this one addressed to Brackett and in Ross's handwriting. It instructed Brackett to hire a motorcycle rider from Harley-Davidson who was to take $50,000 in unmarked, nonconsecutive bills of various denominations and deliver the money at night on a highway to be designated later.

When the money had been assembled and the motorcycle rider had been hired, an ad was to be placed in the "used cars for sale" section of the *Chicago Tribune*: "Dodge. Good cond. No defect. (amount)"

But the kidnappers were about to become increasingly elaborate in their demands. They acquired a typewriter on which they prepared additional demand letters. The next one was postmarked October 2 in Chicago and addressed to Olden Armitage, a friend who belonged to the same fraternal lodge as Ross.

"YOU are Chas. S. Ross' last hope," the letter said. "His own choice as middleman." The letter demanded that the motorcycle delivery man dress in white, and it warned against any contact with "the feds."

Yet another letter, postmarked October 6 in Chicago, was sent to Armitage. This one declared that Ross himself was "very incenced over delays" caused by "pied pipers and rat hunts," apparently meaning the presence of federal agents in the investigation. Most significantly, it promised proof that Ross was alive and well. The proof could be obtained at a camera company on South Wabash Street in pictures left for Armitage.

Sure enough, eight photographs of Charles Ross were found at the camera company. They showed him amid a thicket of birch trees, looking haggard, wearing the clothes he'd had on the night he was kidnapped. Ross was holding up a late edition of a Chicago paper from Saturday, October 2, displaying that day's college football scores.

Hope!

And the final message, received Friday, October 8, by Elton Armitage and postmarked two days earlier in Chicago: "EVERYTHING SET. LETS GO." It laid out the long itinerary, some four hundred miles, that the motorcycle delivery man (dressed in white!) was to take before dumping the ransom money. "ROSS OPINES AS HOW THERES TOO MUCH VITAMIN G IN THIS MESS. WE AGREE." The allusion to vitamin G apparently meant federal agents, or "G-men," as they were beginning to be called.

That very night, the motorcycle rider set out. About six miles east of Rockford, Illinois, he became aware of a car close behind him. The car's lights flashed—the signal for the ransom package to be thrown to the side of the road. After tossing it, the rider drove another few hundred yards and dismounted. One of the kidnappers emerged from the darkness, picked up the money, and vanished.

But where was Charles Ross?

We don't know the moment when lawmen broached the subject with May Ross. But at some point, someone told her it was it was time to concentrate on catching the kidnappers. We can only imagine her emotions at that moment. On October 18, she issued a statement calling for her husband to be freed at once. The next day, the FBI distributed lists of the serial numbers on the ransom bills across the country.

———————

In early January 1938, ransom bills began showing up at the Federal Reserve Bank in Los Angeles. The bills were traced to the nearby Santa Anita racetrack. Hoover, who was no stranger to racetracks, traveled to Los Angeles and enlisted the help of track officials in setting a trap. Agents were stationed behind the betting windows and nearby, ready to pounce on any bettor passing a bill from the Ross ransom. This was no easy mission. Up to a million dollars a day passed through several hundred cashier windows, all amid the hubbub that was normal for a racetrack.

But the vigilance paid off. On Friday, January 14, 1938, a man walked up to a window to bet on a horse and handed over money from the ransom. Whether by luck or alertness or both, agents spotted the bills at once, and the would-be bettor was soon on his way to the Los Angeles FBI office—but not before some $5,600 in ransom money was found on his person, in his hotel room, and in his car.

The man gave his name as "Peter Ander" and said he had obtained the money from bank robbers at a large reduction. In other words, he didn't mind admitting that he had laundered the money. He denied any part in the kidnapping of Charles Ross. Then, questioned at length by Hoover, he changed his story.

He said his real name was John Henry Seadlund. He was twenty-seven years old and had once been a logger. He had shot Ross to death, along with his own partner, in a dispute over how to divide the ransom. He signed a twenty-eight-page confession laying out the details and agreed to show agents where the bodies were.

Flown to Minnesota, Seadlund guided agents across snow-covered fields. Near an abandoned stretch of train track, he pointed to a mound beneath the snow. There, agents found a typewriter case with some $32,000 in ransom money inside.

Horses and sleds were hired for the rest of the search. There were no major highways in the region at the time, and the existing roads were buried under snow. They came to the first hideout, near Emily, Minnesota, where Ross had been kept in a wood-lined dugout for almost *two weeks* after he was taken. Then Seadlund guided the searchers into Wisconsin, near the little community of Spooner. Agents brushed away snow and brush where Seadlund indicated, thus exposing a coffin-sized hole. Inside lay the bodies of Seadlund's partner, James Atwood Gray, and the victim, Charles Ross.

Seadlund admitted killing Ross and Gray on October 10, or two days after the ransom was delivered.

Back in Chicago, Seadlund pleaded guilty in Federal District Court on February 28, 1938, to violating the Federal Kidnapping Statute—the Lindbergh Law. A few weeks later, he was sentenced to the electric chair. He shouted a vulgarity and was led out of the courtroom to begin his stay on death row.

The body of Charles Ross was transported to Chicago for private services.

―――――――

John Henry Seadlund was born in Wisconsin and grew up in that state and in Minnesota, where his father worked in the iron mines. He liked engines and motors more than textbooks and preferred hunting in the woods to sitting in the classroom.

His father died when Seadlund was thirteen. Seadlund also worked in the mines until, one by one, they closed during the Depression. He worked as a logger, at a service station, and as a grocery store deliveryman.

If there was a moment that changed his life, it may have been a chance meeting with a gangster named Tommy Carroll, an associate of John Dillinger, when Seadlund was an adolescent. The encounter took place while Seadlund was hunting in a patch of woods where Carroll was hiding out. They struck up a friendship of sorts, and Carroll persuaded Seadlund to bring him some food.

The FBI file on the meeting between the young Seadlund and Carroll is sparse, but it seems to have convinced Seadlund that a life on the wrong side of the law could be more exciting than a dreary existence on the straight and narrow.*

He began his criminal career by pulling off store robberies and stealing cars while he was still in his teen years. Soon, he graduated to bank heists, committing several in Wisconsin. Then he traveled to Spokane, Washington, where he did honest work for a while. But he grew homesick for the Upper Midwest and returned there, intending to rob more banks in Wisconsin and Minnesota.

On his trip eastward, Seadlund picked up James Atwood Gray, who was hitchhiking and who was similarly eager to commit crimes. A few weeks before kidnapping Charles Ross, the pair kidnapped the wife of a café owner in Lake Geneva, Wisconsin. The enterprise didn't go well. The woman was released after two days as Seadlund and Gray were unable to persuade her husband to pay.

Seadlund traveled up and down the Eastern Seaboard and across the country in the weeks after the kidnapping of Charles Ross. Although he seems to have been missing some connections in his emotional circuitry, it was clear that Seadlund was not devoid of feelings. On October 20, 1937, while he was in Denver, he bought a small dog for companionship. Six weeks after the kidnapping, he was in Spokane, where he asked an

---

* Carroll was killed at Waterloo, Iowa, on June 7, 1934, just weeks before Dillinger was slain in Chicago.

eighteen-year-old to marry him after only their second date. She turned him down. "There was something about him—I don't know what—that gave me a queer feeling," she said later.[186]

After Seadlund was captured, the gossipmonger Walter Winchell reported on his radio show that Seadlund had once considered kidnapping the baseball stars Joe DiMaggio of the New York Yankees and Dizzy Dean of the St. Louis Cardinals. Hoover refused to comment on Winchell's report, at least publicly. Odds are that Hoover fed Winchell the "scoop" in the first place.

A few minutes past midnight on July 14, 1938, Seadlund walked unassisted into the death chamber at the Cook County Jail in Chicago and sat down in the electric chair, sitting impassively as the straps were adjusted. The current flowed, and he was soon pronounced dead.

CHAPTER FORTY-FIVE

A MAN OF GOD IS TAKEN

Huntington, West Virginia
Tuesday, November 2, 1937

Dr. James Seder was a retired minister who seems never to have wondered why God put him on this earth. It was to preach against the evils of alcohol, which he had done for much of his adult life. He and other members of the "dry" movement had lost the good fight four years before with the repeal of Prohibition, but the minister never doubted that their cause was right, socially and morally. He held forth on the evils of drink and other issues in articles that he wrote for English- and German-language religious publications.

He was unusually vigorous for a man of seventy-nine, though his eyesight was fading, and he lived alone in a unit of an apartment building he owned in Huntington. His wife had fallen ill on a visit to St. Paul, Minnesota, to visit one of their sons, Arthur, and had remained there. Arthur was a comptroller for a railroad. Another son, Willard, was an official with the Bethlehem Steel Corporation in Pittsburgh.

All in all, the Seders were prosperous, especially for those hard times. The man of God had also shown himself to be quite competent in the ways of the world.

Photographs of Seder show a smiling, friendly face, nothing like the fire-and-brimstone look one might have expected. Even with his fervid opposition to alcohol, he did not seem like a man who made enemies.

But where was he?

———

"I'm afraid something may have happened to Dr. Seder," a man who lived in the same building told the police this Tuesday evening. "The lights burned in his place all night, and I noticed today that his mail is still in the box and his evening newspaper is still on the porch."[187]

A patrolman rushed to the building and found Dr. Seder's unit empty. But the rear door was unlocked. Immediately, the patrolman summoned detectives.

Right away, investigators saw reasons for alarm. The sheets and blankets on the minister's bed had been yanked off; a remaining sheet, next to the mattress, was ripped. And the three white canes that Seder owned were present. It was inconceivable, said the resident who had called the police, that Seder would have left home at night without one of them, given his poor vision. (A fourth cane, a red one, was missing.)

The minister's sons were summoned to Huntington, as was his daughter, who lived in New York City. Willard Seder asked the FBI to investigate. He was convinced his father had been kidnapped. What other explanation could there be?

Dr. Seder had last been seen the previous Monday evening when one of his tenants stopped by to pay the November rent. Now, as Tuesday night became Wednesday morning, lawmen waited for messages from whoever had taken the minister. FBI agents had special cellophane envelopes to enclose the messages on their way to the laboratory.

Anxiety turned to dread as the days ticked by with no contact. Finally, a week after the minister vanished, a ransom letter arrived. It had been mailed in Huntington the previous Saturday, four full days after the police discovered that Seder was missing. The sender knew enough about the Seder family to address the letter to the minister's son Arthur (though he was referred to as Raymond, his middle name). "Your father being held for $30,000 ransom," it began. "Call all law off—pretend you found him in St. Paul." The message went on to demand the money in small bills—"no serial no's taken"—and instructed that an ad be put in the Huntington newspaper: "Peg—Am Waiting Call Sally."

It was clear that the message sender was not highly educated. "We want axion now at once," the message said. It was also clear that whoever had sent it had indeed abducted the minister. The message alluded to Dr. Seder's red cane, which it said was in the kidnappers' possession, and it described one of the blankets that had been ripped from the bed.

Most ominously, it ended with a crude but clear threat: "Act at once and dont for get if you dont follow instructions you will not see him alive again."

The use of the U.S. mail, plus the considerable time that had elapsed since the victim's disappearance, conferred jurisdiction on the FBI. Agent R. E. Vetterli (a survivor of the Union Station Massacre in Kansas City) was in charge of ten agents on the case, and he advised the family to cooperate and maintain contact. So the Seders put an ad in both city dailies: "PEG—Anxious to see you but haven't enough money to make trip. Write and advise. Am waiting call—SALLY."

The ads brought no response.

Arthur Ronk was used to the sounds of the woods at night. He was a farmer in Gragston Creek, a mountainside community in Wayne County. On the night of Wednesday, November 10, he thought he heard a man moaning in the dark. No, he thought. Probably an animal. Anyhow, sounds could carry considerable distances at night. No telling where the noise had come from.

But even as he was about to fall asleep, the sound bothered Ronk. Haunted him, really. So the next morning, he fetched his nephew, Edgar Ronk, and the two of them set off along a road that Arthur thought might bring them close to where the sound had originated.

On a wooded slope several feet from the entrance to an abandoned coal mine, they saw an old man. His body bore cuts and bruises, and he was mumbling incoherently. The Ronks found someone who had a car, and Dr. Seder was gently put inside for the trip to the little town of Wayne. There, a crowd had begun to gather.

The old minister moaned and cried out as he was removed from the vehicle. It was clear from his blackened eyes and the cuts on his head that he had been badly beaten.

Onlookers recalled this exchange between Dr. Seder and his son Willard:

"Do you know me, Father?"

"It's Willard!"

"Yes. You're all right now, Father. Everything is all right. You're going to be just fine. Arthur and all the family are in Huntington."

"Thank God! It is like Heaven to be here, Willard. It is like Heaven!"

Taken inside, the minister asked for something to eat. An officer gave him milk to sip. "I was gagged and thrown in the mine," he said. "It rained in there, and the stones were sharp." He had been left tied up, able to capture some warmth by squirming into the bedclothes his captors took with them—bedclothes that became stained with his blood.

Drawing on the last bit of his physical and spiritual strength, Seder freed himself from his bonds at last, crawling out of the cave and moaning for help—the sounds that Arthur Ronk heard at night and returned to investigate.

Then the minister said something that stunned investigators: "I knew one of the kidnappers well. I can't recall his name, but he lives in one of my apartments. He is bald-headed, and he gave me a check that was bad."

Immediately, lawmen knew the man they were looking for: Arnett A. Booth, forty-six, who lived around the corner from Seder and had indeed recently passed a bad check—one that Seder, with characteristic kindness, had made good on.

Federal agents found Booth in his apartment, listening to the radio. Searching his apartment, agents found stationery and envelopes similar to the kind used to convey the ransom demands. Then the agents gave Booth a little quiz: write down what was in the first ransom message, they requested.

Booth did—and wrote the non-word *axion* for *action*, as in the first message. When this was pointed out to Booth, he confessed—sort of. "Okay," he said. "I sent the letter hoping to cash in on the minister's kidnapping. But I had nothing to do with it."

At first, Booth said, he had no definite plan to get the money, although he recalled reading about a kidnapping case in Michigan in which the ransom bundle had been thrown from a car. He said he didn't see the newspaper ads responding to the ransom demand, didn't even look in the papers, as a matter of fact, since he had heard that the Seder sons had gone home.

The story didn't wash. It sounded like a spur-of-the-moment account cooked up by a criminal who wasn't terribly bright, which was just what it was. So agents started questioning Booth again, and this time, he cracked, laying out the whole ugly episode on Friday, November 12. And he named two accomplices, Orville (Pete) Adkins and John Travis, both twenty-five, who lived in Huntington.

———————

The plot was inspired, as so many crazy ideas are, with the aid of alcohol. But maybe the plot didn't seem crazy to the three comrades in crime. All had done jail time and seemed unable to make it in the real world, whatever that meant to them.

"On November 1, while we were in various saloons drinking, Pete and I decided that we ought to make some money," Booth recalled. They decided to enlist John Travis in their scheme.

With a pint of whiskey for company, the three talked things over. Travis suggested blowing up a safe somewhere. No, Booth said. Kidnapping someone would be easier. Booth said he was sure Dr. Seder had a lot of money, especially for a minister, and could be parted from it.

"We then had to think of a place where we could keep him," Booth related. He said he knew of a log cabin at the confluence of three creeks in Wayne County. As for spiriting the minister from his home, Booth entered the place while the other two waited outside nearby. He confronted the old man in a hallway. Subjected to cajolery mixed with intimidation, Seder went with his treacherous tenant. A short time later, Booth picked up Adkins (his account did not make clear where Travis was) and headed for the hideout.

By this time, Seder had grown increasingly suspicious and asked where they were going. "You're being kidnapped," Booth said.

After one night in the cabin, Booth decided that the minister should be hidden in an abandoned mine where Booth had once worked. He explained that another accomplice whom he had recruited to guard the captive in the cabin had failed to show up.

Meanwhile, Booth sent Adkins and Travis back to the minister's home with the keys to the house and instructions to pick up any money they found (the minister said about $25 was on a shelf) and bring back bedding. The pair did as instructed and headed back to the mine after buying sandwiches and whiskey, none of which they shared with their captive.

Just before dawn, the victim was taken to the old mine. Then Adkins and Travis headed back to Huntington with instructions from Booth to mail the letter demanding ransom and to return to the mine with food. Booth said he planned to stay at the mine hideout for several days. Instead, he rejoined his two accomplices in Huntington the very next day—and said that he had killed the minister.

As Booth told interrogators, "I was of the opinion that Dr. Seder was either dead or dying at the time I left him." Booth explained that he had thrown stones at the old man while he was in the mine, hitting him on the head, shoulders, and upper body and seeing no response.

═════════

But James Seder had refused to die. Inspired by his faith, determined to be reunited with his sons, he had somehow survived and crawled out of the mine. As he was examined in the hospital, it became sadly clear how cruelly he had been treated. Besides being left to shiver in the cold dampness of the mine without food, he had suffered a broken nose. His right eardrum had been punctured. His entire left side was paralyzed, the result of a blood clot in his brain caused by blows to the head.

Travis was arrested at the home of his mother just after returning from his honeymoon. He had gotten married three days after the kidnapping. Adkins was arrested in Kentucky at the home of a relative. Both defendants admitted taking part in the kidnapping but said they had been led into the endeavor by Booth, the ringleader. Besides, they said, they were drunk when events were set in motion. Later, they said they had planned to free Seder on the second day after the kidnapping but had gotten drunk and forgotten their intention. State prosecutors announced that they would try the three defendants under West Virginia's new law on kidnapping. It would be the first trial under the law. Modeled after the federal Lindbergh Law, the West Virginia statute provided for the death penalty *even if* the victim survived. And prosecutors were determined to gain death sentences.

The prosecutors' task was made easier early on the morning of November 15 when Dr. James Seder died.

_____

The case proceeded with remarkable speed. Booth went on trial first. He had no defense, really, as psychiatrists opined that he was not insane. (Just evil, perhaps?) On December 11, 1937, jurors took less than an hour to convict him. Four days later, a judge sentenced him to death.

Perhaps Travis and Adkins hoped for mercy since they had been led into the whole mess by Booth and, well, they were drunk much of the time. Besides, they testified, they really had meant to free Seder, but again, they got drunk.

Jurors were in no mood to show mercy. They took just forty-two minutes to find Travis and Adkins guilty. Knowing that they faced death, the two cried uncontrollably as they were led out of the courtroom.

On March 21, 1938, the state prison in Moundsville, West Virginia, carried out its first executions for kidnapping and the state's first triple execution in decades. Adkins and Travis went to the gallows first and together, since the scaffold could accommodate two at a time.

Things didn't go smoothly. As straps were being fastened about their arms and legs, a mechanical malfunction caused the trapdoor under Adkins to open before the noose was in place. He fell eight feet to the concrete floor below, cutting his head. Then he was hoisted back up through the open trapdoor for the final plunge. Both men offered prayers of a sort before they dropped.

A short time later, Booth stood alone on the gallows. He prayed aloud that God would take care of Adkins and Travis. He asked for blessings on the warden and guards and prayed that the Lord would receive him. Surely, he knew that he was asking for more mercy than he had shown to an old minister.

Then he dropped to his death.

CHAPTER FORTY-SIX

THE LUCKLESS ONE

Holdenville, Oklahoma
Wednesday, October 24, 1934

He had come of age in the Dust Bowl of Oklahoma. He had never had much in life, and he didn't expect much. He was a career criminal, though not a vicious one, and his name was Arthur Gooch. In the autumn of 1934, he was twenty-six, and he was soon to become one of the saddest figures of those hard times.

On this particular Wednesday, he and another prisoner, Ambrose Nix, broke out of the jail in Holdenville, a little town in the east-central part of the Sooner State, along with several other prisoners. Gooch, who had been jailed to await trial on robbery charges, and Nix stole a car, drove south to nearby Texas, pulled off a robbery in Tyler the next day, then hoped to stay out of sight for a while.

On November 26, they pulled into a service station in Paris, Texas, just south of the Oklahoma border. The car they had swiped had a flat tire. Wherever they were going, they needed good tires to get there.

Maybe it was the flat tire, or maybe Gooch and Nix looked like the nickel-and-dime criminals they were. For whatever reason, two local cops who happened to stop at the station were suspicious. They approached Gooch and Nix to check the papers for the car. Immediately, there was a struggle. Nix knocked one of the cops into a display case. The glass on the case broke, and the cop suffered a minor cut on one hip. Nix managed to pull out a pistol, and he ordered the cops into the back seat of their patrol car. With Nix training his gun on the cops, Gooch went to the stolen car and retrieved the several weapons he and Nix had acquired.

With Nix at the wheel and Gooch pointing a gun on the cops in the back seat, the patrol car sped off—fatefully, it would turn out—across the state line and into Oklahoma, first into Choctaw County then into Pushmataha County. The fugitives stuck to the back roads. The next night, some forty-two hours after seizing the cops, Gooch and Nix let them go after Gooch had dressed the hip injury one cop had sustained.

And off went Nix and Gooch again, not to be heard from until late December.

On December 22, several bandits robbed two banks in Okemah in east-central Oklahoma, netting about $17,000. Not surprisingly, the area was soon teeming with local, state, and federal lawmen. There was a farm whose owner was suspected of happily shielding criminals for money, so police and federal agents staked out the place, thinking the bank robbers might stop there.

During the stakeout, a strange car drove up. Two lawmen drew their guns as two men got out of the car. Gunfire was exchanged, and one of the men who had just alighted from the car fell dead. He was not one of the bank robbers. He was Ambrose Nix. The other man was Arthur Gooch, who surrendered and was soon on his way to Muskogee, Oklahoma, where he was charged with automobile theft and with violating the Federal Kidnapping Act, since the police officers they had seized weeks earlier had been taken across state lines.

No doubt, Gooch expected to go back to prison for a long stretch, a prospect that probably didn't scare him. He had been committing crimes since dropping out of school after the sixth grade and had done several stretches behind bars. His misdeeds consisted mostly of robbery and theft.

Maybe he even looked forward to resuming the prison life he was used to. He could be sure of three square meals a day, a routine he had never enjoyed in his life outside.

———————

Arthur Gooch was born on January 4, 1908. His father, James, was a member of the Muscogee-Creek tribe and his mother, Adella, was illiterate. James Gooch died when Arthur was eight, and Adella struggled to earn money as a laundress and pecan picker. Three of her seven children died. Eventually, the household included her widowed brother and his son and two daughters. Arthur became a petty thief early on, sometimes to bring money home to his mother.

Oklahoma may have suffered more than any other state from the Depression and Dust Bowl. The unemployment rate in the state reached twenty-nine percent, wheat prices collapsed, and many people were hungry much of the time.[*]

By his twenties, Arthur Gooch had married, fathered a son, and split with his wife, who tired of his stealing. But Gooch's life path had been set. He continued to steal, shuttled in and out of jail, and when he was on the outside, was one of the first suspects the police looked for after a burglary or theft.

And so his life went until he broke out of jail in Holdenville and

———————

[*]　I wish to express my gratitude to Leslie Tara Jones, whose 2010 thesis about Arthur Gooch and the Oklahoma of his era, was invaluable to me. Ms. Jones submitted her thesis for a master of arts degree in history from the University of Central Oklahoma.

he and Ambrose Nix took two cops hostage in Paris, Texas, and drove into Oklahoma.

⸻

It is likely that Gooch did not understand, at least at first, the implications of crossing a state line. That act made him subject to the federal Lindbergh Law, which had recently been amended to provide for the death penalty if a jury so recommended. But a death sentence was *not* to be imposed if the kidnapped person or persons were released unharmed.

But one of the kidnapped cops had suffered a cut in the struggle with Gooch's partner in crime, Ambrose Nix, which under the law made Gooch just as guilty of inflicting that injury.

When Gooch tried to plead guilty to the kidnapping charge, Federal Judge Robert Lee Williams wouldn't let him.** The judge wanted to be able to impose the death penalty, which required a jury recommendation.

It is impossible to know what influenced the judge and jurors. Few people in our time can appreciate the crushing poverty and everyday hardships endured by Oklahomans of that time. Kidnappings were being committed with dismaying frequency. Arthur Gooch was a fourth-rate citizen who seemed incorrigible, though he was not the kind of monster the drafters of the Lindbergh Law had in mind.

Whatever the reason or reasons, the jury found Gooch guilty of kidnapping—not that there was any factual doubt—and recommended that he be put to death. Judge Williams was happy to oblige.

After pronouncing the sentence, the judge asked Gooch if he had anything to say.

** Williams helped to write the Constitution for Oklahoma. A Democrat, he was the state's third governor, serving from 1915 to 1919. He was also the first chief justice of the Oklahoma Supreme Court. He was a federal judge for the Eastern District of Oklahoma from 1919 to 1937, then served on the U.S. Court of Appeals for the Tenth Circuit.

"I think there have been worse crimes than mine, and I don't see why I should hang," Gooch said.[188]

Gooch had a limited intellect, but he had a point. However, Judge Williams, who had earned a reputation for being tough on repeat offenders, responded that other juries had been "cowardly" in declining to recommend the death penalty. He said that it was "no pleasure for me to sentence a man to die but when they roam about the country like a pack of mad dogs, killing and robbing and kidnapping, I am going to do it."

Governor E. W. Marland of Oklahoma applauded the sentence, expressing the hope that it would help to "exterminate the kidnappers." President Roosevelt declined to commute the sentence. His attorney general, Homer Cummings, praised the judge for doing his part in the "national battle against crime."

Gooch's appeals went nowhere, and he climbed the steps to the gallows on Friday, June 19, 1936. "It's kind of funny—dying," he said. "I think I know what it will be like. I'll be standing there, and all of a sudden everything will be black, then there'll be a light again. There's got to be a light again—there's got to be."[189]

Just before the trap door was released, he offered farewell advice to his six-year-old boy: "Don't get into any trouble, son."[190]

Gooch's hard luck persisted to the end. The executioner was used to throwing the switch on the electric chair, but he was unaccustomed to carrying out hangings, the federal method for executions at the time. He mistimed the trapdoor release, and Gooch slowly strangled, becoming the only kidnapper put to death under the Lindbergh Law who had not killed a victim.*

---

* In modern times, five people have been executed under federal law for kidnappings in which the victim was killed, according to the Death Penalty Information Center. Besides Gooch, they included John Henry Seadlund, executed for kidnapping and murdering Charles Ross.

CHAPTER FORTY-SEVEN

TUBBO AND TOUHY (ACT II)

Statesville, Illinois
Friday, October 9, 1942

There was never any doubt that Roger Touhy wasn't cut out for a law-abiding life, even though he was the son of a policeman. Eight years into a ninety-nine-year sentence for the "kidnapping" of Jake "the Barber" Factor, Touhy knew he wasn't cut out for life in prison either.

"I never made a good adjustment," he recalled years later. "I tried to obey the rules and I did my work as long as I had a job assignment. But the thought nagged me constantly that I was innocent, that I had been framed."[191]

Yes, he had once profited mightily as a bootlegger, and he was friendly with all kinds of men on the wrong side of the law. He had been a Prohibition-era gangster. But he insisted that what he was *not*, for all his sins, was a kidnapper.

Touhy's claim that there had been no kidnapping, that Factor had faked the whole thing and been aided and abetted by Daniel "Tubbo"

Gilbert, the mob-friendly investigator for the Cook County (Chicago) prosecutor's office, would in fact be validated one day, though Touhy had no way of knowing that. Having just turned forty-four, Touhy longed to be reunited with his wife, Clara, and their two sons. He had even urged her to move far away, to cut ties with him and start a new life. But she had stood by him.

In the fall of 1942, Touhy picked up prison scuttlebutt that several long-term convicts were plotting an escape. One of them was Basil "the Owl" Banghart, Touhy's old associate who had also been found guilty and sentenced to ninety-nine years in the Factor case. Not surprisingly, Touhy wanted to be part of the breakout. After all, with his appeals going nowhere, what did he have to lose?

"This is going to be a high-class break, with no dummies allowed in the group," one of the plotters assured Touhy.[192]

A date was settled upon: Friday, October 9, 1942. Though Joliet Prison was thought of as a hard place to do time and a hard place to break out of, Touhy believed the chances of escape were fair to good. He had observed that with able-bodied men away at war or working in defense plants, a lot of the prison guards seemed middle-aged and soft. And some guards were so friendly with the prisoners that they would pay them a few dollars in return for extra food (beef, coffee, bacon, sugar) smuggled out of the prison kitchen and destined for the guards' homes.

Early in the afternoon of October 9, Touhy rushed out of the prison bakery where he worked and surprised and overpowered the driver of a garbage truck. He was a little rusty behind the wheel, not having driven in eight years or so, but he managed to steer the truck across the prison yard to the mechanical shop, where Banghart worked.

Banghart was armed with one of several handguns that the break-out plotters had managed to have smuggled into the supposedly high-security prison (apparently with the aid of the plotter's brother). A guard in the mechanical shop was quickly overpowered, and Touhy and Banghart seized two ladder sections. Then they took the guard hostage, along with a lieutenant who supervised the shop and had the bad luck to show up just as the escape was unfolding. Five other prisoners who were in on the plot climbed aboard.

Touhy drove to a watchtower near the main gate. The would-be escapees had trouble fitting the ladder sections together, yet somehow the guards missed the commotion or were afraid to react to it. According to Touhy, the guards did not carry firearms, though there were weapons in the tower.

But as Touhy recalled it, the guards were in no mood to resist once they realized what was happening. "Please don't take me with you," one guard pleaded. "I'm an old man."

In no time, the escapees were on the other side of the wall where Touhy knew a car belonging to one of the guards was parked nearby, ready to be loaded with home-bound food from the prison.[*]

The escapees crammed into the car and sped off toward Chicago, where they planned to hide out, probably not in a high-rent neighborhood. On the way, they abandoned the guard's car and procured another with the aid of an outside friend of one convict.

Once in Chicago, Touhy and Banghart found a cheap flat with rats and roaches for company. Two other escapees were cornered by police and killed in a gun battle. Another turned himself in. Perhaps hoping for leniency, he told everything he knew about the fugitives' plans.

—————

A friend of an escapee had obtained some civilian clothes for Touhy and Banghart, but Touhy still wondered if they looked like the fugitives they

—————

[*]   Three guards were fired after an investigation into the escape debacle.

were. During the day, he might take in a movie or even go for a walk—anything to pass the time.

Touhy found the taste of freedom bittersweet. He couldn't contact his wife and sons. No doubt, the police were watching them. And with a war on, there was a larger than usual number of lawmen on the streets, with FBI agents helping the police look for draft dodgers and deserters. Touhy half expected his stay outside to be a short one.

Touhy and Banghart were asleep in the predawn blackness of Tuesday, December 29, 1942, when their apartment was suddenly filled with light from the outside. A voice boomed over a loudspeaker: "This is the Federal Bureau of Investigation. You are surrounded. You cannot escape. Come out with your hands up—immediately. If you resist, you will be killed."[193]

Touhy and Banghart surrendered peacefully. Their short vacations would add 199 years to their original ninety-nine-year terms. The other three remaining fugitives were captured around the same time. In an attempt to insinuate himself into events, Hoover had traveled to Chicago so he could be close to the arrests.

———

"Nights are the worst time in prison," Touhy wrote in his book. "Cons yell in their sleep. Some of them weep and call out for their mothers. The sense of shame for the present and remorse for the past rides them constantly."[194]

The years crawled by, and Touhy kept insisting he'd been framed in the Factor case. Hardly anyone listened, and no wonder. He had never been a sympathetic figure in the first place—he had been a gangster in the Prohibition years—and he had broken out of prison. And the people in Chicago, like Americans everywhere, were preoccupied with the war in Europe and the Pacific. But things were changing.

In 1947, the *Chicago Tribune* reported that Daniel "Tubbo" Gilbert's name was on a Department of Agriculture list of one hundred elected officials "gambling in the wheat market...when inside knowledge of administration market moves would have enabled a speculator in wheat to reap enormous profits."[195]

And in 1950, Senator Estes Kefauver of Tennessee brought his Senate committee to Chicago for hearings into organized crime. One of the witnesses was Gilbert. Amazingly, considering the public interest in the subject, he was allowed to give his testimony in private.

Or perhaps it wasn't amazing. Just cynical. Kefauver was known to have presidential ambitions, and he surely didn't want to alienate the Chicago Democratic organization.

But in an act of trickery that was a great public service, a *Chicago Sun-Times* reporter, Ray Brennan (who would later cowrite Roger Touhy's book), obtained a copy of Gilbert's testimony from the transcription service by posing as a Senate staff member. The revelation caused a sensation.

In 1950, Gilbert was making $9,000 a year in his investigative post. Remarkably, though, he was worth about $360,000, he told the senators. How to explain a net worth equal to forty years of his salary? Simple, Gilbert said. He was good at gambling and commodities trading. No one believed that Gilbert was that good at poker or bridge or picking horses. But Gilbert's success in commodities trading was much more plausible, given what the *Tribune* had uncovered in 1947.

The Kefauver committee concluded that Gilbert's time in office had been marked by neglect of his official duties and "shocking indifference to violations of the law."[196]

In 1950, Gilbert gave up his post of Cook County chief investigator to run for sheriff. But the stink he had given off for his entire career had become too much, even for Chicago voters, after the findings of the Kefauver committee.

Meanwhile, Touhy's family had hired a private detective who uncovered witnesses who said that John Factor had gone into hiding during the time he was supposedly a kidnapping victim. They recalled him playing cards, drinking liquor, and growing a beard.

Eventually, Touhy's appeals and other legal maneuvers caught the attention of Federal Judge John P. Barnes of the Northern District of Illinois. He had been put on the bench by President Herbert Hoover, a Republican. Did that make him more receptive than other jurists to delve into mischief by Democratic politicians? Perhaps no one has a right to say. But there seems to be little doubt that he was thorough.

On August 9, 1954, in an opinion that ran to a remarkable 556 pages and 216 pages of notes, Judge Barnes concluded that there had been no kidnapping of Factor, that the whole thing was "a hoax, engineered by Factor to forestall his extradition to England to face prosecution for a confidence game."[197]

He found that Touhy's conviction had been obtained by perjured testimony, with the full knowledge and indeed the connivance of Gilbert and Thomas J. Courtney, then the Cook County prosecutor. The judge found that Gilbert knew that Factor had been hiding out during his supposed kidnapping ordeal and had "suppressed important evidence on this point."

Prosecutors engaged in numerous shabby tricks "consistent only with a design to bring about the conviction of Touhy at any and all costs," Barnes wrote. He found that the "sinister motives" of Gilbert "and the political-criminal syndicate" that he was part of lay behind the desire to exile Touhy so that what was left of Al Capone's old mob could thrive.

Nor did federal investigators and prosecutors, who had claimed they had a strong case against Touhy in the kidnapping of William Hamm, escape criticism. "That Touhy was indicted at all on the Hamm matter is something for which the Department of Justice should answer. They knew it was a very weak case."

Judge Barnes declared that Touhy should be released at once. He wasn't, amid a debate over whether he had exhausted all his appeals in Illinois courts before turning to the federal system. The back-and-forth dragged on for *five years* before Touhy was freed in November 1959, having served twenty-six years for a "kidnapping" that probably never happened.

On the evening of Wednesday, December 16, 1959, three weeks after his release, Touhy and his coauthor, Ray Brennan, discussed their book at the Chicago Press Club. Then Touhy and a friend and bodyguard, a retired police sergeant, drove to see Touhy's sister. As they were going up the front steps, two men emerged from the darkness. There were five shotgun blasts, and Touhy's thighs were riddled by the pellets.

Roger Touhy died on an operating table a short time later. He was sixty-one. He had kept company with gangsters for most of his life. Gangsters hold grudges.

By the time he died of a heart attack on July 31, 1970, at the age of eighty, Daniel "Tubbo" Gilbert had richly earned the label of "the world's richest cop," as the headline writers had dubbed him.[198] He had amassed a fortune that enabled him to live on Chicago's fashionable Lake Shore Drive; he also spent time in Southern California, where he had "extensive property and contracting interests," as the *Tribune* put it.

The funeral mass for Gilbert at Holy Name Cathedral in Chicago was attended by Mayor Richard J. Daley, one of the last of the big city political bosses, along with various businessmen and union people and an assortment of political trough feeders and hacks from the good old days. It was as though Gilbert had devoted his life to public service instead of lying down with mobsters, misusing his investigative powers, and using his office to gorge himself financially.

One has to wonder if Gilbert ever felt guilty, ever confessed to a priest that he had committed one of the biggest sins of his life in pointing the finger at Roger Touhy. Did flights of angels take "Tubbo" to his eternal rest? Or did they drop him off in purgatory for some soul cleansing before heading for the pearly gates?

==========

A law, after all, is only a collection of words, and not always very clear words at that. So was passage of the Lindbergh Law, spurred if not inspired by the murder of a golden child, a good thing or not? Better to ask was it always used appropriately? The answer is no, as the execution of the hapless Arthur Gooch demonstrated. Did the Lindbergh Law deter some would-be kidnappers? Impossible to say. How much did the FBI contribute to solving kidnapping cases in which it played a secondary, even marginal, investigative role? Again, impossible to say. The Lindbergh Law was a reaction to a crime wave, a wave that some public officials rode to power. No one rode this wave more skillfully than J. Edgar Hoover, who survived early blunders by his agency, blunders that would have doomed a less skilled, less ruthless bureaucrat. Perhaps he could have built his FBI without the Lindbergh Law, as Congress responded to the Depression-era crime wave by federalizing various interstate offenses. But it was the kidnapping epidemic of the 1930s, most infamously the Lindbergh tragedy, that inflamed public sentiment and paved the way for a national police force.

After the thirties passed into history and the kidnapping epidemic subsided, there was a new mission for Hoover, one that involved the very security of the United States: hunting down Nazi spies and saboteurs. In 1942, his men caught eight Nazi agents who had been put ashore on

Long Island and the coast of Florida from German submarines. They were carrying explosives they planned to use to sabotage American factories. Six of the Nazis were soon executed; the remaining two were sentenced to long prison terms.

During the Cold War, as the Soviet Union acquired the atomic bomb and loomed as the new menace, Hoover's men pursued Communist spies. But as the threat from the Kremlin subsided or at least seemed less existential, Hoover's zeal was unabated. He saw Communist threats behind civil rights demonstrations and antiwar protests. He even viewed the Communist Party of the United States as a security threat, while virtually everyone else saw it as a tiny collection of harmless and naïve idealists.

That was quintessential Hoover: stuck in amber, forever seeing America and the world through his personal lens.

Hoover built the FBI into a modern crime-fighting force, with a laboratory relied upon by lawmen across the country and a police academy that has sharpened the skills of legions of local police officers. Along the way, he trampled on individual liberties and intimidated politicians with his collection of secrets. While he acted the part of a strict moralist, he had no compunctions about spending bureau money and using bureau people for strictly personal ends—improvements to his Washington home, for example.

And no wonder he felt so entitled. From the day he took office, May 10, 1924, until the day of his death, May 2, 1972, at the age of seventy-seven, the name J. Edgar Hoover was synonymous with the FBI. No director since has achieved such power and inspired such fear, and none ever will again. Since 1968, Senate confirmation has been required to seat an FBI director, and his term is limited to ten years.

How many Americans could name the present director? (At the time of writing, Christopher Wray.)

It is remarkable, even amazing, how time changes images. The building that houses the Department of Justice, the FBI's parent agency, is named after Robert F. Kennedy. When Robert Kennedy became attorney general in 1961, it was because his brother, President John F. Kennedy, wanted someone in his cabinet whom he could trust totally—a consigliere, if you will. Robert Kennedy was thirty-five when he became attorney general. He had a law license. Otherwise, he had *no* qualifications, save one: his last name. The appointment of Robert Kennedy was shameless nepotism. Yet today, he is respected, even revered.

The building that has housed the Federal Bureau of Investigation since 1974 is named after J. Edgar Hoover. There are still people who admire him and what he stood for. There are many others who would like to take a crowbar, pry Hoover's name off the building, and rename it for almost anyone else.

Today's FBI is still struggling with "his complex and enduring legacy," as the agency acknowledges on its website.[199] "Fairly or unfairly, Hoover was criticized for his aggressive use of surveillance, his perceived reluctance to tackle civil rights crimes, his reputation for collecting and using information about U.S. leaders, and his seeming obsession with the threat of communism."* Fairly or unfairly? I'd say fairly.

_____

The post-Hoover FBI has had its triumphs. One notable one came in 1994 when agents caught Aldrich Ames, a case officer for the Central Intelligence Agency who for years had been passing secrets to the Kremlin

---

* Hoover's "perceived reluctance" to tackle civil rights issues was in keeping with his neo-Confederate attitude toward people of color. As Curt Gentry notes in his book, in 1943, Hoover remarked in a memo to President Roosevelt that recent racial unrest in Washington, DC, was most likely caused by "the sporting type negro."

and living the good life with payoffs from Moscow. Ames pleaded guilty and was sent to prison for life.

Then there was the disgraceful episode of Robert Hanssen, a veteran FBI counterintelligence agent who was arrested in 2001 for passing secrets to the Soviet Union and Russia. Like Ames, Hanssen was motivated by greed, impure and simple. He, too, pleaded guilty and was sentenced to life behind bars.

Had a Judas like Hanssen been caught while Hoover was still in power, the director probably would have erupted into purple-faced, spittle-flying rage. He also would have been heartbroken to see his beloved bureau exposed for what it had always been: human and imperfect. It would have been small consolation to Hoover that the FBI itself nabbed the traitor in its midst.

The other giant figure whose image was sullied with the passage of years was Charles Lindbergh, who suffered mightily because of his fame.

Charles and Anne Lindbergh were hounded so mercilessly by reporters and photographers that in 1935, months after Bruno Hauptmann was convicted, they fled to Britain with their son, Jon, who had been born on August 16, 1932, and for whose safety they feared in America. (The Lindberghs eventually had two other sons and two daughters.)

The Lindberghs did enjoy far more privacy in Britain than they had in the United States. They moved easily in conservative political and social circles. They also traveled across the Channel to France and Germany. Lindbergh voiced admiration for the new Germany that Hitler seemed to be building, and he was impressed by Germany's growing military power.

In 1938, at a stag dinner at the U.S. embassy in Berlin, Lindbergh was given a medal by Hermann Goering in honor of his epic 1927 flight and his contributions to aviation. Anne Lindbergh predicted, presciently, that the medal would one day be an "albatross" and urged her husband to return it.[200] He declined.

The Lindberghs returned to the United States in 1939. When war erupted in Europe, Lindbergh became prominent in the America First Committee, which wanted to keep the United States out of a conflict an ocean away. In a speech in Des Moines, Iowa, on September 11, 1941, he urged his countrymen not to let "the British, the Jews and the Roosevelt administration" drag the United States into war. Later, he denied that he was anti-Semitic, asserting that he had Jewish friends. But the damage was lasting.

After the United States entered the war, Lindbergh sought to atone, sharing his deep knowledge of airplane engines and aerodynamics with the companies designing the planes that would battle the Germans and Japanese. He even flew on combat missions in the Pacific as a civilian after President Roosevelt rebuffed his entreaties to give him a military post.

Before and after the war, Lindbergh prospered as a commercial aviation consultant. In later life, he devoted himself to conservationist causes.

In 2003, a German newspaper published an article contending that on a visit to Germany in 1957, Lindbergh met and fell in love with a woman a quarter century younger than he was. The relationship produced three children, the newspaper said. But Lindbergh biographer A. Scott Berg said he doubted the veracity of the report.

Lindbergh died of cancer in Hawaii on August 26, 1974, at the age of seventy-two. President Gerald R. Ford issued a statement acknowledging the "political controversy" stirred by some of Lindbergh's views. As for his epic flight, Ford said, "the courage and daring of his feat will never be forgotten."

Anne Morrow Lindbergh enjoyed great literary success with her

1955 book *Gift from the Sea*, which, despite its title, was a philosophical meditation on the lives of women in the twentieth century. The book was on bestseller lists for weeks. She wrote numerous other books of prose and poetry and died at her home in Vermont on February 7, 2001. She was ninety-four.

———————

During the trial of Bruno Hauptmann in 1935, there was an incident, little known at the time, that said much about the pettiness to which Hoover could descend.

Charles Lindbergh was talking with Elmer Irey, an agent of the Internal Revenue Service, whose idea it had been to include gold certificates in the ransom money in the theory—which proved correct—that gold notes would be easy to spot.

"If it had not been for you fellows being in the case, Hauptmann would not now be on trial, and your organization deserves full credit for his apprehension," Lindbergh told Irey.[201]

Hoover heard about Lindbergh's remark and never forgave him for it, probably because it reflected the truth, which was that the FBI, while involved in the Lindbergh investigation, had not played the central, all-important role that Hoover had coveted for it. What's more, Hoover had tried to nudge the Internal Revenue Service onto the sidelines.

"Irey was a good Christian who didn't cuss," one of his longtime aides recalled later, "but the air would be blue when the subject of the Lindbergh kidnapping case came up."

EPILOGUE

By the late 1930s, the epidemic of kidnappings was over. Of course, there would be others in the following years, but nothing like what the country experienced in the decade before the Second World War.

What caused the plague to fade away? More effective law enforcement and the obvious willingness of the law to put people to death? The availability of factory jobs as war loomed and then came? Some combination of events and trends? No one can say.

The central figures in the sensational cases of the thirties fared differently as the years went on. I was not able to learn the fates of all of them. But I do know what happened to some of the people.

Adolphus "Buppie" Orthwein, who was kidnapped as a boy, graduated from Yale, served as an intelligence officer in the navy during World War II, tracking German submarines, and joined the family business, the Anheuser-Busch beer empire. He also had other business interests. He married twice and had five children. He died in 2013 at the age of ninety-six.

Nell Donnelly, the dressmaker with a vision, divorced her

husband and married James A. Reed, who had been widowed. She lived until 1991 when she died at the age of 102. (Reed died in 1944 at eighty-two.)

David Wilentz became one of the most powerful Democratic politicians in New Jersey. He practiced law until shortly before his death in 1988 at the age of ninety-three.

John Condon, the eccentric go-between in the Lindbergh case, died on January 2, 1945, at the age of eighty-four. Herbert Norman Schwarzkopf, the first superintendent of the New Jersey State Police, died in 1958 at sixty-three. Arthur Koehler ("the man who loved trees"), to whom Schwarzkopf wisely turned over the kidnapper's ladder for study, died in 1967 at eighty-two.

Dr. Dudley Shoenfeld, the pioneer criminal profiler who advised the police on what kind of man to look for in the kidnapping case, died in 1971 at the age of eighty-two after a distinguished career in psychiatry. He was among the doctors who took part in a study of the effects of marijuana for the New York Academy of Medicine for Mayor Fiorello La Guardia—and concluded that marijuana was not much more addictive than cigarettes.

Anna Hauptmann continued her futile attempts to prove her husband innocent of the Lindbergh kidnapping before she faded into obscurity. She died in 1994 at age ninety-five.

Charles Boettcher, who was kidnapped in 1933 by Verne Sankey and accomplices, was found dead by his wife, Mae, in 1963. He apparently had had a heart attack. He was sixty-one. Boettcher's first wife, Anna, who had been all but ignored as her husband returned home from his kidnapping ordeal, had committed suicide in 1941.

William Hamm, kidnapped in 1933 by the Barker-Karpis gang, died in 1970. He was eighty-seven. Edward Bremer, another prominent kidnapping victim of the Barker-Karpis gang, died of a heart attack in

1965 as he was emerging from a swimming pool at his summer home in Florida. He was sixty-seven.

Jake "the Barber" Factor, the supposed victim in a "kidnapping" that probably never occurred, died in 1984. He was ninety-one.

Charles Urschel, the fabulously wealthy oil tycoon kidnapped in 1933, died at eighty in 1970. The man who engineered the kidnapping, George "Machine Gun" Kelly, spent seventeen years in Alcatraz, where he earned the nickname "Pop Gun" Kelly because of his friendly demeanor and model behavior. In 1951, he was transferred to Leavenworth prison, where he died of a heart attack on July 18, 1954, his fifty-ninth birthday.

Basil "the Owl" Banghart served a long stretch in Alcatraz where he worked in the kitchen with Alvin "Creepy" Karpis. Eventually, Banghart was transferred back to the Illinois state prison. The kidnapping charges against him in the Factor case were dropped, and he was released in 1960. He spent much of his later life living quietly on an island in Puget Sound and died in 1982 at age eighty.

———

Alvin Karpis is said to have served the longest sentence of any inmate at Alcatraz, twenty-six years. In 1962, as the federal government was preparing to close the prison, he was transferred to McNeil Island Penitentiary in Washington State. Paroled in 1969, he moved to Montreal, then settled in Spain in 1973. He died there on August 26, 1979, at seventy-two.

While he was at McNeil Island, Karpis showed a softer side. He also became a link, in a way, between two vastly different eras.

As Karpis told the writer Robert Livesey, who collaborated with Karpis on the gangster's 1980 autobiography, a young prisoner approached him one day and mused that he would like to take music lessons. Karpis learned that the young man had been in institutions much of his life—orphanages, reformatories, and finally prisons—after a childhood utterly lacking in stability and parental guidance. So Karpis became protective of the young man, finding his personality pleasant enough, and rather mild for a convict. The young prisoner's name was Charles Manson.

READING GROUP GUIDE

1. Prior to reading this book, how much did you know about the lawlessness of the Great Depression? Did you recognize any of the cases covered in the book?

2. How do you feel about the kidnapping of Buppie Orthwein by Charles Abernathy, where the kidnappers were not cruel or malicious, merely desperate? Discuss your feelings regarding crimes like these. Are they comparable to violent kidnappings? Should these crimes be treated similarly?

3. Before the advances in forensic science and technology of today, investigating violent crimes was especially difficult. Were there any investigations that you found impressive? Which ones did you find lacking?

4. Discuss which unsolved cases you think could be solved by modern-day forensics.

5. Some instances of kidnapping, like Marion Parker's, are especially gruesome. Which cases were the most difficult for you to read about?

6. During the "kidnap years," it became common for people to be

taken from their homes, schools, and places of work. Imagine you lived during this time. How would you feel going about your day-to-day routine?

7. While this kidnapping epidemic terrorized the States, they produced some positive results. Discuss the good that came out of such a dark history.

8. Many of these stories involve poorer people kidnapping wealthier ones. Given the desperate poverty suffered by many at the time, how do you feel about the motives behind some of these abductions? Does this change the way you think about crime and those who commit it?

9. As the kidnapping epidemic continued, people became violent in their fear, like when a mob took justice into their own hands by lynching Thurmond and Holmes. Citizens and officials alike supported this action, and many encouraged further vigilante justice. Do you think it's important for the government to reserve the right to dictate punishment? How did you feel reading about the mob?

10. Charles Lindbergh's celebrity status granted him a certain amount of freedom in the investigation of his son's kidnapping. If he hadn't been famous, how do you think the case would have been different? Would the investigation have been more or less successful?

11. The press was clearly biased during the Lindbergh trial—do you think they influenced the outcome of the investigation or the trial? Do you think the impartial reporting of crimes is important?

A CONVERSATION WITH THE AUTHOR

How has your career as a journalist informed the way you approach writing books?

A journalist wants to learn as much as he can about a subject. He won't write everything he knows, but his depth of knowledge makes his prose more muscular, gives him access to vivid examples and vignettes, and lets him use shorthand with far more confidence. It's far less satisfying for a journalist to have to concede, or spackle over, gaps in his information.

This book necessitated an incredible amount of research. Can you talk a little bit about your methods?

I relied a lot on microfilm from the *New York Times*, where I worked for twenty-eight years, and other newspapers. Plus, I read a number of books on important individuals, like J. Edgar Hoover, and especially noteworthy cases, the most famous being the Lindbergh kidnapping. And with some persistent internet surfing, I came across a magazine article and a book from the 1930s. The article was by a wood expert who traced the source of the Lindbergh kidnapper's ladder, and the book was by a psychiatrist who pioneered criminal profiling and predicted—accurately—the kind of man the kidnapper would turn out to be, once the police caught him. A little extra digging can pay big dividends!

This kidnapping epidemic has been largely forgotten—why do you think that is?

Years went by, and other events seemed far more important: World War II, the Korean War, the Cold War, and so on. A lot of the kidnappings that were front page news at the time then faded from memory.

In this book you discuss dozens of cases of kidnapping. How did you decide to structure the project?

I decided early on that it would be a mistake to recount every case in a single chapter, although I treated a number of cases that way. But I felt that the Lindbergh case was so fascinating, from the kidnapping through the arrest of suspect Bruno Hauptman two and a half years later and through his trial, that I needed to make the most of it. So I spaced the events of the case throughout the book to create suspense. I used the same technique with the 1928 kidnapping of little Grace Budd and the arrest of the kidnapper more than six years later. It would have been a mistake to use a strictly linear time line. Incidentally, I had to decide which of the many kidnapping cases of that era to include in the book and which to leave out. How did I decide? Instinct.

The Lindbergh case was hugely influential in shaping legislature, and the case itself was widely publicized—is this simply because the victim was a celebrity, or were other factors at play? Why was this case so culturally significant?

Lindbergh's celebrity status was the main factor. Plus, his wife was an appealing person (and from a famous family), and their baby was adorable. And Lindbergh was more than a celebrity; he was an idol. His great courage in flying utterly alone across the Atlantic, his all-American good looks, his "aw shucks" smile—all contributed to his image. And there was far less debunking of famous people than there is today.

The prevalence of kidnapping during the Great Depression was enabled by the lack of technology and forensic science available to law enforcement. Do you think it would be possible, in the present day, for a crime epidemic to occur on a similar scale?

Probably not, given the instant, multi-state communications available today, making it possible for police agencies across the country to talk to one another. But there is still the human factor. For instance, the investigation into the 1969 murders of actress Sharon Tate and several others was hampered by poor communication within the Los Angeles Police Department.

Your body of work largely covers the investigation of violent crimes. What is it about this topic that interests you?

Let's stick with murder. A murder changes everything forever, at least for the victim and those close to him or her. There is nothing on this earth than can undo it, and there is no true justice this side of heaven. Even if the killer is caught and punished, the victim is gone forever, and those close to him or her are scarred forever. And I have occasionally reflected on how issues of profound legal importance reach the Supreme Court after originating in, say, a shabby rooming house or a grimy saloon or pool hall.

BIBLIOGRAPHY AND LIST OF SOURCES

BOOKS

Aymar, Brandt, and Sagarin, Edward. *A Pictorial History of the World's Greatest Trials, From Socrates to Jean Harris*. New York: Bonanza Books, 1985.

Bjorkman, Timothy W. *Verne Sankey: America's First Public Enemy*. Norman: University of Oklahoma Press, 2007.

Burrough, Bryan. *Public Enemies: America's Greatest Crime Wave and the Birth of the FBI, 1933–34*. New York: Penguin Books, 2004.

Cahill, Robert T. Jr. *Hauptmann's Ladder: A Step-by-Step Analysis of the Lindbergh Kidnapping*. Kent, OH: Kent State University Press, 2014.

Gentry, Curt. *J. Edgar Hoover: The Man and the Secrets*. New York: W. W. Norton & Company, 1991.

Nash, Jay Robert. *Bloodletters and Badmen, Volume 3*. New York: Warner Books, 1975.

Neibaur, James L. *Butterfly in the Rain: The 1927 Abduction and Murder of Marion Parker*. Lanham, MD: Rowman & Littlefield, 2016.

Schechter, Harold. *Deranged: The Shocking True Story of America's Most Fiendish Killer!* New York: Pocket Books, 1990.

Shoenfeld, Dudley. *The Crime and the Criminal: A Psychiatric Study of the Lindbergh Case.* New York: Covici-Friede, 1936.

Touhy, Roger, and Ray Brennan. *The Stolen Years.* Cleveland, OH: Pennington Press, 1959.

Unger, Robert. *The Union Station Massacre: The Original Sin of J. Edgar Hoover's FBI.* Kansas City, MO: Kansas City Star Books, 2005.

Wood, Larry. *Murder & Mayhem in Missouri.* Charleston, SC: The History Press, 2013.

ARTICLES

Beason, Robert G. "Floyd Takes Sheriff for Buggy Ride," *The Bolivar Herald-Free Press*, March 8, 2000.

Cushman, Barry. "Headline Kidnappings and the Origins of the Lindbergh Law." *Saint Louis University Law School Journal*, 2011. https://scholarship.law.nd.edu/law_faculty_scholarship/268.

Farris, David. "Massacre Suspect Bailey Drew FBI Scrutiny," *Edmond Life and Leisure*, June 14, 2018. www.edmondlifeandleisure.com.

Jones, Leslie Tara. "Arthur Gooch: The Political, Social, and Economic Influences That Led Him to the Gallows." MA thesis, University of Central Oklahoma, 2010. http://citeseerx.ist.psu.edu/viewdoc/download?doi=10.1.1.428.3355&rep=rep1&type=pdf.

Koehler, Arthur. "Techniques Used in Tracing the Lindbergh Kidnapping Ladder." *Journal of Criminal Law and Criminology* 27 (Winter 1937): 712–24.

Koehler, Arthur. "Who Made That Ladder?" *Saturday Evening Post*, April 20, 1935.

Lindell, Lisa. "No Greater Menace: Verne Sankey and the Kidnapping of

Charles Boettcher II." Hilton M. Briggs Library Faculty Publications, 2004. https://openprairie.sdstate.edu/library_pubs/30/.

McClary, Daryl. "Ten-Year-Old Charles F. Mattson Is Kidnapped in Tacoma and Held for Ransom on December 27, 1936." *HistoryLink. org*, December 13, 2006. https://historylink.org/File/8028.

McClary, Daryl. "Weyerhaeuser Kidnapping." *HistoryLink.org*, March 27, 2006. https://historylink.org/File/7711.

Nash, Jay Robert. "Who Was Behind the Kansas City Massacre?" http://www.annalsofcrime.com/index.htm#03–05.

O'Neil, Tim. "A Look Back: The New Year's Eve Kidnapping of a Busch Family Heir in 1930." *St. Louis Post-Dispatch*, January 1, 2019. https://www.stltoday.com/news/archives/a-look-back-busch-family-heir-kidnapped-on-new-year/article_8ffb7345-9214-5c18-a7f6–51d89c1cc78f.html.

O'Neil, Tim. "A Look Back: A Post-Dispatch Reporter Takes the Hostage Home in One of the Most Bizarre Kidnapping Cases St. Louis Has Ever Seen." *St. Louis Post-Dispatch*, April 26, 2019. https://www.stltoday.com/news/local/metro/a-look-back-reporter-got-his-story-first-then-took/article_03ee06ac-b2cd-5f72-9966-386544c54af8.html#1.

Park, Sharon. "Gangster Era in St. Paul, 1900–1936." MNopedia, Minnesota Historical Society. http://www.mnopedia.org/gangster-era-st-paul-1900–1936 (accessed July 9, 2019).

Stillwell, Ted W. "Portraits of the Past: The Nelly Don Kidnapping Sensation." *Leavenworth Times*, July 31, 2014. https://www.leavenworthtimes.com/article/20140731/NEWS/140739835.

Tuohy, John William. "The World's Richest Cop/Tubbo Gilbert, the Mob and the Power of the Press." *American Mafia*, June 2002. www.americanmafia.com.

INTERVIEWS

Byeff, Dr. Peter. For his personal recollections of Dr. Dudley Shoenfeld, 2018.

Cahill, Robert T. Author of *Hauptmann's Ladder*, 2018.

DeJute, David Anthony. For his personal recollection of his uncle, James DeJute Jr., 2018.

Unger, Robert. Author of *The Union Station Massacre*, 2018.

ACKNOWLEDGMENTS

This book would not exist were it not for my agent, Deborah Hofmann of the David Black Agency. She believed in the idea from the beginning and has been tireless in her support and encouragement. She has been a terrific agent, yet so much more. Her editing and storytelling instincts are superb, and they have made me a better writer. She is my friend as well as my agent.

And I am grateful to Anna Michels of Sourcebooks, my steady navigator from the start. She is that rare editor who sees the big picture *and* the tiny details that go into shaping a manuscript. Her questions and suggestions have been on the mark every time.

Finally, there is my wife, Rita, without whom my life would not be worth living. She, too, has been encouraging and supportive. As I say in my dedication, she is truly my rock and my light.

ENDNOTES

1   "Gang Chief Jailed in Hamm Abduction; Three Aides Held," *New York Times*, July 25, 1933.

2   "Abduction Arrests Grow/Hamm Kidnapping Charges Add to Long List of Recent Cases," *New York Times*, July 25, 1933.

3   Touhy, Roger, *The Stolen Years* (Cleveland: Pennington Press, 1959), 19.

4   Cushman, Barry. "Headline Kidnappings and the Origins of the Lindbergh Law." *Saint Louis University Law School Journal*, 2011. https://scholarship.law.nd.edu/law_faculty_scholarship/268.

5   "Hunt for Slayers of Lindbergh Baby Centres on Gangsters Who Got Ransom; President Orders Relentless Search," *New York Times*, May 14, 1932.

6   Ibid., "President Orders Relentless Hunt."

7   "Kidnapping: A Rising Menace to the Nation," *New York Times*, May 6, 1932, Section 9.

8   "Six States in Drive Against Kidnapping," *New York Times*, March 2, 1932.

9   "Kidnapping Wave Sweeps the Nation," *New York Times*, March 3, 1932.

10   "Kidnapping: A Rising Menace to the Nation," *New York Times*, March 6, 1932.

11   "J. Edgar Hoover Made the F.B.I. Formidable with Politics, Publicity and Results," *New York Times*, May 3, 1972.

12   "Costly Mercy Hit by J. Edgar Hoover," *New York Times*, August 1, 1933.

13   "August Busch Heir Freed by Abductor," *New York Times*, January 2, 1931.

14   "Dr. Kelley's Story of Experiences in Kidnapers' Hands," *St. Louis Post-Dispatch*, April 28, 1931.

15   "Dr. Kelley Released to Post-Dispatch Man," *St. Louis Post-Dispatch*, April 28, 1931.

16   "Dr. Kelley's Story of Experiences in Kidnapers' Hands," *St. Louis Post-Dispatch*, April 28, 1931.

17   "Dr. Kelley Released to Post-Dispatch Man," *St. Louis Post-Dispatch*, April 28, 1931.

18   "Dr. Kelley's Story of Experiences in Kidnapers' Hands," *St. Louis Post-Dispatch*, April 28, 1931.

19   Cahill, Richard T. Jr., *Hauptmann's Ladder, a Step-by-Step Analysis of the Lindbergh Kidnapping* (Kent, OH: Kent State University Press, 2014), 12.

20   Gentry, Curt, *J. Edgar Hoover, the Man and the Secrets* (New York: W.W. Norton & Company, 1991), 149–151.

21   "Kidnapping of Baby Speeds Federal Law," *New York Times*, March 2, 1932.

22   Gentry, Curt, *J. Edgar Hoover, the Man and the Secrets* (New York: W.W. Norton, 1991), 151.

23   "DeJute Boy Found Concealed in Wall," *New York Times*, March 6, 1932.

24   "DeJute Abductor Gets a Life Term," *New York Times*, March 17, 1932.

25   Neibaur, James L., *Butterfly in the Rain: The 1927 Abduction and Murder of Marion Parker* (Lanham, MD: Rowman & Littlefield, 2016), 3.

26   Ibid., 114.

27   Ibid., 15.

28   Ibid., 17.

29   Ibid., 22.

30   Ibid., 33.

31   "Mexicans Welcome Lindbergh's Mother with Rush on Field," *New York Times*, December 23, 1927.

32   Neibaur, James L., *Butterfly in the Rain: The 1927 Abduction and Murder of Marion Parker* (Lanham, MD: Rowman & Littlefield, 2016), 59.

33 Ibid., 77.

34 Ibid., 169.

35 Daniell, F. Raymond, "Progress Made in Search of the Lindbergh Baby," *New York Times*, March 9, 1932.

36 Daniell, F. Raymond, "Lindbergh Search Pressed Near Home," *New York Times*, March 10, 1932.

37 Cahill, Richard T. Jr., *Hauptmann's Ladder, a Step-by-Step Analysis of the Lindbergh Kidnapping* (Kent, OH: Kent State University Press, 2014), 55.

38 "Hitler's Prospects Regarded as Slight," *New York Times*, March 10, 1932.

39 Daniell, F. Raymond, "Lindbergh Hopeful, Is Ready to Ransom Son," *New York Times,* March 3, 1932.

40 "Kidnapping: A Rising Menace to the Nation," *New York Times*, March 6, 1932.

41 Schechter, Harold, *Deranged: The Shocking True Story of America's Most Fiendish Killer!* (New York: Pocket Books, 1990), 30.

42 ibid., 54.

43 Gentry, Curt, *J. Edgar Hoover, the Man and the Secrets* (New York: W.W. Norton & Company), 150.

44 Cahill, Robert T. Jr., *Hauptmann's Ladder, a Step-by-Step Analysis of the Lindbergh Kidnapping* (Kent, OH: Kent State University Press, 2014), 84.

45 "Condon Deals Anew with Kidnappers and Reassures Them," *New York Times*, April 13, 1932.

46 "Flier Asks Secrecy to Deal with Gang," *New York Times*, April 15, 1932.

47 "Lindbergh Baby Found Dead Near Home," *New York Times*, May 13, 1932.

48 Cahill, Robert T. Jr., *Hauptmann's Ladder, A Step-by-Step Analysis of the Lindbergh Kidnapping* (Kent, OH; Kent State University Press, 2014), 113.

49 "Morrow Maid Ends Life; Suspected in Kidnapping," *New York Times*, June 11, 1932.

50 "Brinkert Supported in Kidnapping Alibi," *New York Times*, June 12, 1932.

51 Koehler, Arthur. "Techniques Used in Tracing the Lindbergh Kidnaping Ladder." *Journal of Criminal Law and Criminology* 27 (Winter 1937): 712–24.

52 Bjorkman, Timothy W., *Verne Sankey, America's First Public Enemy* (Norman: University of Oklahoma Press, 2007), 23.

53   Ibid., 62.

54   Ibid., 42.

55   Ibid., 62.

56   Bjorkman, Timothy W., *Verne Sankey, America's First Public Enemy* (Norman: University of Oklahoma Press, 2007), 94.

57   "Hamm Writes His Story," *Associated Press*, as published in the *New York Times*, June 20, 1933.

58   "Kidnappers Seize St. Paul Brewer," *New York Times*, June 17, 1933.

59   Beason, Robert G. "Floyd Takes Sheriff for Buggy Ride," *The Bolivar Herald-Free Press*, March 8, 2000.

60   "5 Slain in Battle by Gang to Free Oklahoma Bandit," *New York Times*, June 18, 1933.

61   Ibid.

62   "No Clues to Killers in Kansas City," *New York Times*, June 19, 1933.

63   "5 Slain in Battle by Gang to Free Oklahoma Bandit," *New York Times*, June 18, 1933.

64   "Seek 'Pretty Boy' Floyd; Federal Agents Seek Arrest in Kansas City Massacre," *New York Times*, July 7, 1933.

65   Unger, Robert, *The Union Station Massacre: The Original Sin of J .Edgar Hoover's FBI* (Kansas City, MO: Kansas City Star Books, 2005), 218.

66   Ibid., 219.

67   Ibid., 218.

68   Ibid., 236.

69   Ibid., 239.

70   Ibid., 167.

71   Ibid., 169.

72   "M'Gee Kidnapper, Miss M'Elroy Says," *New York Times*, July 26, 1933.

73   "Kidnappers Take Kansas City Girl; Return Her after Day for $30,000," *New York Times*, May 29, 1933.

74   "Kidnapping Hunt Gets Federal Aid," *New York Times*, May 30, 1933.

75   "Girl Pleads to Save Her Kidnapper's Life," *New York Times*, April 27, 1935.

76   "Miss M'Elroy Dies by Her Own Hand," *New York Times*, January 22, 1940.

77   "Kidnappers Mourn 'Best Friend,'" *New York Times*, January 22, 1940.

78   "Factor Kidnapped; Held for $100,000," *New York Times*, July 2, 1933.

79   Ibid.

80   "Factor Released by Kidnap Gang," *New York Times*, July 13, 1933.

81   "Factor's Freedom Cost Him $50,000," *New York Times*, July 14, 1933.

82   "Factor Released by Kidnap Gang," *New York Times*, July 13, 1933.

83   "Factor's Freedom Cost Him $50,000," *New York Times*, July 14, 1933.

84   "Editorial on Thompson," *Chicago Daily Tribune*, April 9, 1933.

85   "Hamm Case Band Lose Bail Protest," *New York Times*, July 26, 1933.

86   "J.J. O'Connell Jr. Seized by Kidnappers in Albany; $250,000 Ransom Sought," *New York Times*, July 11, 1933.

87   "O'Connells Name New Negotiators in Ransom Demand," *New York Times*, July 13, 1933.

88   "O'Connell Captors Force New Agents," *New York Times*, July 15, 1933.

89   "Look for Release of O'Connell Soon," *New York Times*, July 19, 1933.

90   "O'Connells Paid in Marked Bills," *New York Times*, August 2, 1933.

91   "Story of Banker's Weary Trudge over Lonely Road at Midnight," *Alton Evening Telegraph*, July 17, 1933.

92   "Luer Kidnapper Confesses, 6 Held," *New York Times*, July 21, 1933.

93   "August Luer Identified Pit That Was His Prison When Held by Gang of Kidnappers," *Alton Evening Telegraph*, July 20, 1933.

94   "Kidnap Case May Go to the Jury Late Thursday," *Alton Evening Telegraph*, September 27, 1933.

95   "Hitler Troopers Beat New Yorker," *New York Times*, July 22, 1933.

96   "Oklahoma Oil Man Seized for Ransom," *New York Times*, July 24, 1933.

97   "David Farris, Massacre Suspect Bailey Drew FBI Scrutiny," *Edmond Life and Leisure*, June 14, 2018.

98   "Kidnapped Oklahoma Man Among the Richest," *The Austin American*, July 24, 1933.

99   "Federal Men Halt Hunt for Urschel," *New York Times*, July 25, 1933.

100 FBI History, Famous Cases and Criminals, www.fbi.gov.

101 "Urschel Relates His Own Story of Seizure and Nine-Day Captivity," *New York Times*, August 2, 1933.

102 Godfrey, Ed, "'Machine Gun' Kelly Kidnaps Wealthy Oilman," *The Oklahoman*, April 18, 1999. (Originally published July 22, 1933)

103 Gentry, Curt, *J. Edgar Hoover, the Man and the Secrets* (New York: W.W. Norton & Company, 1991), 159.

104 "Payer of Ransom Called a Traitor," *New York Times*, August 2, 1933.

105 "Roosevelt in Thanksgiving Proclamation Deals Rebuke to 'Greed and Selfishness,'" *New York Times*, November 22, 1933.

106 "Smith Denounces Nazis as 'Stupid,'" *New York Times*, September 11, 1933.

107 "End of Army Rule in Japan Predicted," *New York Times*, September 15, 1933.

108 "Juror Says Hamm Case Climax Was in Failure to Identify Eddie McFadden," *Minneapolis Tribune*, November 29, 1933.

109 "Touhy and Trio Are Acquitted in Kidnap Trial," *Chicago Daily Tribune*, November 29, 1933.

110 Barker/Karpis Gang, FBI History, www.fbi.gov.

111 "Hamm Ransom Money Is Found in Chicago Bank," *Chicago Daily Tribune*, May 6, 1935.

112 "G-Men Chalk Up One of Their Greatest Victories in Cleanup of the Hamm Kidnapping Gang," *New York Daily News*, August 16, 1936.

113 "California Youth Is Held by Kidnappers; $40,000 Ransom Asked for Merchant's Son," *New York Times*, November 11, 1933.

114 "Young Hart Slain; Kidnappers Threw His Body into Bay," *New York Times*, November 17, 1933.

115 "Gov. Rolph Backs San Jose Lynching as Kidnap Warning," *New York Times*, November 28, 1933.

116 "Hoover and Rolph in Sharp Exchange," *New York Times*, December 1, 1933.

117 "Rolph Restates His Attitude; Sees 'Criminals' Day at an End," *New York Times*, November 30, 1933.

118 "Reich Bishop Wars on Nazis' Enemies as Revolt Widens," *New York Times*, November 27, 1933.

119 "Rush U.S. Liquor Rules to Meet Repeal Tuesday," *Chicago Daily Tribune*, December 4, 1933.

120 "99 Years for Three Touhys," *Chicago Daily Tribune*, February 23, 1934.

121 "Slay One Touhy; Convict One," *Chicago Daily Tribune*, March 14, 1934.

122 "Kidnappers Hold St. Paul Banker; Note Asks $200,000," *New York Times*, January 19, 1934.

123 "Bremer Held Alive; Negotiations Near, the Ransom Ready," *New York Times*, January 21, 1934.

124 "Hunt for Bremer by Federal Men Covers 350 Miles," *New York Times*, January 22, 1934.

125 Koehler, Arthur. "Techniques Used in Tracing the Lindbergh Kidnaping Ladder." *Journal of Criminal Law and Criminology* 27 (Winter 1937): 712–24.

126 Ibid., 153.

127 Ibid., 171.

128 Ibid., 175.

129 Koehler, Arthur. "Who Made That Ladder?" *Saturday Evening Post*, April 20, 1935.

130 "Adolph Fiedler Names Eight Men and Woman as Kidnapers of Dr. Kelley," *St. Louis Post-Dispatch*, February 7, 1934.

131 "Held for 'Protection' in Kidnapping Case," *New York Times*, May 14, 1934.

132 "License Plates Mysteriously Lost in State Bureau Were on Auto Used in Murder of Star Witness," *St. Louis Post-Dispatch*, May 14, 1934.

133 "Woman Is Acquitted in Kelley Kidnapping," *New York Times*, October 6, 1935.

134 "Anna Ware Wins Baby Suit; Commissioner Finds Muenches Had Her Child," *St. Louis Post-Dispatch*, December 5, 1935.

135 Schechter, Harold, *Deranged: The Shocking True Story of America's Most Fiendish Killer!* (New York: Pocket Books, 1990), 89.

136 Ibid., 93.

137 Ibid., 95.

138 Ibid., 92.

139 Ibid., 106.

140 Ibid., 115.

141 "Budd Girl's Body Found; Killed by Painter in 1928," *New York Times*, December 14, 1934.

142 Schechter, Harold, *Deranged: The Shocking True Story of America's Most Fiendish Killer!* (New York: Pocket Books, 1990), 163.

143 Nash, Jay Robert, *Bloodletters and Badmen, Book 3* (New York: Warner Books, 1975), 121.

144 Gentry, Curt, *J. Edgar Hoover, the Man and the Secrets* (New York: W.W. Norton & Company, 1991), 172.

145 "New Dillinger Killings Stir the President and He Asks Quick Action on Crime Bills," *New York Times*, April 24, 1934.

146 "Cummings Says Slaying of Dillinger Is 'Gratifying as Well as Reassuring'," *New York Times*, July 23, 1934.

147 "Key Clue Provided by Chance Remark," *New York Times*, September 21, 1934.

148 "Arrest Pleases Mayor," *New York Times*, September 21, 1934.

149 "Floyd Called Last of Massacre Gang," *New York Times*, October 23, 1934.

150 "2 Bremer Kidnappers Slain," *New York Times*, January 17, 1935.

151 "Outlaw Escapes on a Plane Trip," *New York Times*, February 8, 1935.

152 Burrough, Bray, *Public Enemies, America's Greatest Crime Wave and the Birth of the FBI, 1933–34* (New York: Penguin Books, 2004), 331.

153 Gentry, Curt, *J. Edgar Hoover, the Man and the Secrets* (New York: W.W. Norton & Company, 1991), 185.

154 Ibid., 186.

155 Ibid., 187.

156 "Karpis Captured in New Orleans by Hoover Himself," *New York Times*, May 2, 1936.

157 "Col. and Mrs. Lindbergh on Stand; Mother Identified Baby's Garments; Father Says He Heard Ladder Crash," *New York Times*, January 4, 1935.

158 "Text of Trial Testimony by Col. and Mrs. Lindbergh," *New York Times*, January 4, 1935.

159 "Col. Lindbergh Names Hauptmann as Kidnapper and Taker of Ransom; Cool in 3-Hour Cross-Examination," *New York Times*, January 5, 1935.

160 "Hauptmann Is Calm After Ordeal; Showed Wide Range of Emotions," *New York Times*, January 30, 1935.

161 "Hauptmann Near the Scene with Ladder, Says Witness; Linked to a Ransom Note," *New York Times*, January 9, 1935.

162 "Condon Names Hauptmann as 'John' Who Got Box; Parries Defense's Attack," *New York Times*, January 10, 1935.

163 "'You Stop Lying,' Hauptmann Rages at Federal Agent," *New York Times*, January 18, 1935.

164 "Woman Says Hauptmann Limped after Kidnapping; 'You're Lying,' Wife Cries," *New York Times*, January 19, 1935.

165 "Hauptmann Says He Expects Acquittal, Has 'No Fear of Cross-Examination,'" *New York Times*, January 23, 1935.

166 "Koehler Tells of 18-Month Jury That Traced Ladder to Bronx," *New York Times*, January 24, 1935.

167 "Koehler Gives Demonstration of Plan to Show It Was Used on Kidnap Ladder," *New York Times*, January 24, 1935.

168 Cahill, Robert T. Jr., *Hauptmann's Ladder, a Step-by-Step Analysis of the Lindbergh Kidnapping* (Kent, OH: Kent State University Press, 2014), 278.

169 "'No Mercy,' Wilentz Plea; Intruder Shouts at Court; Case Goes to Jury Today," *New York Times*, February 13, 1935.

170 "Hauptmann Guilty, Sentenced to Death for the Murder of the Lindbergh Baby," *New York Times*, February 14, 1935.

171 Aymar, Brandt, and Sagarin, Edward, *A Pictorial History of the World's Greatest Trials, From Socrates to Jean Harris* (New York: Bonanza Books, 1985), 194.

172 "Heir to Millions Seized in Ransom; Held in Tacoma," *New York Times*, May 26, 1935.

173 "Weyerhaeusers in Secret Parley on Kidnap Clues," *New York Times*, May 28, 1935.

174 "Tacoma Boy Free, $200,000 Is Paid; HE Names Karpis," *New York Times*, June 2, 1935.

175 Gentry, Curt., *J. Edgar Hoover, the Man and the Secrets* (New York: W.W. Norton & Company, 1991), 176.

176 "Demented Man Is Hunted as Mattson Kidnapper," *New York Times*, December 29, 1936.

177 "Ransom Payment for Mattson Boy Is Declared Near," *New York Times*, December 30, 1936.

178 McClary, Daryl. "Ten-Year-Old Charles F. Mattson Is Kidnapped in Tacoma and Held for Ransom on December 27, 1936." HistoryLink.org, December 13, 2006. https://historylink.org/File/8028.

179 "Every Federal Resource to Be Used in Kidnap Hunt," *New York Times*, January 12, 1937.

180 McClary, Daryl. "Ten-Year-Old Charles F. Mattson Is Kidnapped in Tacoma and Held for Ransom on December 27, 1936." *HistoryLink.org*, December 13, 2006. https://historylink.org/File/8028.

181 FBI History, *Charles Ross Kidnapping*, www.fbi.gov.

182 "Kidnap Chicagoan from Car on Road," *New York Times*, September 27, 1937.

183 FBI History, *Charles Ross Kidnapping*, www.fbi.gov.

184 "Kidnap Chicagoan from Car on Road," *New York Times*, September 27, 1937.

185 FBI History, *Charles Ross Kidnapping*, www.fbi.gov.

186 "Will Justice Triumph?" *New York Daily News*, February 6, 1938.

187 "When Justice Triumphed," *New York Daily News*, June 12, 1938.

188 Jones, Leslie Tara. "Arthur Gooch: The Political, Social, and Economic Influences That Led Him to the Gallows." MA thesis, University of Central Oklahoma, 2010. (http://citeseerx.ist.psu.edu/viewdoc/download?doi=10.1.1.428.3355&rep=rep1&type=pdf.)

189 "Arthur Gooch, the Only Execution Under the Lindbergh Law," *Executed Today*, June 19, 2014, originally published in 1936.

190 "First Kidnapper Hanged Under Lindbergh Law," *New York Times*, June 20, 1936.

191 Touhy, Roger, *The Stolen Years* (Cleveland, OH: Pennington Press, 1959), 226.

192 Ibid., 19.

193   Ibid., 46.

194   Ibid., 227.

195   "Who Was Chicago's Dan Gilbert? 'The World's Richest Cop,'" *Chicago Tribune*, February 25, 2016.

196   Tuohy, John William. "The World's Richest Cop/Tubbo Gilbert, the Mob and the Power of the Press," *American Mafia*, June 2002. www.americanmafia.com.

197   "Judge Calls Factor Kidnapping Hoax, Finds Conviction Was Based on Perjury; Holds Law Illegal," *Chicago Tribune*, August 10, 1954.

198   "Who Was Chicago's Dan Gilbert? 'The World's Richest Cop,'" *Chicago Tribune*, February 25, 2016.

199   FBI History/Directors, Then and Now, www.fbi.gov.

200   "Obituary: Daring Lindbergh Attained the Unattainable with Historic Flight Across the Atlantic," *New York Times*, August 27, 1974.

201   Gentry, Curt, *J. Edgar Hoover, the Man and the Secrets* (New York: W.W. Norton & Company, 1991), 163.

INDEX

ABOUT THE AUTHOR

© Rita Stout

David Stout spent nearly 28 years as a reporter and editor for the *New York Times*. His first novel, *Carolina Skeletons*, 1988, won an Edgar Award and was adapted for a television movie. There has been renewed interest in the case that inspired the novel: the 1944 execution of a 14-year-old boy in South Carolina for the murder of two little girls. A South Carolina judge threw out the conviction in December 2014, declaring that the quick trial and execution constituted "a great and fundamental injustice." Stout's other novels are *Night of the Ice Storm*, 1991, and *The Dog Hermit*, 1993 (renamed *A Child Is Missing* for a 1995 TV movie). His other two nonfiction works are *Night of the Devil*, 2003, about the killing of two New Jersey policemen in 1963, and *The Boy in the Box*, 2008, about one of America's most famous unsolved murders. He lives in Washington, D.C., with his wife, Rita, a former Soviet policewoman.